entrepreneurship

Starting
and
Operating
a Small
Business

Steve Mariotti

PEARSON

Prentice
Hall

Upper Saddle River, New Jersey 07458

Library of Congress Cataloging-in-Publication Data

Mariotti, Steve
  Entrepreneurship : starting and operating a new business / Steven Mariotti.
    p. cm.
  Includes bibliographical references and index.
  ISBN 0-13-119767-3 (alk. paper)
  1. New business enterprises—Management. 2. Entrepreneurship. I. Title.
  HD62.5.M3567 2006
  658.1′1—dc22

2005018791

Director of Production and Manufacturing:
  Bruce Johnson
Senior Acquisitions Editor: Gary Bauer
Editorial Assistant: Jacqueline Knapke
Development Editor: Deborah Hoffman
Case Studies: Nancy Rosenbaum
Editors (NFTE): Debra DeSalvo, Tony Towle
Marketing Manager: Leigh Ann Sims
Managing Editor—Production: Mary Carnis
Manufacturing Buyer: Ilene Sanford
Production Liaison: Denise Brown
Full-Service Production: Emily Bush/Carlisle Publishing
  Services

Composition: Carlisle Publishing Services
Manager of Media Production: Amy Peltier
Media Production Project Manager: Lisa Rinaldi
Director, Image Resource Center: Melinda Reo
Manager, Rights and Permissions: Zina Arabia
Manager, Visual Research: Beth Brenzel
Manager, Cover Visual Research and Permissions:
  Karen Sanatar
Image Permission Coordinator: Richard Rodrigues
Senior Design Coordinator: Mary E. Siener
Cover Design: Lisa Klausing
Printer/Binder: Courier Kendalville
Cover Printer: Lehigh Press

Photo Credits

Page 1: PunchStock, Page 2: SuperStock, Inc., Page 10: Frank Moore Studio, Corbis/Bettmann, Page 23: Matthew Simmons, Getty Images, Inc., Page 32: Landon Nordeman, Getty Images, Inc—Liaison, Page 34: Getty Images—Digital Vision, Page 58: Dave King, © Dorling Kindersley Media Library, Page 61: Corbis RF, Page 62: PunchStock, Page 75: Michael L. Ambramson, Getty Images/Time Life Pictures, Page 84: Ray Tamarra, Getty Images, Inc., Page 86: Corbis RF, Page 94: Nick Ruechel, Eyesoar Inc., Page 104: Chris Buck, Corbis/Outline, Page 115: Andre Perlstein, Getty Images Inc.—Stone Allstock, Page 118: Sam Roberts, Photodisc/Getty Images, Page 121: AP Wide World Photos, Page 138: Dan Nelken, Dan Nelken Studio Inc., Page 143: Ryan McVay, Photodisc/Getty Images, Page 144: PunchStock, Page 156: Bob Kaufman, Page 160: Getty Images Inc.—Hulton Archive Photos, Page 177: Shelley Rotner, Omni-Photo Communications, Inc., Page 180: PunchStock, Page 192: John Todd, AP Wide World Photos, Page 196: Robert Daly, Getty Images Inc.—Stone Allstock, Page 200: Mel Yates, Photodisc/Getty Images, Page 208: Frank Franklin II, AP Wide World Photos, Page 209: AFP PHOTO John G. MABANGLO, [Photographer]/Agence France Presse/Getty Images, Page 222: © David Young-Wolff/PhotoEdit, Page 226: SuperStock, Inc., Page 242: © Mark Langello Photography, Page 228: Keystone, [Photographer]/Hulton Archive/Getty Images, Page 247: Jose Luis Pelaez, Inc., CORBIS- NY, Page 248: Corbis RF, Page 260: Old Dartmouth Historical Society/New Bedford Whaling Museum, Page 276: Keith Philpott, Getty Images, Inc., Page 278: Jeff Maloney, Photodisc/Getty Images, Page 297: Ed Quinn, Corbis/SABA Press Photos, Inc., Page 301: Getty Images, Inc—Stockbyte, Page 302: SuperStock, Inc., Page 324: Getty Images, Inc.- Photodisc., Page 309: Bill Pugliano, Getty Images, Inc., Page 334: PunchStock, Page 349 : AP Wide World Photos, Page 337: Keystone, [Photographer]/Hulton Archive/Getty Images, Page 352: Corbis RF, Page 366: David Turnley, Getty Images, Inc.

Pearson Education Ltd.
Pearson Education Singapore, Pte. Ltd.
Pearson Education Canada, Ltd.
Pearson Education—Japan

Pearson Education Australia PTY, Limited
Pearson Education North Asia Ltd.
Pearson Educación de Mexico, S.A. de C.V.
Pearson Education Malaysia, Pte. Ltd.

10 9 8 7 6 5 4
ISBN: 0-13-119767-3

Special thanks to Shelby Cullom Davis. Also thanks to Kathryn Davis, Shelby M.C. Davis, Kimberly La Manna, Abby Moffat, and Diana Davis Spencer.

Brief Contents

*Includes material adapted from the NFTE/Merrill Lynch Global Philanthropy Collaboration, *Investing Pays Off*

Contents

> *The discussion of what it takes to be an entrepreneur is excellent. I think the examples that deal with entrepreneurs and their ideas are excellent.*
>
> —Marsha Wender Timmerman, LaSalle University, Philadelphia, PA

> *The examples given are very effective—e.g., the start-up investment, Bob's Discount Furniture, and the example on how to allocate costs.*
>
> —Samira Hussein, Johnson County Community College, Overland Park, KS

> *Very good coverage of marketing concepts and establishing a marketing strategy.*
> —Larry Weaver, Navarro College, Corsicana, TX

Chapter 4   Developing the Right Marketing Mix   86

> *Great Discussion of the Sales Process and how to actually sell.*
> —Dr. Laura Portolese Dias, Shoreline Community College, Seattle, WA

Chapter 7   Using an Income Statement to Guide a Business   180

Chapter 8   Financing Strategy: Debt or Equity?   200

> *I have just started two new businesses and find that the information in Chapter 9 is right on target.*
> —Emily Martin, Faulkner Community College, Bay Minette, AL

> *The introduction of the legal structure and taxes is the best.*
> —Timothy R. Mittan, Southeast Community College, Lincoln, NE

Chapter 11   **Effective Leadership: Managing Resources and Employees**   278

> *I think the exercises at the end of the chapters are very comprehensive.*
>
> —Eileen M. Kearney, Montgomery County Community College, Blue Bell, PA

Help Your Students Build a Future

Why Use *Entrepreneurship: Starting and Operating a Small Business?*

Because It Works!

Entrepreneurship: Starting and Operating a Small Business is based on the National Foundation for Teaching Entrepreneurship (NFTE). Since 1987, the NFTE organization has reached over 120,000 students and professionals, and certified over 3,200 instructors to teach innovative entrepreneurship curriculum. NFTE is widely viewed as a world leader in promoting entrepreneurial literacy and has a proven track record of helping students start a wide variety of successful new ventures.

Steve Mariotti, President and Founder of NFTE, developed and refined the entrepreneurship program presented in this book with feedback from hundreds of instructors, students, and successful entrepreneurs. The effectiveness and impact of the NFTE programs have been documented by research conducted at Harvard and Brandeis. The studies found that students completing NFTE's entrepreneurial training programs demonstrated a greater interest in college education, an increase in occupational aspirations and goals, and an increase in independent reading, compared to a control group.

Here is what leaders in the educational and business community have to say about this book:

"This is the book we've been waiting for —the essentials of how to start and operate a small business taught clearly and energetically for the college student by Steve Mariotti, who has built a national and international movement in entrepreneurship education."

—Tommy Goodrow, Vice President of Economic and Business Development, Springfield Technical Community College

"Entrepreneurship is the engine of our economy, but its true purpose lies in building community. Through the businesses we create, we become of service to our community and the world. In Entrepreneurship: Starting and Operating a Small Business, *Steve Mariotti teaches not only the nuts and bolts of how to start and operate a small business, but also energizes that knowledge with a strong sense of purpose that will inspire students to go forth and make a difference."*

—John Whitehead, former Co-Chairman of Goldman Sachs

"Never underestimate the power of a simple idea executed with a lot of energy and persistence. This book will enable college students to execute their ideas, grow their businesses, and tap into a greater power—the ability to use their ideas and energy to achieve social and political goals that will empower their communities."

—Russell Simmons, Chairman & CEO, Rush Communications

xix

» Combining Street Smarts and Academic Smarts

Entrepreneurship: Starting and Operating a Small Business unites Steve Mariotti's experience as an entrepreneur with relevant academic theory and practice with stories and practices from NFTE program graduates who have started their own businesses.

Chapter 4
Developing the Right Marketing Mix

"I found that if you give the consumer a snapshot where he could see himself as he really is and the way he wants to be portrayed, people really respond to it."

—Thomas Burrell, founder, the Burrell Communications Group

Performance Objectives

1. Combine the four P's—product, price, place, and promotion—into a marketing mix.
2. Choose where and how to advertise your business.
3. Use press releases and pitch letters to generate publicity for your business.
4. Decide how your business will help your community philanthropically.
5. Use breakeven analysis to evaluate your marketing plan.

All of BMW's marketing—from the price of the cars to the advertisements in magazines catering to people who buy expensive things—is designed to convince customers that it makes luxury automobiles. If BMW lowers the price of its sedan, would that damage the customer's belief in BMW's competitive advantage as a provider of luxury cars? This is the question that working through the next step of the marketing process will help answer. BMW illustrates the importance of getting your marketing mix—product, price, place, and promotion—right. Without an effective mix of these elements, your business is likely to fail.

A marketing mix is the combination of four factors, called the four P's, that together communicate your competitive advantage to your customer:

‹1. Performance Objective

- Product
- Price
- Place
- Promotion

If you tweak one "P," you must pay attention to how it affects the others. If you raise your price, for example, are you now still selling the product in the right place? Or will you need to move to a location that will put you in contact with consumers willing to pay the new price? Where will you promote your product at the higher price? Will you have to take out an ad in a different magazine or newspaper to reach these more affluent consumers?

Your marketing goal is to bring the right product to the right place at the right price with the right promotion.

Chapter Openers Set the Stage

Each chapter starts with an inspirational quote, Performance Objectives that provide a "road map" so readers know where they are headed. Readers connect with a real company story that sets the stage for upcoming material.

[Step Into The Shoes]

Russell Simmons Makes Rap Happen

In the late 1980s, Russell Simmons was promoting rap concerts at the City University of New York. At the time, rap was considered a passing fad, but Simmons really loved it. Even though most record executives thought rap would be over in a year or two, Simmons truly believed it was a business opportunity. He formed Def Jam Records with fellow student Rick Rubin for $5,000. Within a year, they produced hit records by Run DMC and LL Cool J, and Simmons became a multimedia mogul.

Simmons took a chance on this "internal" opportunity because he felt that, if you personally know ten people who are eager to buy your product or service, ten million would be willing to buy it if they knew about it. Luckily for him, he was right about rap's popular potential, but he could have been wrong. That can be a problem with in-

ternal opportunities—you may be passionate about something but there may not be enough consumer interest in it to sustain a business.

Simmons loved rap and hoped that other people would, too. That was the internal factor—he had the passion to sustain himself as he worked 24/7 to make his dream come true. As it turned out, music fans were a little bored with rock at that time, and looking for a fresh sound. Rap filled the bill. This was an external opportunity that happened to coincide with Simmons's internal commitment.

"Step into the Shoes" of the Experts

"Step into the Shoes" boxes appear in all chapters and give insights into the business practices of successful entrepreneurs.

Biz Facts

Biz Facts impart useful information regarding a company practice or a business application.

Biz Facts

- There are about 22.4 million non-agricultural small businesses in the United States, according to 2001 data (Small Business Administration).
- The small businesses in America employ more than half of the country's private workforce, create three of every four new jobs, and generate a majority of the country's innovations (Small Business Administration).
- Fourteen percent of *Inc.* magazine's 500 fastest-growing companies in the United States started with less than $1,000 (*Inc.*, October 2002).
- Small businesses represent more than 99 percent of all employers (Small Business Administration, December 2000).

Entrepreneurial Wisdom

Entrepreneurial Wisdom boxes contain insights or advice that will help students in the preparation of a business plan.

[Entrepreneurial Wisdom]

A useful way to evaluate a business idea is to look at its **S**trengths, **W**eaknesses, **O**pportunities, and **T**hreats (**SWOT**). This is called SWOT Analysis.

- **S**trengths—All of the capabilities and positive points that the entrepreneur has, from experience to contacts
- **W**eaknesses—All of the negatives that the entrepreneur faces, such as lack of capital or training, or failure to set up a workable accounting system
- **O**pportunities—Any lucky break or creative insight that can help the entrepreneur get ahead of the competition
- **T**hreats—Anything that can jeopardize the existence of the business or intimidate the entrepreneur, from competitors to legal issues

Global Impact

Global Impact boxes, in all chapters, illustrate areas entrepreneurs should consider when doing business in other countries.

[Global Impact]

Cell Phones in the Sauna?

The Finnish telecommunications company Nokia is tremendously innovative. The company is codeveloping a device that will enable people to make payments for anything, from a bar tab to a bank loan, using their cell phones. But when a reporter from *Wired* magazine asked a Nokia spokesman if anyone was working on making heatproof cell phones for Finns to take into the saunas, where they spend a significant amount of time, the spokesman fixed the reporter with a look of disdain and explained, "In sauna, we do not even want to hear Bach" (*Wired,* "Just Say Nokia," by Steve Silberman, September 1999).

When you know your market, you know how to market to the people in it. This is why it is so important to spend time conducting market research before you open your business. You may be impatient to get started, but do not do so until you've come to know your market intimately.

≫End-of-Chapter Learning Portfolio

End-of-chapter materials help students develop a working understanding of key concepts and develop critical thinking skills. All chapters include the following:

- Summary in outline format.
- Key Terms list.
- Key Concept Objective Questions that review core topics.
- Critical Thinking Exercises that require readers to ponder critical issues and support a thoughtful response.
- Application Exercises that give readers a chance to apply what they have learned.
- Exploring Your Community and Exploring Online assignments that allow readers to go into the business community or search online material for information.
- Cases for Analysis include one short and one long case with analytical questions. Cases cover a variety of issues and draw on real and realistic business scenarios. Business examples include David Neeleman (Jet Blue Airlines), Honest Tea Company, Russell Simmons (Rush Communications), Excelsior Henderson Motorcycles, Kickin' It Apparel, and more.

[Entrepreneurship Portfolio]

Critical Thinking Exercises

1. Use the following charts to define a business you want to start and analyze your competitive advantage. (**Business Plan Practice**)

Business Definition Question	Response
1. *The offer*—What products and services will be sold by the business?	1.
2. *Target market*—Which consumer segment will the business focus on?	2.
3. *Production capability*—How will that offer be produced and delivered to those customers?	3.

Competitive Advantage Question	Competitive Difference (USP)
1. *The offer*—What will be better and different about the products and services that will be sold?	1.
2. *Target market*—What customers should be the focus of the business to make it as successful as possible?	2.
3. *Production and delivery capability*—What will be better or different about the way that offer is produced and delivered to those customers?	3.

2. Are there customers for your business in other countries? How do you plan to reach them? (**Business Plan Practice**)

3. Describe any international competitors you have found who may be able to access your customers. How do you intend to compete? (**Business Plan Practice**)

4. Describe three core beliefs you will use to run your own company. (**Business Plan Practice**)

CASE STUDY Excelsior-Henderson Motorcycles

In 1993, brothers Dave and Dan Hanlon, along with Dan's wife Jennie, announced their plans to launch a motorcycle company called Excelsior-Henderson in their hometown of Belle Plain, Minnesota. The trio shared a passion for motorcycle riding and they wanted to turn their hobby into a business. Locals were thrilled that Excelsior-Henderson would provide badly needed jobs to people in the area. Skeptics questioned whether the Hanlons could successfully compete with big name brands like Harley Davidson, manufactured in neighboring Wisconsin, which dominated (over 80 percent) of the motorcycle market.

The Hanlons felt that they were ready for the challenge. In Dave's words, "Everybody in the industry who heard about us said: 'This has never been done. It cannot be done. And it will not be done.' And it was that kind of attitude that made us very, very tough." Their goal from the outset was to corner a small niche—1.5 percent—of the upscale motorcycle cruiser market. High-end leisure bikes account for over 50 percent of all [mo]torcycle revenue. Riders like them because [en]gines run loud and slow, they feature a lot [of] chrome, and their wide saddles make [them c]omfortable to ride.

[On]e of the partners had prior business own[ership] experience—let alone experience designing [or] manufacturing motorcycles. At heart, they [were] motorcycle riders who were passionate [about] bikes. During the time of Excelsior-[Hender]son's start-up, Jennie was working as a [model] and her husband Dave was em[ployed] as a middle manager for a truck-leasing [compan]y. With degrees in business and account[ing al]ong with past work experience as a me[chanic,] Dan was probably the most qualified of the three. But what the partners lacked in hands-on experience they believed they could make up for with hard work, passion, and commitment.

To raise funds for their start-up investment, the Hanlons reached out to their personal network of family, friends, and local investors. Within two years, they had secured $600,000 in financing. In 1996, the state of Minnesota provided them with a $7 million dollar business development loan. They even convinced Governor Anne Clarkson to pose atop one of their motorcycles for a photo op in St. Paul, the state capitol. It looked as if the Hanlons were on their way.

In 1997, the Hanlons decided to put out an "IPO" (Initial Public Offering) so that they could sell equity in their company in exchange for cash flow that would help them to build the business. Shares of Excelsior-Henderson were introduced on the NASDAQ at a price of $7.50. Dan Hanlon felt that the company was proceeding too quickly with taking the company public. Excelsior-Henderson was operating with a negative cash flow and Hanlon had wanted to wait until the financial position had improved before it sold shares in the open market. However, a local newspaper had obtained a copy of Excelsior-Henderson's business plan, which outlined its intention to go public at some point. Once the story ran—against the company's wishes—the partners felt pressured to move ahead with the IPO sooner than they had intended.

All told, the IPO brought close to $100 million into Excelsior-Henderson's coffers. However, the Hanlons did not succeed in translating these resources into a profitable company. Excelsior-Henderson's stock price peaked at $10.50 in 1999 but then plummeted to below $3. Things were not looking good for the Hanlons.

Why did Excelsior-Henderson fail despite the company's success in designing and producing a quality product? One factor was the company's production costs. It had intended to manufacture at a cost of $9,000 per motorcycle. But, in reality, the company was spending between $10,000 and $14,000 to produce each bike.

The company also failed to meet its sales targets. In 1999, the Hanlons set out to sell 4,000 motorcycles. By the end of their fiscal year, they reported 1,800 units sold. They fell short of their sales target by over 50 percent. During the life span of their business, the Hanlons devoted seven years to designing their product and building their manufacturing plant. But by the time they were up and running, they had gone through a good percentage of their start-up investment. All told, they were only manufacturing motorcycles for eight months before they were forced to file for Chapter 11 bankruptcy protection.

According to Don Brown, an independent motorcycle analyst with DJB Associates LLC, in Irvine, California, "It takes about $150 million these days to field a new motorcycle of that type. They probably overestimated the market, and they probably did not do enough research to determine the styling and performance elements and the price point that would stand the best chance."

Excelsior-Henderson was rescued from bankruptcy when a Florida-based investment firm, under the name of "EH Partners," decided to acquire the failing company in 1999. The terms of the agreement stipulated that the Hanlons would remain with the company, but in nonexecutive positions. However, within a year, EH Partners had defaulted on its payments to creditors and ultimately filed for bankruptcy protection in its own right. Despite the company's difficulties, some locals hoped that Excelsior-Henderson would rise from the ashes. But Dan Hanlon no longer shared this dream: "Let [Excelsior-Henderson] have its peace," he said. "There is nothing left to restart. Let's be real about it."

Case Study Analysis

1. Excelsior-Henderson raised $100 million in debt and equity investment and yet it still went bankrupt. List three ways that the company could have better managed its cash flow.

»Building a Business Plan Step-by-Step

Students begin thinking about and planning a new business start-up from Chapter One onward. Business Plan fundamentals are presented in Chapter One.

Business Plan Practice

Assignments appear at the end of each unit.

BizBuilder Business Plan CD: Worksheets, Templates, Example Plans

Students are directed to progressively build an effective Business Plan, utilizing the BizBuilder Business Plan Worksheets included on the BizBuilder Student Resources CD packaged with the book. Students follow a three-step process:

■ **Step 1:** Students use the BizBuilder Business Plan Worksheets to work through every aspect of a business plan

■ **Step 2:** Students use the BizBuilder Business Plan Template to create a professional-looking business plan from their worksheets

■ **Step 3:** Students use the BizBuilder Business Plan Presentation Template to create a PowerPoint presentation of their business plan.

The BizBuilder CD also includes a set of sample Student Business Plan Worksheets, a Student Business Plan Template and a Student Business Plan Presentaiton that students can use as a guide. Appendices include instructions on how to create a business plan using Business Plan Pro software, and the business plan for *Venture* magazine.

Unit 1 BUSINESS PLAN PRACTICE

At the end of each unit, you will have an opportunity to work on your own business plan. Please go to the Business Plan Worksheet Template section for Unit One on the BizBuilder CD now to develop the following segments of your plan:

Your Business Idea

1. Describe your business idea. What is the name of your business?
2. Explain how your business idea will satisfy a consumer need.
3. Provide contact information for each owner.
4. If there is more than one owner, describe how the ownership will be shared.

Economics of One Unit

1. Do you intend to pay yourself a salary, wage, dividend, or commission? Explain.
2. What type of business are you starting?
3. Define your unit.

Technology

1. Identify which technological tools you plan to use for your business, and why.
2. Write a memo explaining how you plan to get access to the technology you need.

Core Beliefs

... core beliefs you will use to run

4. Calculate the economics of one unit for your business.

Evaluating Your Business Idea

1. What resources and skills do you (and the other owners) have that will help make your business successful?
2. Perform a SWOT analysis of your business.

Your Goals

1. What are your short-term business goals (less than one year)?
2. What are your long-term business goals (from one to five years)?

Supply and Demand

1. What factors influence the demand for your product or service?
2. What factors influence the supply for your product or service?

Competitive Advantage

1. What type of business are you starting—manufacturing, wholesale, retail, or service?
2. Describe your competitive advantage.
3. Find three competitors and describe:

| | Weaknesses | Strengths |

... charts to define your business and analyze your competitive advantage.

Question	Response
roducts and services will be sold?	1.
hich consumer segment will the	2.
y—How will that offer be produced customers?	3.

PROJECTED 1-YEAR BALANCE SHEET

BALANCE SHEET

	Opening	Closing
ASSETS		
Current Assets:		
Cash		
Accounts Receivable		
Total Current Assets		
Fixed Assets (Property and Equipment):		
Headphones		
Additional Records for my collection		
Blank CD Stock		
Speakers		
Protective Cases for Records		
Amplifier		
Total Property and Equipment		
Less Accumulated Depreciation		
Total Property and Equipment (net)		
Total Assets		
LIABILITIES AND OWNER'S EQUITY		
Current Liabilities:		
Accounts Payable		
Total Current Liabilities		
Long-term Liability (Bank Loan)		
Total Liabilities		
Owner's Equity		
Total Liabilities and Owner's Equity		

Accrued means have increased periodically.

STARTUP INVESTMENT

List the items you will need to buy to start your business.

Item	Quantity	Cost
Equipment		
Computer (includes CD burner)	1	$650.00 (in kind)
Cell Phone	1	$80.00 (in kind)
Printer	1	$75.00 (in kind)
Turntables and Mixer	1	$2000.00 (in kind)
Headphones	2	$100.00
CD Player	1	$100.00 (in kind)
Additional Records for my collection	Multiple	$150.00
Blank CD Stock	25 CDs at $1 each	$25.00
Speakers	2	$500.00
Protective Cases for Records	5 at $30 each	$150.00
Amplifier	1	$550.00
Other Costs		
Promotional Cards	300	@.05/each = $15.00
Legal Fees	1 day	$500.00
		$35.00
		$5000.00
		$2000.00
		$7000.00

Oldies But Goodies DJ Service

■ **MISSION:**
■ Offer customers the best selection of popular and rare recordings from the Motown-era. We enhance the life of every party we service by listening to our customers and playing the music that they like best.

»Business Planning Software Package

BizBuilder Student Resources CD

Packaged with the text is the BizBuilder Student Resources CD which includes the following:

- BizBuilder Business Plan Worksheets that provide step-by-step instructions on building a business plan
- BizBuilder Business Plan Template which is a professional-looking format into which content from the business plan worksheet can be inserted
- BizBuilder Business Plan Presentation Template that guides students through creating a PowerPoint presentation for their business plan
- Sample Business Plans that use the Worksheet Template and the Professional Business Plan format
- Several Business Plans
- PowerPoint Review of each chapter

"The Business Plan Practice is great!"
**—Dr. Laura Portolese Dias,
Shoreline Community College,
Seattle, WA**

Students build their business plans using the BizBuilder worksheets. Appendix 8 provides students with instructions on how to use the worksheets that mirror the planning process in the book and contains more questions in some areas than found in commercially available planning software. Once they have created a plan using the worksheets, they can generate a professional-looking document using the BizBuilder Business Plan Template or Business Plan Pro software.

Business Plan Pro® Software CD

Business Plan Pro (BPP) software, the most widely used professional business-planning software, is also packaged free with every text. Once a student has created a business plan using the BizBuilder worksheet, it will be easy to cut and paste that information into Business Plan Pro. BPP includes a number of very useful features:

- Over 400 sample business plans students can study and compare with their own. Use the Sample Plan Browser to search the extensive library.
- Easy Plan Wizard that guides students through writing a plan.
- Spreadsheet tables with columns, rows, and formulas to automatically calculate totals.

- Pie and bar charts that can be automatically created from your spreadsheets.
- Financial statements that can be customized.
- Plan Review Wizard that reviews the plan for completeness, compares the financial statements to standard accounting practices, and checks for errors.
- Professional-looking printout of the business plan.
- Appendix 7 provides students with an overview of how to get started using Business Plan Pro.

Students can access a wealth of study aids at www.prenhall.com/mariotti

»Online Resources

Companion Website

The online Companion Website includes the following:

- Test-Prep Quizzes for each chapter, including true/false, multiple choice, and short essay. All questions include immediate feedback.
- Business Plan Examples.
- PowerPoint Chapter Review of Key Topics.
- Web Links to Additional Resources.

OneKey Distance Learning Solutions: Convenience, Simplicity, Success

Ready-made WebCT and Blackboard online courses! If you adopt a OneKey course, student access cards will be packaged with the text, at no extra charge to the student. OneKey courses include Research Navigator, a premium online research tool.

Research Navigator: A Premium Research Tool

»Instructor Resources

Instructor's Resource CD: Instructor's Manual, Answer Key, Test Item File, and PowerPoint slides are available on the Instructor's Resource CD or can be downloaded from the Prentice-Hall Instructor's Resources website.

Instructor's Manual Includes the following:

- Answers to all end-of-chapter material, including teaching notes for short and long case studies
- Additional instructional material on how to teach writing a Business Plan and to supplement end-of-unit Business Plan sections
- Course outlines for 8-week term (short course), 12-week term (3 hours/week), and 15-week term (3 hours/week)
- Additional resources (print and Web sites) for each chapter
- Test Item File

TestGen computerized Test Generator

PowerPoint Lecture Presentation Package

»Entrepreneurship Videos

The following commercially produced videos are available free of charge to qualified adopters of the textbook. Please contact your local representative to place an order.

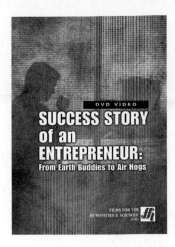

Success Story of an Entrepreneur: From Earth Buddies to Air Hoggs:

It all began in 1994 with Earth Buddies, little heads that sprout grass hair. Four months, a deal with Kmart, and $400,000 in profit later, young Canadian entrepreneur Anton Rabie and his company, Spin Master, were well on their way to becoming a major power in North America's toy industry. Filmed over eight years, this program tracks Spin Master's meteoric rise—and the manufacturing pressures that nearly blew the company apart. Subsequent successes involving other signature product lines—Air Hoggs and Flick Trix Finger Bikes, to name two—are also covered, along with the stresses of trade shows and negotiating with top retailers, including Toys "R" Us. (17 minutes, color)

Warren Buffett: The Ultimate Entrepreneur:

Having sustained its annual growth for decades, Berkshire Hathaway is one of the most profitable companies in existence today. In this rare interview, ABC News anchor Ted Koppel and billionaire CEO Warren Buffett—second only to Bill Gates in personal wealth in the U.S.—discuss how to target businesses for acquisition, the future of investment in a volatile stock market, why Berkshire Hathaway's stock has never split, and Buffett's ultimate entrepreneurial goal: to amass an immense endowment fund to benefit society. (25 minutes, color)

CEO Exchange: Major League Entrepreneurs:

Filmed at the Kellogg School of Management at Northwestern University, this program teams up Mark Cuban, billionaire owner of the Dallas Mavericks and cofounder of Broadcast.com, and Daniel Snyder, owner of the Washington Redskins, who made his team one of the most valuable franchises in sports history. Together they discuss being an entrepreneur in the world of professional sports, while MBA students and faculty ask questions about management styles, the lure of owning a sports team, and the impact of salary caps. (57 minutes, color)

NFTE/Pearson Prentice Hall Business Plan Award

You and Your Students Can Compete on the National Stage

NFTE and Pearson/Prentice Hall are jointly sponsoring a national competition that rewards the best business plan author and his or her instructor. The competition is open to students enrolled in an entrepreneurship or small business management course at any school using this book. Please visit www.prenhall.com/mariotti for official contest rules.

Ten plans will be chosen to be recognized as outstanding plans and two plans will be chosen as the best overall business plans.

The authors of the top 10 business plans and their instructors will each receive the following recognition:

- an award plaque
- a letter of achievement from NFTE
- acknowledgment on the NFTE Web site and the Pearson Prentice Hall book Web site

The authors of the top two plans and their instructors will each additionally receive an award of $500.00 and feedback from NFTE regarding the viability of their plan.

The winners will be announced on July 1st of each year over three years, for submittals made during the prior school year. The first award will be made on July 1st, 2007, following the 2006/2007 school year.

Entries must be accompanied by a submittal form, downloadable from www.prenhall.com/mariotti, and must be received by June 1st of each year to be considered for consideration. Please send business plans along with the completed submittal form to the following:

Steve Mariotti
NFTE
120 Wall Street—29th Floor
New York, NY 10005

About the Author

Steve Mariotti, Founder and President of the National Foundation for Teaching Entrepreneurship (NFTE), is an expert in education for at-risk youth. He has been helping young people develop marketable skills by learning about entrepreneurship for more than 20 years.

Mariotti received an M.B.A. from the University of Michigan and has studied at Harvard University, Stanford University, and Brooklyn College. His professional career began with serving as a Treasury Analyst for Ford Motor Co. (1976–79). He then founded Mason Import/Export Services in New York, eventually acting as sales representative and purchasing agent for 32 overseas firms. In 1982, he made a significant career change and became a Special Education/Business Teacher in the New York City school system, choosing to teach in such notorious neighborhoods as Bedford-Stuyvesant in Brooklyn and the "Fort Apache" section of the South Bronx. It was at Jane Addams Vocational High School in the Bronx that he developed the insight and inspiration to bring entrepreneurial education to low-income youth. This led to founding NFTE in 1987.

Steve Mariotti and NFTE have received numerous awards, including the 2004 Ernst & Young National Entrepreneur of the Year Award; the Golden Lamp Award from the Association of Educational Publishers (2002); and the ACE/Currie Foundation Humanitarian Venture Award (1990), as well as major media exposure that includes profiles on ABC News and CNN. Mariotti has co-authored eight books and eight manuals that have sold over a quarter million copies.

Acknowledgments

First, sincere thanks to the team of reviewers who provided insightful feedback to this book and to the 9th and 10th editions of *How to Start and Operate a Small Business* by Steve Mariotti with Tony Towle, on which it was based.

Consultants and Reviewers

Elaine Allen, National Director Not-for-Profit Services Group, Ernst & Young

Larry Bennett, Johnson & Wales University—Providence, RI

Sunne Brandmeyer, Retired Lecturer/Advisor, Center for Economic Education, University of South Florida

Stanlee Brimberg, Teacher, Bank Street School for Children

Howard W. Buffett, Jr.

John D. Christesen, SUNY Westchester Community College, Valhalla, NY

Steve Colyer, Adjunct Professor, School of Business, Miami Dade College

Laura Portolese Dias, Shoreline Community College, Seattle, WA

Alex Dontoh, New York University

Alan Dlugash, CPA Partner, Dlugash & Kevelson

Thomas Emrick, Ed.D.

George Gannage, Jr., West Central Technical College—Carrollton, GA

Thomas Goodrow, Springfield Technical Community College—Springfield, MA

Janet P. Graham, E. Craig Wall, Sr. College of Business Administration, Coastal Carolina University

John Harris, Teacher of Business, Bristol Eastern High School, CT

Deborah Hoffman, Audit Manager, Ernst & Young

Donald Hoy, Benedictine College—Atchison, KS

Samira Hussein, Johnson County Community College, Overland Park, KS

Eileen M. Kearney, Montgomery County Community College, Blue Bell, PA

Sanford Krieger, Esq., Partner, Fried, Frank, Harris, Shriver & Jacobson

Dr. Jawanza Kunjufu, President, African American Images

Corey Kupfer, Esq., Founding Partner, Kupfer, Rosen & Herz, LLP

Emily H. Martin, Faulkner Community College, Bay Minette, AL

Alaire Mitchell, Former Assistant Director of Curriculum Research, New York City Board of Education

Timothy R. Mittan, Southeast Community College, Lincoln, NE

Eric Mulkowsky, Engagement Manager, McKinsey and Company, Inc.

Raffiq Nathoo, Senior Managing Director, The Blackstone Group, LLP

Ray E. Newton, III , Managing Director, Perseus Capital, LLC

Arnold Ng, Pepperdine University—Rancho Palos Verdes, CA

William H. Painter, Retired Professor of Law, George Washington University

Peter Patch, Patch and Associates

Alan Patricof, Founder and Chairman, Apax Partners

Carolyn J. Christensen Perricone, CPA, Associate Professor and Curriculum Chair, Accounting, SUNY

Robert Plain, Guilford Technical Community College—Jamestown, NC

Christopher P. Puto, Dean and Professor of Marketing, Georgetown University, McDonough School of Business

Richard Relyea, NY Penn

Ira Sacks, Esq., Partner, Fried, Frank, Harris, Shriver & Jacobson

Dr. William Sahlman, Professor of Business Administration, Harvard Business School

Dr. Arnold Scheibel, Professor of Neurobiology, University of California at Los Angeles

Sandra Sowell-Scott, State Director, Youth Entrepreneurship Education, Fox School of Business & Management, Temple University

LaVerne Tilley, Gwinnett Technical College—Lawrenceville, GA

Marsha Wender Timmerman, LaSalle University, Philadelphia, PA

Liza Vertinsky, J.D., Ph.D., Attorney, Hill & Barlow

Peter Walker, Managing Director, McKinsey and Company, Inc.

Walter Lara, Florida Community College—Jacksonville, FL

Larry Weaver, Navarro College—Corsicana, TX

Dr. Donald Wells, Professor of Economics, University of Arizona

I would like to thank Debra DeSalvo, without whose assistance this book would not have been possible; Tony Towle, who from NFTE's inception has helped me organize my thoughts and experiences; and Nancy Rosenbaum and Stephen Spinelli, for contributing the wonderful business cases. I must single out the help of two great educators: John Harris and Peter Patch, and would like to acknowledge the significant contributions of Pete McBride, John Robb, and NFTE executives Michael J. Caslin, III, J. David Nelson, Julie Silard Kantor, Leslie Pechman Koch, Del Daniels, Margaret Dunn, Dianna Maeurer, Jean Mahoney, Christine Poorman, Jane Walsh, Joel Warren, and Katerina Zacharia. Special thanks as well to the Young Entrepreneurs of Prudential program and the Prudential Foundation for initial funding of this project, to Gary Bauer, Brandon Elliott and Peter McCarthy from Prentice Hall for being wonderful friends, to Tom Goodrow of the Springfield Enterprise Center and the National Association for Community College Entrepreneurship (NACCE), and to John Christesen of SUNY Westchester Community College.

Thanks also to Howard Stevenson, Jeffry Timmons, William Bygrave, Bob Pritzker and NFTE Board Member Stephen Spinelli, for their expertise and to Richard Fink of Koch Industries, Carl Schramm of the Ewing Marion Kauffman Foundation, and Mike Hennessy and John Hughes of the Coleman Foundation. Special thanks to Eddy Bayardelle and Melanie Mortimer of Merrill Lynch Global Philanthropy, and Kim Davis of the JPMorganChase Foundation.

I would also like to recognize the efforts and contributions of members of NFTE's National Board of Directors: Albert Abney, Bart Breighner, Jay Christopher, John Fullerton, Verne Harnish, Tom Hartocollis, Landon Hilliard, James Holden, Robert Hurst, Loida N. Lewis, James Lyle, Alan Patricof, Arthur Samberg, Andrew Sherman, Diana Davis Spencer, Kenneth I. Starr, and Peter Walker. I would like to acknowledge the inspired guidance provided by our National Executive Committee: Lewis Eisenberg, Theodore Forstmann, the Hon. Jack Kemp, Elizabeth Koch, Jeff Raikes, and the Hon. John Whitehead. I am deeply grateful as well to the many philanthropists who have supported our work, including Raymond Chambers, Charles G. and David H. Koch, Joanne Beyer of the Scaife Family Foundation, Barbara Bell Coleman of the Newark Boys' and Girls' Clubs, Chris Podoll of the William Zimmerman Foundation, Stephanie Bell-Rose of the Goldman Sachs Foundation, The Shelby Cullom Davis Foundation, Jeff Raikes and the Microsoft Corporation, The Nasdaq Educational Foundation, and Ronald McDonald House Children's Charities.

Further, I would like to acknowledge Steve Alcock, Harsh and Aruna Bhargava, Lena Bondue, Dawn Bowlus, Stephen Brenninckmeyer, Shelly Chenoweth, Janet McKinstry Cort, Erik Dauwen, Clara Del Villar, Christine Chambers Gilfillan, Andrew Hahn, Kathleen Kirkwood, Sheena Lindahl, Dianna Maeurer, Cynthia Miree, Victor Salama, Michael Simmons, Henry To, Carol Tully, Dilia Wood, and Elizabeth Wright, as well as Peter Cowie, Joseph Dominic, Paul DeF. Hicks, Jr., Ann Mahoney, David Roodberg, Phyllis

Ross Schless, and Remi Vermeir, who have provided countless insights into providing entrepreneurial opportunities to young people.

In addition, I would like to thank my brother, Jack, the best CPA I know, and my father, John, for financing much of NFTE's early work, and for their continuing love and guidance. Thanks are due to all the other teachers, students, experts, and friends who were kind enough to look over this book and help me improve it. Finally, I want to thank my mother, Nancy, a wonderful special education instructor who showed me that one great teacher can affect eternity. Any errors are mine alone.

Steve Mariotti

What Business Do You Want to Start?

Entrepreneurs Recognize Opportunities

"Everyone lives by selling something."

—Robert Louis Stevenson, Scottish author

Performance Objectives

1. Explain what entrepreneurs do.
2. Describe how free-enterprise economies work and how entrepreneurs fit into them.
3. Explain how profit works as a signal to the entrepreneur.
4. Find and evaluate opportunities to start your own business.
5. Explain why entrepreneurs write business plans.

» What Is an Entrepreneur?[1]

Have you ever eaten a Mrs. Fields cookie? Used an Apple computer? Listened to a hip-hop CD? An entrepreneur brought each of these products into your world.

Debbi Fields was a young mother with no business experience when she started selling her chocolate chip cookies. Today, Mrs. Fields' Original Cookies has over 380 stores in the United States, and over 80 locations in 11 other countries. Steve Jobs and Stephen Wozniak were barely out of college when they invented the personal computer in a garage in Cupertino, California. Now Apple sells millions of iBooks, iPods, and other innovative products each year. Russell Simmons used his own passion for hip-hop to turn rap artists like Run DMC and LL Kool J into international pop stars. Simmons and his businesses—Def Jam Records, Rush Communications, etc.—have come to be worth over $300 million.

Most Americans earn money by working in **business.** Business is the buying and selling of products or services in order to make money.

- A **product** is something that exists in nature or is made by human beings. It is *tangible*, meaning that it can be touched.

- A **service** is work that provides time, skills, or expertise in exchange for money. It is *intangible*. You cannot actually touch it.

Someone who earns a living by working for someone else's business is an **employee** of that business. There are many kinds of employees. At Ford Motor Company, for instance, some employees build the cars, some sell the cars, and some manage the company. But employees all have one thing in common—they do not own a business; they work for others who do. They know how much money

---

[1] The ideas and concepts in this chapter are adapted from the works of Jeffry A. Timmons, Howard W. Stevenson, and William Bygrave.

Performance Objective 1.〉

> ! *A scarce resource is something of value that can be used to make something else or to fill a need.*

> ! *America's small business owners and their employees represent more than half of the private workforce. These entrepreneurs, who create more than 75 percent of net new jobs nationwide and generate more than 50 percent of the Nation's gross domestic product, and the employees who work in small businesses, deserve our thanks. We salute them.*
>
> *—President George W. Bush, from speech celebrating Small Business Week*

they can earn, and that amount is limited to salary, plus bonuses and any stock options they may receive.

Some people start their own businesses and work for themselves. They are called **entrepreneurs**. Entrepreneurs are often both owners and employees. For an entrepreneur, the sky is the limit as far as earnings are concerned. Unlike an employee, an entrepreneur owns the profit that his or her business earns and may choose whether to reinvest it in the business or use it to pay him- or herself.

An entrepreneur is someone who recognizes an opportunity to start a business that other people may not have noticed—and jumps on it. As economist Jeffry Timmons writes in the preface of *New Venture Creation: Entrepreneurship for the 21st Century*, "A skillful entrepreneur can shape and create an opportunity where others see little or nothing—or see it too early or too late."

The word *entrepreneur* first surfaced in France in the seventeenth century. It was used to describe someone who undertook a project, but after awhile it came to mean someone who starts a new business—often a new kind of business or a new (and improved) way of doing business. The French economist Jean Baptiste Say wrote at the turn of the nineteenth century: "The entrepreneur shifts economic resources [like wood or coal] out of an area of lower and into an area of higher productivity and greater yield." By doing this, Say argued, entrepreneurs added value to **scarce resources**. Oil is a resource because it is used as fuel. Wood is a resource because it can be used to make a house or a table or paper. Economists consider all resources that cost money "scarce."

Debbi Fields took resources—eggs, butter, flour, sugar, and chocolate chips—and turned them into cookies. People liked what she did with those resources so much that they were willing to pay

Debbie Fields, a young mother with no business experience, opened her first Mrs. Fields cookie store in California in 1977. (Arizona Daily Star)

her more for the cookies than it cost her to buy the resources to make them. She added value to the resources she purchased by what she did with them—and created a multimillion dollar business in the process.

»The Economic Questions[2]

Since time began, people have had to answer the same basic questions:

- What should be produced?
- When will it be produced?
- How will it be produced?
- Who will produce it?
- Who gets to have what is produced?

Families and individuals, as well as businesspeople, charities, corporations, and governments, all have had to answer these questions. The system a group of people creates through making these decisions is called an **economy**. The study of how these different groups answer these questions is called **economics**.

An economy is a country's financial structure. It is the system that produces and distributes wealth in a country. The U.S. economy is called a **free enterprise system** because anyone is free to start a business. You do not have to get permission from the government to start a business, although you do have to obey laws and regulations.

This economic system is also called **capitalism** because the money used to start a business is called **capital**. Anyone who can raise the capital is free to start a business. *You* can start a business!

⟨2. **Performance Objective**

»Voluntary Exchange

The free enterprise system is also sometimes referred to as a "free-trade system" because it is based on **voluntary exchange**. Voluntary exchange is a trade between two parties who agree to trade money for a product or service. No one is *forced* to trade. Each is excited by the opportunity the trade offers. Both parties agree to the exchange because they both benefit.

Let's say you have a contracting business and your busy neighbors hire you to renovate their kitchen. You need money and are willing to use your skills and time to earn it. They want their kitchen renovated and are willing to give up money to get it done. You each have something the other wants, so you are willing to trade. Trading only takes place when both parties believe they will benefit. Robbery, in contrast, is an *involuntary* trade.

---

[2] Source of definitions: Small Business Administration.

[Global Impact]

Free Trade

For centuries, international trade was very difficult. To sell products in another country required long and dangerous journeys overland or by ship. Many countries were closed to outside trade. Governments also used their power to give their own businesspeople a competitive advantage over those from other countries by imposing trade barriers, such as taxes on foreign goods that made them too expensive to buy. Governments could also enforce restrictions on how many imports or exports could cross a country's borders.

Today, trade barriers are falling in most parts of the world. The North American Free Trade Agreement (NAFTA) of 1994 ended trade barriers between the United States, Mexico, and Canada. This turned the entire continent into a free trade zone. The General Agreement on Tariffs and Trade (GATT) cut or eliminated tariffs between 117 countries. Where people are free to trade voluntarily to as large a market as possible, their ability to find someone to buy their goods or services increases. So does their ability to meet consumer needs.

Meanwhile, the Internet has made it much easier for entrepreneurs to sell to customers all over the world. Shipping, too, has become much faster and less expensive. It is an exciting time to be in business!

»Benefits of Free Enterprise

We all benefit from living in a free enterprise system because it discourages entrepreneurs who waste resources—by driving them out of business. It encourages entrepreneurs who use resources efficiently to satisfy consumer needs—by rewarding them with profit.

We also benefit because free enterprise encourages competition between entrepreneurs. Someone who can make cookies that taste as good as Mrs. Fields' Original Cookies, and sells them at a lower price, will eventually attract Mrs. Fields' customers. This will force Mrs. Fields' to lower prices to stay competitive. Consumers benefit because they get to buy cookies at a lower price.

»What Is a "Small" Business?

The public often thinks of business only in terms of "big" business—companies such as General Electric, Ford, Microsoft, McDonald's, and Nike. A big business is defined by the Small Business Administration as having more than one hundred employees and selling more than $5 million worth of products or services in a year.

Most of the world's businesses are small businesses. A neighborhood restaurant or a clothing boutique are examples of small businesses. A small business employs fewer than one hundred employees and has yearly sales under $5 million.

Surprisingly, the principles involved in running a large company, like MTV, and a corner deli are the same. In fact, most multimillion-dollar businesses in this country started out as small, entrepreneurial ventures. This is why entrepreneurship is often called the "engine" of our economy. It "drives" the economy, creating wealth and jobs and improving our standard of living. It is no coincidence

Biz Facts

- There are about 22.4 million non-agricultural small businesses in the United States, according to 2001 data (Small Business Administration).
- The small businesses in America employ more than half of the country's private workforce, create three of every four new jobs, and generate a majority of the country's innovations (Small Business Administration).
- Fourteen percent of *Inc.* magazine's 500 fastest-growing companies in the United States started with less than $1,000 (*Inc.*, October 2002).
- Small businesses represent more than 99 percent of all employers (Small Business Administration, December 2000).

that the United States is both the most entrepreneurial country in the world and the richest.

»A Business Must Make a Profit to Stay in Business

No matter how big or small, a business must make a **profit;** that is, the amount of money coming in must be greater than the amount of money required to pay the bills. Most businesses do lose money initially because they have to lay out cash to set up operations, and advertise to attract customers. If the business cannot make a profit, eventually the entrepreneur will be unable to pay the bills and will have to close.

Closing a business is nothing to be ashamed of if you learn from the experience. In fact, most successful entrepreneurs open and close more than one business during their lives. If your venture is not making a profit after you have gotten it up and running, that is a signal that you may be in the wrong business. Closing it may be the smartest decision.

An entrepreneur may change businesses many times over a lifetime in response to changing competition and consumer needs. The great economist Joseph Schumpeter called the process of constantly changing businesses "creative destruction."[3]

> ! *When starting a business, it is a good rule of thumb to expect to lose money for the first three months. It usually takes at least that long for a business to start selling enough to earn a profit.*

»Profit Is the Sign That the Entrepreneur Is Adding Value

Profit is the sign that an entrepreneur has added value to the scarce resources he or she is using. Debbi Fields added value to scarce resources by creating something with them that people were willing to buy for a price that gave her a profit. In contrast, not making a profit is a sign that the entrepreneur is not using resources very well and is not adding value to them.

⟨3. **Performance Objective**

---

[3] Joseph A. Schumpeter, *Capitalism, Socialism and Democracy* (New York: Harper & Row, 1942).

»Profit Results from the Entrepreneur's Choices

An entrepreneur's choices directly affect how much profit the business makes. Say, like Debbi Fields, you have a business selling homemade cookies. You might decide one week to buy margarine instead of butter because it is cheaper, even though your cookies may not taste as good made with margarine. This type of choice is called a **trade-off**. You are giving up one thing (taste) for another (money).

If your customers do not notice the change and continue to buy your cookies, you have made a good choice. You have conserved a resource (money) and increased your profit by lowering your costs. The increase in profit confirms that you have made the right choice.

If your customers notice the change and stop buying your cookies, your profit will decrease. The decrease in profit signals that you have made a bad choice. Next week you should probably buy butter again. The profit signal taught you that your consumers are dissatisfied and the trade-off was not worth it. Every choice an entrepreneur makes is a trade-off.

»Why Be an Entrepreneur?

Entrepreneurs put a great deal of time into launching their own businesses. While establishing a business, an entrepreneur may also pour all his or her money into it. He or she may not be able to buy new clothes or a fancy car, or go on vacation, or spend much time with family until the business becomes profitable.

If so much work and sacrifice is involved, why be an entrepreneur? The entrepreneur is working for the following rewards:

1. ***Control over Time***—Do you work better at midnight than at 8 A.M.? If you start your own business, you have control over how you spend your time. Are you the type of person who would rather work really hard for two weeks nonstop and then take a break? If you are an entrepreneur, you can. You can also choose to hire other people to do tasks that you do not want to do or are not good at, so you can stay focused on what you do best. Bill Gates likes to spend his time designing software. He hires other people to manage Microsoft's operations and market and sell its products.

2. ***Fulfillment***—Successful entrepreneurs are passionate about their businesses. They are excited and fulfilled by their work. Entrepreneurs are almost never bored. If something about running their business is boring to them, they can hire someone to do that task.

3. ***Creation/Ownership***—Entrepreneurship is a creative endeavor. Entrepreneurs put their time into creating something that they hope will survive and become profitable. Entrepre-

Real estate tycoon Donald Trump was asked on his national TV series *The Apprentice* If he ran his many ventures for the money. He replied: "No, I do it for the challenge."

neurs own the businesses that they create and the profits that the businesses earn. Ownership is the key to wealth. Your goal is to create a business that makes a continuing profit. Eventually, you may be able to sell that business for a multiple of earnings. That is how entrepreneurs create wealth.

4. ***Control over Compensation***—Entrepreneurs choose how they are paid. As owner of your company you can decide to

   ● Pay yourself a **salary**—a fixed payment made at regular intervals, such as every week or every month. No matter how much time you put in, the salary remains the same.

   ● Pay yourself a **wage**—a fixed payment per hour.

   ● Take a share of the company's profit—as the owner you can pay yourself a portion of the business's profit. This payment is called a **dividend**.

   ● Take a **commission** on every sale you make. A commission is a percentage of the value of a sale. If you decide to pay yourself 10 percent commission and you sell one of your products for $120, your commission on the sale would be $12.

5. ***Control over Working Conditions***—As an entrepreneur, you can create a working environment that reflects your values. If you believe in recycling, you can make sure your company recycles. You also evaluate your own performance. No one else has the power to hire or fire you.

Some of the greatest entrepreneurs in the world have dealt with problems growing up such as extreme poverty, abuse, learning disabilities, and other issues. Richard Branson, for example, had such bad dyslexia that he dropped out of high school. He became a successful entrepreneur, however, creating Virgin Airlines and Virgin Records. Today he oversees 200 companies and is worth about $4 billion. As an entrepreneur, he was able to create an environment in which he could succeed.

❯❯The Desire to Make Money Is Not a Good Reason to Start a Business

Starting a business is an opportunity, and like any opportunity it should be evaluated by taking a careful look at the costs and benefits it offers. One thing is for certain, though, *the desire to make money, alone, is not a good enough reason to start one's own business.*

[Step Into The Shoes]

Henry Ford's Vision

Henry Ford dreamed of a "horseless carriage" that the average American could afford. Ford needed this strong vision to sustain him through years of business failure. By the time he was almost forty, Ford had been trying to get his vision off the ground for many years. Several of his attempts to produce and sell cars had failed. His neighbors considered him a daydreaming mechanic. He continued to direct all his efforts toward making his vision real, and created the Ford Motor Company. By the time he was fifty, however, Ford was one of the richest and most famous men in the world. After a hundred years, Ford Motor Company is still a major American company.

The dream provides the motivation to succeed. What vision will sustain you?

The financial rewards of owning your own business may not happen until you put in years of hard work. The desire to make money may not be enough to keep you going through the difficult early period. Most successful companies have been founded by an entrepreneur with a powerful and motivating dream.

Entrepreneurs say they are not in business for the money so often that it has almost become a cliché but, like all clichés, it is based on a degree of truth.

»Costs and Benefits of Becoming an Entrepreneur

Even if you do have a strong dream that you believe will motivate you through the ups and downs of running a business, look closely at the costs and benefits of being an entrepreneur before you decide whether this is the life for you.

Benefits include the following:

- **Independence:** Business owners do not have to follow orders or observe working hours set by someone else.
- **Satisfaction:** Turning a skill, hobby, or other interest into your own business can be highly satisfying.
- **Financial Reward:** Through hard work, the sky can be the limit. Entrepreneurs built most of our country's great fortunes.
- **Self-Esteem:** Knowing you created something valuable can give you a strong sense of accomplishment. It makes you feel good about yourself.

Costs include the following:

- **Business Failure:** About one in five new businesses fails in the first eight years, although this is largely due to entrepreneurs not getting proper training.[4] Another third close because the entrepreneurs become discouraged and give up. You risk losing not only your money but also money invested in your business by others.

- ■ *Obstacles:* You will run into problems that you will have to solve by yourself. Your family and friends may discourage you or not support your vision.
- ■ *Loneliness:* It can be lonely and even a little scary to be completely responsible for the success or failure of your business.
- ■ *Financial Insecurity:* You are not guaranteed a set salary or benefits. You may not always have enough money to pay yourself. You will have to set up your own retirement fund.
- ■ *Long Hours/Hard Work:* You will have to work long hours to get your business off the ground. Some entrepreneurs work six or even seven days a week. Also, do not forget to look at the opportunities you will give up to start your own business. What are the "next-best opportunities" for your money and time? Some might include these:
  - Going to college or graduate school
  - Working for someone else

Not everyone is cut out to be an entrepreneur. Entrepreneurs have to be able to tolerate a higher degree of risk and uncertainty than people who work steady jobs for established employers. With higher risk, however, comes the possibility of higher rewards.

»Cost/Benefit Analysis

Using a comparison of costs and benefits to make a decision is called **cost/benefit analysis**. It is a helpful tool because we tend to make decisions with our emotions, not by using our intellect to evaluate the pros and cons. Strong emotions may overwhelm you to the point where you see only the benefits and not the costs of an action (or vice versa).

Say you plan to buy a car. You might be overwhelmed by the idea of making such a large purchase, even if the benefits are greater than the costs. On the other hand, you might decide to buy a car at a cost that outweighs the benefits it will bring you because you are temporarily blinded by a desire to own a really impressive vehicle. Making a list—in dollars and cents—of the costs and benefits of your purchase is a concrete way to take the emotion out of the decision.

To turn an opportunity into a business you will have to invest both time and money. Before making this investment, look carefully at two factors:

Costs. The money and time you will have to invest

Benefits. The money you will earn, and the knowledge and experience you will gain

---

[4] "Self-Employment on Rise," by Linda Yu, *Metro* magazine, June 2004.

»Opportunity Cost

Cost/benefit analysis can be inaccurate, however, without including **opportunity cost**. This is the cost of your "next-best investment." Perhaps your goal is to become a composer who writes scores for movies. You get a full-time job at a local store for $400 a week to support yourself, so you can write and record music in the evenings that you hope to sell to producers, agents, or film companies.

You find, however, that whenever a producer or agent wants to meet with you, you cannot get out of work to go. You realize that, even though you are making $400 a week, you are missing some important opportunities. Perhaps it would be smarter to take a part-time job for $300 a week that would leave your mornings free for meetings. The opportunity cost of the $100 a week you will lose is made up for by the potential income from film-scoring jobs you are missing by not being free to see people in the business. If your first film-scoring job pays $5,000, for example, you definitely would have made the right decision to earn $100 a week less for a few months.

People often make decisions without considering opportunity costs and then wonder why they are not happy with the outcome. Each time you make a decision about what to do with your time, energy, or money, think about the cost of the opportunities that you are giving up. Figure 1-1 presents a quiz to determine if you have what it takes to be an entrepreneur.

Figure 1-1 The "Do You Have What It Takes?" quiz.

Take the following quiz to learn more about yourself and whether you have what it takes to be an entrepreneur. Circle the answer that best represents how you feel.

1. You are at a party and a friend tells you that the guy in the expensive-looking suit recently invested in another friend's business. What do you do?
   a. Race over to him, introduce yourself, and tell him every detail of your business idea while asking if he would be interested in investing in it.
   b. Ask your friend to introduce you. Once introduced, you hand the potential investor your business card and politely ask whether you might be able to call on him sometime to present him with your business plan.
   c. Decide that it is probably not a good idea to bother the man at a party. After all, he is here to relax. Maybe you will run into him again somewhere else.

2. Your boss puts you in charge of researching office supply stores and choosing the one that you think would be best for the company to use. What is your response?
   a. Yes! Finally, a chance to show the boss what you are made of—plus, you will be able to spirit a few of the supplies away for your own business.
   b. You are terrified; this is more responsibility than you really want. What if you make a mistake and cost the company money? You do not want to look bad.
   c. You are excited. This is a good opportunity to impress your boss and also learn how to compare and negotiate with suppliers . . . something you will need to do for your own business.

3. You are already going to school full-time when you are offered a part-time job that is in the same field as the business you want to start when you graduate next year.
   a. Take the job, after talking with your student advisor about how to juggle your schedule so it will fit, because you believe the experience and the contacts you will develop will be invaluable when you start your business.
   b. Take the job. In fact, you ask for extra hours so you can finally start making some real money. Who needs sleep?
   c. Turn down the job. School is hard enough without working, too. You do not want your grades to suffer.

4. You are offered a job as a survey-taker for a marketing firm. The job pays really well but will require you to talk to a great many people.
   a. Take the job. You like people and this job will be a good way to practice getting to know what consumers want.
   b. Turn down the job. Just the thought of approaching strangers makes you queasy.
   c. Take the job so you can conduct some market research of your own by also asking the people you survey what they think about your business idea.

5. Your last job paid well and was interesting, but it required you to put in long hours and sometimes work on the weekends. What is your response?
   a. You put in the extra hours without complaint, but mainly because you felt that the rewards were worth it.
   b. You went a little overboard and worked yourself into a state of exhaustion. Moderation is not your strong suit.
   c. You quit. You are strictly a 9-to-5 person. Work is definitely not your life!

6. You are such a good guitar player that friends keep offering to pay for you to give them lessons. What is your response?
   a. You spend some money to run a six-week advertisement in the local paper, announcing that you are now available to teach at the same rate that established teachers In the area charge.
   b. You start teaching a few friends to see how it goes. You ask them what they are willing to pay and what they want to learn.
   c. You give a few friends some lessons but refuse to take any money.

7. Your best friend has started a business designing Web sites. He needs help because the business is really growing. He offers to make you a partner in the business even though you are computer illiterate. What is your response?
   a. You jump in, figuring that you will learn the ropes soon enough.
   b. You ask your friend to keep the partnership offer open but first to recommend a class you can take to get your skills up to speed.
   c. You pass. You do not see how you can work in a business you know nothing about.

Analysis of the "Do You Have What It Takes?" Quiz

Scoring

1. a = 2	b = 1	c = 0
2. a = 2	b = 0	c = 1
3. a = 1	b = 2	c = 0
4. a = 1	b = 0	c = 2
5. a = 1	b = 2	c = 0
6. a = 2	b = 1	c = 0
7. a = 2	b = 1	c = 0

12 Points or More: You are a natural risk-taker and can handle a lot of stress. These are important characteristics for an entrepreneur to have to be successful. You are willing to work hard but have a tendency to throw caution to the wind a little too easily. Save yourself from that tendency by using cost/benefit analysis to carefully evaluate your business (and personal!) decisions. In your enthusiasm do not forget to look at the opportunity costs of any decision you make.

6 to 12 Points: You strike an excellent balance between being a risk-taker and someone who carefully evaluates decisions. An entrepreneur needs to be both. You are also not overly motivated by the desire to make money. You understand that a successful business requires hard work and sacrifice before you can reap the rewards. To make sure that you are applying your natural drive and discipline to the best possible business opportunity, use the cost/benefit analysis to evaluate the different businesses you are interested in starting.

6 Points or Fewer: You are a little too cautious for an entrepreneur, but that will probably change as you learn more about how to run a business. You are concerned with financial security and may not be eager to put in the long hours required to get a business off the ground. This does not mean that you will not succeed as an entrepreneur; just make sure that whatever business you decide to start is the business of your dreams, so that you will be motivated to make it a success. Use the cost/benefit analysis to evaluate your business opportunities. Choose a business that you believe has the best shot at providing you with both the financial security and the motivation you require.

Figure 1-1 The "Do You Have What It Takes?" quiz. (Continued)

»How Do Entrepreneurs Find Opportunities to Start New Businesses?

In the 1900s, Joseph Schumpeter expanded on Say's definition of entrepreneurship by adding that entrepreneurs create value "by exploiting an invention or, more generally, an untried technological possibility for producing a new commodity or producing an old one in a new way, by opening up a new source of supply of materials or a new outlet for products, by reorganizing an industry and so on."[5] Schumpeter's definition describes five basic ways that entrepreneurs find opportunities to create new businesses.

1. Use a new technology to produce a new product.
2. Use an existing technology to produce a new product.
3. Use an existing technology to produce an old product in a new way.
4. Find a new source of resources (that might enable the entrepreneur to produce a product more cheaply).
5. Develop a new market for an existing product.

[How Do Entrepreneurs Come Up with Business Ideas?]

1. They listen. By listening to others, entrepreneurs get ideas about improving a business or creating a new one.

Come up with a business idea by listening. Describe how you got the idea:

_____

_____

_____

2. They observe. By constantly keeping their eyes open, entrepreneurs get ideas about how to help society, about businesses to start, and about what customers need.

Come up with a business idea by observing. Describe how you got the idea:

_____

_____

_____

3. They think. When entrepreneurs analyze a problem, they think about solutions. What product or service could solve that problem?

Come up with a business idea by thinking. Describe how you got the idea:

_____

_____

_____

---

[5] Joseph A. Schumpeter, *Capitalism, Socialism and Democracy* (New York: Harper & Row, 1942).

»Entrepreneurs Creatively Exploit Changes in Our World

Today's economists and business experts have defined entrepreneurship even more sharply. Management expert Peter Drucker has pointed out that for a business to be considered entrepreneurial, it should exploit changes in the world. These changes can be technological, like the explosion in computer technology that led Bill Gates to start Microsoft, or cultural, like the collapse of Communism, which led to a great many new business opportunities in Eastern Europe.

Nothing changes faster than **technology**, which is defined as science that has been applied to industry or commerce. Just a few years ago, there were no bar codes, no electronic scanners, and hardly anyone used a fax or cell phone. Today, even small sole proprietorships need to use these technologies to stay competitive. Smart entrepreneurs multiply their efficiency by taking advantage of the latest breakthroughs in business technology. To keep up, check out TechWeb:

- The Business Technology Network, www.techweb. com
- BusinessWeek Tech Supplement, www.businessweek.com/technology.

Drucker defines an "entrepreneur" as someone who "always searches for change, responds to it, and exploits it as an opportunity." Could that someone be you?

»Where Others See Problems, Entrepreneurs Recognize Opportunities

Here is a simple definition of "entrepreneur" that captures the essentials: *An entrepreneur recognizes opportunities where other people see only problems.*

Many famous businesses have been started because an entrepreneur turned a "problem" into a successful business. The entrepreneur recognized that the problem was actually an opportunity. Where there are dissatisfied customers, there are definitely opportunities for the entrepreneur.

Anita Roddick is an excellent example of an entrepreneur who started off as a dissatisfied customer. She started The Body Shop International because she was tired of paying for unnecessary perfume and fancy packaging when she bought makeup—and she thought other women might feel the same way. Bill Gates is another problem solver—before he started Microsoft, most software was complicated and confusing (even scary) to the average person. Gates decided to use his programming aptitude to create software that would be "user-friendly"—fun and easy for the average person to use.

»Train Your Mind to Recognize Business Opportunities

The first step in becoming an entrepreneur is to train your mind to recognize business opportunities. The next step is to let your creativity fly. Roddick has suggested that you develop your entrepreneurial instincts by asking yourself such questions as the following:

■ What frustrates me the most when I try to buy something?
■ What product or service would really make my life better?
■ What makes me annoyed or angry?
■ What product or service would take away my aggravation?

»Entrepreneurs Use Their Imaginations

Businesses are also formed when entrepreneurs not only fume about products or services that annoy them but fantasize about products or services they would love to have in their lives. Jump-start your imagination by asking yourself questions like the following:

■ What is the one thing you would love to have more than anything else?
■ What would it look like? Taste like?
■ What would it do?

Consider posing these questions to friends and family members, as well. You might hear about an opportunity you have not recognized yet.

Figure 1-2 shows some simple business ideas to get your imagination jump-started.

Biz Facts

Entrepreneurship has proven to be an effective way for minorities and women to enter the business world.

■ More than three million businesses are minority-owned, and this number has grown (Dun & Bradstreet, 2001).
■ There are more than 9.1 million women-owned businesses—accounting for more than a third of all U.S. companies, and this number has grown (Dun & Bradstreet, 2001).

The Small Business Administration estimates that women formed businesses 1.5 times faster than men did during the 1990s, and that women will own 50 percent of all businesses by 2010.

Advertising
Design flyers and posters
Distribute flyers, posters, and brochures
Image consultant
Publlclst

Animals
Cat sitter
Dog walker
Pet grooming
Pet bowls

Art
Artist
Art gallery
Calligraphy
Pottery

Baking
Baked goods for people in need
Bake sales
Cookie delivery business

Bicycles
Bicycle repair
Messenger service
Bike design

Bilingual
Translation
Teach another language
Teach English as a second language

Birds
Birdcage service
Birdwatching guide
Raise birds for sale

Books
Book selling
Used book selling
Write a book

Children
Baby-sitting service
Mother's helper
Teach activities
Children's stories

Cleaning
Car washing
House/office cleaning
Laundry and ironing

Clothing
Clothing design
Vintage clothing
Buying wholesale for resale

Collecting
Vinyl records
Comics

Computers
Computer repair/software installation
Word-processing service
Desktop publishing
Web site design
Graphic arts

Cooking
Catering
Pasta
Organic baby food
Cookbook

Crafts
Candle-making
Greeting-card design
Handbags
Jewelry-making

Dancing
Dance lessons
Hip-hop dance troupe

Driving
Errand service
Meal delivery
Messenger service

Entertainment
Clown
Magician
Party DJ
Balloon decorating

Fish
Aquarium care
Fishing

Gardening
Fresh herbs and flowers
Yardwork
Plant care
Window boxes

Hair
Hairstyling
Hair clips
Hair wrapping

Holidays
Gift baskets
Seasonal sales

Internet
Geneaology
Web site
EBay auctions

Music
Band
Music lessons
Stickers and buttons
String quartet

Painting
Housepainting
Furniture
Signage

People
Dating newsletter
Wake-up service

Photography
Wedding photography
Photo journalist

Sales
Candy
Jewelry, hats, pens

Silkscreening
T-shirts
Creative clothing

Teaching
Tutoring
Giving lessons

Video
Videotaping events
Videotaping concerts
Digital moviemaking

Woodworking
Carpentry
Bird cages
Decorative carving
Board games

Writing
Pennysaver newspaper
Fanzine

Figure 1-2 Sample business ideas.

»An Idea Is Not Necessarily An Opportunity

Not every business idea you may have is an opportunity. An opportunity has one unique characteristic that distinguishes it from an ordinary idea. *An opportunity is an idea that is based on what consumers need or want.* A successful business sells products or services that customers need, at prices they are willing to pay. Many a small business has failed because the entrepreneur did not understand this.

In addition, according to Jeffry Timmons, "An opportunity has the qualities of being attractive, durable, and timely and is anchored in a product or service which creates or adds value for its buyer or end user."[6]

Timmons defines a business opportunity as an idea, plus these four characteristics:

1. It is attractive to customers.
2. It will work in your business environment.
3. It can be executed in the window of opportunity that exists.
4. You have the resources and skills to create the business, or you know someone who does and who might want to form the business with you.

The "window of opportunity" is the amount of time you have to get your business idea to your market. You might have a great idea, but if several other competitors have it, too, and have already brought it to the marketplace, that window of opportunity has been closed.

Remember, not every idea is an opportunity. For an idea to be an opportunity, it must lead to the development of a product or service that is of value to a customer.

[Entrepreneurial Wisdom]

A useful way to evaluate a business idea is to look at its **S**trengths, **W**eaknesses, **O**pportunities, and **T**hreats (**SWOT**). This is called SWOT Analysis.

- ■ **S**trengths—All of the capabilities and positive points that the entrepreneur has, from experience to contacts
- ■ **W**eaknesses—All of the negatives that the entrepreneur faces, such as lack of capital or training, or failure to set up a workable accounting system
- ■ **O**pportunities—Any lucky break or creative insight that can help the entrepreneur get ahead of the competition
- ■ **T**hreats—Anything that can jeopardize the existence of the business or intimidate the entrepreneur, from competitors to legal issues

---

[6] *New Venture Creation: Entrepreneurship for the 21st Century,* 5th Edition, p. 7 (New York: Irwin/McGraw-Hill, 1999).

»Opportunity Is Situational

A problem is one example of an opportunity that entrepreneurs need to be able to recognize. A changing situation or trend is another. Opportunity is situational, meaning it is dependent on situations. You cannot generalize about when or where an opportunity might appear. Change and flux create opportunities.

Think about the recent changes in computer technology. The conventional wisdom was that only the biggest telecommunications companies were going to be in a position to exploit the Internet and all of the opportunities that it had to offer. How could entrepreneurs compete with established, resource-loaded companies such as AT&T, for example? The opposite has been true, however. Entrepreneurs have penetrated, and indeed, dominated the market for Internet-based services. Think of AOL, Earthlink, Google, Netscape, and Yahoo!. Each one is an entrepreneurial venture that left the telecom giants scrambling to catch up.

As Timmons has pointed out, it can take a huge corporation (think dinosaur) over six years to develop and implement a new business strategy. Entrepreneurs, in contrast, can dart in and out of the market like roadrunners.

> *According to a study by the National Science Foundation, 95 percent of technological innovations since World War II have been developed and exploited by entrepreneurial companies.*

»The Five Roots of Opportunity in the Marketplace

There are "five roots of opportunity" in the marketplace that entrepreneurs can exploit.[7] Notice how similar these are to Schumpeter's definition of entrepreneurship!

〈4. **Performance Objective**

1. ***Problems*** that your business can solve.
2. ***Changes*** in laws, situations, or trends.
3. ***Inventions*** of totally new products or services.
4. ***Competition.*** If you can find a way to beat the competition on price, location, quality, reputation, reliability, or speed, you can create a very successful business with an existing product or service.
5. ***Technological Advances.*** Scientists may invent new technology, but entrepreneurs figure out how to use and sell it.

»Get Your Hands on a Computer

Advances in technology that ordinary people without scientific backgrounds can use have been a tremendous part of the entrepreneurial wave of the last decade. With this in mind:

- Every entrepreneur should have access to a computer.
- Every business should have a Web site.

---

[7] Adapted from the *Master Curriculum Guide: Economics and Entrepreneurship*, ed. by John Clow et al. (New York: Joint Council on Economic Education, 1991).

■ Every business should hire employees who are conversant and comfortable with technology.

The World Wide Web came into being in 1989, when an Englishman named Tim Berners-Lee invented "hyperlinks." These were words that, when clicked on, transferred the reader to a new document page, anywhere on the Internet. Now pictures, and even video, can be links. Every Web page has an address, called a URL (Uniform Resource Locator), and you can surf from one URL to another using hyperlinks. Web pages are *hypertext* documents. This means that they combine text with graphics. Sound and video can also be included. Web documents are much more fun to look at than the documents that used to be exchanged on the Internet—which consisted of text and numbers and were written in a special, programming language. The Internet is now the world's largest computer network, connecting over 300 million users.

One of the best investments you can make for your business is to buy or borrow a computer. You do not need to buy the latest model; older ones can be purchased inexpensively. Even the most basic model can do the following:

■ Surf the Web
■ Create stationery and business cards
■ Type professional-looking letters and check your spelling
■ Keep financial records
■ Make flyers and posters
■ Keep a mailing list of customers and print labels for mailing

If you do not own a computer, consider making arrangements to borrow or use one part time. You can also rent computer time at Internet cafés or some office supply stores. Most public libraries and community colleges even offer free Internet access.

Visit Web sites like http://officeupdate.microsoft.com to see the latest software products that can help you run your business.

»Maximize Your Phone!

Do not forget, however, that technology does not have to be new to be useful to an entrepreneur. The phone is still one of the businessperson's most important technological tools. Obviously, you can turn your phone into an answering service for your business by buying an answering machine. But some companies offer answering services for only a few dollars a month, which would not require you to buy a machine. Using a voice-mail service that provides you with a number for customers to call is another inexpensive option.

Whether you use an answering machine or an answering service, make sure the message that callers hear is clear and professional and gives the full name of your business. Change your message often to advertise specials and sales and to keep customers listening. Use beepers and cell phones to stay in touch with customers, employees, and suppliers.

If you can afford it, consider a separate telephone line for your business. That way you can have it listed by your business name in the phone book and you will know to always answer with your business name when the "work" phone rings.

Developments in phone technology include devices that allow you to check your e-mail using any phone and text messaging. Broadband telephone plans from such companies as Vonage (www.vonage.com) and Optimum Online (www.optonline.com) may help you cut your phone bills.

What technology do you already own or know how to use? Brainstorm four technologies to which you have access, and explain how you would use each to create a business.

Technology	Business Idea
1. _____	1. _____
2. _____	2. _____
3. _____	3. _____
4. _____	4. _____

»Protect Your Computer and Data

The information you store on your computer is called **data**. Important business data on your computer might include mailing lists, invoices, letters, and financial records. Since your computer is an electronic device, you will need to protect it from three things that can wipe out your data:

1. ***Power Surges or Outages***—A power blackout can destroy data that you have not saved yet. You can purchase an uninterruptible power supply (UPS) at office supply stores that will keep your computer running when the lights go out. A power surge can damage your computer. Plug all your computer equipment into a "power strip" with a surge protector, available at office supply or hardware stores.

2. ***Computer Viruses***—A virus is computer software that can attach itself to your software or files and ruin them. Protect your computer with virus protection software like Norton Antivirus or McAfee.

3. ***Disk Failure***—Hard drives can crash, destroying valuable data. To prevent this, save everything you do to back-up floppy disks or CDs. An even better method—especially for people who know they do not have the patience to make back-ups—is to attach a Zip drive or Syquest or other type of removable hard drive to your computer and periodically back up your entire drive.

Keep up to date with methods of protecting your data by visiting sites like Microsoft's "Protect Your Computer" site, (www.microsoft.com/athome/security/protect/default.mspx) and PC Security News (www.pcsecuritynews.com).

»The Younger Generation's Advantage

If you are a young entrepreneur, you may have an advantage over businesspeople twice your age, because so many innovations in computing and communication technologies have occurred while you were growing up. Twenty years ago, most entrepreneurs kept their financial records in handwritten accounting journals, not on the computer. Almost no one used a cell phone or a fax, and e-mail was just an idea.

We tend to be most comfortable with the technology we learned to use while we were growing up. Your generation's familiarity with the Internet, laptop computers, beepers, faxes, and cell phones can be a competitive advantage for your business. Maybe there is a video rental store in your neighborhood run by an entrepreneur who does the store's ordering and recordkeeping by hand. If you open a technologically savvy store that uses scanners and computerized lists, you will probably attract the other store's customers, once they realize they will not have to wait as long in line at your store.

Computer technology has led entrepreneurs to create new products and new businesses, such as the following:

- Ring tones for cell phones
- Web-site design firms
- Internet animations, or "smileys"
- Music-sharing Web sites

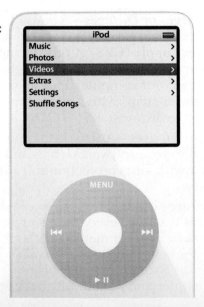

Apple led the digital music revolution with its iPod portable music players.
(Apple Computer, Inc.)

- Online radio stations
- Online networks, such as Myspace and Friendster

»Internal Opportunities

It is helpful not only to be aware of the "five roots of opportunity" in the marketplace, but to think also about how we perceive opportunities ourselves. Opportunities fall into two classes: internal and external. An **internal opportunity** is one that comes from inside you—from a hobby or an interest, or even a passion. An **external opportunity**, in contrast, is generated by an outside circumstance that you notice.

»External Opportunities

External opportunities are circumstances you notice that make you say to yourself, "Hey! That would make a great business!" You notice that people in your neighborhood are complaining about the lack of available day care, for example, so you start a day care center. But what if you find out after a month that two-year-olds get on your nerves? That's a drawback with external opportunities. Your idea may fill a need for the market, but you may not have the skills or interest in putting in the necessary time and energy to make it a successful business.

The best business opportunities often combine both internal and external factors. Ideally, a business that you are passionate about fills a huge need in the marketplace.

[Step Into The Shoes]

Russell Simmons Makes Rap Happen

In the late 1980s, Russell Simmons was promoting rap concerts at the City University of New York. At the time, rap was considered a passing fad, but Simmons really loved it. Even though most record executives thought rap would be over in a year or two, Simmons truly believed it was a business opportunity. He formed Def Jam Records with fellow student Rick Rubin for $5,000. Within a year, they produced hit records by Run DMC and LL Cool J, and Simmons became a multimedia mogul.

Simmons took a chance on this "internal" opportunity because he felt that, if you personally know ten people who are eager to buy your product or service, ten million would be willing to buy it if they knew about it. Luckily for him, he was right about rap's popular potential, but he could have been wrong. That can be a problem with in-

ternal opportunities—you may be passionate about something but there may not be enough consumer interest in it to sustain a business.

Simmons loved rap and hoped that other people would, too. That was the internal factor—he had the passion to sustain himself as he worked 24/7 to make his dream come true. As it turned out, music fans were a little bored with rock at that time, and looking for a fresh sound. Rap filled the bill. This was an external opportunity that happened to coincide with Simmons's internal commitment.

»Do Not Rip Off Someone Else's Creativity

You would be upset if someone made money off your invention or art, so resist the urge to base your business on someone else's creative work. Not only is it unethical, it is against the law. Be sure that any business you start respects the intellectual property of others.

- Do not sell counterfeit knockoffs of popular brands.
- Do not take graphics, music, or content from the Web without permission and/or payment.
- Always know the source of the goods you buy from suppliers, to avoid the risk of receiving stolen property.

»Seven Rules for Building a Successful Business

Simmons and Rubin were also successful because they instinctively applied the seven basic rules of building a successful business:

1. ***Recognize an Opportunity***—Simmons believed that rap music was an untapped business opportunity.
2. ***Evaluate It with Critical Thinking***—He tested his idea by promoting concerts and observing consumer reaction.
3. ***Build a Team***—Simmons formed a partnership with Rick Rubin.
4. ***Write***—a realistic business plan.
5. ***Gather Resources***—Simmons and Rubin pooled their $5,000.
6. ***Decide Ownership***—Simmons and Rubin formed a legal partnership.
7. ***Create Wealth.***

»The Team Approach

Let's take a closer look at step 3: Build a Team. Alone, neither Simmons nor Rubin had enough money to launch a record label, but together they were able to do it. Their business was also helped by the fact that they each knew different artists and had different contacts in the record industry.

Every person you know is a potential business-formation opportunity. Your friends or family members may have skills, equipment, or contacts that would make them valuable business partners. Say you really want to start a Web site design business because you know many businesses in your community want to put up Web sites. You are a graphic artist but you do not know how to use Web site development programs. If you have a friend who has that knowledge, you could start a business together. Or maybe you

[Entrepreneurial Wisdom]

Build Your Brain

Becoming a successful entrepreneur is all about making connections—those "Aha!" moments when you realize what your business opportunity is or when you figure out how to do something better than the competition. Research indicates that mental exercise will help your brain become better at making such connections. Even the most erudite scientists recognize the value of activities that encourage their brain cells to make new connections. Robotics engineer Hugo De Garis, who is building an artificial brain for an artificial cat, plays classical piano every day before he sits down at the computer. "This helps to build my own brain," he told the *New York Times* ("Robokitty," by Nicholas D. Kristof, Aug. 1, 1999). Arnold Scheibel, head of the University of California–Los Angeles Brain Research Institute, suggests the following brain-builders:

■ Solve puzzles.

■ Play a musical instrument.

■ Fix something—learn to repair cars or electrical equipment.

■ Create art: write poetry, paint, or sculpt.

■ Dance.

■ Make friends with people who like to have interesting conversations.

would like to start a DJ business, but you only have one turntable or laptop computer. If you form the business with a friend, you can pool equipment. (When forming a business team, organize the venture so that everyone involved shares in the ownership and profits. People work much harder when they are working for themselves.)

Now carry this idea a step further—every person you meet is a potential contact for your business. Thinking this way will encourage you to **network**, or exchange valuable information and contacts with other businesspeople. Keep your business cards on you at all times and truly view every individual you meet as an opportunity for your business.

»What Is a Business Plan?

By the time you complete this book, you will have written a **business plan** that you can use to start and operate your own venture. A business plan is a document that thoroughly explains a business idea and how it will be carried out. The plan should include the following:

■ All costs and a marketing plan

■ A description of how the business will be financed

■ An estimate of what the earnings are expected to be

The number one reason to write a business plan is to organize your thoughts *before* starting a business. Most of the entrepreneurs mentioned in this book wrote a business plan before they made a single sale. A well-written plan will guide you every step of the way as you develop your business. It can also help you raise money from investors.

≫ Why Do You Need a Business Plan?

Performance
Objective   5.

Bankers, and other potential investors, will refuse to see an entrepreneur who does not have a business plan. You may have a brilliant idea, but if it is not written out, people will be unlikely to invest in your business.

A well-written plan will show investors that you have carefully thought through what you intend to do to make your business profitable. The more explanation you offer investors about how their money will be used, the more willing they will be to invest. Your plan should be so thoughtful and well written that the only question it raises in an investor's mind is: "How much can I invest?"

≫ Writing a Business Plan Will Save You Time and Money

As you work on your plan, you will also be figuring out how to make your business work. Before you serve your first customer, you will have answered every question you can. How much should you charge for your product or service? What exactly *is* your product or service? What is one unit? What are your costs? How are you going to market your product or service? How do you plan to sell it? Figuring all this out in advance will save you time and money.

If you start your business without a plan, these kinds of questions can overwhelm you. By the time you have completed the exercises in this book, though, you will have answers—and you will have a road map for your own business! You will be able to use the Biz Builder CD to create a professional plan and a PowerPoint presentation that will hit the highlights of your strategy.

There are several software packages on the market designed to help you write a business plan, including the following:

- Tim Berry's Business Plan Toolkit (Palo Alto Software, www. paloalto.com)—for Macintosh users
- Success, Inc. (Dynamic Pathways, www.dynamicpathways.com)

Using the Web, you can present your business plan to several investors at a time—no matter where they are located. With a presentation program like PowerPoint 2000, you can broadcast your presentation in real time over the Web. As long as you and your audience both have PowerPoint 2000 and Internet Explorer 4.0 or later, you can attach a microphone to your computer and even broadcast audio (or just use the phone and save the computer for the visual part of the presentation!). PowerPoint contains instructions for online broadcasting. This can be an effective way to present your business plan to investors at their convenience. You can use e-mail to stay in touch with investors, schedule a presentation, and remind them when your scheduled presentation is coming up.

»Chapter Summary

Now that you have studied this chapter you can do the following:

1. Explain what entrepreneurs do.

   ■ Entrepreneurs start their own businesses and work for themselves.

   ■ Entrepreneurs recognize opportunities to start businesses that other people may not have noticed.

2. Entrepreneurs shift economic resources from an area of lower and into an area of higher productivity and greater yield. By doing this, they add value to scarce resources.

3. Describe how free-enterprise economies work and how entrepreneurs fit into them.

   ■ The free enterprise system is based on voluntary exchange. Voluntary exchange is a trade between two parties who agree to trade money for a product or service. Both parties agree to the exchange because they both benefit from the trade.

   ■ The free enterprise system encourages entrepreneurs who use resources efficiently to satisfy consumer needs—by rewarding them with profit.

4. Explain how profit works as a signal to the entrepreneur.

   ■ Profit is the sign that an entrepreneur has added value to the scarce resources he or she is using.

   ■ Not making a profit is a sign that the entrepreneur is not using resources very well and is not adding value to them.

5. Find and evaluate opportunities to start your own business.

   ■ Five Roots of Opportunity:
      1. Problems that your business can solve
      2. Changes in laws, situations, or trends
      3. Inventions of totally new products or services
      4. Competition. If you can find a way to beat the competition on price, location, quality, reputation, reliability, or speed, you can create a very successful business with an existing product or service.
      5. Technological Advances. Scientists may invent new technology, but entrepreneurs figure out how to sell it.

6. A business opportunity is an idea plus these three characteristics:

   ■ It is attractive to customers.

   ■ It will work in your business environment.

   ■ It can be executed in the window of opportunity that exists.

7. Use cost/benefit analysis to make decisions.

   ■ Cost/benefit analysis is the process of comparing costs and benefits in order to make a good decision.

   ■ Cost/benefit analysis can be inaccurate without including opportunity cost. This is the cost of your "next-best investment."

8. Use SWOT analysis to evaluate a business opportunity.

■ *Strengths*—All of the capabilities and positive points that the entrepreneur has, from experience to contacts

■ *Weaknesses*—All of the negatives that the entrepreneur faces, like lack of capital or training or failure to set up a workable accounting system

■ *Opportunities*—Lucky breaks or creative insights that can help the entrepreneur get ahead of the competition

■ *Threats*—Things that can jeopardize the existence of the business or intimidate the entrepreneur, from competition to legal issues

9. Explain why entrepreneurs write business plans.

■ To organize their thoughts *before* starting a business, and to help guide the operation of the business.

■ To use to raise money from investors. Bankers and other potential investors will refuse to see an entrepreneur who does not have a business plan.

Key Terms

business	free enterprise system
business plan	internal opportunity
capital	network
capitalism	opportunity cost
commission	product
cost/benefit analysis	profit
data	salary
dividend	service
economics	scarce resources
economy	technology
employee	trade-off
entrepreneur	voluntary exchange
external opportunity	wage

[Entrepreneurship Portfolio]

Critical Thinking Exercises

1. What would be the best thing about owning your own business? What would be the worst?

2. Identify three nonfinancial benefits of entrepreneurship that might be important to you. Write a paragraph about each.

3. If you were to start a business, what would be your opportunity cost? In other words, what is the next-best use of your time? How much money could you make working at a job, instead? The answer to this question will give you a rough idea of how to value your time when you start a business and have to figure out how much to pay yourself.

My time is worth approximately $_____ per hour.

4. Describe an idea for a business that you have. Explain how it could satisfy a consumer need. **(Business Plan Practice)**

5. Explain how a business opportunity differs from a business idea.

6. Give an example of a change that has occurred or is about to occur in your neighborhood. Discuss any business opportunities this change might create.

7. List five business opportunities in your neighborhood and the need(s) each would satisfy. Determine whether each opportunity you describe is internal, external, or a mix.

Business Opportunity and Type: **Need(s) or Wants Satisfied:**

1. _____   1. _____

2. _____   2. _____

3. _____   3. _____

4. _____   4. _____

5. _____   5. _____

Key Concepts Questions

1. Define *small business*.

2. Explain how profit works as a signal to the entrepreneur.

3. Do you agree that it will probably take about three months for your business to start earning a profit? Why or why not?

4. Describe three things you have learned about capitalism.

5. Identify which technological tools you plan to use for your business, and why. Write a memo explaining how you plan to get access to the technology you need and describe how you will use it. **(Business Plan Practice)**

6. Working with a partner, make a list of the technology you each have access to and brainstorm how you might combine your technological resources to create a successful business. Describe in detail how the partnership would work. For example, would the person contributing more technology have a bigger share of the business, or would profits and expenses be split 50-50?

7. Call a phone company and ask whether it offers any special programs for small businesses. If it does, ask to have an information package sent to you.

8. Visit the Small Business Administration for brochures and other materials. Find an office in your area or go to www.sba.gov.

Application Exercises

Have a conversation with a friend or relative. Ask this person to tell you about which things he or she finds frustrating in the neighborhood. Write down these complaints.

Step 1: Generate at least three business opportunities from this conversation.

Step 2: Use the checklists below to evaluate your three business ideas as opportunities.

Step 3: Choose the best of the business opportunities and write a SWOT analysis for it.

Step 4: Write a cost/benefit analysis for yourself to analyze the costs and benefits actually starting this business. Use the analysis to explain why you would or would not start it.

Business Idea	**Critical Evaluation**
Would it be attractive to potential customers?	Yes ___ No ___
Would it work in your business environment?	Yes ___ No ___
Is there a window of opportunity?	Yes ___ No ___
Do you have the skills and resources to create this business?	Yes ___ No ___
If you do not have the skills and resources to create this business, do you know someone who does and might want to create this business with you?	Yes ___ No ___

Business Idea	**Critical Evaluation**
Would it be attractive to potential customers?	Yes ___ No ___
Would it work in your business environment?	Yes ___ No ___
Is there a window of opportunity?	Yes ___ No ___
Do you have the skills and resources to create this business?	Yes ___ No ___
If you do not have the skills and resources to create this business, do you know someone who does and might want to create this business with you?	Yes ___ No ___

Business Idea	**Critical Evaluation**
Would it be attractive to potential customers?	Yes ___ No ___
Would it work in your business environment?	Yes ___ No ___
Is there a window of opportunity?	Yes ___ No ___
Do you have the skills and resources to create this business?	Yes ___ No ___
If you do not have the skills and resources to create this business, do you know someone who does and might want to create this business with you?	Yes ___ No ___

Interview an entrepreneur in your community. Entrepreneurs are busy people but most are willing to spend some time talking with someone who is interested in what they are doing. Meeting over a meal might be the most efficient use of the entrepreneur's time. Before the interview, brainstorm ten questions in the following four categories. If you can, tape the interview (with the entrepreneur's permission). After the interview, be sure to write a thank-you note to the entrepreneur.

a. *Information gathering*—Open the interview with questions about the entrepreneur's family (any other entrepreneurs?) and educational and work background.

b. *About the business*—Next, ask questions about how the business was started. How did the entrepreneur recognize an opportunity and develop it?

c. *Running the business*—Ask about what problems came up as the business got underway and how they were solved.

d. *Reflection*—Ask the entrepreneur to reflect. What advice would he or she give to an aspiring entrepreneur? Has running a business been rewarding?

Visit the following Web site:

http://officeupdate.microsoft.com/2000/focus/articles/smbizres.htm.

Find three software products you would like to use to run your business. Pretend that you have to make a speech to the chief financial officer explaining why the company should make these purchases. Prepare a five-minute presentation that describes the cost of the products, what they can accomplish, and why the company should buy them.

CASE STUDY: Online Auto Sales

Pete Ellis was an extremely successful car dealer. At one time he operated the largest Jeep, Eagle, and Chrysler dealership in the United States. Ellis was a true entrepreneur. For the entire time he was in business, he disliked the antagonism between buyers and sellers and believed that the auto industry's sales and distribution systems were inefficient. This led Ellis to create Autobytel, an Internet auto-buying service that gave bargain hunters the information they needed to negotiate a good price, and delivered a no-hassle, no-haggle transaction. Through Autobytel, a car buyer indicates the car he or she wants to buy, including the options. The nearest participating car dealer e-mails back an offer. There is no charge to the customer and no obligation to accept the offer. Autobytel makes money by charging a fee to the dealer.

Autobytel had processed one million online requests, resulting in 600,000 purchases in the first two years. By the third year, the company had gross revenue in excess of $50 million. As could be expected, Autobytel's success resulted in many other companies entering the online market. Then the major car manufacturers themselves came in. These programs required participating dealers to respond to online requests within 24 hours and adhere to a no-haggle policy. Although it may seem that the Internet would allow car manufacturers to sell directly to the consumer, automakers in the United States are prohibited from selling directly because laws require a dealership to be an intermediary.

Despite Autobytel's rapid increase in sales, it had not made a profit as of the end of its third year. Many analysts believe that the concept of selling cars online is just not feasible. However, a partnership between General Motors and Autobytel may be the answer. GM announced that it would start testing Chevrolet sales through Autobytel in a major metropolitan area. Consumers will be able to get information and quotes on all cars and trucks at regional dealerships.

Case Study Analysis

1. What unmet needs of the customer or conditions in the car-buying process contributed to the early success of Autobytel?

2. Do you think Peter Ellis thought through the Autobytel idea well enough before he launched the product?

3. Is there a future for Autobytel? What might that future look like?

CASE STUDY: JetBlue Airlines

Natural-Born Entrepreneur

Ten years ago, JetBlue Airlines® CEO David Neeleman had $25 million in the bank but was out of a job. A lifelong veteran of the travel industry, Neeleman had started an economy airline called Morris Air that had been acquired by Southwest Airlines in the early 1990s. All of a sudden, Neeleman went from being the captain of his own ship to an employee in someone else's corporation. The adjustment was difficult for the multitasking executive. At Southwest, there were protocols to follow and soon Neeleman was stepping on people's toes. Within a year's time, he was fired. Southwest awarded him a $25 million severance package and required him to sign a five-year noncompete agreement, which meant that he could not go out and work for another airline. This forced Neeleman to take some time off to regroup and plan his next venture.

Opportunity Analysis

Entrepreneurial by nature, Neeleman began analyzing the state of the struggling airline industry to see

if he could find a way to do things differently and better. One of the first things Neeleman noticed was that flying had become a miserable and expensive experience. In the 1960s, when air travel was just coming into vogue, taking a plane trip was viewed as a glamorous activity. By the 1990s, getting on an aircraft was like being rounded up for a cattle call—cabins were cramped, the food and service were poor.

It did not take long for Neeleman to brainstorm creative ways that he could make flying fun again *and* turn a profit. One of the first things he vowed to do with his new company was eliminate airplane meals. After all, these "chicken or steak" dinners and lunches were expensive to deliver and they usually were not very good. Instead, he would serve snacks and drinks, which were less costly. Neeleman also had an important revelation about the importance of customer service. Before, he used to think of himself as being in the travel industry. His job was to help people get from one place to another. He concluded that his new company needed to be built from the ground up as a *service* enterprise. This changed his whole way of thinking. If he was going to succeed, he needed to put service first and have his employees focus their energies on making flying a positive experience for the customer.

But a successful business cannot be built on good customer service alone. Neeleman needed to think strategically about *where* he would fly his airplanes. What untapped needs existed in the marketplace? He researched the competition and zoned in on flight routes that were overpriced, in demand, and underserviced.

For example, in 1999, it was not uncommon for a passenger to pay between $500 and $800 for a round-trip ticket from New York to Fort Lauderdale. Neeleman resolved to offer lower fares and give customers more flexibility, by not requiring them to stay over on a Saturday night. Over time, JetBlue has taken aggressive steps to corner the New York–Florida market by offering special $69 one-way fares to other popular Florida destinations, such as West Palm Beach, Orlando, and Tampa.

Embracing Technology

A champion of technology, Neeleman also noticed that his competitors had been slow in adopting it as a cost-saving tool. Earlier in his career, Neeleman had pioneered the development of efficient, Internet-based reservation and ticketing systems. Making it easy for customers to book their tickets online would translate into savings for the company in the form of reduced labor costs. Today, 40 percent of JetBlue's sales are made over the Internet. JetBlue rewards its customers for buying tickets online by charging $5 less per one-way ticket.

JetBlue has perhaps become best known for offering live satellite Direct TV to all of its passengers. Every JetBlue seat comes with a small television screen where people can choose from 24 channels. This service costs the company as little as $1.00 per customer per flight to provide. While satellite TV may have JetBlue's customers buzzing, in Neeleman's opinion, this feature is "overrated." What makes JetBlue great, he thinks, is the quality of customer service that passengers receive. This is the strategy he would like JetBlue to champion.

Operating Lean and Mean

Neeleman also was zealous about keeping his cost structure as lean as possible, without compromising on quality. Instead of buying an aging fleet of used planes to save money, Neeleman invested his start-up capital in 50 new Airbus A320 aircraft. The A320s were fuel-efficient and cheaper to maintain than their Boeing 737 counterparts. The Airbus held 35 more seats than the Boeing 737, which meant that Neeleman would be able to sell more tickets per flight and increase his profit margin. Because he bought in bulk from one supplier, Neeleman was also able to negotiate on the price of the planes. He especially liked the fact that the Airbus had leather seats. These were more comfortable than fabric and also sent a message to customers that JetBlue was a quality operation.

Beating the Competition

While other airline giants like American and United are teetering on the brink of bankruptcy, JetBlue—now five years old—has managed to turn a profit. JetBlue averages a per-passenger–mile cost of about 6 1/2 cents, one of the very lowest in the industry. The company's mission is to "bring humanity back to air travel" and Neeleman continues to be vigilant about finding small, yet significant ways to make flying an enjoyable experience for his customers. While market forces are always changing and the airline industry in particular is notorious for being volatile, Neeleman has identified the right mix of ingredients for success.

Case Study Analysis

1. List the things that David Neeleman did to assess whether or not his plan for JetBlue was actually a good business opportunity.

2. If you had been in Neeleman's shoes, what else could you have done to research this opportunity?

3. List the problems Neeleman identified that he wanted to solve with his business.

4. Would you describe Neeleman's business idea as an internal opportunity or an external one, or both? Explain.

5. If you had been Neeleman's business advisor, what suggestions would you have given him? List some examples.

6. Describe how Neeleman used technology to make his business more competitive. Brainstorm three additional ways for enhancing JetBlue's competitive advantage through technology.

CASE SOURCES

"JetBlue Skies," Forbes.com, January 31, 2001. See http://www.forbes.com/2001/01/31/0131jetblue_print.html

"JetBlue CEO says airline's employees are key to success," by Meg Learson Grosso, WestportMinuteman.com, April 8, 2004. http://www.zwire.com/ site/news.cfm?newsid=11266216&BRD=1654PAG=461dept_id=12915&rfi=8

"The Amazing JetBlue," by Arlyn Tobias Gajilan, *Fortune Small Business,* May 17, 2003. See http://www.fortune.com/fortune/print/0,15935,444298,00.html

> ## "Problems are only opportunities in work clothes."

—Henry J. Kaiser, American industrialist

Performance Objectives

1. Define your business.
2. Analyze your competitive advantage.
3. Define unit of sale for a business.
4. Analyze the economics of one unit for each of the four types of business: manufacturing, wholesale, service, and retail.
5. Calculate gross profit per unit.

Sometimes entrepreneurs see a consumer need even before consumers do! When automobiles were invented, for example, they were considered playthings for the rich. Henry Ford, however, imagined an automobile in front of every American home—long before most Americans ever thought they would need their own cars. Similarly, Stephen Wozniak envisioned a computer inside every American home at a time when computers were huge and unaffordable. His company, Apple Computer (cofounded with Steve Jobs), became a leader in the development of personal home and office computers. Both Ford Motor Company and Apple Computer became powerhouses, meeting consumer needs that consumers were not aware they had.

≫Apple Creates the Personal Computer

In 1943, IBM's founder Thomas Watson said, "I think there is a world market for about five computers." A **market** is a group of people who may be interested in buying a given product or service. When Watson made his statement, computers were forbiddingly expensive machines that only the government, universities, and a few giant corporations could afford. That was the market for computers at the time.

By the 1970s, however, a few people were talking about creating personal computers. These enthusiasts were considered dreamers. One such visionary was Stephen Wozniak, who had landed his first job at Hewlett-Packard, a major computer company. He was also attending meetings of the Homebrew Club, a group of amateur computer whizzes. Wozniak was determined to build a small "personal" computer to show the Club. He believed that there was a larger market for computers than Watson had thought.

Apple co-founder Stephen
Wozniak participating in a panel
discussion of Mac OS X operat-
ing software at the Macworld
Expo in downtown San Francisco
(AP Wide World Photos)

Wozniak offered Hewlett-Packard a chance to co-develop his
small computer. The company failed to recognize that this was a
great opportunity staring them in the face and turned him down. To
be fair to Hewlett-Packard, though, most people were unable to see
a market for personal computers at that time. This is a classic example of why we like to say that what entrepreneurs do best is to
recognize opportunities.

Wozniak's good friend Steve Jobs did recognize this opportunity,
however. Jobs and Wozniak started Apple Computer in Wozniak's
parents' garage in Cupertino, California, with only $1,300.

Wozniak worked on his design until he created the Apple II, now
considered one of the great achievements in the computer industry.
Jobs, meanwhile, searched for an investor for the company. After
being turned down by friends and family, he found Mike Markkula.
Markkula agreed to back the company in return for a share of the
profits. He also put together Apple's business plan.

By 1984, Apple had sales of $1.5 billion. The company was suc-
cessful because Wozniak and Jobs recognized an opportunity that
led to a product that satisfied the needs of a market that the giants
of the computer industry had failed to recognize.

》Business Definition[1]

Apple began as a **manufacturing** business, meaning a business that
makes a product from the beginning. There are four basic types of
business:

1. *Manufacturing*—Makes a tangible product.
2. *Wholesale*—Buys in bulk from the manufacturer and sells
   smaller quantities to the retailer.

---

[1] Special thanks to Peter Patch for providing many of the ideas for this chapter.

3. *Retail*—Sells one piece at a time to consumers.

4. *Service*—Sells an intangible product to consumers.

Before you can start your business, you must define it. The *business definition* answers three questions: Who, What, and How?

1.❬ **Performance Objective**

1. *Who* will the business serve? In other words, who is in the market for your product or service?

2. *What* will the business offer the customers? What are the products (or services) the business will sell?

3. *How* will the business provide the products or services it offers? What are the primary actions and activities required to conduct this business? For example:

   ● Buying or developing or manufacturing the product

   ● Identifying its potential customers and selling the product to them

   ● Producing and delivering the product or service

   ● Receiving payment

The business definition has three elements:

1. **The Offer**—What will you sell to your customers? That is called your *offer.* This includes exactly which products and services you will bring to the market and how you will price them.

2. **Target Market**—Which segment of the consumer market are you aiming to serve? This is called your *target market.* Defining your target market in a way that helps you to identify potential customers is an important factor in achieving success.

3. **Production and Delivery Capability**—How will you provide your offer to your targeted customers? This includes how you will perform all key activities required to produce the product or service, deliver it to your customers, and ensure that they are satisfied.

[Exercise]

Imagine you are Stephen Wozniak. Define your business:

1. *Who* will the business serve?

_____

2. *What* will the business offer? What are the products (or services) the business will sell?

_____

3. *How* will the business provide the products or services it offers? What are the primary actions and activities required to conduct this business?

_____

_____

»What Is Your Competitive Advantage?

Performance Objective 2.» For your business to be successful, you will need a strategy for beating the competition. This is your **competitive advantage.** It is whatever you can do better than the competition that will attract customers to your business.

- Can you supply your product at a lower price than other businesses serving your market?
- Can you attract more customers than your competitor by offering better quality or some special service?

If you are running a video game rental business, perhaps you could deliver the games, so the customers would not have to come to the store. That would be your competitive advantage. If you can beat your competitors on price *and* service, you will be very strong.

»Find Your Competitive Advantage by Thinking about What Consumers Need

Bill Gates did not invent computer software, but he did recognize that consumers were frustrated and intimidated by it. He created user-friendly software applications that consumers wanted, and packaged them in bright, attractive cartons with easy-to-read manuals. That was his competitive advantage over other software companies.

»You Have Unique Knowledge of Your Market

You may be wondering: "How do I figure out what consumers need? I do not know anything about consumers." Actually, you do. Your market is composed of your friends, neighbors, classmates, relatives, and colleagues. You already have the most important knowledge that you need to succeed. You know your own market very well.

Richard Branson, the CEO of Virgin Corporation, chose the name "Virgin" for his company because it reflected his total inexperience in business. His empire, which includes Virgin Megastores, Virgin Atlantic Airways, and Virgin Mobile, began as a tiny discount mail-order record company, which he started at age 19 after he had given up on finishing high school. "I realized I'd be hopeless at studying," Branson, who is dyslexic, told *Woman's Journal* magazine in 1985. "So I quit to do something I knew I could do and which interested me." Branson knew his market—other young people who were into music—very well.

How will you know if a business idea is going to be successful? Again, your market will tell you. The communication will be loud and clear and will come in the form of the signal called *profit*.

[Entrepreneurial Wisdom]

A new business may need some time before it can turn a profit. Federal Express, in fact, suffered initial losses of a million dollars a month! But if you just are not making enough money to stay in business, that is your market talking. It is telling you that your business is not satisfying consumer needs. Do not take it personally. Many famous entrepreneurs opened and closed many businesses during their lifetimes.

Henry Ford went bankrupt twice before the Ford Motor Company was a success. If you want to be a successful entrepreneur, start growing a thick skin and decide right now that you intend to learn from failures and disappointments. Do not let them get you down.

"Failure is the opportunity to begin again more intelligently."

—Henry Ford

»Competitive Strategy: Business Definition + Competitive Advantage

Your business will only succeed if you can offer the customers in your market something more than the competition does. This is your competitive advantage. It is whatever you can do better, cheaper, or faster than your competitors that will attract customers, satisfy them, and keep them coming back.

Once you are clear about your competitive advantage, or **core competency,** your business decisions will start to fall into place. Every ad, every promotion, even the price of your product and the location of your business, should be designed to get customers excited about your competitive advantage.

Your **competitive strategy** combines your business definition with your competitive advantage.

A competitive advantage must be *sustainable,* meaning that you can keep it going. If you decide to beat the competition by selling your product at a lower price, your advantage will not last long if you cannot afford to continue at that price. Small business owners should realize that price alone is probably not going to work as an advantage for long. A bigger business can almost always beat you on price because it can buy larger quantities from its suppliers, who will be more willing to give them a lower wholesale price, as a result.

Being able to temporarily undercut the competition's prices is not a competitive advantage. Being able to *permanently* sell at a lower price because you have discovered a cheaper supplier *is* a competitive advantage.

»Strategy vs. Tactics

Your **strategy** is the plan for outperforming the competition. Your **tactics** are the ways in which you will carry out your strategy.

If you plan to open a bookstore, how will you compete with the chain outlet in the neighborhood? This competitor buys more books and will receive higher discounts from wholesalers. So you probably will not be able to compete on price. How else could you attract customers?

Perhaps you could make your bookstore a kind of community center so that people will want to gather there.

What tactics could you use to carry out this strategy?

- Hold poetry readings and one-person concerts to promote local poets and musicians.
- Offer free tea and coffee.
- Provide comfortable seating areas for conversation and reading to encourage customers to spend time in your store.
- Set up a binder of personal ads as a dating service.

If your tactics attract enough customers to make a profit, you will have found a strategy for achieving a competitive advantage.

To find a competitive advantage, think about everything your business will offer. Look at your

Location

Product

Design

Price

What can you do to be different, and better in some way, than the competition?

»Sometimes Giving Away Your Product Is a Smart Tactic

Surprisingly, a lot of software is available for free or low cost on the Internet. Free software is called *freeware* and is free for one of two reasons:

1. The individual who developed it is eager to share it with others.
2. A company wants to start you using the program so you will be interested in buying other, related merchandise. Apple used this strategy effectively with QuickTime multimedia software, and Microsoft used it with the Internet Explorer Web browser.

Freeware does not include upgrades or technical support. The supplier of a freeware program gambles that people who use it will like it so much that they will decide to pay for the program that includes those upgrades and support.

Shareware is also distributed for free or for a suggested donation. It usually stops working after a stated expiration date. Then you will have to pay a fee to use or upgrade the program. The supplier basically uses the shareware as a "test drive" for the consumer. If you are using an online server, such as America Online or MSN, the server can direct you to shareware. If you are using a direct connection to the Internet, visit Download.com (http:// www.download.com) and Shareware.com for a list of popular programs.

> *Be sure to run all software through your virus detection program before installing it on your hard drive.*

»Is Your Competitive Advantage Strong Enough?

According to Jeffry Timmons,[2] a successful company needs the following:

- *To sell to a market that is large and growing.* The market for digital cameras is a good example. New products are being marketed to meet the demand, such as printers that turn digital photos into prints.

- *To sell to a market where the competition is able to make a profit.* It will be interesting to observe what happens in the market for hybrid cars. Right now the jury is out as to whether the companies selling them can make a profit—so most automakers are not yet entering the market.

- *To sell to a market where the competition is succeeding but is not so powerful as to make it impossible for a new entrepreneur to enter the market.* Microsoft has been taken to court several times by competitors arguing that it is so big that new software companies cannot enter the market.

- *To sell a product or service that solves problems consumers may have with the competition (such as poor quality or slow delivery).* This is how FedEx beat its competition—the U.S. Postal Service and the United Parcel Service—when it entered the market with its overnight delivery service.

- *To sell a product or service at a competitive price that will attract customers.* Now UPS is fighting back by offering a less-expensive overnight delivery service than that of FedEx.

If all of these are in place, you need to do the following:

1. Understand the needs of your customers.
2. Have a sustainable competitive advantage.
3. Deliver a product or service that meets your customers' needs at a fair price. If you do, you should be able to beat the competition and make a healthy profit.

> *Sometimes the best competitive strategy is to cooperate with the competition.*

---

[2] Jeffry Timmons, *New Venture Creation*, 6th edition. (New York: McGraw-Hill/Irwin, 2003).

»The Six Factors of Competitive Advantage

Competitive advantage comes from one (or a combination) of six factors:

1. Quality—Can you provide higher quality than competing businesses?
2. Price—Can you offer a lower price than your competition?
3. Location—Can you find a more convenient location for customers?
4. Selection—Can you provide a wider range of choices than your competitors?
5. Service—Can you provide better, more personalized customer service?
6. Speed/Turnaround—Can you deliver your product or service more quickly than the competition?

»Naming Your Business

What are you going to name your business? This is a very important decision. The name of your business will be the first impression you make on customers. Ideally, it will convey your competitive advantage to your market.

Using your first name to identify your business—showing the pride you take in it—can be a good idea (Joe's Deep Dish Pizza). If you use your last name for your business, however, there are several risks:

■ If the business fails, your name will be associated with the failure. This can hurt you if you decide to start a new business. Potential customers and investors may associate you with the old one.

■ If the business succeeds, you might decide to sell it for a profit. But what if you hate what the new owner does with it? What if he or she engages in dishonest business practices? Your name is still on the door.

Keep it simple: *The best name is one that tells customers what the company does, sells, or makes.* Here are some classic examples:

Federal Express

America Online

Burger King

Microsoft

As Joe Mancuso says in his best-selling book, *Have You Got What It Takes? How To Tell If You Should Start Your Own Business,* "Naming the company is the first move of many in which you should keep the customer's needs first and foremost in mind."

Shops and cafes line the narrow
street around Taos Plaza in Taos,
New Mexico.
(Francesca Yorke © Dorling Kindersley)

»Your Company's Core Beliefs

When you start your own company, what beliefs will you use to
guide it? These are the **core beliefs** of your business.

Examples of core beliefs in business might be the following:

- "At Superior Printing, we believe in business practices that affect the environment as little as possible."

- "At Sheila's Restaurant, we believe in supporting local organic
  farmers."

Core beliefs affect your business decisions. The owner of Superior
Printing, for example, will choose an ink that is less harmful to the
environment over a cheaper ink that is more so. Superior Printing
may also have a paper-recycling program to minimize its paper consumption. The owner of Sheila's Restaurant will only buy fruits and
vegetables from organic farmers with farms in the same area as the
restaurant. Your core beliefs will affect everything from the cost of
your materials to the prices you charge and how you treat customers.

> *Tom Watson, Jr., built his
> father's company, IBM, into a
> huge international success with
> these three core beliefs: respect
> for the individual, unparalleled
> customer service, and the pur-
> suit of superiority in all that the
> company undertakes.*

»Analyzing Your Competitive Advantage

To determine whether you have a competitive advantage that will
enable you to outperform your closest and strongest competitors,
ask these questions:

1. *Competitive offers*—How does your offer compare with those of
   your leading competitors? What are the key features of each?

2. *Unique selling proposition*—Based on that comparison, what is your **unique selling proposition** (USP)? This will require a comparison of offers and identifying what is unique about yours. What is it about yours that your competitors cannot or will not match?

3. *Cost structure*—What is different about your business activities, and "the cost of doing business," from that of your competitors? Overall, are you at a cost advantage or disadvantage?

To be successful, you must have a unique selling proposition that will attract customers to buy from you.

Second, you must have a cost structure that is sufficiently advantageous so that, when all of your costs are deducted from your revenue, you will have some profit left over. If you can achieve a cost advantage or, at least, minimize any cost disadvantage, this will help you achieve a profit in the business. This profit is your reward for operating a successful business.

»The Most Chocolate Cake Company

In this example, our entrepreneur makes and sells chocolate cakes. She chose this product because she loves chocolate and she enjoys baking cakes. She decided to make the most *chocolate* cakes possible. From this decision, she came up with the concept for her product and the name of her business: The Most Chocolate Cake Company.

Her target market was the segment of the public that loved chocolate cakes. Because cakes are usually purchased for special occasions, our entrepreneur believed she could charge a good price—at least as much as a bakery store cake.

She decided she would make the cakes "special" in three ways:

■ By using the finest ingredients

■ Through expert custom-decorating, to personalize each cake

■ By baking the cakes to order, so they would be fresh for the event

She baked her cakes at home, which made them literally "homemade" and reduced the costs of making them—she was not renting commercial space or paying a staff.

The following chart shows how our entrepreneur answered the key questions about business definition.

Business Definition Question	Response
1. *The offer*—What products and services will be sold?	1. Chocolate cakes, for special events, at a price competitive with neighborhood stores.
2. *Target market*—Which consumer segment will the business focus on?	2. People who love chocolate and those who want a special cake for a special event.
3. *Production capability*—How will that offer be produced and delivered to those customers?	3. Homemade and baked to order to ensure freshness, using high-quality ingredients.

»Checking Out the Competition

At this point, our entrepreneur has defined the business in terms of the offer, the target market, and the capability required to produce and deliver that offer to customers. Now she needs to compare her approach to the business to that of her competitors.

One useful exercise is to notice everything you can about a particular competitor—especially one that has earned the respect of the marketplace. Try to figure out why they do the things they do, and identify the sources of their competitive advantage.

You will also need to keep an eye on your competition *after* you have started your business, because new factors might be undermining your competitive advantage.

Before the Internet, researching was both time-consuming and expensive. Today's entrepreneurs, even those starting very small ventures, may face competition from far beyond their neighborhoods because customers can go shopping on the Web. Most entrepreneurs are *optimistic*—optimism is a trait that goes with entrepreneurship—so they tend to get excited about their potential customer base via the Web. What they often do not realize is that "The world already is selling to their customers—aggressively and seamlessly."[3] Therefore, get online yourself and conduct a thorough search of your industry. Check out your competition's Web sites.

Competitive Advantage Question	Competitive Difference (USP)
1. *The offer*—What will be better and different about the products and services that will be sold?	1. Most Chocolate will use more and higher-grade chocolate; better ingredients in general, especially in frostings and fillings; will have personalized decorations; and will be freshly baked to order.
2. *Target market*—What customers should be the focus of the business to make it as successful as possible?	2. People who love chocolate and those who want a special cake for a special event.
3. *Production and delivery capability*—What will be better or different about the way that offer is produced and delivered to those customers?	3. Homemade and baked to order to ensure freshness; using highest-quality ingredients.

Our entrepreneur is making the bet that her more chocolaty cake, with its special frosting and decoration, as well as its freshly homemade quality, will be successful in the marketplace. This is her USP (unique selling proposition). She hopes this will be a source of competitive advantage, along with the cost advantage of baking the cakes at home.

If all of the following are in place, you should be able to find a way to beat the competition and make a healthy profit:

1. Understand the needs of your customers.
2. Have a sustainable competitive advantage, based on a comparison of your offer to that of your competitors, identification

---

[3] Fred Hapgood, "Foreign Exchange," *Inc.* magazine (June 1997).

of your "unique sales proposition" (USP), and an understanding of how your costs compare with the competition.

3. Produce and deliver a product or service that meets your customers' needs at a fair price.

Based on these principles, she has determined how she wants to make her offering better and different from those of her competitors. These differences will form the basis of her USP.

»Mission

Your mission as an entrepreneur is to use your competitive advantage to satisfy your customers. Most great entrepreneurs have discovered that the true mission of business is to meet a consumer need better than anyone yet has. A commitment to serve your customers, and to satisfy their needs, is at the heart of a strong mission statement.

The **mission** of your business, expressed in a **mission statement,** is a concise communication of your strategy, including your business definition and your competitive advantage. The function of a mission statement is to clarify what you are trying to do, and it can provide direction and motivation to people who are involved in the business.

A clearly stated mission statement not only tells your customers and employees what your business is about, but also it will be a guide for every business decision you make. It should capture your passion for the business and your commitment to satisfying your customers.

Here is an example of a mission statement, based on our example of The Most Chocolate Cake Company:

The Most Chocolate Cake Company will create the richest, tastiest, most chocolaty cakes in our area. They will be made from the finest and freshest ingredients with our own special frostings and fillings. Baked to order and individually decorated for that special occasion, they will make any event as special as our cakes!

The Most Chocolate Cake Company's mission statement defines the business and its competitive advantage, the core of its strategy.

»Can You Make a Profit?

Once you have chosen a business idea and determined your competitive advantage, you need to figure out if the business is financially viable. In other words, can you provide your product or service at a price that will cover your costs and provide you with a profit? Wozniak and Jobs were able to move out of the garage once they were making enough profit to hire people to make the computers for Apple. This freed them to create new products and new strategies for their business.

Entrepreneurs use profits:

1. To pay themselves
2. To expand their businesses
3. To start or invest in other businesses

Every entrepreneur, therefore, needs to know how much **gross profit** (price minus cost of goods sold) the business will earn on each item it sells. To do this, entrepreneurs study the **economics of one unit of sale (EOU).** The EOU tells you how much gross profit you will earn on each unit of your product or service that you sell.

»Defining the Unit of Sale

Begin with the **unit of sale,** which is one unit of the product or service a business sells. Entrepreneurs usually define their unit of sale depending on the type of business:

3.⟨ **Performance Objective**

Manufacturing. One order (any quantity; e.g., 100 watches)

Wholesale. A dozen of an item (e.g., 12 watches)

Retail. One item (e.g., 1 watch)

Service. One hour of service time (e.g., one hour of lawn-mowing service) or a standard block of time devoted to a task (e.g., one mowed lawn)

If the business sells a combination of differently priced items (such as in a restaurant), the unit of sale is more complicated. The entrepreneur can use the average sale per customer minus the average cost of goods sold per customer for the economics of one unit of sale. The formula would be as follows:

Average sale per customer − Average cost of sale per customer = Average gross profit per customer

A business that sells a variety of items may choose to express one unit of sale as a combination of items that comprises the average sale per customer. (See Figure 2-1.)

UNIT OF SALE AND ECONOMICS OF ONE UNIT OF SALE			
Type of Business	**Unit of Sale**	**Economics of One Unit of Sale**	**Gross Profit per Unit**
1. Retail & Manufacturing	One item (e.g., one tie)	$7 − $3 = $4	$4
2. Service	One hour (e.g., one hour of mowing a lawn)	$20 − $10 = $10	$10
3. Wholesale	Multiple of same item (e.g., one dozen roses)	$240 − $120 = $120	$120
4. Combination	Average sale per customer minus average cost of goods sold per customer (e.g., restaurant meals)	$20 − $10 = $10	$10 average gross profit

Figure 2-1 Unit of sale as a combination of different items.

»Cost of Goods Sold and Gross Profit

To get a closer look at the costs involved in making one unit, entrepreneurs analyze the **cost of goods sold (COGS)** of one unit, which are the costs associated specifically with each unit of sale. These are:

- The costs of materials used to make the product (or deliver the service).
- The costs of labor used to make the product (or deliver the service).

Performance Objective 4.〉

For a product, these are called the cost of goods sold (COGS). For a service business, they are the **cost of services sold (COSS).**

Costs of goods sold can be thought of as the cost of selling "one additional unit." If you buy watches and then resell them, your COGS per unit is the price you paid for one watch. Once you know your COGS, you can calculate gross profit by subtracting COGS from revenue. (See Figure 2-2.)

»Your Business and the Economics of One Unit

The economics of one unit of sale (EOU) is a method for seeing whether your business idea might be profitable. If one unit of sale is profitable, the whole business is likely to be profitable, too. On the other hand, if one unit of sale is not profitable, then no matter how many units you sell, the business will never be successful. (See Figure 2-2.)

Say you have a simple business selling decorative hand-blown wineglasses that you buy from a local artist for $12 each wholesale, and resell to friends for $20 each. The cost of goods sold for each wineglass is the wholesale price of $12 (gross profit: $8).

Assume you buy a dozen glasses for $12 each wholesale. Your unit of sale is one glass. Your cost of goods sold is $12 per unit.

Assume you sell all the glasses for $20 each. Here is how you would calculate your gross profit.

	Economics of One Unit (EOU)	Total Gross Profit for 12 Units (@$10 per Unit Sold)
Price Sold/Revenue	$20	$240 (12 × $20)
− Cost of Goods Sold	− 12	$144 (12 × 12)
Gross Profit	$8	$96 (12 × 8)

Figure 2-2 Economics of one unit of sale versus total gross profit.

Total Revenue = 12 glasses × $20 selling price		=	$240
Total Cost of Goods Sold = 12 glasses × $12 selling price		=	−120
Total Gross Profit (Contribution margin) =			$144
$240 revenue −$120 COGS		=	$96

Total Revenue − Total Cost of Goods Sold = Total Gross Profit

> *Never reveal your cost of goods sold. Customers will use it to try to get you to lower your selling price.*

You made a gross profit of $96.

For a manufacturing business, one unit might be one pair of sneakers. The costs would include the money paid to the people who make the sneakers (the labor) and the supplies, such as fabric, rubber, and leather. (See Figure 2-3.)

The manufacturer makes a gross profit of $3.00 for every pair of sneakers sold. That may not seem like much, but manufacturers sell in *bulk*. In other words, a manufacturer might sell several million pairs of sneakers per year.

The economics of one unit also applies to wholesale, retail, and service businesses. Assume the wholesaler buys each set of one dozen sneakers from the manufacturer for $180 and can sell them to the retailer for $240. (See Figure 2-4.)

The retailer pays the wholesaler $240 for one dozen sneakers. The retailer's COGS, therefore, is $20 ($240/12). The store sells each pair to its customers for $35. (See Figure 2-5.)

Here is the economics of one unit for a hair stylist who charges $50 per cut. (See Figure 2-6.)

ECONOMICS OF ONE UNIT (EOU)			
Manufacturing Business: unit = 1 pair of sneakers			
Selling Price per Unit:			$15.00
Labor Cost per Hour:	$4.00		
No. of Hours per Unit:	2 hours	$ 8.00	
Materials per Unit:		4.00	
Cost of Goods Sold per Unit:		$12.00	12.00
Gross Profit per Unit:			$ 3.00

Figure 2-3 Economics of one unit, manufacturing.

ECONOMICS OF ONE UNIT (EOU)	
Wholesale Business: unit = 1 dozen pair of sneakers	
Selling Price per Unit:	$240.00
Cost of Goods Sold per Unit:	180.00
Gross Profit per Unit:	$ 60.00

Figure 2-4 Economics of one unit, wholesale.

ECONOMICS OF ONE UNIT (EOU)	
Retail Business: unit = 1 pair of sneakers	
Selling Price per Unit:	**$35.00**
Cost of Goods Sold per Unit:	20.00
Gross Profit per Unit:	**$15.00**

Figure 2-5 Economics of one unit, retail business.

ECONOMICS OF ONE UNIT (EOU)		
Service Business: unit = 1 hour		
Selling Price per Unit:		**$50.00**
Supplies per Unit (hair gel, etc.):	$ 2.00	
Labor Costs per Hour:	25.00	
Cost of Goods Sold per Unit:	**$27.00**	27.00
Gross Profit per Unit:		**$23.00**

Figure 2-6 Economics of one unit, service business.

ECONOMICS OF ONE UNIT (EOU)		
Manufacturing Business: unit = 1 bookmarker		
Selling Price per Unit:		**$4.50**
Materials:	$1.00	
Labor:	1.50	
Cost of Goods Sold per Unit:	**$2.50**	2.50
Gross Profit per Unit:		**$2.00**

Figure 2-7 EOU example.

»The Cost of Labor in the EOU

Janet has a business designing handmade bookmarkers. Her unit of sale is one bookmarker. Below is additional information about Janet's business:

■ She sells forty bookmarkers per week to a bookstore in her neighborhood.

■ Her selling price is $4.50 each, including an envelope.

■ Her costs are 80¢ per card for materials (construction paper, glue, and paint) and 20¢ each for the envelopes.

■ On average, it takes her one hour to make six bookmarkers.

■ Janet pays herself $9 an hour.

The labor for each bookmarker is $1.50 ($9/6). Janet wisely realizes that she must include the cost of her labor in the EOU. See how she did this in Figure 2-7.

Janet's gross profit was $2 per bookmarker sold. Assuming no other expenses, she will keep this as owner of the business. She also earned $1.50 per bookmarker by supplying the labor, thus ending up with $3.50 per bookmarker.

»Hiring Others to Make the Unit of Sale

Janet realizes that, if the bookstore wants to order more bookmarkers, or if she can sell them to additional bookstores, she will not have enough time to make them all herself. To solve this issue, she hires a friend to make the bookmarkers for $9 per hour. Although the EOU stays the same, Janet will have more time to look for new opportunities for her business. Her income from the business will now come solely from the gross profit, which is currently $2.00 per unit.

»Going for Volume

Janet meets a bookstore supply wholesaler. He offers to buy 2,000 bookmarkers if Janet can deliver them in one month and sell them for $3.50 each, $1 less than she had been getting for them. This would reduce her gross profit but offer more revenue. Three questions immediately came to her mind:

1. *Can I produce the 2,000-unit order in the required time frame?*

   After doing some calculations, Janet realized that, if she hired ten people each to work 35 hours a month, she could deliver the order in time. Janet convinces ten people to take on the one-month commitment by offering $12 per hour.

2. *If I lower the price to $3.50 for each bookmarker (instead of $4.50), will I still make an acceptable gross profit per unit?*

   To answer this question, Janet created a chart (Figure 2-8) and realized that her new gross profit per unit would be $1.00. Let us look at the EOU if she factors in her labor at $12.00 per hour or $2 per bookmarker.

ECONOMICS OF ONE UNIT (EOU)		
Manufacturing Business: unit = 1 bookmarker		
Selling Price per Unit:		$3.50
Materials:	$1.00	
Labor:	1.50	
Cost of Goods Sold per Unit:	$2.50	2.50
Gross Profit per Unit:		$1.00

Figure 2-8 EOU example.

GROSS PROFIT PROJECTION (BASED ON EOU)		
Janet's Total Gross Profit		
Revenue ($3.50 × 2,000 bookmarkers):		**$7,000.00**
Materials ($1 × 2,000):	$2,000.00	
Labor ($2.00 × 2,000):	4,000.00	
Cost of Goods Sold:	**$6,000.00**	6,000.00
Gross Profit:		**$1,000.00**

Figure 2-9 Gross profit projection.

3. *How much in total gross profit will I make from the order?*

    To answer this question, Janet created another chart (Figure 2-9) and realized that her total gross profit would be $1,000.

Janet concluded that $1,000 in gross profit was much better than earning $80 a week in gross profit and $60 a week for her labor, which is what she would earn making the bookmarkers herself each week at a selling price of $4.50. Even though the wholesaler was asking for a lower selling price, her total revenue, and therefore her total gross profit, would be much higher. When Janet realized that she could deliver the order in the required time and make $1,000, she accepted the offer.

    Five breakthrough steps entrepreneurs can take are these:

1. Calculating the unit of sale
2. Determining the economics of one unit of sale
3. Substituting someone else's labor
4. Trying to sell in volume
5. Creating jobs and operating at a profit

»Becoming a Business Leader

By taking these steps, the entrepreneur is "promoting" him/herself as being a *leader* of a business, the chief executive officer. Janet promoted herself by hiring her friends. Janet was able to make $0.50 for every bookmarker that her employees made on the order for the wholesaler. Meanwhile, she had freed her time to seek further opportunities for her business.

»How Entrepreneurship Creates Wealth

Janet discovered how entrepreneurship leads to wealth. When the entrepreneur figures out how to make something for a profit, she can hire others to do the labor.

    Janet created part-time jobs for ten people to each make 200 bookmarkers per month (10 people × 200 units each = 2,000 units).

[Global Impact]

Selling Your Product around the World

Through the Internet, even a very small business run by one person can reach customers internationally. What if a customer from Germany contacts you through your Web site and wants to buy your product—in euros? The euro is a currency. **Currency** is money that can be exchanged internationally. In the United States, the currency is the dollar. In Japan, it is the yen. In many countries in Europe, it is the euro. In Mexico, it is the peso.

The **foreign exchange (FX) rate** is the relative value between one currency and another. It describes the buying power of a currency. The foreign exchange rate, or FX rate, is expressed as a ratio. If one dollar is worth 1.25 euros, to figure out how many euros a certain number of dollars is worth, multiply that number by 1.25.

$$\$5 = \$5 \times €1.25 = €6.25$$

How would you figure out how many dollars €6.25 is worth? Simply divide 6.25 by 1.25 to get $5.00.

TIP: There are currency converters available online, such as http://finance.yahoo.com/currency?u.

By creating jobs for others, Janet is making far more money than she could ever have made alone. She is fulfilling the entrepreneur's role as the driving force for job- and wealth-creation.

At first, an entrepreneur can be part of his or her own economics of one unit. If you start making (manufacturing) computers in your garage, like Steve Jobs and Stephen Wozniak did when they started Apple, you should include your labor on the EOU worksheet.

Over time, though, Jobs and Wozniak made enough profit to hire others to manufacture the computers. This left them free to develop new ideas for Apple that brought more business and profit to the company. Jobs and Wozniak took themselves out of the economics of one unit so they could be the creative leaders of the company. And by lowering prices they were able to sell millions of units.

》Chapter Summary

Now that you have studied this chapter you can do the following:

1. Define your business.

2. Identify the four basic types of business.

   - *Manufacturing*—makes a tangible product.
   - *Wholesale*—buys in quantity from the manufacturer and sells to the retailer.
   - *Retail*—sells to the consumer.
   - *Service*—sells an intangible product to the consumer.

3. Find and analyze your business's competitive advantage.

   - Your competitive advantage is whatever you can do better than the competition that will attract customers to your business.
   - Find your competitive advantage by thinking about what consumers in your market need. You have unique knowledge of your market.

4. Calculate the economics of one unit of sale.

■ The EOU is the basis of business profit.

■ Entrepreneurs use profits to do the following:

a. Pay themselves.

b. Expand the business.

c. Start or invest in new businesses.

■ The entrepreneur chooses how the unit is defined:

a. One item (unit).

b. One hour of service time (if the business is a service business).

c. If the business sells differently priced items (such as in a restaurant), use the average sale per customer as the unit. The average would be total sales divided by the number of customers:

Total Sales/Number of Customers = Average Unit of Sale

■ To get a closer look at the costs involved in making one unit, entrepreneurs analyze the cost of goods or services sold (COGS or COSS) of a unit.

a. The costs of materials used to make the product (or deliver the service)

b. The costs of labor used to make the product (or deliver the service)

■ Once you know your cost of goods sold, you can calculate gross profit. Subtract total COGS from your total revenue to get your gross profit.

Revenue – COGS = Gross Profit

5. Eventually entrepreneurs have enough gross profit and business volume to replace their own labor with their employees' labor.

■ This frees the entrepreneur to seek out new opportunities to grow the business.

■ This is how entrepreneurs create wealth and jobs.

Key Terms

competitive advantage
competitive strategy
core belief
core competency
cost of goods sold (COGS)
cost of services sold (COSS)
currency
economics of one unit of sale
  (EOU)
foreign exchange rate
gross profit

manufacturing
market
mission
mission statement
retail
service
strategy
tactics
unique selling proposition
unit of sale
wholesale

[Entrepreneurship Portfolio]

1. Use the following charts to define a business you want to start and analyze your competitive advantage. (**Business Plan Practice**)

Critical Thinking Exercises

Business Definition Question	Response
1. *The offer*—What products and services will be sold by the business?	1.
2. *Target market*—Which consumer segment will the business focus on?	2.
3. *Production capability*—How will that offer be produced and delivered to those customers?	3.

Competitive Advantage Question	Competitive Difference (USP)
1. *The offer*—What will be better and different about the products and services that will be sold?	1.
2. *Target market*—What customers should be the focus of the business to make it as successful as possible?	2.
3. *Production and delivery capability*—What will be better or different about the way that offer is produced and delivered to those customers?	3.

2. Are there customers for your business in other countries? How do you plan to reach them? (**Business Plan Practice**)

3. Describe any international competitors you have found who may be able to access your customers. How do you intend to compete? (**Business Plan Practice**)

4. Describe three core beliefs you will use to run your own company. (**Business Plan Practice**)

1. Gross profit is a business's profit before which other costs are subtracted?

Key Concept Questions

2. What is the average unit of sale for the following businesses?

- ■ Business 1: A restaurant that serves $2,100 in meals to 115 customers per day.
- ■ Business 2: A record store that sells $1,500 worth of CDs to 75 customers per day.

3. For the following business, define the unit of sale and calculate the economics of one unit.

Sue, of Sue's Sandwich Shoppe, sells sandwiches and soda from a sidewalk cart in a popular park near her house. She sets up her cart in the summers to earn money for college tuition. Last month she sold $1,240 worth of product (sandwiches and sodas) to 100 customers. She spent $210 on the sandwich ingredients and buying the sodas wholesale. Her unit is one sandwich ($4) plus one soda ($1).

4. Explain why a monopoly can charge any price for the products it sells. Can monopolies last in a free market system? Why or why not?

5. When Stephen Wozniak and Steve Jobs envisioned a computer in every home, computers were large, expensive machines. They were only available to the government, universities, scientists, and large companies. What technology currently available today to only a few people can you envision meeting a need for many consumers in the future?

6. Is there a service presently available to only a few consumers? Or one that is not available yet? Write about a service that you can imagine eventually becoming very popular, and the need(s) it will meet.

7. If the FX rate between the U.S. dollar and the Japanese yen is 1:119, how many yen will it take to equal $20?

8. If the FX rate between the Japanese yen and the euro is 189.35:1, how many yen will equal 10 euros?

Application Exercises

You own a small record label. You sell CDs through your Web site for $15, including shipping and handling. You get e-mail from someone who owns a record store in Germany who would like to sell your CDs. He wants to buy them at $10 each and sell them for $30. He says his profit from each sale would be $12 and he will split it with you. Assuming the exchange rate between the dollar and the euro is $1 = €2:

a. How much profit would you get from the sale of each CD in the German store?

b. How much is that profit in dollars?

c. Is this a good business opportunity for you? Why or why not?

d. If the FX rate between the dollar and the euro falls to $1 = €1 will this still be a good business idea for you? Why or why not?

Exploring Online

Use the Internet to research suppliers for a business you would like to start. Below, describe the business you want to start and list the URL, e-mail, phone and fax, and street address for five suppliers you located via the Internet.

Visit www.download.com and find three shareware programs that would be of value to you as an entrepreneur.

Some people argue that NAFTA is not a good idea because American companies can now move their factories to Mexico, where wages are much lower. Research this issue on the Internet and write a short essay exploring the pros and cons of free trade.

In Your Opinion

CASE STUDY: Entrepreneurs in the Beverage Industry

Entrepreneurs have been a driving force in the beverage industry for more than a century. In 1886, John Pemberton began marketing Coca-Cola as an over-the-counter medicine, and in 1929, Charles Grigg developed Bib-Label Lithiated Lemon-Lime Soda, which today is known as 7-Up. The beverage industry has always provided opportunities for entrepreneurs. More than 3,000 new beverage products were launched in 1997. However, entrepreneurs who attempt to succeed in this industry have to be aware of the changing consumer tastes and industry trends.

There are many good examples of recent success in the beverage industry. Specialty coffee outlets experienced explosive growth in recent years. In 1989, there were only 200 specialty coffee outlets in the United States. By 1995, there were approximately 4,000 and over 10,000 by 2000. The most well-known name in the gourmet coffee industry is Starbucks, but there are also standout performers like New World Coffee–Manhattan Bagel, Quick-ava Coffees, and Krispy Kreme. Just in the caffeine arena we have also seen new beverages such as Jolt, RC Edge Maximum Power Cola, and Walter Joe.

Herbal drinks first became popular in 1970, when Morris J. Siegel founded Celestial Seasonings, Inc., which markets herbal teas. In 1998, Celestial Seasonings jumped into the fastest-growing segment in the tea industry—the green tea category. The market for green tea has been growing steadily. Joe Bello, of SoBe Beverage Co., states that his company is "taking the concept of herbal remedies to the mass market." SoBe's products include a variety of teas containing plant extracts that improve alertness. Nantucket Nectars, Ame, and Norfolk Punch are other examples of new beverages in this area.

Proponents of smoothies state that the beverage is one of the most promising new items in this field since specialty coffees. One company, Smoothie King, was in business for more than 20 years before great demand for the product developed. Smoothies are often sold at juice bars and are marketed as low-fat, high-nutrition meals. These characteristics make smoothies a favorite with the rapidly growing diet-conscious population.

Case Study Analysis

1. What other beverage success stories can you think of? Why are there so many successes in the beverage industry?

2. Not every new beverage idea is successful. (New Coke was a disaster.) What factors might predict success in this industry?

3. What marketing knowledge can help you decide on the strength of a business concept?

CASE STUDY: Honest Tea

Seth's Problem: "I Was thirsty!"

Seth Goldman likes to say that his business got started because he was thirsty. A natural-born athlete, Seth was always searching for a satisfying drink to quench his thirst after a tough workout. While there were plenty of sports drinks and sodas he could buy, not to mention water, none of these options ever appealed to him. So he started to experiment.

A Hobby Evolves into a Business Idea

After he graduated with an MBA from Yale, Seth began concocting fruity beverages in his kitchen as a hobby. But he was not satisfied. One day he decided to call his old business school professor Barry Nalebuff to discuss the problem. Nalebuff had just returned from India, where he had been studying the country's tea industry. He explained that beverage companies which purchased their raw materials from Indian tea plantations did not use whole tea leaves in their manufacturing. Instead, they took whatever was left over after the quality leaves had been packaged and used for other products, such as tea bags. Seth and Barry had a hunch that they were circling in on an opportunity. Even better, Barry had already come up with a name for a company that would make beverages using top-of-the-line tea leaves. The company would be called Honest Tea. Seth loved the name and what it represented. He hung up the phone and resolved to continue his experiments by brewing tea leaves in his kitchen until he came up with the perfect product.

That was seven years ago. Today, Honest Tea® sells twelve different kinds of bottled iced teas as well as a growing line of bagged and loose teas. In 2001, the company generated $1.9 million in sales; in 2002, this increased to $3.2 million. Seth is aiming for a 75 percent growth rate each year, and the company seems to be on track to do it. So, how did Seth do it? How did this drink hobbyist succeed in competing with big-time beverage companies?

Honest Tea's Competitive Advantages

Seth has worked hard to define the company around the features that make Honest Tea stand out from its competitors. In Seth's own words, "Given that this is a highly competitive market, the most important factor in our favor is that we offer a differentiated product. A company like Coca-Cola is a thousand times our size. What we are offering is a very strong brand that is consistent with what is in the package and very meaningful to customers."

For example, Honest Tea is the only bottled tea company whose products are all 100 percent USDA organic certified. What does this mean and why does it matter? Well, when a product is labeled "USDA organic," it confirms that harmful pesticides and other toxic chemicals have not been used in growing or producing the product. Increasingly, consumers, particularly the health-conscious, are seeking out organic goods in the marketplace.

Honest Tea also uses up to two-thirds less sugar in its teas compared with its competitors, such as Snapple and Arizona iced teas. Seth likes to say that his teas are "lightly sweetened." This feature appeals to consumers who care about their health and diet.

Socially Responsible Business

The "honest" part of Honest Tea extends beyond using organic ingredients. Seth goes to great lengths to educate customers about the company's ethical and socially responsible business practices. For example, Honest Tea purchases peppermint leaves for its "First Nation Peppermint" iced tea from a woman-owned herb company on the Crow Indian reservation in Montana, where the unemployment rate is a staggering 67 percent. By purchasing its peppermint leaves from this supplier, Honest Tea is promoting economic activity in a location where many suffer from poverty and joblessness. A percentage of the revenue from the sale of this product is donated to nonprofit organizations that help at-risk Native American youth.

Seth wants customers to know that, when they buy Honest Tea, they are also doing something good for the community. As Seth puts it, "A commitment to social responsibility is central to Honest Tea's identity and purpose. The company strives for authenticity, integrity, and purity in our products and in the way we do business."

Staying in the Game

The beverage market is highly competitive, but Honest Tea appears to be thriving because it is delivering a differentiated product that customers feel good about buying, and it uses organic ingredients. Comparable brands like Snapple, Lipton, and Arizona iced teas may be 25 to 50 cents less per bottle, but do not offer the same quality and health benefits. However, some high-end tea purveyors, such as Tazo iced and loose teas, sold exclusively at Starbucks and other retail locations, may pose a threat to Honest Tea in the long run. In order to stay in the game, Seth needs to continue to enhance and market the features that make Honest Tea a specialty product.

Case Study Analysis

1. What are Honest Tea's competitive advantages?

2. Brainstorm a list of Honest Tea's competitors. What are the competitive advantages of their products?

3. Look at the list you generated of Honest Tea's competitive advantages. Which is most important to you as a consumer and why?

4. Given what you already know about Honest Tea's business philosophy and practices, if you were Seth's business advisor, what additional competitive advantages would you encourage him to develop?

5. In your opinion, what does it mean for a company to engage in "socially responsible business practices"?

6. Assume the following. An 8-oz. bottle of the following iced tea products costs the following:

   - Snapple: $1.25
   - Arizona Iced Tea: $1.50
   - Honest Tea: $1.75

   Would you be willing to pay between 25 and 50 cents more to purchase an Honest Tea beverage because you know that the company engages in socially responsible business practices and uses organic ingredients? How much are these features worth to you and why?

CASE SOURCES

Honest Tea Web site: www.honesttea.com

"A Boston Tea Party: Seth Goldman of Honest Tea Visits HBS," by Brian Duchovnay, *Harbus News*, February 23, 2004. See www.harbus.org

"Honest Tea's Best Policies," by Jon Goldstein, *Baltimore Sun*, August 5, 2003.

Net-Impact Success Story: Seth Goldman. See "Member Success Stories" at www.net-impact.org

Unit 1 BUSINESS PLAN PRACTICE

At the end of each unit, you will have an opportunity to work on your own business plan. Please go to the Business Plan Worksheet Template section for Unit One on the BizBuilder CD now to develop the following segments of your plan:

Your Business Idea

1. Describe your business idea. What is the name of your business?
2. Explain how your business idea will satisfy a consumer need.
3. Provide contact information for each owner.
4. If there is more than owner, describe how the ownership will be shared.

Economics of One Unit

1. Do you intend to pay yourself a salary, wage, dividend, or commission? Explain.
2. What type of business are you starting?
3. Define your unit.

4. Calculate the economics of one unit for your business.

Evaluating Your Business Idea

1. What resources and skills do you (and the other owners) have that will help make your business successful?
2. Perform a SWOT analysis of your business.

Your Goals

1. What are your short-term business goals (less than one year)?
2. What are your long-term business goals (from one to five years)?

Technology

1. Identify which technological tools you plan to use for your business, and why.
2. Write a memo explaining how you plan to get access to the technology you need.

Core Beliefs

1. Describe three core beliefs you will use to run your company.

Supply and Demand

1. What factors influence the demand for your product or service?
2. What factors influence the supply for your product or service?

Competitive Advantage

1. What type of business are you starting—manufacturing, wholesale, retail, or service?
2. Describe your competitive advantage.
3. Find three competitors and describe:

Competitor	Weaknesses	Strengths

Use the following charts to define your business and analyze your competitive advantage.

Business Definition Question	Response
1. *The offer*—What products and services will be sold?	1.
2. *Target market*—Which consumer segment will the business focus on?	2.
3. *Production capability*—How will that offer be produced and delivered to those customers?	3.

Competitive Advantage Question	Competitive Difference (USP)
1. *The offer*—What will be better and different about the products and services that will be sold?	1.
2. *Target market*—What customers should be the focus of the business to make it as successful as possible?	2.
3. *Production and delivery capability*—What will be better or different about the way that offer is produced and delivered to those customers?	3.

International Opportunities

1. Are there customers for your business in other countries? How do you plan to reach them? **(Business Plan Practice)**

2. Describe any international competitors you have found who might be able to access your customers. How do you intend to compete? **(Business Plan Practice)**

Who Are Your Customers?

And Why Should They Buy from You?

Chapter 3

What Is Marketing? Analyzing Customers and Your Market

"In my factory we make cosmetics, but in my stores we sell hope."

—Charles Revson, founder of Revlon cosmetics

Performance Objectives

1. Explain how marketing differs from selling.
2. Analyze the consumer your marketing plan will target.
3. Write a mission statement describing the strategy, tactics, and competitive advantage of your business.
4. Choose your market segment and research it.
5. Position your product or service within your market.

The original McDonald's was a modest burger restaurant in San Bernardino, California. It was owned by two brothers, Maurice and Richard McDonald, and they lived nearby. Ray Kroc was a 52-year-old salesman of Multimixer milkshake machines, and the McDonald brothers' restaurant was his best customer. When Kroc received an order from the McDonalds for eight Multimixers—enough to make forty milkshakes at once—he had to see the operation for himself.

What Kroc saw was that the McDonald brothers had hit upon a unique combination that drew customers from miles around. The restaurant combined three factors:

1. Fast, friendly service

2. Consistent quality for its burgers, shakes, and fries

3. Low prices

The McDonald brothers had stumbled onto the magic formula for fast-food success. They knew they could expand their business, but they both hated to fly. In 1955, Kroc offered to form a partnership to create identical McDonald's restaurants around the country.

In 1961, Kroc bought out the brothers for $2.7 million, but he strictly adhered to their original recipes. Kroc wanted every McDonald's customer, from Anchorage to Miami, to eat an identical product. According to Bill Bryson's fascinating history of McDonald's, *Made in America*, Kroc "dictated that McDonald's burgers must be exactly 3.875 inches across, weigh 1.6 ounces, and contain precisely 19 percent fat. Big Mac buns should have an average of 178 sesame seeds." Today there are 30,000 McDonald's outlets in 118 countries.

»What Is Marketing?

Marketing is satisfying the customer at a profit.[1] A **market** is a group of people with the potential interest of buying a given product or service. Marketing is the business function that identifies these customers and their needs and wants.

Through marketing, the name of your business comes to mean something clear and concrete in the customer's mind. As an entrepreneur, your current and future customers should always be your top priority.[2] Above all, marketing is the way a business tells its customers that it is committed to meeting their needs. Marketing should constantly reinforce your competitive advantage, which is what makes customers choose your business over the competition. Ray Kroc understood what customers wanted from McDonald's and he did not tinker with it.

Nike sells sneakers. It puts them in stores where customers can buy them. But Nike also *markets* sneakers. Nike creates advertisements and promotions designed to convince customers that Nike sneakers will inspire them to *Just Do It*. You can choose sneakers from many companies, but Nike hopes you will feel inspired by its marketing to seek out and buy its brand.

> Ray Kroc invented a new way of marketing hamburgers by realizing that customers cared more about fast service, consistent quality, and a low price than about the "ultimate hamburger."

Performance Objective 1.〉

»A Business That Markets vs. a Market-Driven Business

Do not make the mistake of treating marketing as a separate business function, instead of the engine that drives all business decisions. Most experts agree that, to be successful, a business must develop its marketing vision first, and then use it as the basis for all subsequent decisions.

Give an example of a company that you believe operates as a market-driven organization, and why.

Example: _____

Why: _____

Give an example of a company that functions as an organization that markets.

Example: _____

Why: _____

---

[1] Adapted from Philip Kotler and Gary Armstrong, *Principles of Marketing*, 9th ed. (Upper Saddle River, NJ: Prentice Hall, 2001).
[2] Ibid.

»How Customers Decide to Buy

How will you figure out who the potential customers are for *your* business?

Step One: Ask yourself what need your product serves. Arm & Hammer has turned this marketing question into a gold mine by developing its simple baking soda powder into toothpaste, air and carpet fresheners, and deodorants.

Step Two: Think about who might actually *buy* your product. Remember that the people who use a product are not always the buyers. Mothers buy children's clothes, for example; so, if you are making kids' playsuits, they should offer a benefit that appeals to mothers. They could be marketed as very easy to clean, for example.

Step Three: Analyze the "buying process" that leads consumers to your product.

1. *Awareness*—The consumer realizes a need. Advertising is designed to make consumers aware of potential needs for everything from dandruff shampoo to cars.
2. *Information Search*—The consumer seeks information about products that could fulfill the need. A consumer looking for a multivitamin might pick up a brochure on the counter of the local health food store.
3. *Evaluate Alternatives*—The consumer looking for a multi-vitamin might check out the kinds available in the local health food store and compare them for price and content with more commercial brands found in the local supermarket or drug store.
4. *Decide to Purchase*—The first purchase is really a test; the consumer is trying your product to see how well it performs.
5. *Evaluation of Purchase*—If your product performs well, the consumer may begin to develop loyalty to your brand and tell others about it, as well. How do you keep this consumer for life?

»Owning a Perception in the Customer's Mind

More valuable to McDonald's than all the Big Macs it sells every year is the perception it owns in the minds of its customers that every time they patronize a McDonald's, they will receive food that

Biz Facts

Minority business owners (often defined to include women) should contact local corporate offices and ask about minority purchasing programs. Many companies and most government agencies are committed to buying up to 25 percent of their supplies and services from minority-owned businesses.

tastes exactly the same as at every other McDonald's, that the prices will be cheap, and that service will be friendly and fast.

For Burger King to compete with McDonald's, it had to fight for a "mind share" of the fast-food customer. Burger King opened its attack with "Have It Your Way," which targeted McDonald's mass-manufacturing approach to hamburgers. It followed up with "Broiled, not Fried" and "The Whopper Beats the Big Mac."

It is almost impossible to topple a leading brand in a market. Burger King's executives wisely decided that their goal was to be a strong number two. As "number two," you try to create a new category (broiled instead of fried hamburgers, for example) rather than trying to take over the competitive advantage of the number one company in the market. Avis lost money for fifteen years because it kept trying to overtake Hertz. Once Avis accepted its number two position, however, and turned it into a competitive advantage by declaring, "We Try Harder!" it became a very profitable company.

You do not have to be first to be successful; you just have to discover a competitive advantage and attack the market by creating a new category in the customer's mind. Domino's Pizza, for example, decided its competitive advantage was going to be delivering orders in under thirty minutes. That marketing insight created a hugely successful company.

≫Developing a Marketing Plan

Performance Objective 2.≫ Now that you understand how marketing should permeate your business, you are ready to develop a plan for introducing your product to your market. We begin with consumer analysis because, before you can develop a marketing vision for your business, you will need to know who your customers are and what they want.

Q: Why does a customer go to a hardware store to buy a drill?

A: Because she needs to make a hole.

The *hole* is what the customer needs, not the drill. If the hole could be bought at the hardware store, the customer would not bother to buy the drill.[3] If you are marketing a drill, therefore, you should explain to the customer what good holes your drills make! If someone invents a better hole-maker, drill manufacturers will soon be out of business.

≫Features Create Benefits

There is a subtle, but important, difference between the *benefits* and the *features* of a product. The features are facts. The features of a drill might include its hardness and sharpness, but the benefit is the fact that it makes an excellent hole. You might be selling a pan with Teflon coating. This feature creates a benefit: Food cooked in the pan will not stick and the pan will be easy to clean. The essence of

---

[3] Special thanks to Joe Mancuso for this concept.

selling is showing how and why the outstanding features of your product or service will benefit customers. Smart marketers always emphasize benefits, not features.

»Home Depot: Teaching Customers so They Will Return

Home Depot's marketing vision is not just to sell tools and materials but to teach people how to *use* them to improve their homes and lives. Home Depot's marketing vision focuses on what customers need Home Depot products to do.

Successful businesses are not built on single sales but on repeat business. The owners of Home Depot have calculated that a satisfied customer is worth over $25,000 in sales over the customer's lifetime. Bernie Marcus, one of the company's founders, has said, "All of our people understand what the Holy Grail is. It is not the bottom line. It is an almost blind, passionate commitment to taking care of customers."

Home Depot's million-dollar insight was that its customers not only need the products it sells but also need help in using them.

> *The owners of Home Depot have calculated that a satisfied customer is worth over $25,000 in sales over the customer's lifetime.*

»Needs, Wants, and Demands

Home Depot is meeting its customers' needs for help with home improvement, not just tools. What are needs, really, and how do they differ from desires (wants) or demands?

- **Needs:** Northwestern University Professor Philip Kotler's classic marketing textbook defines human needs as "states of felt deprivations."[4]
- **Wants:** Kotler defines wants as "the form taken by human needs as they are shaped by culture and individual personality."[5] Wants are objects that will satisfy a need. "I'm hungry; I want a hamburger," a New Yorker might say. "I'm hungry; I want jerk chicken," a Jamaican might say.
- **Demands:** Demands, Kotler says, are wants that are backed by buying power. A poor student might translate hunger into a demand for a Big Mac, while a well-to-do lawyer might translate it into a demand for an expensive steak dinner. *People demand the products and services that best satisfy their wants within the limitations of their resources.*

The most successful companies pay close attention to consumer demands. They constantly observe their customers, survey them, and analyze their wants, needs, and demands. They train salespeople to keep an eye open for customer needs that might be going

---

[4] Philip Kotler and Gary Armstrong, *Marketing: An Introduction*, p. 6 (Upper Saddle River, NJ: Prentice Hall, 1997).
[5] See Kotler and Armstrong, p. 7, *Marketing*.

unfulfilled. This is all part of consumer analysis, the first step in developing a marketing plan.

»Your Company's Mission Is to Satisfy Customers

Your mission as an entrepreneur is to use your competitive advantage to satisfy your customers. Great entrepreneurs have discovered that the true mission of business is to meet a consumer need better than anyone yet has.

Performance Objective 3. ❯

The **mission statement** describes a company's **mission**—its reason for existing. A concise mission statement not only tells your customers and employees what your business is about, it will be a guide for every business decision you make.

A mission statement does not need to be longer than three sentences. It should express both a business's strategy and its primary tactics. Here is a good example from the Chrysler Corporation:[6]

"Chrysler's primary goal is to achieve consumer satisfaction. We do it through engineering excellence, innovative products, high quality and superior service. And we do it as a team."

Chrysler's mission statement states its competitive advantage, strategy, and tactics:

- Chrysler believes its competitive advantage is creating "consumer satisfaction."
- Chrysler's strategy is to attempt to deliver greater consumer satisfaction than its competition—the other automakers.
- Chrysler's tactics: excellent engineering, innovation, high quality, superior service, and encouraging its employees to work together as a team.

»Market Research Helps You Visualize Your Customer

Before you can put a marketing plan in place and deliver your competitive advantage to your customers, you need to find out who your customers *are*. **Market research** is the process of finding out the following:

- Who your potential customers are
- Where you can reach them
- What they want and need

Through market research, business owners ask consumers questions and listen to their answers. Think of market research as access to other people's brains. President Woodrow Wilson once stated proudly, "I not only use all the brains that I have, but all that I can borrow."

---

[6] Steven Silbiger, *The Ten-Day MBA*, p. 312 (New York: William Morrow, 1993).

Woman conducting a market survey about banking habits with pedestrians at the Lincoln Road Mall in Miami Beach.

(© Jeffrey Greenburg/Photo Researchers, Inc.)

You will want to get into your current and potential customers' brains and find out what they really think about the following:

- Your product or service
- The name of your business
- Your location
- Your logo
- Your prices
- Your promotional efforts

Market research helps you get a fix on who your customers are.

- How old are they?
- What kind of income do they earn?
- What is the benefit your product or service offers that would best attract them?

The ideal customer should be at the center of your marketing plan. This profile will guide every marketing decision you make. If your target customer is affluent, for example, you might decide to price your product fairly high to reflect its quality. If your target market is not affluent, you might choose lower price to beat the competition.

»Do You Know Ten People Who Love Your Product? You May Have a Winner!

Not everbody has to like your product. What's important is that some people love it—a lot.

As we have seen, Russell Simmons started one of the first rap record labels, Def Jam Records, and became a multimillionaire. His perception was that if you personally know ten people who love your product, you could have a winner.

What if you conduct your market research and learn that you do not have a winner? Is your business dead? Only the one you thought of first! Think positively: This is an opportunity to come up with an even better idea.

»Types of Market Research

You will want to find out everything you can about your ideal customers. What do those people eat, drink, listen to, watch on TV? How much do they sleep? Where do they shop? What movies do they like? How much do they earn? How much do they spend?

Where can you find this kind of information?

- *Internet Research:* Search online for reports and statistics about the industry you want to enter.
- *Magazine Articles:* Whenever a major magazine does an article about an industry, the piece often includes statistics about the size of the target market and its preferences.
- *Business Library:* Most major cities have libraries specializing in business. Befriend the reference librarian! He or she can help you find almost anything.

A large corporation might hire an advertising agency to conduct market research, or may have its own marketing division. Small business owners can—and should—conduct market research, too. This can vary from a simple survey of your friends and neighbors that can be carried out in a day, to detailed statistical studies of a large population.

The four types of market research are the following:

1. *Surveys and Focus Groups*—Surveys ask people directly, in interviews or through questionnaires, what they would think about a product or service if it were available. Your marketing surveys should ask about the following:
   - Product use and frequency of purchase.
   - Places where consumers purchase the product (the competition!). Ask consumers why they like to purchase from these businesses.
   - Business names, logos, letterheads—everything that represents your business in a consumer's mind.

   Make sure your marketing surveys also gather general information about consumers, such as the following:
   - Interests and hobbies
   - Reading and television-watching habits
   - Educational background
   - Age

- Annual income
- Gender

Another way to survey people about a product or service in development is to hold "focus group" discussions. A focus group is composed of approximately a dozen people who do use or might use a certain product. The group is typically led by a facilitator trained in market research who questions the group about a product or service. The resulting discussion is usually videotaped for later analysis.

Competing phone companies, such as AT&T and Verizon, regularly hold focus groups to stay on top of how consumers feel about their respective services and to determine how consumers will react to any new calling plans or promotions.

2. *General Research*—Libraries, city agencies, the chamber of commerce, and the Internet are good sources of marketing information. If you want to start a neighborhood sporting-goods shop, for instance, you will need to know how many such stores are already in the area.

3. *Statistical Research*—**Statistics** are facts collected and presented in a numerical fashion, often as percentages. For example: "Of the 30 students in my class, 40 percent are women and 60 percent men."

Market research firms are paid by other companies to gather information. The federal government can also provide statistics on consumers in a given area from the census data the government gathers. These sources can provide statistics based on the following:

- Age
- Annual income
- Ethnic or religious background
- Gender
- Geographic location (zip code)
- Interests
- Occupation
- Type of dwelling (house or apartment)

Market research companies keep records of the typical consumer in a given area. They can then provide statistics based on age, occupation, geographic location, income, or ethnic/religious background. Market researchers also delve into consumers' hobbies and interests and whether they own or rent their homes. Consumer statistics dealing with the behavior of groups of people are called **demographics.**

Many kinds of statistics are available from the U.S. Government Printing Office. The latest edition of *The Statistical Abstract of The United States* is sold for $25 (paperback) and provides 1,400 statistical tables. Call (202) 738–3238.

4. *Industry Research*—This focuses not on individual consumers, but on the industry as a whole. If you want to start a

record label, you will need to know how the record industry is doing. Is it growing? Are people buying more CDs this year or fewer? Who are the major consumers of CDs? What age group buys the most records? What kind of music is selling the most?

To answer such questions, start with the Internet.

- Look for recent articles on trends in the industry and its major players by using Google or other search engines.
- Look on your competitors' Web sites to find their annual reports. These are likely to have valuable industry information.
- Check out the Internet Public Library at http://www.ipl.org/div/subject/browse/bus82.00.00/

Another source of industry research is interviews. Large competitors may be quite willing to arrange for a young entrepreneur to interview one of their executives about the industry and its trends. Do not hesitate to call and ask. If you get an interview, go in with a structured list of questions.

Additional sources of industry information include the following:

- Local Small Business Administration
- Local Chamber of Commerce
- Business schools at local colleges whose libraries and career centers are great sources.

» Your Research Method Matters

When you design your market research surveys, bear in mind that *the method you use may affect the answers you get.*

Some people may be less honest when you interview them face to face. They might not want to hurt your feelings by telling you personally that they do not like your business name, for example. Or perhaps they might feel embarrassed admitting to something they feel is a weakness—such as liking junk food.

If you think a direct interview might result in dishonest answers, consider handing out surveys that people in your market can complete *anonymously* (without signing their names).

[Global Impact]

Cell Phones in the Sauna?

The Finnish telecommunications company Nokia is tremendously innovative. The company is codeveloping a device that will enable people to make payments for anything, from a bar tab to a bank loan, using their cell phones. But when a reporter from *Wired* magazine asked a Nokia spokesman if anyone was working on making heatproof cell phones for Finns to take into the saunas, where they spend a significant amount of time, the spokesman fixed the reporter with a look of disdain and explained, "In sauna, we do not even want to hear Bach" (*Wired*, "Just Say Nokia," by Steve Silberman, September 1999).

When you know your market, you know how to market to the people in it. This is why it is so important to spend time conducting market research before you open your business. You may be impatient to get started, but do not do so until you've come to know your market intimately.

»Research Your Market *before* You Open Your Business

Large corporations spend a great deal of money on market research before they introduce a product or service. You may be impatient to get your business started, but take a lesson from the big companies. Do not begin until you've researched your market thoroughly. Be open to criticism. It is not always pleasant to hear, but it is valuable. Criticism can help you fine-tune your business.

Large corporations with nationally distributed products will spend a great deal of time and money on market research in order to get a product "just right." Ford and Chrysler each spent millions on market research before producing, respectively, the Mustang and the minivan. It was worth millions of dollars to these companies to determine if the public wanted these automobiles, because it was going to cost tens of millions to produce them.

»Focus Your Brand

The key to building a successful brand is to focus tightly on the one benefit you want to make sure customers associate with your business. In *Focus: The Future of Your Company Depends on It,* Al Ries explains that the most successful businesses focus their marketing so that they come to own a category in the customer's mind. You want to own a benefit the way Volvo owns "safety" or Federal Express owns "guaranteed overnight delivery."

Even entertainers can become a brand. By developing a consistent image and sound, pop singer Britney Spears became a brand that sold not only millions of records, but also over $50 million worth of dolls, T-shirts, posters, etc., that used her image.

»Ford's Costly Failure—The Edsel

One of the most notorious examples of a product that failed due to lack of focus is a car Ford introduced in 1956 called the Edsel.

Ford tried to cram every kind of gadget and design element it thought consumers might want in a car. Ford also manufactured more than 20 different models, at different prices. The goal was to try to appeal to everybody, but Ford soon learned that a car with something to appeal to everyone appealed to no one! The Edsel had no outstanding benefit that could be clearly marketed. When it was introduced on the market, it bombed.

Even millions of dollars of marketing will not make consumers buy a product they do not want. Ford spent more money on advertising the Edsel than had ever been spent before on marketing any product. Two years and $350 million later, Ford pulled the plug on the Edsel assembly line.

»Ford's Focus on Success— The Mustang

Ford learned from the Edsel mistake, however. When it introduced the Mustang in the 1960s, it focused very clearly on a target market of people from twenty to thirty years old. Everything about the car—from its design to the colors it came in—were focused on appealing to young drivers. The marketing described the Mustang as "for the young at heart." Only one model was offered. The Mustang was a huge success.

Interestingly, Ford tried to offer some luxury and four-door versions of the Mustang a few years later. Sales dropped—perhaps because the brand started losing focus. Today the Mustang remains one of Ford's strong sellers.

»How to Build Your Brand

You can build your own brand with these steps:

1. ***Choose a business name that is easy to remember, describes your business, and helps establish "mind share."*** Mind share is the degree to which *your* business comes to mind when a consumer needs something that your product or service could provide.

2. ***Create a logo that symbolizes your business to the customer.*** Logo is short for "logotype." A **logo** is a distinctive company trademark, or sign. The Nike "swoosh" is an example of a logo. So are McDonald's Golden Arches.

3. ***Develop a good reputation.*** Make sure your product or service is of the highest quality you can afford to offer. Always treat your customers like gold. You want people to feel good when they think of your brand or hear it mentioned.

The Nike "swoosh"—A logo recognized worldwide.
(Sandy Feisenthal, Corbis Bettmann)

[Step Into The Shoes]

How Thomas Burrell Became a Leader in Marketing to African Americans

To market a product or service to a specific market segment, you must research what the people who comprise it want. In the late 1960s, major corporations became more conscious of the potential clout of African-American consumers but were unsure how to market to them.

In 1971, Thomas Burrell opened one of the first black-owned advertising agencies in the United States. By 1972, Burrell had convinced McDonald's that Burrell Advertising could help the huge company expand into the African-American market. Burrell came to be the fastest-growing and largest black-owned advertising agency in the United States, with annual billings of over $60 million.

Burrell Advertising has created over one hundred commercials for McDonald's. Other Burrell clients include Coca-Cola, Ford Motor, Johnson Products, Schlitz Brewing, Blockbuster Entertainments, Proctor & Gamble, Jack Daniel Distillery, Polaroid, Stroh Brewing, and First National Bank of Chicago.

Burrell himself could probably quote the demographics of the African-American market off the top of his head. Demographics are statistics that describe a population in detail. He has combined his company's thorough market research with his own personal experience as a black man to create powerful appeals to the targeted market. Burrell describes his marketing philosophy as "positive realism." He adds: "We wanted to make sure the consumer understood the advertiser was inviting that consumer—that black consumer—to participate as a consumer of their product. Black consumers have not felt they were being extended an invitation."

4. ***Create a brand personality.*** Is your brand's "personality" youthful and casual, like the Gap? Safe and serious, like Volvo? Customers will respond to brand personality and develop a relationship with your brand. Personality will reinforce your name and logo.

5. ***Communicate your brand personality to your target market.*** What type of advertising will best reach your target market? Where should you put flyers? Which newspapers or magazines does your target market read?

Always present yourself and your business in such a way that people will have confidence in your product or service. Anything that harms your reputation will damage your sales and profits. Anything that boosts your reputation will have a positive impact on your business.

Here are seven things you can do to build and maintain your brand and its reputation.

1. Provide a high-quality product or service.
2. Maintain the highest ethical standards.
3. Define your product or service clearly—focus!
4. Treat your employees well.
5. Make all your ads positive and informative—whether they are simple posters and flyers, or television commercials.
6. Associate your company with a charity.
7. Become actively involved in your community.

»Make Market Research an Ongoing Part of Your Business

Market research is not something you only do once. Make it an ongoing part of your business. Just as your tastes and desires change as you learn about new ideas and products, so do those of your customers. By continuing to survey your customers as you run your business, you will stay current with their needs and how they feel about your product.

»Which Segment of the Market Will You Target?

Performance Objective 4.

If the best marketing strategies are focused on the consumer, a company clearly has to choose which consumers to target. After all, you cannot please all of the people all of the time! Chances are, your product will not be needed by every individual in the marketplace. You will need to figure out which segments of the market to target.

There is a huge market for home repair, including professional carpenters and builders. Home Depot's competitive advantage would not be strong in the **market segment** composed of professionals. A market segment is composed of consumers who have a similar response to a certain type of marketing. Home Depot chose to market primarily to the nonprofessional, private-individual segment of the market.

In the cosmetics industry, one segment responds positively to luxuriously packaged, expensive products. Another is most responsive to products that claim to reduce signs of aging. Another's primary concern is price. A company that recognizes these segments and chooses one or two to market to will do better than a company that tries to sell its cosmetics to every single female in the country.

It is difficult to target simultaneously two very different segments of a market. Volvo, for example, has established a reputation as a safe family car. It targets parents with young children. Volvo would have a difficult time also trying to market a two-seat convertible sports car to young adults who are concerned more with style and speed than safety.

»Successful Segmenting: The Body Shop

The Body Shop is a good example of the success that can result from choosing the right market segment. Founder Anita Roddick was fed up with paying for expensive packaging and perfuming when she bought cosmetics. She was also offended by the extravagant claims made by many cosmetics companies and by the high prices for their perfumes and skin-care lotions. Price became part of the image for many products. A perfume called Joy, for example, was marketed as the most expensive perfume in the world!

Roddick saw an opportunity to create a different line of cosmetics. She decided to use natural products that would be packaged inexpensively and marketed without extravagant claims. Roddick believed that what the cosmetics houses were doing was wrong. As she said in her book, *Body & Soul: Anita Roddick tells the story of the Body Shop, Inc.:* "It is immoral to deceive a customer by making miracle claims for a product. It is immoral to use a photograph of a glowing sixteen-year-old to sell a cream aimed at preventing wrinkles in a forty-year-old."[7]

Roddick tapped into a segment of the cosmetics market that had been neglected and her business grew explosively as a result. Her success proves that selling an honest product honestly can be the best marketing strategy of all.

What if Roddick had found out that there were very few women interested in natural cosmetics? Her business would not have survived because, even though the cosmetics market is very large, her segment would have been too small to support a business. As *The Ten-Day MBA* author Steven Silbiger points out, "The easiest mistake to make is to believe that your *relevant* market includes the total sales of your product category."[8]

It is possible to go after a small, "niche" segment, but then your price must be high enough to make a profit. Jaguar and Rolls Royce each sell far fewer cars than Honda or Ford, but at *much* higher prices. Jaguar and Rolls Royce target the luxury segment of the car market.

»Applying Market Segmentation Methods

Marketers have developed four basic ways to analyze a market:

- *Geographic segmentation*—Dividing a population by location.
- *Demographic segmentation*—Dividing a population based on a variable like age, gender, income, or education.
- *Psychographic segmentation*—Dividing a population by psychological differences, such as opinion (conservative vs. liberal) or lifestyle.
- *Behavioral segmentation*—Dividing the market by purchase behaviors that have been observed, such as brand loyalty or responsiveness to price.

Say you want to make and sell hacky-sacks on your college campus. Twenty thousand students attend your college. To which students do you direct your marketing? If 50 of the 200 students surveyed seem interested in your hacky-sack, you can expect that roughly 5,000 of the 20,000 students would represent your market. Which segments of that market should you target?

If your company has very limited resources, you might choose to target only one segment. A very large company might decide to

[7] Anita Roddick, *Body & Soul, Anita Roddick Tells the Story of the Body Shop, Inc.,* (Crown Publishers, 1991).

[8] Steven Silbiger, *The Ten-Day MBA,* p. 31 (New York: William Morrow, 1993)

appeal to the entire market by designing a product tailored for each segment. Gap Inc., for example, has three product lines—Old Navy, Gap, and Banana Republic—each priced for and tailored to a different segment of the sportswear market.

You could use any of the four segmentation methods to define your market segment. For example:

- *Geographic*—You could decide that your market is everyone who lives within two miles of the campus.
- *Demographic*—You could decide to limit your marketing efforts to people between the ages of 18 and 23 who are enrolled in the college.
- *Psychographic*—You could decide to market to people who like rock music or play soccer.
- *Behavioral*—You could decide to market to people who buy Frisbees.

One way to gauge your market would be to survey a random sample of 200 students, showing them the product and asking questions such as the following:

- Do you play Frisbee? How often?
- Would you be interested in purchasing this hacky-sack, if it were available?

Once you have chosen your market segment, you can really fine-tune your market research because you now have to focus only on these consumers—not every potential consumer in your market. Collecting data from the people in your market segment can be fun as well as financially rewarding. Here are a few questions you can adapt to your own product or service:

1. Would you buy this product/service?
2. How much would you be willing to pay for it?
3. Where would you buy it?
4. How would you improve it?
5. Who are my closest competitors?
6. Is my product/service worse or better than my competitors'?

»The Product Life Cycle

Performance Objective 5.❭ You will also need to analyze where your market is in its **product life cycle (PLC).** The PLC has four stages:

1. *Introduction*—Consumers are curious about your product but not familiar with it. Marketing at this stage will require a lot of education and experimentation with price and presentation. When the personal home computer was first introduced, Apple's marketing was focused on convincing consumers how easy it would be to use. Apple is using the same strategy—only in regard to the Internet this time—with the introduction of the iMAC.

2. *Growth*—Attracted by your growth in sales, competitors now start entering your market, so efforts at this stage will have to focus on communicating your competitive advantage to consumers.

3. *Maturity*—At this stage, consumers have become savvy about both you and your competitors. Advertising needs to focus on promoting brand loyalty.

4. *Decline*—Even reluctant consumers have bought or are aware of your product by now. New developments will be necessary to revive the market's interest.

»Is Your Market Saturated?

Figuring out where your product is in the PLC will tell you whether your market is close to saturation. In other words, have all 3 million people in your market already bought a competitor's product? Nokia, for example, has sold 41 million of the 165 million cell phones that have been sold. But that market is nowhere near saturation. Meanwhile, Nokia has introduced its Short Message Service (SMS), which will allow e-mail messages to be sent between mobile phones in Finland. SMS has quickly become Finnish teenagers' favorite way to communicate, and observing how the technology has spread among them is giving the company invaluable hints about how to market SMS in the 140 countries where it sells cell phones.

»Market Positioning—Drive Home Your Competitive Advantage

After deciding which market segments to target, an entrepreneur will need to decide what position the company should try to occupy in the market segments. *Position* is defined by Kotler as "the place that the product occupies relative to competitors in consumers' minds."[9] The goal of market **positioning,** therefore, is to distinguish your product or service from others being offered to the market segments you have targeted. You can do that by focusing on your competitive advantage. "Have It Your Way," Burger King promised, driving home its competitive advantage—that at Burger King you can specify exactly how you want your hamburger prepared and garnished.

As you can see from the Burger King example, positioning involves clearly communicating your competitive advantage to the consumer by demonstrating how your product/service differs from that of the competition. Your goal is to position your product/service clearly in the mind of your target market as the brand that provides that difference. Try using the following positioning-statement format to develop a positioning statement for your business:

(Your business name/brand) is the (competitive industry/category) that (provides these benefits, or points of difference) to (audience/target market).

---

[9] Adapted from Philip Kotler and Gary Armstrong, *Principles of Marketing,* 9th Edition (Upper Saddle River, NJ: Prentice Hall, 2001).

Here is an example: (General Motors) is the (leading U.S. automobile maker) that (provides affordable cars, trucks, and vans) to (American families).

By the time you complete the four steps of your marketing plan, you will know your potential customers, your competitors, and your market intimately. It is a lot of work, but well worth it. Make a commitment to let marketing drive your business decisions, and you will greatly increase the odds that your business will be successful.

»Chapter Summary

Now that you have studied this chapter you can do the following:

1. Explain how marketing differs from selling.

   ■ Marketing is the business function that identifies your customers and their needs and wants.

   ■ Through marketing, the name of your business comes to mean something clear and concrete in the customer's mind. Above all, marketing is the way a business communicates its competitive advantage to its market.

2. Before you can develop a marketing vision for your business, you will need to know who your customers are and what they want.

   ■ Choose your market segment and research it.

      1. A market segment is composed of consumers who have a similar response to a certain type of marketing.

      2. Segmentation methods:

         a. *Geographic segmentation*—Dividing a population by location.

         b. *Demographic segmentation*—Dividing a population based on a variable like age, gender, income, or education.

         c. *Psychographic segmentation*—Dividing a population by psychological differences such as opinion (conservative vs. liberal) or lifestyle.

         d. *Behavioral segmentation*—Dividing the market by purchase behaviors that have been observed, such as brand loyalty or responsiveness to price.

3. Market research is the process of finding out who your potential customers are, where you can reach them, and what they want and need.

   ■ Survey research—Surveys are sets of questions that you ask consumers—either in interviews or through written questionnaires.

   ■ General research—Check libraries, city agencies, and other resources for information.

   ■ Statistical research—Statistics are facts collected and presented as numbers.

   ■ Industry research—This focuses not on individual consumers, but on the industry as a whole.

4. Position your product or service in your market.

■ The goal of market positioning is to distinguish your product or service from others being offered to the market segments you have targeted. You can do that by focusing on your competitive advantage.

■ Use the following positioning statement format to develop a positioning statement for your business:

(Your business name/brand) is the (competitive industry/ category) that (provides these benefits, or points of difference) to (audience/target market).

Key Terms

demographics	mission
logo	mission statement
market	positioning
marketing	product life cycle (PLC)
market research	statistics
market segment	

[Entrepreneurship Portfolio]

1. What three concepts should a business's mission statement contain and why?

2. Write a mission statement for your business. **(Business Plan Practice)**

3. *Step One: Consumer Analysis* **(Business Plan Practice)**

Describe the typical consumer your business plans to target.

Gender:_____

Age:_____

Education: _____

Income: _____

Interests: _____

Other: _____

What need do you plan to satisfy for this consumer? _____

4. *Step Two: Market Analysis* **(Business Plan Practice)**

■ How large is the total market for your product or service? How did you arrive at this figure?

■ Which segment of this market do you intend to target? Why? How large is the segment?

■ Describe your segmentation method. Why did you choose this method?

Critical Thinking Exercises

5. Choose five people from your market segment to research with a survey. Write ten questions and ask the survey participants "yes-or-no" questions on a scale of one to four, or design your own range. Also ask five open-ended questions (questions that do not have a yes-or-no answer). **(Business Plan Practice)**

Key Concept Questions

1. What four factors should market research include, and why?

2. Write a positioning statement for your business. **(Business Plan Practice)**

3. Describe where you think your product or service is in the product life cycle.

4. Read and interpret the chart in Figure 3-1.
   a. Which single provider has the largest market share? What is the percentage?
   b. What share do the two largest suppliers enjoy together?
   c. How much bigger is IBM's share than Apple's?
   d. If there are approximately 100 "Other" smaller makers of personal computers, about how much market share would each have on average?

5. Research can give you a great deal of information, but you will have to use your math skills to make it more useful. For example, imagine you are interested in opening a dog care service, and you have gathered the following facts:

   ■ In 2000, the U.S. Census Bureau estimated that there were 2.67 people per household.

   ■ According to your city's public records, the population of your community is 80,000.

   ■ The *U.S. Pet Ownership & Demographics Sourcebook* estimates that the number of dog-owning households in a community = 0.361 multiplied by the total number of households.

   ■ The *Sourcebook* also estimates that the number of dogs in a community = 0.578 multiplied by the total number of households—or 1.6 multiplied by the number of dog-owning households.

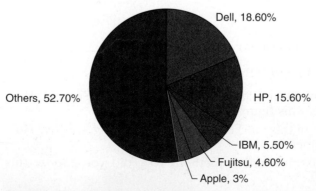

Figure 3-1 Global PC market share.

Determine:

a. The number of dog-owning households in your community.

b. The number of dogs in your community. Round your answers off to the nearest whole number.

Order a sandwich at three different fast-food restaurants; then answer the following questions.

1. Did you observe any differences in how the employees handled your order? Describe them.

2. Describe what you believe to be the marketing vision of each restaurant based on what you observed. Write a positioning statement for each restaurant.

3. Analyze the market for each restaurant using the four methods of market analysis: geographic segmentation, demographic segmentation, psychographic segmentation, and behavioral segmentation.

4. Where do you think each restaurant is in the product life cycle?

Application Exercises

Go online and conduct an industry-wide search for competition for your business. Create a profile of the competition (this may be written using a word-processing program or shown as a graph using Excel). It should include minimum and maximum prices, minimum and maximum ordering times, and any other information you feel is pertinent. **(Business Plan Practice)**

Exploring Online

CASE STUDY: Choosing a Business

Mark and Mary Smith are interested in starting a business. Mark has an engineering background and has worked for ten years in the design department of an aircraft parts manufacturing company. Mary is an elementary school teacher with a specialty in remedial mathematics. The Smith family, including two teenage girls, resides in a fast-growing Midwest suburban community. The desire to control their earnings and time while building their own security are the ideas motivating Mark and Mary to start a business.

A large computer manufacturer has opened a facility in their community, creating over 7,000 new jobs. This amount of new employment will create demand for new homes, schools, roads, restaurants, shopping, and many other services. The new company will require all types of construction, local supply outlets for a wide range of products, and contract services for the business areas that are commonly outsourced, such as maintenance, information processing, technical services, and employment assistance. There have been several articles in the local newspaper about the new business opportunities in the area. Mark and Mary attended a course on "Starting a Small Business" at the local community college and they were both impressed with the importance placed on marketing.

The Smiths decide to make a list of businesses they feel are good opportunities to explore. Mark's list includes engineering, computer-aided design, computer maintenance and repair, network administration, and engineering employment services. Mary is interested in tutoring services, training workers in computer and math skills, a food-services franchise, and temporary employment services. The couple has sufficient resources to start one business and maintain their lifestyle for two years. Mark thinks that they should be looking for a new concept or idea that will attract new customers while promoting rapid growth.

Mary believes that they should be starting with customers that they can identify, and find existing services that these customers need.

Case Study Analysis

1. What marketing principles should Mark and Mary focus on?

2. Are there other opportunities for starting a small business that you could suggest to them?

3. What marketing knowledge will help you decide on the strength of a business concept?

CASE STUDY: Russell Simmons—Hip-Hop Entrepreneur

Hip-hop entrepreneur Russell Simmons turned off his cell phone and took a rare moment to admire the view from his fourteenth-floor office in midtown Manhattan. At 47, Simmons knew he had a lot going for him. As the president of Rush Communications, he sat at the helm of a constellation of successful enterprises, including a record label, a clothing line, a philanthropic arts foundation, and a multimedia production company. Lately he had been thinking a lot about how to leverage his influence as a "hip-hop mogul" to inspire young people to get involved in social issues such as voter registration and education reform. Yet when he was growing up in Hollis, Queens, in the 1960s and 1970s, Simmons never could have imagined that his life would have turned out like this.

Window of Opportunity

Early on, Simmons decided that he wanted to make his own way in the world. His father had been a teacher and his mother worked as a recreation coordinator. Both enjoyed stable jobs, but Simmons was not driven by a need for security—he wanted to live a fast-paced life and call his own shots. In 1977, Simmons, who never liked school very much, enrolled at the City College of New York as a sociology major. That year, something happened that permanently changed the course of his life. He went to hear a rap artist named Eddie Cheeba perform at a club and was amazed to see how the rapper had cast a spell over the audience with his freestlye rhymes. In Simmons's own words:

> Just like that, I saw how I could turn my life in another, better way . . . All the street entrepreneurship I'd learned, I decided to put into promoting music.[10]

At that time, "rap" and "hip-hop" were underground musical styles, but Simmons set out to change this. He believed that rap music had the potential to reach a larger audience and so he teamed up with another aspiring rap producer named Rick Rubin. Rubin had built a recording studio for rap artists in his New York University dorm room. Together they decided to transform Rick's studio into a viable and legitimate record label. By 1985, Def Jam Records was officially underway.

---

[10] Russell Simmons, *Life and Def: Sex, Drugs, Money + God* (New York: Crown Publishing, 2002).

Def Jam experienced its first surge of success when it scored a number one hit with RUN DMC's remake of the Aerosmith hard rock classic "Walk This Way." Bridging the worlds of rock and rap music turned out to be a stroke of genius. Simmons and Rubin single-handedly introduced a whole new market of mostly white, suburban heavy metal music fans to hip-hop. Suddenly, RUN DMC was being featured on MTV, and rap was no longer an "underground" fad.

Marketing Insight—Authenticity Matters

Simmons learned an important lesson from RUN DMC's breakout success. He realized that these rap artists had soared to the top of the charts because they had remained true to their street style and musical origins. While RUN DMC may have popularized wearing gold chains, Adidas sneakers, and name-plate belts among suburban teenagers, these were the fashions that its core audience of urban youth had already embraced. Simmons understood that being perceived as *authentic* was key to making it in his segment of the music industry. According to Simmons:

> *You have to tell the truth. It endears you to the community. The [people] can smell the truth, and they're a lot smarter than the people who put the records out.*[11]

Simmons knew how to market his product, and his ability to promote rap music and the hip-hop lifestyle was influenced by how close he was to it.

Simmons has remained true to this philosophy of "keeping it real" throughout his business career. It permeates everything he does and is even reflected in his preference for wearing Phat Farm sweatshirts instead of Brooks Brothers suits. Since those early days, Simmons has gone on to launch many other business ventures, which are all geared toward the same target market—urban teens and young adults. This market is composed of the style-makers who have the power to influence the tastes and preferences of other consumers.

Simmons's Empire Grows

In 1999, Simmons sold his stake in Def Jam records to Polygram Records for over $100 million. He has since focused his energies on developing the various entertainment, fashion, and multimedia companies that are housed under Rush Communications. Simmons's business goals have evolved

from promoting hip-hop music to developing new products and services for the urban youth market. One of his latest pet projects is the "Rush Card"—a prepaid debit card that aims to compete with costly check-cashing services that target urban youth who do not have bank accounts.

These days, Simmons is also using his status as a taste-maker and hip-hop entrepreneur to influence public debate about political issues. In 2002, he organized a "youth summit" in New York featuring hip-hop artists such as Jay-Z and Alicia Keyes. When Simmons put out a call to action over the airwaves, over twenty thousand students showed up at New York's City Hall to protest the mayor's proposed cuts to the education budget. Simmons has demonstrated that he has the skill and sophistication to market ideas as well as products and services. Rumor has it that he may even decide to run for public office at some point. But, for now, he continues to sit at the helm of Rush Communications where he keeps his radar attuned to new opportunities in the marketplace.

Case Study Analysis

1. Why do you think Russell Simmons has been successful?

2. Describe the target market that Simmons is trying to appeal to in all of his business ventures. What does this target market value?

3. Simmons grew up surrounded by hip-hop music and culture. In what ways did this give him an advantage in the marketplace? How might his "insider's knowledge" also function as a limitation?

4. Brainstorm a business idea that you could pitch to Russell Simmons that would be appropriate for Rush Communications to consider. What market research would you need to conduct in advance to assess whether or not your idea has the potential to be successful?

5. Russell Simmons invested $5,000 to start Def Jam and then later sold his business to Polygram Records for $100 million. Calculate Simmons's return on investment (ROI).

CASE SOURCES

Jennifer Reingold, "Rush Hour," *Fast Company Magazine*, no. 76, November 2003.

Russell Simmons, *Life and Def: Sex, Drugs, Money + God* (New York: Crown Publishing, 2002).

[11] "Rush Hour," by Jennifer Reingold, *Fast Company Magazine*, Issue 76, November 2003.

"I found that if you give the consumer a snapshot where he could see himself as he really is and the way he wants to be portrayed, people really respond to it."

—Thomas Burrell, founder, the Burrell Communications Group

Performance Objectives

1. Combine the four P's—product, price, place, and promotion—into a marketing mix.
2. Choose where and how to advertise your business.
3. Use press releases and pitch letters to generate publicity for your business.
4. Decide how your business will help your community philanthropically.
5. Use breakeven analysis to evaluate your marketing plan.

All of BMW's marketing—from the price of the cars to the advertisements in magazines catering to people who buy expensive things—is designed to convince customers that it makes luxury automobiles. If BMW lowers the price of its sedan, would that damage the customer's belief in BMW's competitive advantage as a provider of luxury cars? This is the question that working through the next step of the marketing process will help answer. BMW illustrates the importance of getting your marketing mix—product, price, place, and promotion—right. Without an effective mix of these elements, your business is likely to fail.

A marketing mix is the combination of four factors, called the four P's, that together communicate your competitive advantage to your customer:

◀ **1.** Performance Objective

- Product
- Price
- Place
- Promotion

If you tweak one "P," you must pay attention to how it affects the others. If you raise your price, for example, are you now still selling the product in the right place? Or will you need to move to a location that will put you in contact with consumers willing to pay the new price? Where will you promote your product at the higher price? Will you have to take out an ad in a different magazine or newspaper to reach these more affluent consumers?

Your marketing goal is to bring the right product to the right place at the right price with the right promotion.

As you choose the elements of your marketing plan, always keep your vision in mind. What is the benefit your product or service is providing to consumers?

1. ***Product***—The product (or service) should meet or create a consumer need. The packaging is also part of the product. Your customer might throw away your packaging but that does not mean it is unimportant. Starbucks revolutionized the coffee shop by creating different cup sizes and using Italian names.

2. ***Place***—Place your product where customers who need it do their shopping. Selling bathing suits in Alaska in February is not going to fill a customer need. Where should you go to bring your product or service to the attention of your market? If you are selling a luxury item, you will need to place it in stores that are visited by consumers who can afford it.

3. ***Price***—The product has to be priced low enough so the public will buy it, and high enough for the business to make a profit. Price also should reflect your marketing vision. If you are marketing a luxury item, a relatively low price might not send the right message to the consumer.

4. ***Promotion***—**Promotion** consists of advertising, publicity, and other promotional devices such as discount coupons or giveaways. Publicity is free, while advertising is purchased. If a newspaper writes an article about your business, it's publicity. If you buy an ad in that newspaper, you're advertising.

> *Simply selling at a lower price will not necessarily win you a large market share.*

»Price: What It Says about Your Product

According to *Guerrilla Marketing Attack*, by Jay Levinson, a study of consumers in the furniture industry found that price came ninth when consumers were asked to list factors affecting their decision to make a purchase. Quality was the number two influence on buying patterns, and confidence in the product was number one. Service was third.

Although your business may not behave exactly like the furniture industry, the lesson here is that simply undercutting your competitors' prices will not necessarily win you the largest market share. For one thing, consumers tend to infer things about the quality or specialness of a product or service based on its price. It is important, therefore, for entrepreneurs to consider not only the economics but also the psychology of pricing. Studying the pricing strategies of your competitors will tell you a lot about the importance of psychological pricing in your market.

An increasingly popular strategy is "value" pricing, which began in the 1990s as a reaction to the "Glitzy Eighties," when marketers used high prices to pitch luxury and extravagance. Companies like Wal-Mart and Proctor & Gamble shifted to value pricing—offering more for a lot less by underscoring a product's quality while at the same time featuring its price. Value pricing is not just price-cutting.

It means finding the balance between quality and price that gives your target customers the value they seek.

New entrepreneurs often assume they should simply sell their product or service at the lowest price they can afford. Sometimes, however, consumers assume that a low price indicates low quality.

»Keystoning: The Retailer's Rule of Thumb

Retailers who buy goods wholesale and resell them in stores sometimes **keystone,** or double, the cost of goods sold, as a rule of thumb for estimating what price to charge. If you buy cell phones for $22 each from a wholesaler, for example, selling them for $44 each in your store will probably cover your costs and provide you with an acceptable profit.

Keystoning is a good way to estimate a price. If you are selling hacky-sack balls that cost $4, consider selling them for $8. When pricing, however, the entrepreneur must always be sensitive to the market and to what competitors are charging.

»Other Pricing Strategies

Other pricing strategies include the following:

- *Cost-plus*—This method simply takes your cost and adds a desired profit margin. This method fails to take marketing vision into consideration.

- *Penetration Strategy*—This method uses a low price during the early stages of a product's life cycle to gain market share. Japanese companies used this method to dominate the VCR market.

- *Skimming Strategy*—The opposite of penetration strategy, this method seeks to charge a high price during the introductory stage of the PLC, when a product is novel and has few competitors. RCA used this strategy when it introduced color television.

- *Meet or Beat the Competition*—This is a common strategy in service businesses. Airlines tend to compete intensely by lowering their ticket prices. The more you can show that your business is different from your competition, however, the less you will have to compete with your price. When Richard Branson started Virgin Atlantic Airways, he offered massages and individual videos at each seat. His marketing emphasized how much fun it was to fly on Virgin. This marketing strategy was successful, even though Virgin did not always offer the lowest fares.

Pick a price that communicates your competitive advantage to your market segment. The same goes for the rest of the four P's—make all your business decisions market-driven and you will be successful.

»Place: Location, Location, Location!

Now on to the next P: Place. The type of business you are running will influence your choice of location. For a retail business, location is the key to attracting customers. Ideally, you will want your store or business to be where your market is. Site location is one of the most important decisions for a retailer. This is why you did the work in Step one: Consumer Analysis and Step two: Market Analysis to figure out who your customers were. By now you should know where they shop. Your goal is to find a location you can afford that is also convenient for your customers.

Wal-Mart did an excellent job of choosing locations that were perfect for its customers yet underserved by similar retailers. Wal-Mart was the first mass merchandise store to choose locations in rural and semirural markets. This strategy has been so successful that other stores now seek to be located next to a Wal-Mart!

Of course, the Internet has made it possible for an entrepreneur to start a retail business out of his or her home and reach customers all over the world. This has led many to believe they could succeed in selling merchandise online and could forgo the expense of renting a store in a location that provides foot traffic or other access to customers. As the old saying goes, however, you can lead a horse to water but you can't make him drink. The problem with the Internet is: How do you lead your customers to your site, let alone make them buy? If you are going to start a retail business online, you must figure out first how you will get customers to your Web site.

For nonretail businesses the key to location might be cost or convenience, rather than proximity to the market. Wholesale businesses require a great deal of storage space and are best located in out-of-the-way areas where rent or property costs are low. They look for low-rent, low-tax areas with warehousing and roads for trucks and vans.

As for service businesses, the Internet is making it easier for people who provide services such as graphic or Web site design, writing, or accounting, to start their businesses in their homes. Communication with clients is easy via e-mail, and you cannot beat the start-up costs. On the other hand, working at home requires discipline and a high tolerance for isolation. If you are the sort of person who would be miserable spending your workday alone, it is probably not for you.

»Promotion: Publicity + Advertising

Performance Objective 2.》 Promotion is the use of **advertising** and **publicity** to get your marketing message out to your customers. Publicity is free mention of your business in newspapers and magazines or on radio and TV stations. An advertisement is a paid announcement that a product or service is for sale. Examples of advertising include television commercials, billboards, and magazine ads.

A billboard in the Bronx, New York City.
(Jochen Tack/DAS FOTOARCHIV., Peter Arnold, Inc.)

If your business is providing an unusual service, you might be able to get a local newspaper to do an article. That article would be publicity for your business—you did not pay for it, yet consumers will learn about your service by reading the article. If you buy an ad in that same newspaper, on the other hand, you're using advertising to promote your business.

Publicity is sometimes referred to as **public relations,** or "PR." Always save the publicity you receive. Frame and display articles prominently in your place of business (if you do not have an office, have these in a portfolio that you can easily show to customers). Make copies of the articles to send or hand out to potential customers. Each piece of publicity has enormous value. It has a lot of credibility with consumers because you did not pay someone to write it.

There are many ways you can promote your business, including the following:

■ *Banner Ads*—These are the advertisements that run on Web sites.

■ *Billboards*—Billboards are often in highly visible locations and use short, punchy copy that motorists can grasp at a glance.

■ *Brochures*—Place brochures in "take one" boxes around town.

■ *Business Cards*—This should include the name, address, and contact information (phone and fax numbers, e-mail address, and Web site) of your business, as well as your own name and title. A card can also include a short catchy phrase or motto, such as *For Sound Advice* if you are running a stereo-repair business. Carry some cards with you wherever you go to give to potential clients and contacts.

■ *Direct Mail*—Whenever you make a sale, get the customer's address, and contact information. Once you have developed a mailing list, send out cards or letters regularly to customers, informing them of sales and special events. You can send e-mail updates, but be sure to always include a statement within the e-mail that says: "If you wish to be removed from this list, please type REMOVE in the subject line of your response." You can send out discount coupons that only go out to the mailing list and are not distributed to other customers. This is an excellent way to ensure that your mailings are noticed. Mailing-list software is easy to use—to keep organized and to print labels. Sophisticated customer-tracking programs are also available.

■ *Catalogs*—When you build a list of 10,000 names, you may be able to afford a color catalog. You can produce a two-color catalog with even fewer names.

■ *Discount Coupons*—Give a discount (price break) to first-time customers or for a limited time. This will encourage people to try your product or service.

■ *Flyers*—Flyers are one-page ads you can create by hand or computer. Fax your flyer to customers on your mailing list; photocopy and distribute it at church functions, sporting events, under windshield wipers, or hand them out on the street. Flyers can also include discount coupons.

■ *Free Gifts*—"Freebies" draw customers the way honey draws flies. But do not disappoint with gifts that look and feel cheap. Go to a wholesaler, where you can get good prices on large quantities of calculators, watches, desk pens, or other useful items. When you open your business, you can give away samples of your product to encourage customers to tell their friends about it. You could also offer an initial low price to attract customers, or offer a coupon for a discount on their next purchase.

■ *Promotional Clothing*—T-shirts or caps bearing the name of your business can turn you and your friends into "walking advertisements." You can even put the name of your business on shopping bags.

■ *Samples or Demonstrations*—Offer samples of your product to potential customers who walk by your business. Or take samples to a high-density location, such as a park or town square. If you are selling a service, consider demonstrating it outdoors or in a mall (get permission first!).

■ *Special Events*—Hold contests, throw parties, or put together unusual events to attract attention and customers. Contests and sweepstakes can gather valuable names for your mailing list, too.

■ *Team Sponsorships*—Sponsoring a local sports team is a great way to involve your business in the community and meet customers.

■ *800 Numbers*—Contact your phone company to find out how to set up an 800 number, so customers can call you for free. Some long-distance providers offer special discounts to small-business owners. AT&T, for example, has a program called Small Business Advantage.

»Making Your Own Marketing Materials

You can create most, if not all, of your marketing materials yourself using available software. Some popular programs for creating marketing materials are the following:

■ Microsoft Publisher (included in Microsoft Office) can be used to create professional-looking marketing materials like brochures.

■ Microsoft PhotoDraw can be used to design company logos and create business flyers.

■ Microsoft Direct Mail Manager (also in Office) can be used to buy mailing lists, verify and correct U.S. addresses, check for duplicate addresses, and send documents and lists to a mailing service for quick production.

Marketing software can be ordered online or found at office supply stores such as Staples or Office Depot.

»Logos and Trademarks

Whether you are advertising your business with flyers at the local laundromat or through a storefront on the Internet, you will need an easily recognizable **logo.** A logo (short for logotype) is an identifying symbol for a product or business. A logo is printed on the business's stationery, business cards, and flyers. When a logo has been registered with the U.S. Patent Office to protect it from being used by others, it is called a **trademark.**

Do a search online for the name you intend to use for your business. What did you find?

_____

Will you still use this name? Why or why not?

_____

How do you plan to protect the name of your business?

_____

A company uses a trademark so that people will recognize its product instantly, without having to read the company name or even having to think about it. NutraSweet's red swirl and the Nike "swoosh" are examples of trademarks most people recognize.

[Global Impact]

Protecting Your Trademark Worldwide

If you plan to do business outside the United States, you will need to make sure your trademark is properly registered and protected. The International Trademark Association (www.inta.org) is an excellent resource. It can help you apply for a Community Trade Mark (CTM), for example, which provides protection for a trademark in the 25 current member countries of the European Union (Austria, Belgium, the Czech Republic, Cyprus, Denmark, Estonia, Finland, France, Germany, Greece, Hungary, Ireland, Italy, Latvia, Lithuania, Luxembourg, Malta, the Netherlands, Poland, Portugal, Slovakia, Slovenia, Spain, Sweden, and the United Kingdom).

Rights to a trademark are reserved exclusively for its owner. To infringe on a trademark is illegal.

To file for a trademark, send the Patent and Trademark Office the following:

1. A written application form
2. A drawing of the trademark
3. Three specimens showing the actual use of the mark on or in connection with the product or service
4. A filing fee ($200)

Address: Patent & Trademark Office
U.S. Department of Commerce
Washington, DC 20231
Telephone   (703) 557–4636

[Step Into The Shoes]

Trademarking a Domain

In 1998, Laurel Touby purchased the domain name www. hireminds.com for her online job listings network for New York City journalists and editors, but she failed to trademark it. By 1999, Touby had a thriving site. She was charging publishers looking for writers and editors $100 per ad, and her clients included many national publications.

Soon, however, she got a phone call from a recruiter for Boston computer companies informing her that she had purchased all domain names around hers and was applying for the trademark for her domain name, as well. As your business grows, or if you are starting an online business, you may want to purchase a domain name for your Web site(s).

The domain name is the first part of the URL; it ends in ".com," for a commercial business, ".org," for a nonprofit business, or ".net," for a network. Check out InterNIC, www.internic.net, where you can register the domain name you want. If you purchase a domain name, seriously consider spending an additional $200 to have it trademarked. The U.S. Patent and Trade Office will award the trademark to whichever business can prove it used the domain name in trade first.

»Logos Help Customers Make Quick Decisions

Customers do not have a lot of time to study different products before deciding where to spend their money. If you can consistently offer a quality product or service and create a logo that successfully represents your company, you are on your way to success. Over time, your logo will become associated with your business. It is up to you to make sure that the customer thinks of quality when he or she sees your logo. This association can become an advantage over the competition.

McDonald's Golden Arches are another famous trademark. When you see them you expect fast service, inexpensive prices, and a certain kind of food. The McDonald's logo is a competitive advantage over less recognizable businesses. Customers head for the Golden Arches because they have been primed by McDonald's consistent marketing to know what to expect. At this point, the arches, just by themselves, embody McDonald's entire marketing vision. Using someone else's intellectual property, such as a trademark, is called **infringement,** and is illegal.

»Copyright

Art is another form of intellectual property. If you are a songwriter, author, or painter, you will create works that you might sell. If you do not protect your work, however, someone else can sell it. A copyright is the form of legal protection offered to literary, musical, and artistic works. The owner of a copyright has the sole right to print, reprint, sell and distribute, revise, record, and perform the work under copyright. The copyright protects a work for the life of the author/artist plus seventy years.

The world's most well-known trademark—McDonald's golden arches.
(© James Leynse/CORBIS SABA)

To file for a copyright, request forms from the Copyright Office (202-707-9100). The forms are easy to fill out. To secure a copyright, send a completed form and two examples of the work, with a registration fee of $30, to the following address:

Copyright Office

Information and Publications Section, LM-455

Library of Congress

101 Independence Ave. S.E.

Washington, DC 20231

All copyright application forms are available on the Internet. You must have Adobe Acrobat® Reader software installed on your computer to download the forms. A free version of Adobe can be downloaded through links at the home page for the Copyright Office, http://www.loc.gov/copyright

»Electronic Rights

Now that writing, photographs, art, and music can be posted on the Web, entrepreneurs must protect their intellectual property online, as well. The rights to reproduce someone's work online are called **electronic rights.**

Using artwork without permission, even if it is a song or photo posted online, is Internet piracy. President Clinton dealt a blow to Internet piracy in 1998 when he signed the Digital Millennium Copyright Act into law. The act protects copyrighted software, music, and text on the Internet by outlawing the technology used to break copyright protection devices.

»Protect Your Electronic Rights

Beware of contracts that say the following:

- *"Work-made-for-hire"*—This means you are giving up the rights to your work. Now the buyer can use it anywhere without paying you anything beyond the original fee you negotiated.

- *"All Rights"*—This means you are handing over all rights to your work to the buyer.

Here are some strategies for protecting your electronic rights.[1]

1. Get the buyer to define exactly what is included in "electronic rights"—online publication? CD-ROMs? Anything else?

2. Put a limit on how long the buyer can have the electronic rights—one year, for instance.

3. Ask for an additional fee for each additional set of rights. A good rule of thumb would be to ask for 15 percent of the orig-

---

[1] Adapted from the *National Writers Union Guide to Negotiating Electronic Rights.* For more information see http://www.nwu.org.

inal fee every time your work is used somewhere electronically. If you sell a drawing to a newspaper for $100, you could ask for $15 if the paper wants to use the drawing on its Web site.

»Marketing Materials Should Reinforce Your Competitive Advantage

All promotional items for your business should reflect and reinforce your marketing vision, which in turn will reinforce your competitive advantage. They should include the name of your business, your logo, and a slogan, if you have one. All your business materials, in fact, such as order forms, invoices, and receipts, should also reflect and reinforce your business's competitive advantage.

Good marketing materials serve three functions:

1. Creating them will organize your business thinking.
2. They will enable you to teach others in your company about the business.
3. They will enable you to go into the marketplace and sell your product or service.

»Print, Audio, and Video Brochures

Advertising can get people interested in your business but, before they buy, prospects will almost certainly want more information. Brochures will enable you to provide that information and turn interest into a sale.

At the bottom of every print ad you run, offer your free brochure. When you send the brochure, include a personal letter thanking this prospective customer for requesting it. If you do not hear from him or her within a few weeks, send a follow-up note. You are establishing one-to-one contact with someone you did not know before— the kind of contact that can lead to a sale.

The brochure can actually close the sale itself, by providing an 800 number people can call to place orders or to obtain coupons or order forms that can be faxed or mailed to you.

Whether you use print, audio, or video brochures will depend on your budget and your business. Some suggestions from Jay Levinson's *Guerrilla Advertising* are the following:[2]

■ Print brochures should fit into a standard envelope, make ordering simple, and connect closely with your advertising.

■ Audio brochures work when visuals aren't necessary to sell your product or service and should run between ten and twenty minutes. According to Levinson, 93 percent of U.S. motorists have cars with cassette players and are good candidates for audio brochures.

---

[2]Adapted from Jay Levinson, *Guerilla Advertising* (Boston: Houghton Mifflin, 1994).

■ Video brochures should run between five to ten minutes and describe your business verbally and visually. If your business has ever been profiled on a television show, you've already got the centerpiece of your video brochure!

»Image Is Important

You will have a much stronger impact if all your business materials are tied together with a strong, coordinated image. Desktop publishing and word-processing software can help you create a logo and "look" that can be used for all the ways you present your business:

- Business cards
- Stationery
- Flyers
- Brochures
- Press releases
- Mailing cards

URLs: Desktop Publishing.com, www.desktoppublishing.com
DTP Journal: www.dtpjournal.com

»Where to Advertise? Visualize Your Customer

An effective ad for a small business typically concentrates on the benefit the product or service provides to the customer. This is why it is important that you accomplished Step 1 of the marketing process: consumer analysis. You need to know who your customers are in order to know how to reach them with advertising. If you are advertising a snowboarding trip, for example, it would be a waste of money to take out an ad in a magazine for senior citizens. By visualizing your customer, you avoid wasting money on customers who aren't interested in your product or service.

»The Media

There are many places to advertise and publicize your business. These are referred to collectively as the **media,** which includes print (magazines, newspapers, etc.), television, and radio. The trick will be to choose the most effective places to spend your advertising dollars, which for a small business are usually quite limited.

Print: Newspapers, magazines, and newsletters are examples of print media. Another good spot for a print ad is the *Yellow Pages.* Consider running a coupon in a neighborhood newspaper. The most important thing to know about newspaper advertising is that a year-long study determined that a potential customer needs to see an advertisement at least nine times before the marketing message

A Print Ad Has Five Parts:

1. **Headline** (or Title)
2. **Deck** (or Subhead)
3. **Copy** (or Text)
4. **Graphics** (Photos or Drawings)
5. **Logo**

penetrates.[3] In addition, the study found that, for every three times a consumer sees an ad, he or she ignores it twice. This implies that a consumer will have to see your ad twenty-seven times before actually visiting your business and buying something.

If you take out a newspaper ad that runs three times a week, therefore, commit to running it for nine weeks at the very least. The most common advertising mistake entrepreneurs make is to give up too soon. One gauge of how effective a given advertising medium will be for your business is to observe it for a while and see whether your competitors use it regularly. If they do, they are probably seeing a good return on their investment, so you should, too.

Television: Even though TV advertising rates are very expensive, an entrepreneur with a new business can sometimes have them lowered or even get a free mention (publicity) on local cable stations. If you are in a position to purchase commercial TV or radio advertising, consider going with a media-buying service, instead of purchasing it yourself (to avoid paperwork and confusion), or hiring an advertising agency (which will charge quite a bit of money and probably contract with a media-buying service anyway). Media-buying services are granted the same 15 percent discount by the media as advertising agencies, but they generally return 10 percent of the savings to you, keeping 5 percent for their fee. You can find media buyers in the *Yellow Pages*.

Radio: University and local community radio stations often do not take ads, but are willing to mention a new business venture that has an interesting or unusual angle. To generate this kind of publicity, you will need to mail or fax a **press release.** A press release consists of several paragraphs of factual information about your business that can be used by a writer as the basis of an article or a radio or TV story. Send out a press release when you open your business, when you get involved with a charity, or when you hold special events.

》Generating Publicity

Publicity is very important for a small business, which typically has a low advertising budget. To get publicity, you will need to mail or fax a **pitch letter** and a press release to the magazine, newspaper, TV station, or radio station you hope to interest in your business.

3. Performance Objective

---

[3] Ibid.

A pitch letter "pitches" the story. It tells the person reading it why he or she should be interested in your business. In the press release, you are announcing the who, what, when, where, and why of an announcement. A pitch letter allows you to explain the story behind the press release and why it would be interesting and relevant to the media's readers, listeners, or viewers.[4]

Before mailing or faxing a pitch letter and press release, call the media outlet and ask to whom you should direct the pitch. Say something like, "My name is Jason Hurley and I'm a young entrepreneur with a downtown delivery/messenger service. I'd like to send WKTU a press release about the commitment we have just made to donate ten hours of free delivery service per month to Meals on Wheels for Seniors. To whom should I direct a press release?"

Try to get to know the print, radio, and television journalists in your town so you can get publicity. The most effective way to get notice for your business is to call the reporters yourself. You might be tempted to hire a professional publicist, but most reporters are bombarded by publicists and would rather hear directly from you. Take a whole day to make phone calls pitching your business and explaining why your story is worth writing about. Be totally honest and try to build friendships. Positive reporting develops most often because the writer comes to care about the entrepreneur.

Press releases can generate positive stories about your business in local newspapers and radio stations. Make sure you send the release about a month before the event you are promoting. Follow up with a phone call two weeks before the event will take place and then one week before.

» What's Your Story?

Younger entrepreneurs can have an advantage here, because few young people start their own businesses. The print, radio, and television journalists in your area may want to hear about you.

Bear in mind, however, that reporters are looking for stories. It is fine to send out a press release announcing the opening of your business, but be aware that it would not be a "story" until it is up and running. There is no point sending out a pitch letter and press release until you are actually in business and have a story to tell.

- What has happened to you or what have you done that would make you and your business an interesting story?
- Did you have to overcome any obstacles in order to start your business?
- Is your product or service unique, or is it something your community really needs?
- How has your business changed you and helped members of your community?

---

[4] Special thanks to Tom Philips of COMPTWP and Jan Legnitto for the information in this chapter.

Answers to these questions will help reporters determine whether your story might be of interest to their readers or viewers. Reporters are very busy people, so keep your answers to these questions tight and concise. Try to find one focus or "angle" for your story. What's the "hook"? Figure 4-1 shows a sample pitch letter.

> ! *Avoid using the phrases "hopes to," "plans to," or "expects to" in your press releases. When reporters see those phrases, they know there is no story yet.*

January 1, 2004

Joe Smith
100 Main St.
Anytown, NY   12345

Dear _____ :

When Malik Armstead opened his soul food take-out restaurant the Five Spot on Myrtle Avenue in Brooklyn, in 1996, he was taking a risk. He was putting all his savings into the business in a neighborhood that was far from fashionable. On the other hand, Malik came from a less-than-fashionable neighborhood himself, and, when he was still a teenager, an organization called the National Foundation for Teaching Entrepreneurship (NFTE, pronounced "nifty") believed that he could make it as an entrepreneur and gave him the skills to do so.

"NFTE taught me that you do not necessarily have to have a lot of money to start a business," says Malik. "I started my first business in high school with only $50."

- The restaurant is thriving, based entirely on word-of-mouth advertising, and has become a neighborhood staple, providing generous portions of high-quality soul food at reasonable prices.

- Other entrepreneurs have followed the 29-year-old Malik's lead. And as Clinton Hill has now been "discovered" by Manhattanites who can no longer find affordable apartments in Brooklyn Heights or Park Slope, the area is flourishing.

- Malik has hired many young people from the neighborhood. For two current employees, the Five-Spot was their first job. One of them has been with the restaurant for over three years and has risen from dishwasher to sous chef.

On February 1st, Malik plans to expand the Five Spot from its current 800 square feet to 2,500 square feet, including a 60-foot mahogany bar and a 150-foot stage, as well as a full dining room. He will continue to serve great soul food while providing live entertainment by musicians from the neighborhood.

I invite you to meet and interview this young entrepreneur who has helped to transform a neighborhood. You are also invited to join us at the Five Spot for a special VIP party on February 1st at 9 P.M., where there will be free food, drink, and entertainment.

Sincerely,

Figure 4-1 Sample pitch letter.

> ***FOR IMMEDIATE RELEASE JANUARY 1, 2004***
>
> ***For More Information Contact:***
> ***Malik Armstead — (718) 555-7839***
>
> ***Five Spot Soul Food Restaurant Expands with 60-Foot Bar and 150-Foot Stage***
>
> ***Popular Restaurant Revitalized Myrtle Avenue***
>
> On February 1st , Malik Armstead plans to expand the Five Spot Restaurant at 459 Myrtle Avenue from its current 800 square feet to 2,500 square feet, including a 60-foot mahogany bar and a 150-foot stage, as well as a full dining room. To celebrate, Malik is hosting a special VIP party on February 1st at 9 P.M., where there will be free food, drink, and entertainment.
>
> The Five Spot will continue to serve great soul food while providing live entertainment by musicians from the neighborhood.
>
> - The restaurant is thriving, based entirely on word-of-mouth advertising, and has become a neighborhood staple, providing generous portions of high-quality soul food at reasonable prices.
> - Other entrepreneurs have followed the 29-year-old Malik's lead, and as Clinton Hill has now been "discovered" by Manhattanites who can no longer find affordable apartments in Brooklyn Heights or Park Slope, the area is flourishing.
> - Malik has hired many young people from the neighborhood. For two current employees, the Five Spot was their first job. One of them has been with the restaurant for over three years and has risen from dishwasher to sous chef.

Figure 4-2 Sample press release.

»Sample Press Release

In order to tell your story in a press release or to a reporter, you have to answer six questions: who, what, when, where, why, and how? Who are you; what did you do; and when, where, why, and how did you do it?

A press release must provide contact information (name, phone, e-mail, and Web site, if available) and answer the six questions. (See Figure 4-2.)

»Follow Up a Press Release by Phone

Follow up your press releases with phone calls. Try to reach the journalists directly. Be polite but persistent. Do not wait for a newspaper or radio station to return your call; call again (but do not make a pest of yourself). Remember, they receive many press releases every day.

As we have said, save all publicity you receive to show potential customers. Publicity has enormous value because it can attract more publicity and more customers.

[Entrepreneurial Wisdom]

Be sure to obtain videotapes of any mention you receive on television. There is no more powerful sales tool than a video that includes a story, however brief, on your business.

»Philanthropy

There is a long, proud connection in the United States between entrepreneurs and **philanthropy.** Philanthropy is the giving of money, time, or advice to charities in an effort to help solve a social or environmental problem such as homelessness, pollution, or cruelty to animals. Philanthropists often give their money through **foundations.** A foundation is a nonprofit organization that passes on donated money, through grants, to other nonprofit organizations that help people and social causes.

Many philanthropic foundations in this country were established by entrepreneurs. As a business owner, you have a responsibility to help the communities you serve. The people and causes you choose to support should be those that matter to you. Your philanthropy may also generate positive publicity, because you can choose to promote the giving that you do. For this reason, marketing experts sometimes consider philanthropy as "the fifth P." We prefer to treat it as a separate topic—to emphasize how important philanthropy is to a successful and fulfilling life.

The Bill and Melinda Gates Foundation is one of the world's largest foundations, with over $23 billion in capital. This money comes from the personal wealth that Gates has earned at Microsoft. As a private foundation, it is required by the federal government to give away 5 percent of the fair market value of its assets every year. The Gates Foundation provides a great deal of money annually to other charities. These in turn use the money to finance social and community programs that the Gates Foundation supports, such as education and health care.

You can be philanthropic even if you have very little or no money to donate. You can donate your time by volunteering for an organization that is doing work you would like to support. If you know how to paint a house or if you have some carpentry skills, for example, you could contribute your efforts to help build homes for an organization such as Habitat for Humanity, which provides affordable housing for low-income families. If you love animals, volunteer at your local animal shelter.

‹ **4. Performance Objective**

»Cause-Related Marketing

Cause-related marketing—marketing inspired by a commitment to a social, environmental, or political cause—is a simple way to work philanthropy into your business. You could donate a fixed percentage of your revenue (say, 1 or 2 percent) to a particular charity

[Step Into The Shoes]

The Body Shop's Campaigns

One of the strongest examples of cause-related marketing by an entrepreneur is Anita Roddick's chain of cosmetic and skin-care-product stores—The Body Shop. Roddick pays her employees to volunteer for community service. The company has run media campaigns on causes ranging from saving whales to preserving the rain forest, and each campaign has had the same effect: It has attracted customers in droves.

Roddick estimates that the company gains roughly $4 million per year in publicity from its various campaigns for solving social and environmental problems.

and then publicize this in your marketing. Another way to help is to donate something your business produces. If you own a sporting-goods store, you could donate uniforms to the local Little League team.

Encourage your employees to participate, too. Volunteerism is a great way to improve morale and make a difference. AT&T, for example, pays employees to devote one day a month to doing community service.

»Gaining Goodwill

Many entrepreneurs try to make a difference in their communities by giving money and time to organizations that help people. Microsoft, for example, made it possible for the National Foundation for Teaching Entrepreneurship to develop an Internet-based entrepreneurship curriculum, BizTech. Microsoft has donated both money and computer programming expertise to this project.

Why would Microsoft do this?

- First, Microsoft's founder, Bill Gates, believes in NFTE's mission and wants to help young people learn about business. The Internet-based program makes it much easier to teach entrepreneurship to greater numbers of young people around the world.
- Second, supporting this program is an intelligent business move for Microsoft. Microsoft gains publicity and **goodwill.** Goodwill is composed of intangible assets, such as reputation, name recognition, and customer relations. Goodwill can give a company an advantage over its competitors.

»Nonprofit Organizations

Nonprofit organizations are corporations whose mission is to contribute to the greater good of society. The Internal Revenue Service classifies nonprofits under section 501(c)(3) in the tax code. These corporations are tax exempt. This means they do not have to pay federal or state taxes, and they are not privately or publicly owned. Essentially, a board of directors controls the operations of a 501(c)(3) nonprofit organization.

Such well-known institutions as the Boys and Girls Clubs of America, the YMCA, the Girl Scouts, the Red Cross, and Big Brothers/Big Sisters are all examples of nonprofits. Their founders were social entrepreneurs, and, although they did not earn large sums of money personally and could not sell the organization for a profit, they received great satisfaction and made a difference. Wendy Kopp, of Teach for America, and Michael Bronner of UPromise, are two examples of social entrepreneurs who founded innovative and successful nonprofit organizations described in the next section.

»Teach for America and Upromise

Founded in 1991, Teach for America recruits recent college graduates to become public school teachers. Operating with a budget of over $11 million, the organization has trained some 10,000 young teachers, and placed them in two-year teaching positions in schools where teachers are badly needed.

Michael Bronner, a former marketing executive who became a social entrepreneur, started Upromise in 2001. Bronner felt strongly that the cost of sending a child to college had become much too expensive for most families. He believed that there needed to be a better way of helping families save money for college.

Bronner came up with the idea that a portion of the money that families already spend on popular goods and services, such as groceries and toys, could go into a college savings account for their children. Upromise works with established corporations, such as AT&T, America Online, and Toys "R" Us. Every time a registered family makes a purchase from one of these companies, a percentage automatically goes into a special college savings account.

»What Entrepreneurs Have Built

Many philanthropic organizations in this country were created by entrepreneurs who wanted to give back some of the wealth that they had earned. Entrepreneurs have financed great museums, libraries, universities, and other important institutions. Some foundations created by famous entrepreneurs include the Rockefeller Foundation, the Coleman Foundation, the Charles G. Koch Foundation, the Ford Foundation, and the Goldman Sachs Foundation.

You can always start your own nonprofit to attempt to solve a world problem, but remember that entrepreneurs who run their businesses in socially responsible ways are also positive forces in their communities.

Some of the most aggressive entrepreneurs in American history, such as Andrew Carnegie, have also been the most generous. In 1901, after a long and sometimes ruthless business career, Carnegie sold his steel company to J. P. Morgan for $420 million. Overnight, Carnegie became one of the very richest men in the world. After retiring, he spent most of his time giving away his wealth to libraries, colleges, museums, and other worthwhile institutions that still benefit people today. By the time of his death, in 1919, Carnegie had given away over $350 million to philanthropic causes.

»You Have Something to Contribute

You may not have millions of dollars to give to your community, yet. But there are many ways you can be philanthropic that will help others, get your employees excited, and create goodwill in your community:

- Pledge a percentage of your sales to a nonprofit organization you have researched, believe in, and respect. Send out press releases announcing your pledge.

- Become a mentor to a younger entrepreneur. Help that individual by sharing your contacts and expertise.

- Volunteer for an organization that helps your community. Find out how you can serve on its board of directors.

- Sell your product to a charity that you support at a discount. The charity can then resell it at full price to raise money.

- When you give it a little thought, you will realize that you have a lot to give. Remember, making a contribution does not necessarily mean giving money. You can donate time, advice, and moral support!

> To get some ideas on how to make your business socially responsible, check out Standards of Corporate Responsibility at http://www.svn.org/initiatives/standards.html

These days, customers have access to a lot of information about what companies do with their money. Make sure you can always be proud of your business. Choose to support causes that are important to you and make sense for your business. Philanthropy will strengthen your relationship with your customers because it goes beyond the sale and into what's important in their lives.

»Relationship Marketing

Most companies have moved away from "transaction-oriented" marketing, which focuses on closing a sale with customers, and towards "relationship" marketing, which focuses on creating long-term relationships with customers by making sure they are satisfied. Relationship marketing acknowledges that making the sale is just the beginning of the relationship between a company and a customer.

Companies communicate to their customers through marketing. The most profitable message a company can communicate is that it would like to serve customers over a lifetime in a mutually beneficial relationship.

»Marketing Online

More than 40 million people in 150 countries are connected to the Internet. Your marketing message might only appeal to a tiny percentage, but even a fraction of the online market represents a lot of people. Better still, the online marketplace is organized into special interest groups, so it is not hard to figure out where to promote your business.

The World Wide Web is a subset of the Internet, made up of computers that can deliver graphics and sound as well as text. Web sites are not hard to create and can be a lot of fun. Other ways to market your business online are the following:

- *Online services*—classified ads, billboards, and online shopping malls. Talk to a marketing staff person about setting up your own storefront in such a mall. Online services also have special-interest forums where you can find people who might be interested in your business.

- *Newsgroups*—A "newsgroup" is an online forum where people leave messages for each other on a specified topic. The messages form an ongoing discussion. Although you cannot advertise your business in a newsgroup, you can get to know the other participants and conduct some informal market research. This is also a great way to build a reputation for yourself as knowledgeable about a given subject.

> *Find three online newsgroups or chatrooms that you believe would help you with your business. Explain why and how you plan to participate.*

- *E-mail*—Electronic mail is fast and easy to use, but resist the urge to bombard potential customers with it. Most people greatly resent unsolicited e-mail. If you are going to send this type of advertising, it had better be so informative and entertaining that customers will be happy to get it. Of course, you can develop a mailing list of customers who have indicated that they want to receive e-mail about your business.

- *Electronic storefront*—As mentioned previously, the major online services offer entrepreneurs the opportunity to put up a "storefront" in a shopping area. You can also put up a storefront on the Net. Each has advantages. The online service might get more "hits" from curious browsers, but you are limited to that service's customers. On the Net, your storefront is accessible to anyone in the world who is online.

»Marketing Is a Fixed Cost

Let's say you want to launch a new software program. You've researched the consumers, pinpointed your market segment, and determined your marketing mix. You are now ready to implement a marketing plan that will get your vision "out there." There is one more question: Can you afford your marketing plan?

Marketing is part of your business's fixed costs. Fixed costs are costs that do not vary with sales. They can be remembered as USAIIRD:

- **U**tilities (gas, electric, telephone)
- **S**alaries
- **A**dvertising
- **I**nsurance
- **I**nterest
- **R**ent
- **D**epreciation

There are also variable costs, such as commissions, that vary with sales. For a business to survive, though, it must be able to cover its fixed costs. Most fixed costs, such as rent, insurance, and utilities, are hard to cut back if your sales are slow. You can't go to your landlord and tell him or her you cannot pay the rent this month because business has been slow.

Marketing costs are more flexible. (Some entrepreneurs even choose to treat them as variable.) They fall under **a**dvertising, and may also show up under **s**alaries, if you hire a marketing consultant or a full-time marketing staff.

»How to Calculate Your Breakeven Point

Performance Objective 5.》

The question is this: Can you sell enough units to pay for your marketing plan? **Breakeven** is the point at which a business sells enough units to cover its fixed costs. If you estimate that your market is roughly 3 million people, but you have to sell 5 million units just to cover the cost of your marketing plan. The plan is not viable.

This is why calculating the breakeven point tells you if your marketing plan is viable. It shows whether or not you can cover your fixed costs with the number of units you plan to sell. If not, the one place you can cut costs is advertising—your marketing plan.

David is an artist who supports his painting career by creating unique tank tops with airbrush designs. The shirts are very popular with the hip young women in Manhattan's East Village, and David sells the shirts each weekend at a flea market next to Tower Records, on East 4th Street. Let's say he buys eight-dozen tank tops for $576. He airbrushes them and sells them all at a weekend flea market for $1,152. David considers one tank top his unit of sale. COGS would be calculated as $576/96 = $6 with selling price per unit $1152/96 = $12.

- How much did each tank top cost David? $ _____
  This is his cost of goods sold.
- How much did he charge for each tank top? $ _____
  This is his selling price per unit.
- David's unit of sale is one tank top.

■ David's cost of goods sold is $6.

■ David's selling price is $12.
$12 (selling price per unit) – $6 (cost of goods sold per unit) = $6 (gross profit per unit)

■ David's gross profit per unit is $6 per tank top.

Next, David needs to take a look at his fixed costs. Let's say he spends $150 a month on renting his space at the flea market, and $30 a month on flyers as advertising. His monthly fixed costs are $150 + $30 = $180. How many tank tops does he have to sell to cover his fixed costs? We'll use the following formula:

$$\frac{\text{Fixed Cost}}{\text{Gross Profit per Unit}} = \text{Breakeven Units}$$

$$\frac{\text{Fixed Cost: \$180}}{\text{Gross Profit per Unit \$6}} = 30 \text{ Breakeven Units}$$

David needs to sell 30 tank tops to cover his fixed costs. David typically sells about 20 tank tops each weekend, so in one month he can expect to sell:

20 units × 4 weekends = 80 units

David can definitely afford to spend $30 per month on flyers. He could even afford to add another expense to his marketing plan, such as getting business cards printed, or setting up a Web site where customers could order shirts and find out where he will be selling each weekend.

»Breakeven Analysis of a Restaurant

Here is a breakeven analysis from a chicken restaurant in Florida, called Mary Ann's.

Typically, a customer at Mary Ann's buys a bucket of chicken for $8 and a drink for $2, so the average sale per customer is $10. Therefore, a business unit is defined as a $10 sale. The cost of goods sold for each unit is $3.50 for the sandwich and $0.50 for the drink, so the cost of goods sold is $4.00 per unit.

Mary Ann's fixed costs for a month are:

Utilities	$1,000
Salaries	3,000
Ads	1,000
Interest	0
Insurance	1,000
Rent	2,000
	$8,000

The restaurant is open on average 30 days per month.

To figure out how many units Mary Ann's has to sell each month to break even, divide the gross profit per unit into the monthly fixed costs.

$$\text{Gross Profit per Unit} = \text{Unit Price } (\$10) - \text{COGS } (\$4.00) = \$6.00$$

$$\text{Breakeven Units} = \frac{\text{Monthly Fixed Costs } (\$8,000)}{\text{Gross Profit per Unit } (\$6.00)} = 1,333 \text{ Units}$$

Since the store is open 30 days per month, to break even Mary Ann's has to make 44 average sales per day:

$$\frac{1,333 \text{ units}}{30 \text{ days}} = 44.33 \ (45 \text{ units per day})$$

Breakeven is the point at which fixed costs are recovered by sales but no profit has yet been made. Once you have determined your breakeven point, the next question in the analysis is this: *Can my business reach breakeven in its relevant market?* In the previous example, can Mary Ann's reasonably expect to sell 45 buckets of chicken a day? The answer to this question for you will be in the market research you have conducted to get to this, the last step of creating a marketing plan. You should know the answer to this question. If not, you must conduct further research until you can confidently gauge whether or not you can afford your marketing plan. Revising your plan is another option, of course.

Breakeven analysis is a good tool for looking at all your costs and should be performed frequently. It is especially important after you've completed your marketing plan and before you open your business to see if your plan is realistic.

»The Spreadsheet—A Powerful Tool for Projection

Spreadsheets are a table of numbers organized into rows and columns. Each row or column is governed by a mathematical formula. A row across the top might be monthly sales, for example, and you add them up to get the last number in the row, which is the total yearly sales.

If you have ever worked with Excel software, you were making spreadsheets. Computerized spreadsheets are extremely useful when you are working on financial calculations, such as trying to find your business's breakeven point. They are especially valuable for creating projections, which are your best guesses about future performance because, if you just change one number in the spreadsheet, the computer will make all the calculations showing how that change will affect every other number on the sheet. You can change your monthly sales projections and see how that will affect total yearly sales, for example. Spreadsheets make it easy to manipulate numbers.

»Chapter Summary

Now that you have studied this chapter you can do the following:

1. Combine the four Ps—product, price, place, and promotion—into a marketing mix.

2. Choose where and how to advertise your business.

   ■ Promotion is the use of advertising and publicity to get your marketing message out to your customers. Publicity is free mention of your business—in newspapers or magazines or on radio or TV.

   ■ An advertisement is a paid announcement that a product or service is for sale. Examples of advertising include television commercials, billboards, and magazine ads.

3. Use press releases and pitch letters to generate publicity for your business.

   ■ To get publicity, you will need to mail or fax a pitch letter and/or a press release to the magazine, newspaper, TV or radio station you hope to interest in your business.

   ■ A pitch letter "pitches" the story. It tells the person reading it why he or she should be interested in your business.

   ■ In the press release, you are announcing the who, what, when, where, why, and how.

4. Decide how your business will help your community philanthropically.

   ■ Philanthropy is the giving of money, time, or advice to charities in an effort to help solve a social or environmental problem, such as homelessness, pollution, or cruelty to animals.

   ■ You can be philanthropic even if you have very little or no money to donate. You can donate your time by volunteering for an organization that is doing work you want to support.

5. Use breakeven analysis to evaluate your marketing plan.

   ■ Breakeven is the point at which a business sells enough units to cover its costs.

   ■ Breakeven analysis tells you if your marketing plan is viable. It shows whether or not you can cover your fixed costs with the number of units you plan to sell. If not, the one place you can cut costs is your marketing plan.

Key Terms

advertising
breakeven
cause-related marketing
electronic rights
foundation
goodwill
infringement
logo
keystone

media
philanthropy
pitch letter
press release
promotion
public relations
publicity
trademark

[Entrepreneurship Portfolio]

Critical Thinking Exercises

1. Describe how your product or service will fit into, and complement, your marketing mix.

2. Meet with a partner and discuss the pros and cons of the following pricing strategies—value pricing, keystoning, cost-plus, penetration strategy, skimming strategy, and meet or beat the competition—for each of your businesses. Present your recommendations for each other to the class.

3. Where do you plan to locate your business? Explain.

4. How do you plan to work philanthropy into your marketing mix?

5. Use the following chart to describe your marketing mix.

Marketing Mix Chart (Business Plan Practice)
My Market Segment: _____

Marketing Mix	Decision	Explanation
Product		
Price		
Place		
Promotion		
Philanthropy		

6. Use computer software to create a logo for your business. Do you intend to trademark your logo? Explain.

7. Describe any intellectual property you are developing. **(Business Plan Practice)**

8. How do you plan to protect your intellectual property? Explain why it would qualify for protection. **(Business Plan Practice)**

9. Give an example of a business in your community that you think may be infringing on someone else's intellectual property.

Key Concept Questions

1. What is a drawback of "cost-plus" pricing?

2. What is "penetration" pricing? Can you think of an example of a company that has used penetration pricing to introduce a new product?

3. Brainstorm five creative ways for a small business without much money to advertise and promote its products or services using the latest developments in communications and Internet technology.

4. Visit a "shopping mall" on a major online Internet server, such as America Online, CompuServe, or MSN. List three advantages and three disadvantages of opening a Web site for your business at an online server's shopping mall.

5. Answer the questions below and use them to write a press release for your business. **(Business Plan Practice)**

   a. What was your life like before you began the study of entrepreneurship?

   b. Were you having any problems in school or at home?

   c. What have you learned about business that you did not know before?

   d. What's the best thing about running your own business? What obstacles have you had to overcome to get your business going?

   e. Has running your own business changed how you are doing in school? Has it changed how you get along with your family?

   f. Are you more involved in your community since you started your business?

   g. How has your business changed your life? What would you be doing if you were not an entrepreneur?

   h. If you could give one piece of advice to students who were thinking about starting a business, what would it be?

   i. What are your dreams for the future?

6. Use your press release to write a pitch letter for the opening of your business.

1. Use the following chart to describe your marketing plan in detail.

Application Exercises

Marketing Plan

Date:_____   Product/Service:_____

Methods	Door-to-Door	Online	Street	Store/Office	Other
800 number					
Billboards					
Brochures					
Business cards					
Catalog					
Demonstration					
Direct mail					
E-mail/fax					
Flyers					
Free gifts					
Online store					
Phone calls					
Posters					
Promo items					
Sales calls					
Samples					
Special events					
Web site					

Exploring Your Community

Obtain ad rates from two local radio stations, a local newspaper, and a cable television channel.

Media	**Advertising Rates**
Radio _____	_____
Radio _____	_____
Newspaper _____	_____
Cable _____	_____

Exploring Online

Find out how much it would cost to run a banner ad on the "personal start" pages (the pages subscribers see when they log on) for the following online services: AOL, Earthlink, Panix, and CompuServe.

AOL Banner Ad Price: $_____

Earthlink Banner Ad Price: $_____

Panix Banner Ad Price: $_____

CompuServe Banner Ad Price: $_____

CASE STUDY: Aces Corp.

Jan Peters, Rob Hunter, and Julie King are recent MBA graduates hired by the Aces Corp. to revamp its marketing program. Ellen Aston founded the Aces Corp. in 1965. The company operates 400 combination gas and convenience stores in eleven southern states. The company has most of its stores in shopping plazas with a major grocery chain retailer. The retailer has decided that the convenience side of the Aces business is in too much competition with its grocery items and has notified Aces that its agreement will not be renewed after the contract expires, in one year. Aces will have two more years to close its stores in the plazas.

While the loss of the plaza locations will be a setback, the Aces Corp. executives are optimistic about the future because it has a close association with the NASCAR racing organization and will sign a trademark agreement shortly. This agreement will give Aces the right to use certain symbols, and make references to NASCAR in its signage. The company sees this link to NASCAR as a key to its future. Another positive factor for Aces is a long-term marketing agreement with a major oil retailer that will give the company a guaranteed supply of gasoline for ten years. Aces also has secured beer and wine licenses for the majority of its stores and believes that these will be transferable to most new locations. The company has been very profitable and is willing and able to make substantial investments in the future.

The gasoline and convenience store business operates on a small margin, and volume and repeat business are key to success. Ellen and her two sons built the company through entrepreneurial methods. At this point, Aces is looking to the three MBAs to develop new marketing ideas. The company has a great history, financial resources, and two strong partnerships, but it needs a plan.

Case Study Analysis

1. What strengths and weaknesses does the Aces Corp. have in its marketing mix?

2. Where will the emphasis need to be placed in the short term? On product, place, promotion, or price?

3. How valuable do you think the NASCAR connection for Aces Corp. is?

CASE STUDY: Malia Mills Swimwear

When 38-year-old Malia Mills decided to launch her own swimwear company, she set out to do much more than just sell high-end bathing suits—Mills wanted to inspire a beauty revolution that would fundamentally change the way that women felt about themselves. Before she became an entrepreneur, Mills had worked in the fashion world as a designer for established apparel companies. A native of Hawaii, Mills saved up her startup investment by working for many years as a waitress in New York City. She started Malia Mills Swimwear in 1991.

The slogan of Mills's business is Love Thy Differences™, and Mills is passionate about encouraging all women, regardless of age, weight, or body type to feel good about themselves and to celebrate their uniqueness. In Mills's world, if a woman does not like the way she looks in a swimsuit, it is the suit that has to change, not the woman. As she explains, "We are passionate about inspiring women to look in the mirror and see what is right instead of what is wrong."

The Polaroid Project

If you walk past the Malia Mills Swimwear flagship store in New York's chic SoHo district, the first thing you will notice are the photographs in the window. Instead of showcasing fashion models, the window display features a collage of Polaroid pictures of customers wearing her signature swimwear. According to Mills's sister, Carol, who manages the store, "We've had so many customers walk in off the street because of those photographs. People are thrilled to see actual women in all colors, shapes, and sizes wearing our suits." This "Polaroid project" actually began as an offbeat idea brainstormed by a summer intern on a particularly slow sales day. Mills liked the idea of using photographs of her customers because it resonated with the core mission of her business.

Place Matters: Setting the Right Tone

To create a comfortable environment for her customers, Mills has constructed her stores to look and feel like cozy lounges. Mills always hated trying on bathing suits in department stores under the glare of unflattering fluorescent lights. In her boutiques, the lighting is soft and dressing rooms are located in the back so that her customers will not feel exposed in front of other shoppers. She provides free bottled water to customers so that they can feel relaxed and at home. Sales associates are always on hand to assist with finding the appropriate suits. Mills does not believe in a one-size-fits-all design philosophy. People's bodies do not come in packages of small, medium, and large. Accordingly, her tops are sized like lingerie and bottoms come in sizes 2 to 16. All pieces are sold as separates, which allows customers to mix and match across different style and fabric options.

The Price/Production Connection

Malia Mills's suits are priced at the high end of the swimwear market. A bikini top will cost somewhere between $88 and $96; bikini bottoms are $86; and full-piece suits run an average of $182. Mills's pricing scheme reflects some of the choices she has made as an entrepreneur about how her suits are produced. For example, she chooses to manufacture in New York City instead of outsourcing production to Asia or elsewhere, where labor costs are lower. According to Mills, "It costs us much more per unit to sew our suits locally but supporting our community is worth it. The women (mostly) who sew our suits do so with extra care—we visit them often and they know how important quality is to us."

Mills chooses to import the fabrics she uses from Europe and she typically buys them in small quantities—which is more costly—so that her suit designs stay fresh. Mills also pays a premium to the fabric mills that custom-dye her materials in unique colors, and this also contributes to the bottom line of her manufacturing costs. Her suits are so well made that she sometimes worries about undercutting herself in the marketplace. If the average woman owns 2 to 3 bathing suits and a Malia Mills suit can last several years, it could take a long time for a customer to purchase a replacement.

Smart Selling Requires Trial and Error

Early on, Mills sold her suits wholesale to department stores but she found that this strategy did not fit well with her core mission. Mills's suits got lost on the racks next to other brand-name apparel, and the salespeople did not understand how to answer customers' questions about the unique features of her products, such as how they are sized differently from other swimsuits. So eventually Mills pulled the plug on the department stores and decided to focus on selling directly to the consumer. Maintaining control over the sales process has allowed Mills to stay true to her mission of providing women with an enjoyable and empowering experience—purchasing swimwear in a comfortable environment.

Promotions: Getting the Word Out

Over the years, Mills has been successful in generating PR. Her company has been profiled in major publications such as *The New York Times*, *Sports Illustrated*, and *Harper's Bazaar*. It has helped to have celebrities such as Madonna wearing her suits, especially when they are photographed in public. Recently, Mills began purchasing advertising for the first time in local print media. She is doing this as an experiment to see if it has a noticeable impact on generating new customers. In the meantime, the growth of Malia Mills Swimwear continues to be propelled by word of mouth and customer loyalty. Each day, the business connects with passers-by who are lured into the store by the Polaroid photographs of ordinary women wearing her bathing suits. Once these women walk in off the street, there is a pretty good chance that they will walk out as customers, with shopping bags in hand.

Case Study Analysis

1. Describe the unique features of Malia Mills's product.

2. Malia Mills Swimwear is not inexpensive. Why do you think customers are willing to pay a premium for her suits?

3. The case mentions that Malia Mills Swimwear is currently experimenting with paid advertising. If you were in charge of marketing for the company, how would you assess whether or not it was cost-effective to continue to purchase advertising?

4. What kind of environment is Malia Mills trying to create in her stores? Why is this important?

5. Besides her own boutiques, specialty stores, and through the Internet, what might be some additional sales venues for Malia Mills Swimwear to consider exploring?

6. Why was the "Polaroid project" a successful promotional venture?

7. Imagine a scenario where Malia Mills Swimwear hired you as a media consultant. Answer the following:

   ■ Brainstorm a cause-related marketing strategy for the company.

   ■ Describe three strategies for the company to pursue to obtain media coverage.

CASE SOURCES

Malia Mills Web site: see www.maliamills.com

"Chic to Chic—Turn style into sales with a clothing-design company," by Pamela Rohland. *Business Start-Ups* magazine, December 1999. See http://Entrepreneur.com/article/0,4621,231846,00.html

Chapter 5 | Smart Selling and Effective Customer Service

"The secret of success is to have a self-seller, and if you do not have one, get one."

—William C. (Billy) Durant, founder of General Motors

Performance Objectives

1. Explain the difference between features and benefits.
2. Use the principles of selling to make effective sales calls.
3. Analyze and improve your sales calls.
4. Handle customer complaints effectively.
5. Provide good customer service.

When it sold right, it is an increase on demand.

From 1878 to 1886, in Flint, Michigan, William Durant—invariably called "Billy"—started a variety of entrepreneurial ventures in the fields of insurance, real estate, and construction. None of them took off. He had yet to find his "self-seller." When he was 25, however, Durant hitched a ride to work with a friend. He noticed that his friend's new horse-drawn buggy rode more smoothly than any other he had been in. His friend explained that the buggy had a new kind of spring. Durant was so impressed that he decided he wanted to own the company that made this vehicle.

Durant learned that the Coldwater Road Cart Company made the buggies. The very next day, Durant went to the company and made a deal with the owner to buy it for $1,500. Durant insisted that the arrangement include the patent for the springs, and the transaction was completed in two days. This first of many deals exemplified Durant's business philosophy: "Decide quickly, make your pitch, nail down the details, and do not worry about the money."

Durant was not joking about the last part. When he closed the deal on Coldwater, he did not have $1,500, but he did not let that deter him. He borrowed $2,000 from his local bank and had two sample buggy carts made. He rode one to a county fair in Madison, Wisconsin. The cart "sold itself" and within a week he had orders for 600 carts. By 1893, his original $2,000 had grown to $150,000. By 1901, his company was the largest buggy manufacturer in the country. Then Durant turned to the young automobile industry. In 1904, he took over the Buick Motor Company, which eventually became General Motors.

»From Sales to Owning Your Own Business

Direct selling is dealing with a potential customer face to face and trying to convince him or her to make a purchase. Salespeople often become successful entrepreneurs because they hear what the consumer needs and wants on a daily basis.

For example, many of America's great entrepreneurs started out in sales:

(Ryan McVay, Photodisc/Getty Images)

- Ray Kroc, founder of McDonald's, was selling milkshake machines when he was inspired to turn the McDonald brothers' hamburger restaurant into a national operation.
- Aristotle Onassis was a wholesale tobacco salesman before becoming a multimillionaire in the shipping business.
- King C. Gillette was a traveling salesman when he invented the safety razor.
- W. Clement Stone started out selling newspapers at the age of six before going on to build a great fortune in the insurance industry.
- As we have seen, Billy Durant, the founder of General Motors, began his career as a buggy salesman.

»Selling Is a Great Source of Market Research

If the customer is dissatisfied, the salesperson hears the complaint. In that sense, selling is a constant source of valuable market research. When you start your business, you will probably not be able to hire a sales staff. You will be the sales staff.

Even if you have never sold anything in your life, you can develop into a great salesperson. Being face to face with customers, trying to sell your product, may make you nervous at first. But if you think of even rejections as opportunities for continuous market analysis, you will look forward to every sales encounter throughout your entrepreneurial career.

Biz Facts

Many salespeople earn a **commission,** which is a percentage paid on each sale. A car salesperson who makes a 10 percent commission, for example, would earn $1,000 after selling a $10,000 car.

$.10 \times \$10,000 = \$1,000$

Entrepreneurs can use commissions to motivate sales staff. When you are starting out and cannot afford to pay sales representatives full-time salaries, you can offer commissions instead.

[Step Into The Shoes]

Michael Dell Focuses on Benefits and Scores Big

Let's say you're Michael Dell, sitting in your Texas dorm room, figuring out how to convince your fellow students to let you build computers for them. You know you can build computers that are customized, cheap, and reliable. Those are the features of your product. You could tell your friends this and they might be mildly interested. But there would be a better way to present your case, and that would be to focus on the benefits. These could include the following:

■ If a student cannot figure out how to use a feature on his computer, he or she can come see you personally.

■ If a computer "crashes," or breaks, he or she does not have to send it out for repairs.

■ Less money for a new computer means more money for beer!

■ A customized computer is faster than a generic one because it is not loaded down with software the student will never use.

Dell used this approach to create Dell Computer, and today, at age 38, he earns $3.44 million per year as the company's CEO—all because he understood that *benefits* sell computers, not *features*. The features of a product are just facts. *The creative art of selling is teaching the customer how the features will become benefits.*

»The Essence of Selling Is Teaching

⟨1. Performance Objective

Inexperienced salespeople make a common mistake: They think telling the customer about the features of a product will sell it. But remember, a customer who buys a drill does not need a drill, she or he needs to make a hole. The essence of selling is explaining *why* the outstanding features of your product or service will benefit the customer.

The essence of selling is teaching how and why the outstanding features of your product or service will benefit your customers. Durant succeeded by showing that a new type of spring (feature) made riding in his buggy carts more comfortable (benefit).

»The Principles of Selling

⟨2. Performance Objective

Every entrepreneur has to be able to think through the benefits his or her product can provide and make an effective sales call. Entrepreneurs *sell* constantly—not just to customers but to potential investors, bankers, and people they want to hire. Commit the following selling principles to memory and you will be on your way to becoming a successful salesperson. These principles apply to any product or service:

1. ***Make a good personal impression*** when selling your product or service. Prepare yourself physically. A salesperson must be clean and well dressed, but it is important not to overdress. If you are selling oil to gas station attendants, do not walk in

wearing an $800 suit. For sales calls, use a general business card that does not identify you as president or owner, so your prospects can talk with you more easily.

2. ***Know your product or service.*** Understand how its features can benefit the consumer. It is your chance to teach the customer about the product or service. Explain its benefits to the customer.

3. ***Believe in your product or service.*** Good salespeople believe in what they are selling. If, during this stage, you begin to feel that your product or service does not measure up, do not try to sell it. Your business will fail if you do not believe it is the best available in the marketplace for the price. Always be on the lookout for ways to improve your product or develop a better one.

4. ***Know your field.*** Read the trade literature. Learn about your competitors. Buy their products or try their services and compare them with yours. Make sure you experience a call from one of your competitor's salespeople. Let this person try to sell to you. This can be a gold mine of information. Study the strengths and weaknesses of your competitor's product or service, because your prospects will probably bring them up during your own sales calls.

5. ***Know your customers.*** What are their needs? How does your product or service address them?

6. ***Prepare your sales presentation.*** Know ahead of time how you want to present your product or service.

7. ***Think positively.*** This will help you deal with the rejections you may experience before you sell your product or service. Many people do not realize how mentally strong you have to be to conduct sales calls. One entrepreneur went on over 1,100 calls while running his import-export firm—he went on 400 of these before he closed a sale of more than $1,000. This experience made him an excellent salesperson.

8. ***Keep good records.*** Have your recordkeeping system, including invoices and receipts, set up before you go on your first sales call.

9. ***Make an appointment.*** People are more likely to listen when they have set aside time to hear your sales pitch. They will be less receptive if you interrupt their day unannounced.

10. ***Treat everyone you sell to like gold.*** Joe Girard is a car salesman who has been dubbed "The World's Greatest Salesman" twelve times by *The Guinness Book of Records*. In his best seller *How to Sell Anything to Anybody,* Girard gives his Law of 250 as follows: "Everyone knows 250 people in his or her life important enough to invite to the wedding and to the funeral." He goes on to explain, "This means that if I see 50 people in a week, and only two of them are unhappy with the way I treat them, at the end of the year there will be about 5,000 people influenced by just those two a week."[1] Obviously, if each person you sell to influences 250 others, you cannot afford to alienate even one sales prospect!

---

[1] Joe Girard, *How to Sell Anything to Anybody*, p. 48 (New York: Warner Books, 1986).

»The Sales Call

A **sales call** is an appointment with a potential customer to explain or demonstrate your product or service. During the sales call, you will want to do the following:

- Make the customer aware of your product or service.
- Make the customer want to buy that product or service.
- Make the customer want to buy it from *you*.

»E-Mail and Newsgroups

E-mail is short for "electronic mail," mail sent via the Internet. **Newsgroups** are public message boards that discuss particular topics.

Sending e-mail or posting messages on newsgroups can help contact sales prospects and keep in touch with customers you already have, but you must use these methods carefully. In the physical world you can fish for sales prospects by distributing flyers or by cold-calling people on a list. Using e-mail or newsgroups in a similar fashion can result in your e-mail box being jammed with "flames," or hate mail. Most newsgroups do not appreciate receiving unwanted advertisements, which are called **spam,** and members may respond angrily.

Becoming involved in a newsgroup can lead to sales prospects, however, if done correctly. Let's say you sell photography supplies and you hear about an interesting newsgroup for photographers. Do not blitz it with ads for your business! Instead, before posting any messages, "lurk" for awhile. Just read messages for a week and get a feel for the discussions taking place. Once you are comfortable, try posting a message. For example, see the message in Figure 5-1. Because this is not a sales pitch, no one in the newsgroup will take offense, and your message may attract some potential sales prospects to your Web site.

This week's discussion on the advantages of the new Nikon mini-camera was very interesting. I'm in the photography supply business and am looking for interesting items to add to my Web site. I have already posted articles from Advanced Photography magazine and tips from some of my clients. Does anyone have any other ideas for useful information that I could post? Thanks!

Sandra Bowling
PhotoSupply Online
http://www.photosupply.com
E-mail: "photosupply"AOL.com
The Photographer's Source for Supplies and Advice

Figure 5-1 Message to a newsgroup.

»Prequalify Your Sales Calls

Before calling to make an appointment for any sales call, write down your **prospects.** This is a list of people you think might be receptive to your sales pitch. Include everyone you can imagine, but, after you've made your list, comb through it carefully by asking the following:

- Is this person in my market?
- Does he/she need my product?
- Can he/she afford it?

If the answer to any of these questions is "no," making a sales call on that person will probably be a waste of time. Asking these questions is called "prequalifying" a sales call. Spend plenty of time getting your prospect list organized. Abe Lincoln's famous saying—"If I had ten hours to chop down a tree, I'd spend nine sharpening my axe"—applies here.

»Focus on the Customer

During each call, focus on one thought: What does the customer need? Visualize your product or service fulfilling that need. If you believe in your product or service, you will be able to see this without any problem. In general, focusing on listening to the potential customer will help you overcome self-consciousness in any situation.

Mental visualization will help you perform better when the actual situation arrives. Practice the sales call in your mind, visualizing how you want it to go. Visualization will enlist your subconscious mind in the sales process, instinctively providing you with subtle verbal and body language cues that can convince a customer to buy from you.

»The Eight-Step Sales Call

1. *Preparation*—Prepare yourself mentally. Think about how the product/service will benefit this customer. Have the price, discounts, all technical information, and any other details "on the tip of your tongue." Be willing to obtain further information if your customer should request it. Visualize the sales call in your mind until it goes smoothly and successfully. Use mental visualization to call to your attention any rough spots in your presentation, any doubts you may have about your product or service, or any facts you are missing.

2. *Greeting*—Greet the customer politely and graciously. Do not plunge immediately into business talk. The first few words you say may be the most important. Keep a two-way conversation going. Maintain eye contact and keep the customer's attention. Remember that the customer is first and foremost a human being with whom you would like to form a friendship. The more you can learn about his/her family, hobbies, interests—anything to help develop a genuine relationship—the better your

chances of eventually securing a sale. The best salespeople keep files on their customers with all sorts of information in order to develop genuine friendships with their customers and prospects.

3. ***Showing the Product/Service***—Personalize your product or service by pointing out the benefits for this particular customer. Use props and models (or the real thing) where appropriate.

4. ***Listen to the Customer***—After you pitch your product or service once, sit back and let the customer talk about it. This is how you will get your most valuable information. This is how to learn what the customer needs and wants. Neil Rackham, the author of *SPIN Selling* (1996), had his consulting firm, Huthwaite, analyze more than 35,000 sales. He discovered that in successful calls it was the buyer who did most of the talking.[2]

5. ***Dealing with Objections***—During the listening phase, you will hear a customer's objections to your product or service. Always acknowledge objections and deal with them. Do not pretend you did not hear. Do not overreact to objections and do not be afraid to listen. A famous real estate entrepreneur, William Zeckendorf, said, "I never lost money on a sales pitch when I listened to the customer." Do not hesitate to tell the absolute truth about any negative aspect of your product or service. Each time you admit a negative, you gain credibility in the customer's mind.

6. ***Closing the Sale***—Review the benefits of your product or service. If negatives have come up, point out that, at this price, the product or service is still an excellent buy. Narrow the choices the customer has to make. Close the sale. Do not overstay your welcome. The rule of thumb: If a customer says no three times, you still have a chance. If he/she says it the fourth time, it is really no. If the answer *is* no, take it gracefully. You may make a sale to this customer in the future.

7. ***Follow-up***—Make regular follow-up calls to find out how he/she likes the product or service. Ask if you can be of any further help. If the customer has a complaint, do not ignore it. Keeping the customer's trust after the sale is the most important part of the whole process.

    A successful business is built on repeat customers. Plus, every time you talk to a customer you are deepening your friendship. Your best sales prospects in the future are people who have already bought something from you. Keep them posted on your business by sending postcards or flyers.

8. ***Ask for References***—If you did a good job for customers who needed your product or service, ask them to refer you to other potential customers. Try to set up a system that encourages others to send sales prospects your way. Offer discounts, gift certificates, or other incentives to customers who refer people to you, for example. Give customers a few business cards to pass on to their friends.

---

[2] Neil Rackham, *SPIN Selling* (New York: McGraw-Hill, 1996).

»Three Call Behaviors of Successful Salespeople

Neil Rackham researched thousands of sales calls and discovered that successful salespeople exhibit certain "sales-call behaviors."[3] He concluded that there are three steps that lead to more sales:

1. *Let the customer talk more than you do.* According to *SPIN Selling*, "The more your customer talks, the more you will learn about their needs, which puts you in a better position to offer them the most customized and most helpful solutions." Encourage your customers to talk to you about their situations and problems. As they talk, they begin to understand their own needs better and begin to realize the importance of solving their problems.

2. *Ask the right questions!* How do you get customers to talk to you? Rackham notes that you have to ask the right questions. If your sales calls are leaving you with little information, you're not asking the questions that uncover your customers' needs. Instead of focusing on selling your product, focus on listening to your customer. Try to draw him or her out. Be a friend. You need to fully understand his or her problems *before* trying to suggest that your product or service could provide a solution.

3. *Wait to offer products and solutions until later in the call.* First, let your customer talk. Second, once you've got the customer talking, ask the right questions to help uncover his or her problems. Now you are ready to offer your product or service as a solution to one of these problems. As Rackham writes, "You cannot know what solution to offer if you do not uncover customer needs and decision criteria first. For example, if you spend your time with the customer talking about how quiet your machine is, and noise is not a factor your customer cares about, you've wasted your time."[4] You cannot offer a solution until you know what problem the customer needs to solve.

»Analyze Your Sales Calls to Become a Star Salesperson

Performance Objective 3.〉 Every sales call is an opportunity to improve your selling skills—even if you did not make a sale. The star salesperson analyzes each call by asking him/herself:

■ Was I able to get the customer to open up to me? Why, or why not? Did I do or say anything that turned the customer off?

■ Which of my questions did the best job of helping the customer zero in on his/her problems?

■ Was I able to make an honest case for my product/service being the one that could solve the customer's problem?

■ Did I improve my relationship with this person during the call?

---

[3] Ibid., p. 110.
[4] Ibid., p. 84.

Neil Rackham believes that unless you analyze your selling at this level of detail, you will miss important opportunities for learning and improving your selling skills.

»Turning Objections into Advantages

Getting the customer to open up may lead to your being told things you may not want to hear about your product or service. These objections, however, will be valuable sources of marketing data. Sales expert Brian Tracy recommends writing down objections that customers make about your product. He believes all objections fall into one of six categories, and suggests making a list of every objection you've ever heard, and then grouping them under the following headings:

1. Price
2. Performance
3. Follow-up service
4. Competition
5. Support
6. Warranties and assurances[5]

Once you've listed the objections under these headings, take a close look at them. Try to rephrase each set of objections in a single question of 25 words or less.

Work on developing objection-proof answers to each of these questions—answers that are backed by proof, testimonials from customers, research, and data comparing your product with the competition's. If you make the effort to do this, you will learn to appreciate hearing objections.

■ You will have airtight responses, backed by written proof.

■ If you do hear a new objection for which you have not developed a response, you will be excited to get back to the office and do exactly that.

»Use Technology to Sell

Where appropriate and applicable, use the latest advances in technology to sell your product, help your customers understand and use the product, and stay in touch with them. Some examples include the following:

■ A videotaped demonstration or presentation of your product

■ A Web site customers can visit for updates or product facts

■ Using e-mail and faxes to stay in touch with customers

■ Digital planners and calendars—to keep prospect lists organized and log sales calls

---

[5] Brian Tracy, *Be a Sales Superstar: 21 Great Ways to Sell More, Faster, Easier in Tough Markets*, p. 84 (San Francisco: Berrett-Koehler Publishers, 2003).

[Global Impact]

Keep an Open Mind

Your business may be small but do not forget that, via the Internet, you can participate in an exciting global economy. The more you travel and learn about other cultures, the stronger an entrepreneur and business leader you will become. The best entrepreneurs are tolerant and open-minded. They are curious about other countries, other cultures, other ways of life—because these are all potential sources of business.

Perhaps there is a product you will discover on a backpacking trip in Europe that you can profitably import into the United States. Perhaps there is a consumer need you will find while reading about Panama online that you can meet by exporting your product there. Once you realize you are a citizen of the world, the sky is the limit for your career as an entrepreneur.

To *import* means to bring a product made in a different country into your country to sell.
To *export* means to send a product made in your country to a different country to be sold.

All the technological concepts used to identify customers through market research can be instrumental in selling to your segment of the market.

»The One-Minute Sales Call

Believe it or not, it is a challenge for most people to pay attention to someone for more than a minute. You will do best if you keep your sales calls under a minute. Write down your sales pitch and practice delivering it to a friend or relative. Have yourself timed. You will be shocked at how fast a minute can go by! You cannot practice your sales calls enough. Spending time planning a call is better than agonizing over why a call failed.

Here is an example to get you started. Let's say you make baby food from organic fruits and vegetables. You are trying to convince the owner of Johnson's General Store to buy your products.

Hello, Mr. Johnson. Thank you for agreeing to see me today. I'm excited about this product and think you and your customers will be, too.

I brought you a jar of our baby applesauce. It is nicely packaged, don't you think? We hand-decorate each jar. It makes a nice gift for new or expecting parents. The eye-catching ribbons will be sure to attract your customers.

We use only organic fruits and vegetables, no sugar, and very little salt. Our label explains that some babies are sensitive to the additives and dyes found in certain commercial baby foods. These may give sensitive babies headaches or upset stomachs. Our food is very gentle on the baby—and that makes the parents' life much easier!

I understand your concern that our product costs twenty-five cents more per jar than the brand you presently stock. I think your customers will pay more for our high quality and for knowing that their babies are protected from harmful additives or high levels of sugar and salt. Also, because we add very little water to our product, you actually get more food for the money than some of the less expensive brands.

I really think you could start a trend by stocking our baby food, Mr. Johnson. There has been a shift in the market toward healthy food for adults—and those adults are also looking for healthy baby food. Our products combine an eye-catching look with healthy ingredients that new parents and their friends and relatives will not be able to resist. How many jars would you like to order?

»Do Not Forget the Sales Receipt

Once you make a sale, do not forget to fill out a customer receipt. This must include the date of the sale, the amount, and the item description. The receipt is the customer's proof that the item or service was purchased. The carbon copy is a record of income for you.

»Successful Businesses Need Customers Who Return

Once you have made your first sale, you have a customer! Making the sale is actually only the first step in your relationship with this individual. Your real goal is not the first sale, but to develop repeat business—customers who will buy from you over and over again. Successful businesses are not built on single sales but on repeat business. The management of Home Depot has calculated that one satisfied customer is worth more than $25,000 in sales during his or her lifetime!

> *"It is not the bottom line. It is an almost blind, passionate commitment to taking care of customers."*
> —Bernie Marcus, founder, Home Depot

»Customer Service Is Keeping Customers Happy

Customer service is everything you do to keep your customers happy—especially *after* they've bought something. It includes maintaining and repairing the product or service once it has been sold and dealing with customer complaints. Many businesses do not practice customer service because it requires effort, time, and money. Smart entrepreneurs understand, however, that investing in customer service is likely to have a high return.

Here are some examples:

1. Knowing your customer by name
2. Delivering a product on time
3. Helping a customer carry the product to the car
4. Suggesting a less expensive product that will meet the customer's need
5. Providing a full refund to a customer who is dissatisfied
6. Taking time to listen politely and with empathy to a customer's complaint
7. Providing a toll-free customer-assistance phone line

Smart entrepreneurs pay close attention to their customers. They constantly ask questions and analyze their needs. They train their employees to look for customer needs that might be going unfulfilled.

The most successful entrepreneurs become customer service experts. Excellent customer service combined with smart selling and a product that offers a unique competitive advantage will lead to success.

≫ The Costs of Losing a Customer

Have you heard the expression "The customer is always right"? There will be times when a customer may get angry at you, complain, or make demands that you believe are unreasonable.

In *Customer Service: A Practical Approach*, Elaine Harris describes four costs of losing a customer:[6]

1. Loss of current dollars the customer was spending at your business.
2. Loss of jobs. Harris describes an advertising agency that lost one client because of a lack of courtesy and follow-through by the agency. Losing that client forced the owner of the business to close the office, throwing fifty people out of work.
3. Loss of reputation. Remember Joe Girard's Law of 250. Do you really want to send this person away unhappy? One unhappy customer can keep many people away from your business.
4. Loss of future business.

Use your self-control to stay polite, even when a customer is losing his or her temper. Do your best to find a solution that will send him/her away satisfied. Your effort will protect your business and may even earn you a customer for life.

Customer Service is everything you do to keep the customer happy.
(Studio M., The Stock Connection)

[6] Elaine Harris, *Customer Service: A Practical Approach* (Upper Saddle River, NJ: Pearson Education, Inc., 2003).

»Customer Complaints Are Valuable

You may not enjoy hearing a customer complain about your product or service, but a complaint is full of valuable information that no one else will tell you—and you do not have to pay for it! Listen closely to learn what your customers need and want:

- Always acknowledge complaints and criticism and deal with them. Never pretend that you did not hear a negative comment.
- Do not overreact to negative comments. And, above all, do not take them personally!
- Always tell the truth about any negative aspect of your product or service. When you admit a negative, you gain the customer's trust.

> *Keeping a customer's trust after the sale is the most important part of the transaction.*

Remember, a successful business is built on repeat customers. When you listen to a customer, you are building a friendship. You are encouraging loyalty to your business.

»The Better Business Bureau

If you treat a customer badly, he or she may report you to the Better Business Bureau. This is a nonprofit organization that publishes reports about the reliability, honesty, and performance of businesses. It bases much of its reporting on complaints submitted by customers. Think about that when you are tempted to ignore a customer's request or to lose your temper. Even if you believe you are in the right, you could damage your business's reputation.

‹ **4.** Performance Objective

An angry customer can make you feel angry, too. It is crucial that you stay calm, however, when dealing with a customer that is upset. Ask the customer to explain the situation. Do not interrupt him or her. This will give the customer a chance to vent the anger and will probably help him or her to calm down. If you show that you are willing to listen, you will probably defuse much of the irritation.

If the customer is using profanity, however, say something like "I understand your frustration, but I'm not comfortable with the way you are expressing it. Let's find a solution for you."

Elaine Harris provides a list of words to use and words to avoid when dealing with customers.[7] (See Figure 5-2.)

»Customer Service *Is* Marketing

‹ **5.** Performance Objective

Marketing brings a customer to your business, but it does not stop there. Once the customer is inside your door, the treatment should be consistent with your marketing. If your competitive advantage is speedy service, make sure your employees move fast. If your competitive advantage is a cozy, easygoing environment, make sure

---

[7] Elaine Harris, *Customer Service: A Practical Approach* (Upper Saddle River, NJ: Pearson Education, Inc., 2003), p. 77.

Words to Use	Words to Avoid
Please	Cannot
Yes	Never
May I	Do not
Consider this	You have to
Do	Do not tell me no
Let's negotiate	Will not
Will	Not our policy
Thank you	Not my job
You	Profanity
Us	Vulgarity
Appreciate	Problem
Can	Sorry
Use customer's name	Endearments (honey, sweetie, etc.)
Would you like	We'll try
Opportunity	Haven't had time
Challenge	I do not know
Regret	Hang on for a second

Figure 5-2 Words Matter: Smart Customer Service

each customer is warmly welcomed and made to feel at home. Your customer service must reinforce your marketing.

»Customer Service Is a Valuable Source of Market Research

Market research should not end once you open your business. Each customer is a valuable source of facts. Ways to collect market research as part of your customer service include the following:

- Providing a short survey on a stamped postcard with every item purchased. Or include a survey that can be redeemed for a 10 percent discount on the next item purchased.
- Asking selected customers to fill out a longer survey again, offering a discount as an incentive.
- Always ask, and have your employees ask, standard questions when completing a sale, such as "Do you have any suggestions on how we could improve our product?" or "Were you satisfied with the service you received today?"

The best people to market to are those who have already bought or shown interest in your product or service. When a customer makes a purchase, or a potential customer inquires about your business, ask for his or her e-mail address.

»The Customer Database

A **database** is a collection of information that is organized for easy searching. Create a database on your computer to collect any information you obtain from customers. Your database should include every customer you've ever had, for this or any other business, as well as potential customers—friends, family, and other contacts. The database should include each person's name, e-mail address, phone and fax numbers, and mailing address. Also include the date of your last contact and a note about what the person bought. Start collecting this information now and you will be ahead of the game when you are actually ready to start making sales calls or send out marketing material.

As your mailing list grows, you can organize it by region or customer interest and send out targeted e-mails. If you sell gourmet sauces, for example, your notes could tell you whether a customer is interested in hot sauces or dessert sauces. When you add a new hot sauce to your product line, you will know whom to target with an e-mail announcement introducing the sauce, possibly with a special offer.

Make sure that your subject line is effective and interesting. If it isn't, your prospect may not even bother to read the message. *Remember,* most people resent getting e-mail that does not interest them and may even retaliate by "flaming" you. It is a good idea, in fact, to always include an offer to drop people from your mailing list at the end of each message. This shows that you are respectful of their "cyberspace."

≫Mailing Lists

Your access provider will give you software that your computer will use to browse the Internet and to send and receive electronic mail. You can use e-mail to communicate with suppliers and customers and to create a mailing list.

You can also keep in touch with thousands of special-interest newsgroups. As we have mentioned, there are newsgroups online that discuss every subject imaginable. No matter what your business, you are sure to find potential customers talking about their needs in a newsgroup. Newsgroups are excellent sources of information about markets for your business, too.

You can keep your e-mail mailing list on a program such as Outlook Express. Most word-processing programs will allow you to set up a simple table, like this:

Name	Address	Phone	Fax	E-mail	Last purchase	Note

Stay in touch with your customers and potential customers. Build friendships so they will be loyal to your business for life.

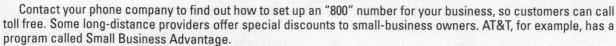

Contact your phone company to find out how to set up an "800" number for your business, so customers can call toll free. Some long-distance providers offer special discounts to small-business owners. AT&T, for example, has a program called Small Business Advantage.

How much will an 800 number for your business cost?

_____

Did you find any special discounts?

_____

» Ask Customers to Refer You to New Customers

If you did a good job for people who needed your product or service, ask them to refer you to others. Offer discounts, gift certificates, and so forth, for referrals. Offer business cards for customers to pass on to their friends.

» Build a Web Site

It is not as hard to design your own Web site as you might think. Many Internet Service Providers (ISPs) are making it easier by offering home pages as part of the deal. Software such as Dreamweaver even enables you to design a Web site without having to learn HTML (HyperText Markup Language), the programming language used to create Web pages.

When you build your own Web site, be sure to register it with at least three of the major search engines. The search engine will allow you to register both your URL and keywords to associate with it.

» Chapter Summary

Now that you have studied this chapter you can do the following:

1. Explain the difference between features and benefits.
   - Features are qualities a product or service has.
   - Benefits are what the product or service can do to fill a need for a customer.
2. Use the principles of selling to make effective sales calls.
   - Make a good personal impression.
   - Know your product or service.
   - Believe in your product or service.
   - Know your field.
   - Know your customers.
   - Prepare your sales presentation.
   - Think positively.
   - Keep good records.
   - Make an appointment.
   - Treat your customers like gold.

3. Analyze and improve your sales calls.

■ Was I able to get the customer to open up to me? Why or why not? Did I do or say anything that turned the customer off?

■ Which of my questions did the best job of helping the customer zero in on his/her problems?

■ Was I able to make an honest case for my product/service being the one that could solve the customer's problem?

■ Did I improve my relationship with this person during this call?

4. Handle customer complaints effectively.

■ A customer complaint is full of valuable information that no one else will tell you.

■ Stay calm when dealing with a customer that is upset. Ask the customer to explain the situation. Do not interrupt. This will give the customer a chance to vent and will probably help him or her to calm down. If you show that you are willing to listen, you will probably defuse much of the customer's irritation.

5. Provide great customer service.

■ Customer service is everything you do to keep your customers happy—especially *after* they've bought something. It includes maintaining and repairing the product or service once it has been sold, and dealing with customer complaints.

■ A successful business is built on repeat customers.

Key Terms

commission	newsgroup
customer service	prospect
database	sales call
e-mail	spam

[Entrepreneurship Portfolio]

1. Describe the features of each product listed below and then create a "benefit" statement for each that you would use as selling points.

   Product

   miniature cell phone

   wristwatch with daily events calendar

   milk-free chocolate

   vegetarian dog food

2. Create a database for your business. Which five questions will you ask every customer? **(Business Plan Practice)**

3. Describe a business that you deal with as a customer. Describe the customer service at this business. What do you like (or dislike) about it? How could it be improved?

Critical Thinking Exercises

4. List five things you intend to do at your business to offer superior customer service.

5. Come up with five sales-call prospects for your business. Prequalify the prospects using these questions: (1) Is the prospect in my market? (2) Does he/she need my product/service? (3) Can he/she afford it?

6. Have you created any marketing materials for your business? If so, have three friends and a mentor (someone older whom you respect and who can give you good business advice) look at your materials and give you feedback. Write a memo listing their suggestions and what you plan to do to improve your marketing materials.

7. Write a one-minute sales call for the product (or service) your business will be selling. **(Business Plan Practice)** Try your pitch out on a partner and write down his or her objections. Rewrite your pitch to incorporate these criticisms. Try your pitch again. Repeat this process until you think you have a strong sales call.

Key Concept Questions

1. Explain Joe Girard's "Law of 250" in your own words, with examples from your own life.

2. Why is customer service an extension of marketing?

3. Give three reasons why you think it is important to keep collecting market research even after you have opened your business.

4. How do you intend to look when you start selling your product/service, and why?

5. Brainstorm ways that you can use technology in order to sell.

6. List three ways you intend to provide superior customer service. **(Business Plan Practice)**

7. Create a company signature for your business e-mail. Keep it under eight words.

Application Exercises

1. Develop a one-minute sales pitch for three items that you are wearing. Try out the pitch for each on a partner. Have your partners help you time the pitches to a minute.

2. Write a memo to your partner discussing his/her sales calls and how they could be improved. Use the Eight Steps of a Sales Call as your guide when analyzing your partner's efforts.

3. Arrange to receive a sales pitch from a competitor in the business field that you intend to enter. After the presentation, write down your objections to purchasing the product/service. Use Brian Tracy's method to categorize your objections and then phrase them in a single question composed of 25 words or less.

Visit three businesses in your community and note how you are treated. Write a memo comparing the customer service at each. Include such information as the following: Were you greeted when you came in? Did anyone offer to help you? If you bought something, were you given a survey?

Exploring Your Community

CASE STUDY: Outrageous Service

If you visit highly successful companies such as Federal Express, Southwest Airlines, or Motorola, you will learn about a series of stories, and heroes that express the organizations' "corporate culture." Often the heroes you hear about are employees who provided some form of customer service that was "beyond the call of duty." Ginger Trumfio, assistant editor of *Sales & Marketing Management*, says that keeping customers happy and coming back requires more than smiles and thank-yous. She believe that building customer loyalty requires "outrageous" service:

In today's business climate salespeople need to do more than follow up on promises, meet deadlines, and create win-win situations to keep clients happy—and coming back. Salespeople need to be outrageous, shocking, even death-defying.

Does good customer service really require this much effort? Trumfio contacted several sales forces to find examples of outrageous service. Two examples follow.

1. The industry standard for morning express air carrier deliveries had been 10:30 A.M. Xerox Corporation had a critical need to get emergency parts to its technicians much earlier. Airborne Express carefully studied Xerox's needs and developed a plan to guarantee delivery times across the United States that ranged from 8:00 to 9:30 A.M. Airborne took several steps to track Xerox packages throughout the process of delivery. For example, every driver's scanner has been coded to beep and read "Xerox" when there is a Xerox package to be delivered. Once the drivers realize they have an urgent Xerox package, the load plan is prioritized to make that delivery first.

2. David Lubelkin, president of Industrial Edge, USA, an apartment house supply company in Orange, New Jersey, gave outrageous service during a winter snowstorm. On a cold January day, after a major snowfall, he received a call from a desperate customer who needed 60 pounds of rock salt to be delivered to a property located 100 miles away. Predictions of sleet and icy rain threatened to bring traffic to a halt. Knowing that his delivery trucks were already on the road and not due back until late in the day, Lubelkin promised to deliver the salt needed. He quickly met with company CEO Stephen Weintraub and a decision was made to rent a truck to make the delivery. The trip, normally an hour and a half drive, turned into a four and a half hour crawl at an average speed of 20 miles per hour. After dropping off the salt, the return trip took even longer. It was 10:00 P.M. when the truck finally returned to the office.

Case Study Analysis

1. Do you believe that outrageous service is needed to build customer loyalty? Explain.

2. Is there a downside to outrageous service after a sale has been made?

3. How do acts of outrageous service influence the organization's "corporate culture"?

CASE SOURCES

Manning, G. *Selling Today*. 8th edition, 2001. Reprinted by permission of Pearson Education, Inc., Upper Saddle River, NJ.

Adelman, Philip J.; Marks, Alan M. *Entrepreneurial Finance: Finance of Small Business*, 2nd edition, 2001. Reprinted by permission of Pearson Education, Inc., Upper Saddle River, NJ.

Lambing, Peggy A.; Kuehl, Charles, R. *Entrepreneurship*, 3rd edition, 2003. Reprinted by permission of Pearson Education, Inc., Upper Saddle River, NJ.

Decenzo, David A.; Silhanek, Beth. *Human Relations: Personal and Professional Development*. 2nd edition, 2002. Reprinted by permission of Pearson Education, Inc., Upper Saddle River, NJ.

CASE STUDY: Jorge Diaz, "Sonic Studio"[8]

Jorge Diaz had always dreamed about owning his own music recording studio. As a teenager growing up on the southwest side of Chicago, Diaz would spend hours in his room mixing different songs on the computer with his friends. He even recorded a few demo tapes and was able to get his tracks played on local radio stations. When he turned 21, Diaz started going to live shows almost every night of the week. If a new band was performing, Diaz could be counted on to show up and stay for the entire set. Over time, he became a well-known fixture in the alternative music scene. People liked Diaz and they trusted his opinions about music.

A Business Is Born

So, in January 1999, when Diaz decided to open a record store and build a makeshift recording studio in the basement, all of his musician friends came over to lend a hand with his new business, Chi-Town Records. After he closed up the store, Diaz and his friends would retreat downstairs to the basement studio where they would experiment with recording new songs. Diaz did not think about the recording studio as an actual business. It was the record store upstairs that consumed most of his time and attention.

After a few years, Diaz noticed that he was spending more time in the recording studio than in the record shop. Word of mouth spread about Diaz's underground studio, and steadily, demand

for his recording services increased. He was especially popular with new bands that did not have a lot of money to invest to record their first albums. Diaz realized that he couldn't continue to let everyone use his equipment for nothing and so he started charging a small fee—just enough to cover his costs and earn a modest profit. Sometimes he bartered with the bands, allowing them to work in the record store in exchange for studio time. He decided to give the studio a formal name—La Nueva Recording Lounge, or "The Lounge," for short. In March 2003, he sold Chi-Town Records so that he could focus on The Lounge full time.

Diaz Negotiates a Deal

Slowly but surely, Diaz's recording equipment started to show signs of wear and tear. He believed that The Lounge had the potential to expand and serve more customers because his studio was consistently booked three months in advance. To take his business to the next level, Diaz concluded that he would need to purchase high-quality audio equipment. But where would he get the money for this? Diaz came up with an idea. He had heard about a studio designer who was looking for a facility to test the new mixing speakers he had invented. Diaz contacted the designer and offered him free rein to redo the studio to his specifications. In return, the designer agreed to lower his fee. Normally, this studio designer would have been far too expensive, but Diaz found a way to negotiate what he thought was a win-win situation. Diaz was so excited about the new high-tech equipment he would be installing that he decided to rename his business "Sonic Studio" to reflect the change.

Poor Planning Leads to Problems

It took the designer four months to transform "The Lounge" into "Sonic Studio." This was much longer than Diaz had anticipated, although he never did sign a formal contract with the designer. When the renovations were finally complete, Diaz had spent more money on the studio upgrade than he had initially planned. The designer kept convincing him that he "just had to have" this latest piece of equipment so that he could maximize the quality of the new mixing speakers. Diaz lost revenue on The Lounge because he was unable to operate his business while the renovations were taking place.

[8] Note: This is a fictional case.

Once the studio had finally reopened, Diaz felt he had no choice but to raise his rates. The new higher fees he was charging were a turn-off to his loyal client base of struggling musicians. Some of his old friends even accused him of "selling out." This made him feel bad. But what could he do? He tried to attract established recording artists to Sonic Studio but discovered that this wealthier clientele preferred to use the more spacious studios located in downtown Chicago.

Plotting Strategy

Diaz was determined to transform Sonic Studio into a profitable business. How could he achieve this goal? Maybe he needed to rethink his pricing (Figure 5-3). He was currently charging clients $110 per hour for studio time. Diaz looked at the other monthly fixed costs (Figure 5-4).

Economics of One Unit (EOU) Analysis		
One Unit of Sale = One (1) hour of studio time		
Selling Price		**110**
COGS (direct cost of the product or service)		
Direct Labor ($40/hr.)	40	
Supplies used per hr. (avg.)	10	
Total COGS	50	50
Gross Profit		60
Other Variable Costs (none)	–	–
Contribution Margin		60

Figure 5-3 COGs and Other Var. Costs

Fixed Costs per Month		
Fixed Costs		**500**
Utilities		
Salaries		
Part-time employees	900	
Salary for Diaz	1,500	
Total Salaries	2,400	2,400
Advertising		250
Interest on Business Loan		350
Insurance		500
Rent		1,000
Depreciation		500
Total Fixed Costs		**5,500**

Figure 5-4 Fixed costs.

A Dilemma

As Diaz examined his finances, many questions troubled him. He figured that, if he somehow lowered his costs, then he could afford to charge his customers less money per hour for studio time. This would make his old clients happy. To reduce his costs, he wondered whether he should pay himself a lower hourly rate for his own labor. Did this make sense? Or maybe he could hire another employee who would do the same work for less money. But Diaz liked helping bands record their albums in the studio. He did not want to give up this aspect of the business.

Diaz had hired a part-time employee who worked an average of 60 hours a month and this was costing him roughly $900. The employee was responsible for bookkeeping, purchasing supplies, and scheduling customers at the studio. Perhaps he ought to terminate the employee and take on the extra workload. Diaz quickly remembered that he hated these organizational tasks. He would rather pay somebody else to do them.

Diaz was also paying himself a monthly salary of $1,500. Since he owned the business outright, Diaz understood that he could structure his salary in untraditional ways. Instead of having Sonic Studio pay him a monthly fixed salary of $1,500, he could defer his compensation until the business was profitable again. At the end of the year he could see how much net profit Sonic had generated and then pay himself a percentage of this amount. But then, what if Sonic Studio lost money and there was no profit remaining at the end of the year? And, in the meantime, how would he pay his own personal bills, which averaged $1,200 per month?

Diaz knew that he did not want to run Sonic Studio forever. At some point he would want to sell his business and use the money for other things, like buying a home or taking a trip around the world. And when this time came, he would want the business to be earning a healthy profit so that he could sell it at a competitive price. Diaz's head hurt. He needed to come up with a plan. He decided to sleep on it and figure things out in the morning.

Case Study Analysis

1. There are five primary ways for an entrepreneur to get paid:
   - Hourly wage (comes out of the cost of goods sold)
   - Salary (fixed cost)
   - Commission (variable cost)

- Ownership (taking a portion of the net profit from the business)
- Selling all or part of the business (trading equity for cash)

Given the circumstances described in the case, decide how Diaz should pay himself. Remember that he can use any combination of the methods just outlined. What are the pros and cons of each of these payment strategies?

2. Under Diaz's current cost structure, how many hours of studio time would he need to sell in order to break even?

3. Should Diaz try to recapture his old target market of struggling musicians, or should he identify a new target market for Sonic Studio? Explain.

4. List the features and the benefits of Sonic Studio. Which should he focus on when selling, and why?

5. Review Diaz's cost structure. If you were his business advisor, what would you suggest that he do differently to transform Sonic Studio into a profitable business?

6. At the end of the case, Diaz mentions that he plans to sell his business at some point in the future. One of the ways that entrepreneurs can make money is by starting a business that delivers value to customers and then selling it to investors or another business. Answer the following:

- Why is Diaz concerned with Sonic Studio earning a profit if his ultimate goal is to sell the business?
- How do you think investors decide how much a business is "worth"?

Unit 2 BUSINESS PLAN PRACTICE

At the end of each unit, you will have an opportunity to work on your own business plan. Please go to the Business Plan Worksheet Template section for Unit Two on the BizBuilder CD now to develop the following segments of your plan:

Use the following chart to determine your tactics for carrying out your business strategy.

Tactical Questions	Issues	Solutions
1. Sales Plan: Where and how will you sell to your customers?	How to identify prospects and convert them to sales.	
2. Market Communications: How will you communicate with your customers and make them aware of your business offer?	How to make customers aware of your offer; how to attract them to the business.	
3. Operating Plan: How will you manage your internal operations?	How to make the business go, and determine who will perform the tasks.	
4. Budget: How do you plan to manage your revenues and expenses?	What are the sources of revenue; what are the items that have to be purchased?	

1. Describe your strategy for outperforming the competition.
2. What tactics will you use to carry out this strategy?

3. Write a mission statement for your business in fewer than three sentences that clearly states your competitive advantage, strategy, and tactics.

Marketing Step 1: Consumer Analysis

1. Describe your market research methods (surveys, focus groups, general research, statistical research).
2. Describe your target consumer:

   Age: _____

   Gender: _____

   Income: _____

   Other: _____

Marketing Step 2: Market Analysis

1. How large is your potential market?
2. Will you analyze your market segment by location, population, personality, or behavior?
3. Use your market-analysis method to describe your market segment. Roughly, how many consumers are in your market segment?
4. Explain how your marketing plan targets your market segment.
5. What percentage of the market do you feel you need to capture for your business to be profitable?

6. Who are the potential customers you plan to approach in the first two months of business?
7. Write a positioning statement for your business.
8. Where is your product/service in the product life cycle?

Marketing Step 3: The Marketing Mix

1. Explain why your product will meet a consumer need.
2. Describe your pricing strategy.
3. Where do you intend to sell your product? Describe the advantages and disadvantages of your location(s).
4. How do you plan to promote your business?

   a. What is your business slogan? Do you have a logo for your business? How do you intend to protect it?

   b. Where do you intend to advertise?

   c. How do you plan to get publicity?

Promotions	Door-to-Door	Online	Street	Store/Office	Other
800 number					
Billboards					
Brochures					
Business cards					
Catalog					
Demonstration					
Direct mail					
E-mail/fax					
Flyers					
Free gifts					
Online store					
Phone calls					
Posters					
Promo items					
Sales calls					
Samples					
Special events					
Web site					

5. How will your business help others? List all organizations to which you plan to contribute. (Your contribution may be time, money, your product, or something else.)

6. Do you intend to publicize your philanthropy? Why, or why not? If you do, explain how you will work philanthropy into your marketing.

Marketing Mix Chart
My Market Segment:

Marketing Mix	Decision	Explanation
Product		
Price		
Place		
Promotion		
Philanthropy		

Marketing Step 4: Breakeven Analysis

Use Excel or Lotus 1–2–3 to create a spreadsheet projecting the marketing expenses for your business for six months. Use this data to perform a breakeven analysis of your marketing plan.

Sales and Customer Service

1. Describe the features and benefits of the product (or service) your own business will focus on selling.
2. Choose three ways you plan to sell your product or service. Describe why you have chosen these three methods and why you think they will work.
3. Write a one-minute sales pitch for your product (or service).
4. Describe five sales prospects you intend to pitch.
5. Show examples of marketing materials you intend to use to sell.
6. List three ways you intend to provide superior customer service.
7. How will you keep your customer database? What five questions will you ask every customer to answer?

Show Me the Money!: How to Track Costs and Find Financing

## Chapter 6

Tracking Fixed and Variable Costs

"All our records had to be hits because we couldn't afford any flops."

—Berry Gordy, founder, Motown Record Company

Performance Objectives

1. Describe the variable costs of starting a business.
2. Analyze your fixed operating costs and calculate gross profit.
3. Choose the right insurance products for your business.
4. Set up financial recordkeeping for your business.

Anyone can spend unlimited amounts of money and create a good product, but the entrepreneur's goal is to create a product that costs less than the consumer is willing to pay for it. An entrepreneur's ability to find creative ways to cut costs often means the difference between a struggling business and a thriving one.

» Ford: Lowering Costs through Assembly-Line Manufacturing*

Entrepreneurs scrambling for ways to lower their costs have created some of our society's most powerful breakthroughs. When Henry Ford was trying to make his vision of an automobile in front of every home in America a reality, it was the *cost* of building a "horseless carriage" that stood in his way. The motorcar was considered a novelty for rich people. But Ford was determined to build one that almost anyone could afford.

In those days, cars were manufactured one at a time. This was a slow, expensive process that involved a lot of labor to build each car. To cut manufacturing costs, Ford had his cars assembled as they moved on a conveyer belt past the workers, with each worker responsible for attaching one item. This **moving assembly line** produced cars quickly with much lower labor costs per unit. The assembly-line concept revolutionized manufacturing and was adopted by many other companies to make products that were previously too expensive to mass-produce. Industrial production exploded in America, as the moving assembly line made it possible for companies to lower their costs enough to sell the average consumer products—from washing machines to refrigerators—that previously only the well-to-do could afford. Ford revolutionized industry by introducing the concept of mass production on a grand scale.

---

*Special thanks to John Harris for reviewing this chapter.

Workers assembling engines on the line at the General Motors plant in Baltimore.
(Jim Pickerell, The Stock Connection)

»Define Your Unit of Sale

To run a successful business, you will need to keep a grip on your costs. A business earns a profit by selling products or services.

Since everything sold has a related cost (or costs), the business can make a profit only if the selling price per unit is greater than the costs per unit. Understanding the **economics of one unit** (EOU) tells an entrepreneur if the business is earning a profit.

Before you can get a grip on your costs, you must determine your unit of sale. Entrepreneurs commonly define the unit of sale as follows:

- One item, or unit (if the product is sold by the piece)
- One hour of time (if work is billed by the hour)
- One job or contract (e.g., mowing one lawn or washing one car)
- One dozen or more of an item (for wholesale businesses, particularly)
- Different combinations of items expressed as an average sale per customer (say, $25 at a restaurant or $15 at a hardware store)

»Costs: Fixed and Variable

After you have clearly defined your unit of sale, you can begin to calculate the economics of that unit for the product or service. You do that by calculating the costs of one unit of sale.

Small business owners divide their costs into two categories: **variable costs** and **fixed costs.**

Performance Objective   1.»

Variable costs vary (change) with sales. They are broken into two subcategories:

1. Cost of goods sold (COGS), which are the costs associated specifically with each unit of sale, include the following:

- The cost of materials used to make the product (or deliver the service)
- The cost of labor used to make the product (or deliver the service)

2. Other variable costs that can figure in the economics of one unit include the following:
   - Commissions
   - Shipping and handling charges, etc.

Fixed costs stay constant whether you sell many units, or very few. Examples of fixed costs include rent, salaries, insurance, equipment, and manufacturing plants.

Henry Ford spent money on efficient manufacturing equipment (a fixed cost) but saved a fortune on labor (COGS) by doing so. This reduced his total costs because labor was used in each of the millions of cars Ford made, but he only had to pay for the plant and equipment once.

For any unit of sale, you can study its EOU to figure out what it cost you to make that sale. Figure 6-1 shows an example from a business that sells hand-painted vintage T-shirts.

»Calculating Total Gross Profit and Contribution Margin

You can use EOU to calculate how much you will come out ahead on each sale. The EOU will help you figure the gross profit per unit (COGS and the **contribution margin** per unit sold—the selling price minus total variable costs (COGS) plus other variable costs).

Economics of One Unit (EOU) Analysis				
(Define the unit of sale)				
Selling Price (per Unit)				**35.00**
COGS (Cost of Goods Sold)				
Materials per Unit		7.00		
Labor per hour	10.00			
# of Hours per Unit	3/4			
Total Labor per Unit	7.50	7.50		
Total COGS (per Unit)		14.50	14.50	14.50
Gross Profit (per Unit)				**20.50**
Other Variable Costs				
Commission (10%)		3.50		
Packaging		0.50		
Total Other Variable Costs		4.00	4.00	4.00
Total Variable Costs (per Unit)			18.50	
Contribution Margin				16.50

Figure 6-1 Manufacturing business: Unit = 1 hand-painted t-shirt.

»Calculating EOU When You Sell More Than One Product

A business selling a variety of products has to create a separate EOU for each to determine whether each product is profitable. When there are many similar products, a "typical EOU" can be used.

Example: Jimmy sells four different kinds of candy bars at his school. He sells them all at $1, but he pays a different wholesale price for each bar. His costs are the following:

a. Snickers   36¢ each
b. Almond Joy   38¢ each
c. Butterfinger   42¢ each
d. Baby Ruth   44¢ each

Rather than make a separate EOU for each similar product, Jimmy uses one EOU with the average cost of his candy bars. (See Figure 6-2.)

Costs of the four candy bars = (36¢ + 38¢ + 42¢ + 44¢) ÷ 4

Average cost of the four candy bars = $1.60 ÷ 4

Average cost of each bar = 40¢

Using an average works if the costs are similar, and as long as Jimmy sells roughly the same number of each type of candy bar. If he can no longer get Snickers and Almond Joy, for example, he might have to change his EOU to reflect the higher price of the other bars.

What if each unit of sale is made up of a complex mix of materials and labor? The economics of one unit can still help you figure the COGS, other variable costs, and gross profit for the product.

Example: Janelle sells turkey sandwiches from her deli cart downtown on Saturdays. She sells each for $5.

The materials and labor that go directly into making each sandwich are the COGS (also called **inventory costs** until the sandwich is sold). There will also be some other variable costs, such as napkins, a paper wrapping for each sandwich, and plastic bags.

Assume the employee making the sandwich earns $7 per hour and can make ten sandwiches in one hour.

First, make a list of COGS, and any other variable costs:

Economics of One Unit (EOU) Analysis		
One Unit of Sale = One (1) candy bar		
Selling Price		1.00
COGS (direct cost of the product or service)		
Average Cost of Candy Bars (COGS)	0.40	
Average Shipping Cost per Unit	0.06	
Total COGS	0.46	0.46
Gross Profit		0.54
Other Variable Costs (none)	–	–
Contribution Margin		0.54

Figure 6-2 Retail business: Unit = 1 candy bar.

COGS

a. Turkey costs $2.60 per lb. Each sandwich uses 4 oz. of turkey meat (16 oz./1 lb.).

b. Bread (large rolls) cost $1.92 per dozen. One roll is used per sandwich.

c. One ounce of mayonnaise is used per sandwich. A 32-ounce jar of mayo costs $1.60.

d. Lettuce costs 80 cents per lb. and 1/16 of a pound (1 ounce) is used on each sandwich.

e. Tomatoes cost $1.16 each. Each sandwich uses a fourth of a tomato.

f. Each sandwich comes with two pickles. Pickles cost 5 cents each.

g. Employees are paid $7 per hour and can make ten sandwiches per hour.

Other Variable Costs

The following supplies are used every time a sandwich is sold:

a. Napkins cost $3 per pack of 100. One napkin is included with each sale.

b. Paper wrapping costs 20 cents per foot (on a roll). Each sandwich uses two feet of paper.

c. Plastic carryout bags cost $7 per roll of 100. Each sandwich sold uses one plastic carryout bag.

The EOU for the turkey sandwich is shown in Figure 6-3.

Retail Business: unit = 1 turkey sandwich					Date: 12/1/2008
Selling Price per Unit:					$5.00
Cost of Goods Sold	Price	Units	Quantity Used	Cost Each	
Turkey (4 oz.):	$2.60	Per lb.	¼ lb.	$0.65	
Bread (roll):	$1.92	Per dozen	½ lb.	$0.16	
Mayonnaise (1 oz.):	$1.60	Per 32-oz. jar	$\frac{1}{32}$ lb.	$0.05	
Lettuce (1 oz.):	$0.80	Per lb.	$\frac{1}{16}$ lb.	$0.05	
Tomato ¼ lb.	$1.16	Each	¼ each	$0.29	
Pickles (2):	$0.05	Each	2 pickles	0.10	
Direct Labor (6 min.):	$7.00	Per hr.	$\frac{1}{10}$ hr.	0.70	
Total Cost of Goods Sold per Unit:				$2.00	**$2.00**
Gross Profit					**$3.00**
Other Variable Costs					
Napkin:	$3.00	Per 100-pack	$\frac{1}{100}$ pack	0.03	
Paper Wrapping:	$0.20	Per foot	2 feet	0.40	
Plastic Bag:	$7.00	Per roll (100)	$\frac{1}{100}$ roll	0.07	
Total Other Variable Costs per Unit:				$0.50	
Total Variable Costs per Unit:					0.50
Contribution Margin per Unit:					$2.50

Figure 6-3 Economics of one unit.

»Fixed Operating Costs

Performance
Objective 2.›

Costs such as rent or the DSL bill are called **fixed operating costs.** Fixed operating costs are not included in COGS (or COSS) because they are not direct costs of creating each product (or service).[1] Fixed operating costs are not included in other variable costs because they do not vary with the number of sales made.

Fixed operating costs do not change based on sales; therefore, they are not included in the EOU. A sandwich shop has to pay the same rent each month whether it sells one turkey sandwich or a hundred.

An easy way to remember the seven common fixed operating costs is USAIIRD:

> *Operating costs are also called* **overhead.** *This is an informal term for "fixed" costs. Overhead comes from the literal "over head"—that is, the roof over the business.*

Utilities (gas, electric, telephone, Internet service)

Salaries

Advertising

Insurance

Interest

Rent

Depreciation

Most of these categories are self-explanatory, but depreciation and insurance are important concepts entrepreneurs use to protect their businesses.

Depreciation is a method used to "expense" expensive pieces of equipment. Fixed costs are "expensed" (meaning counted as an expense) during the year the money is spent. When a company pays for advertising, for example, it subtracts that cost from gross profit for that year. Some items, however, such as a computer, last for a number of years. A business could choose to expense a computer during the year it was bought. That's not very accurate, however, because a computer that will last for four years is only 25 percent "used up" during the year it was purchased. Expensing the entire cost of the computer during that year makes the company's accounting records and financial statements inaccurate. If more than 25 percent of the computer's cost is expensed in the first year, the business income statement will show a lower profit than it really should. Meanwhile, profits in subsequent years will appear to be higher than they should.

This problem is solved by depreciation, which spreads the cost of an item purchased by a business over the period of time during which it is actually in use. If the computer will last for four years, then by expensing 25 percent of the cost each year, the cost of the computer will be spread out realistically and accurately, which is an important accounting principle.

---

[1]Cost of Goods Sold is used for businesses that sell products. Service businesses use the term Cost of Services Sold (COSS).

»How Inflation Hurts Small Business Owners

Inflation, the gradual rise in the prices of goods and services in an economy, is the enemy of the small business owner. If you put aside $600 per year to buy new tables and chairs for your restaurant, but find at the end of five years that the cost of replacing them has risen, due to inflation, to $5,000, you could be driven out of business if you cannot come up with the additional $2,000. Smart entrepreneurs educate themselves about economic trends by reading the financial section of the newspaper and financial magazines.

»Insurance Protects Your Business from Disaster

Insurance protects people and businesses from having property or wealth stolen, lost, or destroyed. There are many kinds of insurance, and almost anything can be insured.

If you owned a restaurant, for example, you would need fire insurance. Your insurance agent would help you calculate how much money it would take to replace everything in the restaurant and rebuild if a fire were to destroy it. If you borrowed money from a bank to buy equipment for the restaurant, the bank would require you to carry insurance.

Assume rebuilding your restaurant would cost $150,000. You would need an insurance policy that would guarantee you $150,000 in case of fire. You might pay $100 per month, for instance. This monthly payment is the **premium.**

Insurance protects your business from disasters like this fire, fought by firefighters in Virginia. (Joe Sohm/Chromosohm, The Stock Connection)

As long as you pay the premiums on your fire insurance policy, you will not have to worry about losing your restaurant to a fire. If it burns down, your insurance policy will pay you to rebuild and continue the business. Insurance prevents random events from destroying you financially.

»Basic Coverage for Small Business

Performance Objective 3. 〉 You will not need insurance if you are simply selling ties on the street or at school, but the moment you move your business into a building, you will need it.

A **deductible** is the amount of loss or damage you agree to cover before the insurance takes over. In the restaurant example, the owner might feel confident that he or she could cover $5,000 in damages from a fire without going bankrupt. The insurance company would have to pay the remaining $145,000 in case of fire. So it would charge a lower premium, say, $90 per month. The policyholder pays a lower premium in return for a higher deductible.

When buying insurance, choose the policy with the highest deductible you can afford to cover. This will give you the lowest possible premium.

Lower deductible = Higher premium

Higher deductible = Lower premium

Although state laws vary, most require business owners who have people working for them to carry the following:

- *Workers' Compensation*—Covers employees for loss of income and medical expenses due to job-related injuries.
- *Disability Insurance*—Covers employees for loss of income due to a disabling injury or illness.

If you have a car or truck, you must carry the following:

- *Auto Insurance*—Covers your liability for personal injuries in an accident, as well as damages to any vehicle involved and injuries to other persons.

Other important types of insurance are the following:

- *Property Insurance*—Replaces any property damaged by fire, flood, vandalism, or other types of damage as specified in the policy.
- *Crime Insurance*—Protects against robberies as well as theft by employees. The federal government has a program that provides crime insurance for small businesses located in high-crime areas where insurance companies usually will not provide coverage.

Still other types of insurance are available that can be tailored to the needs and resources of your business. When you are ready to take this step, ask other businesspeople to refer you to a good insurance agent.

»Liability Insurance Protects You and Your Customers

What if someone visiting your store trips on a loose tile and breaks an arm? Who pays the medical bills? Smart entrepreneurs carry **liability insurance,** which pays the expenses of anyone who is injured while on your property or using your product or service.

Before you decide to sell a product or offer a service, try to imagine how it could cause injury to someone. If you think it might cause injury, do not sell it.

»How Insurance Companies Make Money

By now you may be wondering, "How can an insurance company afford to pay $150,000 to a restaurant owner whose place has just burned down, if the owner has only been paying the insurance company $100 a month?"

The answer is that insurance companies employ experts who calculate the odds of a particular event actually happening. An insurance company that specializes in fire insurance, for example, will have information about fires in restaurants going back many years. Analysts at the company study this information and figure out how often fires tend to occur and how much they cost.

Analysts decide how much to charge for premiums so that, even if some fires do occur, the cost of insurance paid out to one policyholder has been covered by the premiums paid by the many other policyholders.

[Entrepreneurial Wisdom]

Lying about the Risks of Your Product Is Fraud

Failure to inform a customer of potential danger from your product or service is called **fraud.** If a customer proves that you knew your product or service was dangerous but you sold it anyway, you could be forced by a court to pay damages.

The entrepreneur has a moral duty to inform customers of possible danger. The best idea is not to sell a product or service that could cause harm. Even if you are selling something as "safe" as ties, make sure they are not made of highly flammable material!

Before you decide to sell a product or offer a service, try to imagine how it might possibly cause injury to someone. If you think it might injure a customer, do not sell it.

»Keep at Least Three Months of Fixed Operating Costs in Reserve

During the early days of your business, when you are working hard to attract customers and establish your reputation, you may not be making many sales, but you will still have your fixed operating costs. If you are not prepared for this, you could be forced out of business because you did not pay the rent or utilities.

Try to put enough money in the bank to cover at least one-half of your start-up costs *before you open your business.* This money is called a **cash reserve.** A reserve is money you keep for emergencies—such as not being able to sell your handmade swimsuits because it has been raining for a month! A reserve will keep your business going during tough times, while you think of new ways to attract customers.

You can build up a reserve through savings, borrowing, or from investors.

»Fixed Operating Costs Do Change over Time

If you pay your restaurant manager $3,600 per month in salary, you will have to pay that amount whether the restaurant sells one meal or a thousand. The cost is fixed.

Fixed operating costs do change over time—at some point you may give your restaurant manager a raise, for example. The word *fixed* does not mean the cost *never* changes, just that it does not change in response to sales. For instance:

- *Advertising*—The cost of advertising will change based on decisions the entrepreneur makes about how much to spend to reach the consumer, not because of current sales.
- *Heating Costs*—The price of heating goes up and down based on the weather, not on the amount of revenue the business earns.

»Allocate Your Fixed Operating Costs Where Possible

Business owners like to know, whenever they sell a unit, how much of the revenue will have to be used to cover cost of goods sold and other variable costs.

Whatever is left over after you pay COGS and other variable costs is your contribution margin. You will pay your fixed operating costs out of your contribution margin. Whatever is left over after you pay your fixed operating costs (and taxes) is your **net profit.**

Fixed operating costs can be dangerous because they have to be paid whether or not the business makes any gross profit. The entrepreneur should be cautious about taking on fixed costs. An entrepreneur does not have to worry quite so much about variable costs because, if sales are low, variable costs will be low as well.

Wherever possible, the entrepreneur seeks to **allocate** (include) as many costs as possible in the EOU by making them variable.

Here is an example of how to fully allocate your costs, so that you know, each time you sell a unit, how much of your fixed and variable costs the sale covers.

Example: Say you sell 300 watches per month at $15 per watch. (See Figure 6-4.) Your COGS is $2 per watch and your other variable costs are commissions of $1 per watch and shipping charges of $1 per watch.

Gross profit per unit is $13 ($3,900 in gross profit divided by 300 watches sold). Contribution margin per unit is $11 ($3,300 ÷ 300). Some of this gross profit will have to be used to cover the business's fixed operating costs. How much profit will be left over after paying the fixed operating costs? (Figure 6-5 shows the calculation of the total cost per unit.)

For every watch you sell, your total cost, fixed and variable, is $5.50. If you receive $15 for each watch, therefore, your profit before tax is the following:

$15.00 selling price – $5.50 total cost per unit = $9.50 profit before tax

Analysis – 300 watches sold			
Sales (300 watches x $15 per watch):			4,500
COGS ($2 per watch x 300 watches):		600	600
Gross Profit (on 300 watches sold)			3,900
Other Variable Costs			
Commission ($2 per watch)	600		
Shipping ($1 per watch)	300		
Total Other Variable Costs	900	900	900
Total Variable Costs (per Unit)		1,500	
Contribution Margin			3,000

Figure 6-4 Retail business: Unit = 1 watch.

Total Variable Costs (COGS + Other Variable Costs):		$1,500
Fixed Operating Costs (per month):		
Utilities	$50	
Salaries	$100	
Advertising	$50	
Insurance	$50	
Interest	$50	
Rent	$100	
Depreciation	$50	
Total Fixed Operating Costs:	$450	450
Total Costs (Fixed + Variable) =		$1,950
Total Cost per Unit ($1,950/300 watches) =		$6.50 per watch

Figure 6-5 Retail business: Total cost per unit.

[Step into the Shoes]

Bob's Discount Furniture[2]

Bob Kaufman owns 20 furniture stores in New England (with more on the way). Bob's Discount Furniture is one of the largest TV advertisers in Connecticut. When Bob was starting out in the furniture business in 1992, though, he needed to find creative ways to cut his costs.

Bob found a store to rent for his furniture business, but the landlord wanted him to sign a one-year lease. Bob knew that rent was a fixed cost. This meant he would have to pay rent every month, whether he could afford to or not, for a full twelve months. He realized that if sales were low he would get into trouble quickly, because he did not have cash in reserve.

What Bob needed was to change his rent from a fixed to a variable cost. He negotiated with the landlord to pay the rent as a percentage of the monthly sales. That way, if sales were low, Bob's rent would also be low. If sales were high, his rent would go up—but he would be able to pay it. Rent was Bob's largest fixed cost. By changing it into a variable, he cut a lot of the risk out of his new business.

Bob's Discount Furniture became extremely successful. That arrangement helped Bob out when his business was small. Today Bob and his partners own 7 of their 20 locations and pay fixed rents on the rest. Bob is able to allocate his rent now to each unit that he sells, using his economics of one unit.

»The Dangers of Fixed Costs

If a business does not have enough sales to cover its fixed costs, it will lose money. Fixed costs are dangerous to the small business because they must be paid whether or not the business is making enough sales to cover them.

Variable costs, on the other hand, do not threaten a business's survival because they are proportional to sales. If sales are low, variable costs will also be low. If sales are high, variable costs will also be high but the business will have enough revenue to pay them.

Small business owners do not need to worry much about variable costs, as long as they are earning a respectable gross profit from their EOU. They should be wary of taking on too many fixed costs, however.

»Start-Up Investment

There is one more cost to discuss before you can learn how to keep good accounting records for your business. We have talked about the costs of producing one unit and the costs of operating a business, but what about the money required to *start* a business? **Start-up investment** is the one-time expense of opening a business. It is also called seed capital. In a restaurant, for example, start-up capital would include stoves, food processors, tables, chairs, silverware, and other

---

[2]Thanks to John Harris for this story and for reviewing the finance chapters in this book.

items that would not be replaced very often. Also included might be the one-time cost of buying land and constructing a building.[3]

For a hot dog stand, the start-up investment might look like this:

Hot dog cart	$1,500
License from the city	200
Business cards and flyers	50
Beginning inventory (hot dogs, ketchup, buns, etc.)	50
Telephone answering machine	100
Total start-up investment	$1,900

For a more complex business, like a restaurant, the start-up might look like this:

Stove	$ 22,000
Food processors	11,000
Tables and chairs	6,000
Cash register	1,500
Dishes and silverware	8,400
Renovations	15,000
Industrial fans/cooling system	45,000
Industrial dishwashers/dish racks	18,600
Total start-up investment	$127,500

For a manufacturing business, developing a **prototype** for the item being manufactured would probably be a major start-up cost. A prototype is a model or pattern that serves as an example of how a product would look and operate if it were manufactured. Companies that specialize in creating prototypes can be found in the *Thomas Register of American Manufacturers*.

»Brainstorm to Avoid Start-Up Surprises

Before starting your business, make every effort to anticipate every possible cost. Talk to other business owners in your industry and ask them what start-up costs they failed to anticipate. Use Figure 6–6 to estimate your start-up investment.

Once you have brainstormed a list, take it to a couple of advisors and have them look it over. They will probably find start-up costs you have overlooked. You might not have realized that the electric company may require a $500 deposit to turn on services, for example. Or that you will need licenses and insurance you did not expect. Tack on an additional 10 percent for contingencies and emergencies.

---

[3] Some entrepreneurs also choose to consider the time they put into getting their businesses off the ground part of the start-up investment. To do so, place a value on your time per hour and multiply by the number of hours required to get your business started.

Item	Estimated Cost
Beginning inventory	$_____
Your time (valued at $_____ per hour)	$_____
Site improvements (renovation, etc.)	$_____
Furniture and fixtures	$_____
Cash registers	$_____
Computers, software	$_____
Professional consultants	$_____
Supplies	$_____
Deposits	$_____
Registration fees	$_____
Memberships	$_____
Pre-opening salaries	$_____
Training, conventions, seminars	$_____
Pre-opening promotions, advertising	$_____
Contingencies/emergencies (10%)	$_____

Figure 6-6 Start-up investment checklist.

»Keep a Reserve Equal to One-Half of Start-Up Investment

Start-up investment should include one more thing—a cash reserve that equals at least half of your start-up costs. For the hot dog cart, therefore, the reserve would be half of $2,150, or $1,075.

Entrepreneurs must be ready for the unexpected—the only surprise is no surprise. The reserve will provide a cushion of protection when you need it. When your computer goes down or your biggest supplier raises his prices, you will be glad you had this cash on hand!

Having cash reserve will also let you take advantage of opportunities. Say you own a vintage clothing store and you hear from a friend whose great-aunt died and left him a great deal of authentic vintage clothing and jewelry. He is willing to sell you the whole lot for $500, which you figure you can resell in your shop for at least $2,000. If you did not have the extra cash on hand, this opportunity would have been lost.

»Payback

Payback tells you and your investors how long it will take your business to earn enough profit to cover the start-up investment. It is measured in months.

$$\text{Payback} = \frac{\text{Start-up Investment}}{\text{Net Profit per month}}$$

[Global Impact]

Your Competitors Are around the World

Today's entrepreneurs, even those starting very small businesses, face international competition on the World Wide Web. Most entrepreneurs are optimistic, so they tend to get excited by the prospect of selling to customers all over the world via the Net. They often do not realize that the world is already selling to their customers—aggressively.

Today, small American businesses that used to only worry about local competition may have competitors from Asia, New Zealand, Europe—all with sites in English and prices in dollars. Why? Because companies in these countries realize that four out of every five online dollars are spent by Americans.

The good news? The Internet makes researching the competition less costly than ever before. Get online yourself and conduct a thorough search of your industry that includes foreign Web sites.

Example: Business "A" required a start-up investment of $1,000. The business is projecting a net profit per month of $400. How many months will it take to pay back the start-up investment?

$$\text{Payback} = \frac{\$1,000}{\$400} = 2.5 \text{ months}$$

»Using Accounting Records to Track Fixed and Variable Costs

Now you are ready to set up your accounting records. Nothing that you learn as an entrepreneur will be more important than keeping accurate records of the money flowing in and out of your business. Keeping numerical records of inflows and outflows is called **accounting.** Accounting is the language businesspeople use to communicate. When you talk to an investor or a supplier about your business, you will need to use this language. He or she will want to see financial statements for your business that describe its performance at a glance. These are **income statements, cash flow statements,** and **balance sheets.**

Before you can create financial statements, however, you must be able to keep track of your daily money flow. If you develop record-keeping into a habit, you will be ahead of the many businesspeople who tend to stick their heads in the sand when it comes to keeping good records consistently.

‹4. Performance Objective

»Three Reasons to Keep Good Records Every Day

1. ***Keeping good records will show you how to make your business more profitable.*** Perhaps you are making less profit this month than last month. Did your expenses go up? Maybe you need to try lowering your costs. Did your sales drop? Maybe you are not spending enough on advertising. Use accurate records to constantly improve your business.

> *Keeping good records is simple, as long as you do it every day. When you start skipping days, maintaining the journal will become impossible.*

2. ***Keeping good records will prove your business is profitable.*** If you want people to invest in your business, show them that it is profitable. Keep accurate records to create financial statements and ratios that prove that your business is doing well. Remember, you will *always* need to maintain your income statement and balance sheet statement so that you will be up-to-date on your return on investment (ROI) and return on sales (ROS).

3. ***Keeping good records proves that payments have been made.*** Records help prevent arguments because they prove you have paid a bill or that a customer has paid you. Records also prove that you have paid your **taxes** (the percentage of your income paid to the government). Sometimes the Internal Revenue Service, which is the federal agency that collects taxes, will visit a business and check its financial records in a process called an **audit.** If you keep good records, you will have nothing to fear from an audit.

U.S. tax law allows business owners to deduct many expenses from their taxes. These **deductions** save you money, but you must keep receipts to prove you actually had the expenses. Write the purpose of the expense on the back of the receipt.

》Accounting Software

There are lots of good computer software programs on the market that help the small business owner keep good records. Software programs that make bookkeeping easier include Quicken or Quick Books, Microsoft Profit, Peachtree Accounting, and DacEasy Instant Accounting.

There are also programs to help you manage your money. You can use Microsoft Money or Quicken to write checks, balance your bank account, and track your income. Quicken also makes Quick-Invoice, which creates professional-looking invoices, and Quick-Books, an accounting program that includes invoices.

[Step Into The Shoes]

Rockefeller's Recordkeeping

John D. Rockefeller, who founded Standard Oil (now Exxon) and built one of the most famous family fortunes ever, reportedly kept track of every penny he spent from age 16 until his death in 1937, at the age of 98. His children said that he never paid a bill without examining it and being certain that he understood it.

Being up to date with your financial records will give you control over your business and a sense of security. Best of all, you will avoid the confusion and stress (and often needless financial loss, as well) that messy records invariably cause.

■ **Deposit money from sales right away.** When you make a sale, it is not complete until the money is in the bank and, if the payment was made by check, until the check has cleared.

»Get Organized!

You can start your recordkeeping with just an accounting journal and two shoeboxes—but once you get going, consider these other organizational tools:

- File cabinet
- Day Runner organizer
- Accounting software—Quicken, Microsoft Money, etc.
- Palm Pilot
- Personal Digital Assistant (PDA)
- Accounting Software

»"Cash Only" Accounting

This method is called "cash only" accounting because the only time you make a journal entry is when you have paid or received cash or checks. Every time you pay for something, write it down on the left side of the journal. (See Figure 6-7.) Include the check number. Keep a running balance so you always know how much cash you have on hand.

Each column on the right side of the journal has a heading for a category of income or expense. For each entry on the left side of the journal, make a **matching entry** on the right side. Find the column on the left that describes the entry you made on the right side and enter the same amount in the right-hand column. (See Figure 6-8.)

NFTE Journal - 10 ©

	Company:	The City Never Sleeps	Month / Year:	April, 2007				Page 1 of 2
	Student Name:	Kelvin Turner				NFTE		Cash is an ASSET
	Class / Section:	NFTE 101, Per.3						
	Teacher:	Mr. Mariotti		(hint: Write the month and year large so it's easy to see.)				BALANCE FORWARD

						$ IN DEPOSIT	$ OUT PAYMENT	250.00
Ck No.	DATE	TO / FROM	FOR – With Number Details					
1	324	4/15/07	STAPLES	OFFICE SUPPLIES-3 printer inks@ 12.00 ea			38.88	211.12
2	325	4/17/07	JERMEY JONES	10% Commission on 10 radios sold @ $90 ea			90.00	121.12
3		4/21/07	Deposit $ from Sales	Deposit revenue on 10 radios sold @ 90 ea (line 2)		900.00		1,021.12
4	D card	4/22/07	Debit Card, Joe's Online Disc't	SEE PURCHASE ORDER #211			452.20	568.92
5								

Figure 6-7 Journal—Left side.

$ IN INVESTMENT (equity)	$ IN LOANS (debt)	$ IN REVENUE[1]	COGS[4] (COSS)	$ OUT INVENTORY (purchases)	$ OUT OTHER VAR-IABLE COSTS	$ OUT FIXED COSTS	$ OUT CAPITAL EQUIP'T	OTHER COSTS	EXPLANATION for all OTHER COSTS entries
1						38.88			
2					90.00				
3		900.00	625.00						
4				452.20					
5									

Figure 6-8 Journal—Right side.

The URLs for these companies are the following:

Microsoft, www.microsoft.com

Quicken, www.quicken.com

Peachtree Software, www.peachtree.com

DacEasy, www.daceasy.com

Many software companies offer free versions of their software that you can try for a limited period of time or that are free but do not have as many features as the software for sale. This is a great way for you to try out different accounting and other business software before you buy.

»Receipts and Invoices

Records can also prevent disputes because they will prove you have paid a bill or that you have been paid. For a very small business, all you will need is a journal and two files (or boxes) for storing **receipts** and **invoices.** As your business grows, you can add the organizational tools listed on page 162.

- A receipt is a slip of paper with the date and amount of the purchase on it. *Always get a receipt for every purchase you make.*

- An invoice, or bill, shows the product or service sold and the amount the customer is to pay. Once the customer pays the bill, the invoice is marked "PAID." Your invoice becomes the customer's receipt. Keep a copy of each invoice, in numerical order, or organized alphabetically, by customer name.

Buy a carbon-copy receipt book. When you make a sale, give the top copy to the customer as a receipt. Keep the second copy as your invoice (your record of the sale).

»Keep Two Copies of Your Records

Always keep a copy of your financial records in a location separate from your business. If you are using software, back up your data and keep the CD in a different location. At the end of each month, move your new receipts and invoices to this location. This way if anything happens to your journal or your business site, you will still have your financial records.

»Use Business Checks for Business Expenses

Get a checking account and use it only for your business.

- *Avoid using cash for business.* When you pay with cash, there is often no record of your payment. If you must pay in cash, make sure to get an itemized receipt.

Journal Categories

- **Variable Costs (VC)**—Any cost that changes based on the number of units sold. Includes COGS: cost of goods sold. Multiply COGS by the number of units sold to get total COGS. When you receive revenue, write the total COGS in the COGS column. (COGS is not counted in the "balance" of the two sides of your journal because it is not a "cash" transaction.)

- **Fixed Costs (FC)**—Business expenses that must be paid whether or not sales are made (USAIIRD).

- **Capital Equipment**—Money you spend on business equipment that you expect to last a year or more.

- **Investment**—Start-up capital plus any money you (or others) have invested in the business. This column is not for loans. This is only for money invested in exchange for part ownership—*equity*.

- **Loans**—Any money you borrow to start or operate the business is entered in this column.

- **Revenue**—Money you receive from sales. *Whenever you write down revenue, declare your COGS in the next column on the same line!*

- **Inventory**—Anything you buy to resell is *inventory*. Include shipping costs from the supplier.

- **Other Costs**—Anything that does not fit into the other expense categories. Include a brief explanation.

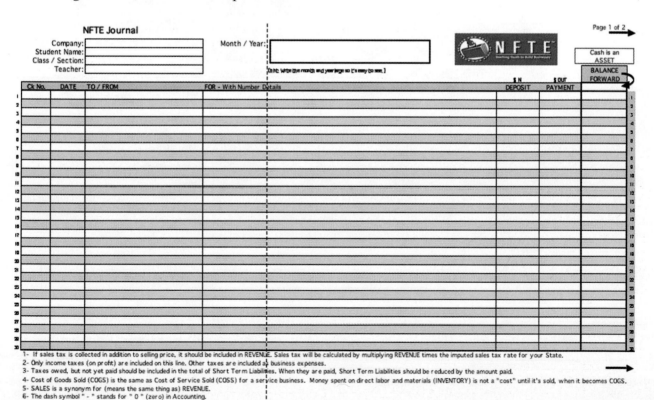

Figure 6-9 Blank Accounting Journal—Left side.

Using the Journal

Please see Figure 6–9 and 6–10 for sample blank accounting journal pages.

- Enter only one **transaction** (payment or deposit) per line.

- Use pencil, so you can erase mistakes. Mechanical pencils are best because they make very thin lines, allowing you to write more in a small space.

- Left- and right-hand entries must match and be on the same line. *The only exception is COGS, which is entered with "Revenue" on the right side.*

- Describe each transaction. Details like "how many" and "at what price" can be helpful later.

- Figure the "new balance" on the left side. This will tell you how much cash you actually have.

- **Reconcile** your journal each month. This means that you will need to go through the journal and check the right side against the left side to make sure you did not make any mistakes. Make adjustments for last month's statement on the next open line of your current journal. Adjustments go in the "Other Costs" column, with an explanatory note.

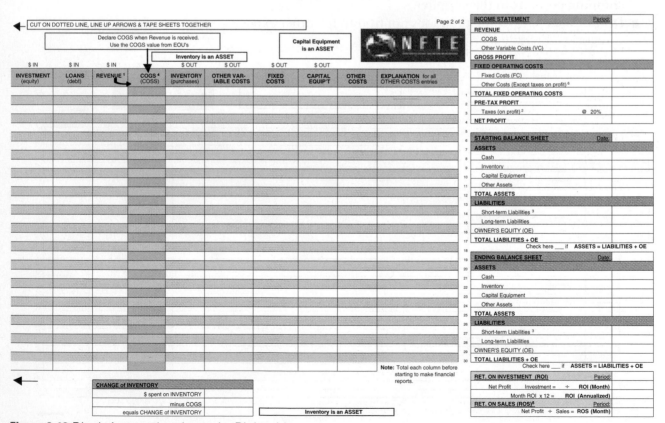

Figure 6-10 Blank Accounting Journal—Right side.

»Creating Financial Statements from the Journal

Entrepreneurs use the following financial statements to run their businesses:

1. Monthly income statement
2. Monthly cash flow statement
3. Monthly ending balance sheet

The monthly income statement and monthly ending balance sheet "fall out of" the accounting journal. The journal also shows you your running cash balance, which you can use to create a cash flow statement and to calculate the return on your investment.

To create a financial statement, simply carry numbers over from the journal to the blank financial statement on the far right side, as will be explained next.

»Monthly Income Statement

The income statement helps the entrepreneur keep track of sales and costs, and shows whether or not the business made a profit in the previous month. If not, the entrepreneur can study the income statement to try to figure out how to cut costs or increase revenue.

1. Put total from Revenue column on the line marked Revenue on your Income Statement.
2. Put total from COGS column on the line marked COGS.
3. Calculate Gross Profit by subtracting COGS from Revenue.
4. Put total Fixed Costs on the FC line.
5. Put total Variable Costs on the VC line.
6. Put total Other Costs on the Other Costs line.
7. Calculate Pre-Tax Profit. Subtract FC, VC, and Other Costs from Gross Profit.
8. Multiply Pre-Tax Profit by the tax rate (use 20%). Put on Taxes line.
9. Subtract Taxes from Pre-Tax Profit to get Net Profit.

»ROI (Return on Investment)

ROI tells you the rate of return on your capital investment in the business. You can calculate it from your income statement in your accounting journal.

Net Profit/Investment = ROI

To express ROI as a percentage, multiply it by 100.

ROI × 100 = ROI%

ROI% is normally expressed as an annual (yearly) figure. If you are figuring it for one month, project annual ROI% by multiplying by 12.

Monthly ROI% × 12 = Annual ROI%

»Monthly Ending Balance Sheet

The balance sheet shows the entrepreneur how the business is doing with regard to paying off debt and increasing equity. Are short-term liabilities being paid off? Is the business making a dent in its long-term liabilities? Is the business growing?

(Note: Your Starting Balance Sheet for this month is your Ending Balance Sheet for the previous month.)

1. Put current cash balance on the Cash line.
2. Figure how much Inventory you added this month. Subtract COGS from INV Costs. Add that to the "Inventory" number from the Starting Balance Sheet for this month to get "Inventory" for the Ending Balance Sheet.
3. Add the Capital Equipment total to "Capital Equipment" from your Starting Balance Sheet. This is Ending "Capital Equipment."
4. *(Off the Journal)* If you have "Other Assets," add them to the "Other Assets" number from the Starting Balance Sheet. This is Ending "Other Assets."
5. *(Off the Journal)* If you have "Short-Term Liabilities" at the end of the month, add them to "Short-Term Liabilities" you still owe from the previous month. Short-Term Liabilities are debts you plan to pay in less than a year. Include taxes you owe on this month's profits in "Short-Term Liabilities."
6. *(Off the Journal)* If you have "Long-Term Liabilities" at the end of the month, add them to the "Long-Term Liabilities" you owe from the previous month.
7. Calculate Ending Owner's Equity: Add Net Profit from the Income Statement *and* the total of this month's Capital Invest column *and* the Owner's Equity number of your Starting Balance Sheet.
8. Add up Assets. Now add up Liabilities + Owner's Equity. If these two numbers are equal, then you did your Ending Balance Sheet correctly. If not, you made a mistake somewhere.

Assets = Liabilities + Owner's Equity

»Sample Accounting Journal

To illustrate how to use the journal and how the financial statements fall out of it, we will fill out a journal for a business called Hernando's T-Shirts. Hernando makes custom-printed T-shirts and hoodies. His transactions for October 2007 are described below. As you read about the entries, try to find them in the journal pages. (See Figures 6-11 and 6-12.)

October 1

1. Hernando invests $3,000 of his own money to start his business. On 10/1 he opens his business checking account with a $3,000 deposit.

October 2

2. Hernando buys a silk-screen printing frame and some equipment for $500 from ACME Printing Supply Co. He pays with check #100.

3. Hernando buys inks and supplies from ACE ARTS. He gets enough to make about 300 T-shirts and pays $300 with check #101.

4. He buys six dozen blank shirts from Big Bob's Wholesale. He pays $36 per dozen. The check is #102.

October 5

5. Hernando pays his friend José Rivera $2 each to screen-print 72 shirts. His check #103 to José is for $144.00.

October 6

6. Hernando pays the monthly $150 registration fee so he can sell at the Grand Flea Market. He pays with check #104.

7. Hernando stops in at the Corner Print Shop and buys 500 business cards for $20.

BizBuilders Journal - 10 ©

Company:	Hernando's T-Shirts
Student Name:	Hernando LaHideaway
Class / Section:	Entrepreneurship 101
Teacher:	Mr. Mariotti

Month / Year: **October, 2007**

(hint: Write the month and year large so it's easy to see.)

Cash is an ASSET

	Ck No.	DATE	TO / FROM	FOR - With Number Details	$ IN DEPOSIT	$ OUT PAYMENT	BALANCE FORWARD	
1	deposit	10/1/07	Hernando	Start-up investment in the business. (Since the account is new, there is no forward balance.)	3,000.00		3,000.00	1
2	100	10/2/07	ACME Printing Supply	Startup; Silk Screen equipment		500.00	2,500.00	2
3	101	10/2/07	ACE ARTS	Start up; Silk Screen Ink and Supplies - Enough to make 300 printed T shirts		300.00	2,200.00	3
4	102	10/2/07	Big Bob's Wholesale	Buy 6 Dozen blank T shirts @ $36.00 / doz. ($3.00 each)		216.00	1,984.00	4
5	103	10/5/07	Jose Rivera	Pay to have T shirts printed; Pay Jose $2.00 each for 72 shirts = $144.00		144.00	1,840.00	5
6	104	10/6/07	Grand Flea Market	Monthly Registration Fee		150.00	1,690.00	6
7	105	10/6/07	Corner Print Shop	Business Cards, for 500 cards		20.00	1,670.00	7
8	106	10/8/07	Corner Print Shop	Color Flyers - quan. 200		65.00	1,605.00	8
9	deposit	10/9/07	Deposit Checks from Flea Market	Deposit money from sales of 6 Dozen T Shirts @ $12.00 each (COGS of $6.00 each)	864.00		2,469.00	9
10	107	10/10/07	Big Bob's Wholesale	Buy 15 Dozen blank T shirts (180 T shirts) $36.00 / doz. ($3.00 each)		540.00	1,929.00	10
11	108	10/12/07	Jose Rivera	Pay to have "T" shirts printed; Pay Jose $2.00 each for 180 shirts = $360.00		360.00	1,569.00	11
12	deposit	10/14/07	Deposit Checks from Flea Market	Dep.$ from sales-15 dz. shirts sold; 12 dz. @ $12.00 ea., 3 dz. @ $10.00 ea.(COGS of $6.00 each)	2,088.00		3,657.00	12
13	109	10/16/07	Big Bob's Wholesale	Buy 15 Dozen blank T shirts (180 T shirts) @ $36.00 / doz. ($3.00 each)		540.00	3,117.00	13
14	110	10/16/07	ACE ARTS	More silk screen ink and supplies - Enough to make 450 printed T shirts		450.00	2,667.00	14
15	111	10/18/07	Jose Rivera	Pay to have "T" shirts printed; Pay Jose $2.00 each for 180 shirts = $360.00		360.00	2,307.00	15
16	112	10/19/07	Corner Print Shop	More color Flyers - quan. 200 more		65.00	2,242.00	16
17	deposit	10/21/07	Deposit Checks from Flea Market	Deposit money from sales; Only 9 dz. @ 12.00 ea. (it rained) (COGS of $6.00 each)	1,296.00		3,538.00	17
18	113	10/25/07	Big Bob's Wholesale	Buy 21 Dozen blank T shirts (252 T shirts) @ $36.00 / doz. ($3.00 each)		756.00	2,782.00	18
19	114	10/26/07	Jose Rivera	Pay to have "T" shirts printed; Pay Jose $2.00 each for 21 doz. (252) shirts = $504.00		504.00	2,278.00	19
20	deposit	10/28/07	Deposit Checks from Giselle's Sales	Deposit money from Sales - 24 doz. @ 12.00 ea. (COGS of $6.00 each)	3,456.00		5,734.00	20
21	115	10/30/07	Giselle Rivera	Commission @ 25% of Sales; $3,456.00 x 25% = $864.00		864.00	4,870.00	21
22								22
23								23
24								24
25								25
26								26
27								27
28								28
29								29
30								30

1- If sales tax is collected in addition to selling price, it should be included in REVENUE. Sales tax will be calculated by multiplying REVENUE times the imputed sales tax rate for your State.

2- Only income taxes (on profit) are included on this line. Other taxes are included as business expenses.

3- Taxes owed, but not yet paid should be included in the total of Short Term Liabilities. When they are paid, Short Term Liabilities should be reduced by the amount paid.

4- Cost of Goods Sold (COGS) is the same as Cost of Service Sold (COSS) for a service business. Money spent on direct labor and materials (INVENTORY) is not a "cost" until it's sold, when it becomes COGS.

5- SALES is a synonym for (means the same thing as) REVENUE.

6- The dash symbol " - " stands for " 0 " (zero) in Accounting.

Figure 6-11 NFTE Journal.

October 8

8. Hernando makes 200 flyers at the Corner Print Shop for $65.00.

October 9

9. He sells all six dozen T-shirts at $12 each at the Grand Flea Market. He deposits $864.00 in his bank account. At the same time he "declares" his COGS on the same line as Revenue, as a matching entry. His COGS is $6 per shirt × 72 shirts = $432.00 ($3 per blank shirt; $2 each, printing; $1 each, ink).

October 10

10. Hernando buys 15 dozen more T-shirts (180 shirts) from Big Bob's Wholesale. They still cost $36 per dozen.

October 12

11. Hernando pays José to print 180 shirts for $360.00.

October 14

12. Hernando deposits $2,088.00 from the flea market sales in the bank. He sold 12 dozen T-shirts at $12 each, and 3 dozen for $10 each. He declares his COGS and records that on the same line. COGS is still $6 per shirt.

October 16

13. Hernando buys 15 dozen more T-shirts from Big Bob's at $36 per dozen.

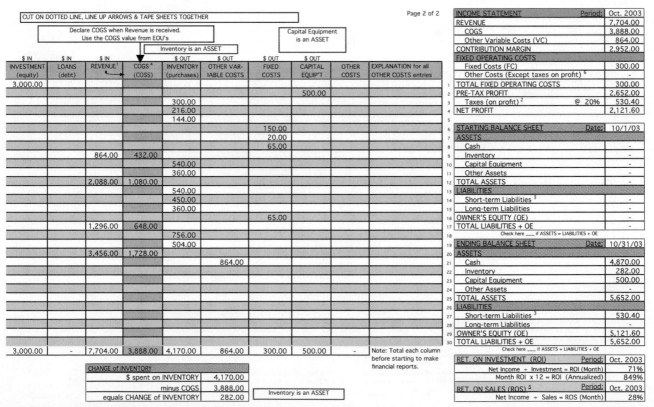

Figure 6-12 NFTE Journal.

14. Hernando is running out of ink, so he buys enough to print another 450 shirts. The ink costs $450.00 at ACE ARTS.

October 18

15. Hernando pays José $360.00 for printing the next order of 180 shirts.

October 19

16. Hernando pays $65.00 for 200 more flyers.

October 21

17. Hernando deposits $1,296.00 from sales at the Grand Flea Market into the business bank account. Because it rained, he only sold nine dozen shirts at $12 each.

October 25

18. Hernando buys 21 dozen shirts from Big Bob's for $756.00

October 26

19. Hernando pays José $504.00 for printing 21 dozen shirts.

October 28

20. Hernando deposits $3,456.00 from sales made by Giselle Rivera, José's little sister. She sold 24 dozen T-shirts at $12. Total COGS is $1,728.00 (288 units × $6).

October 30

21. Hernando pays Giselle a sales commission of 25 percent. He writes her a check for $864.00 (.25 × 3,456.00 = $864.00).

Page 1 of 2 — Page 2 of 2

BALANCE FORWARD	$ IN INVESTMENT (equity)	$ IN LOANS (debt)	$ IN REVENUE[1]	COGS[4] (COSS)	$ OUT INVENTORY (purchases)	$ OUT OTHER VARIABLE COSTS	$ OUT FIXED COSTS	$ OUT CAPITAL EQUIP'T	OTHER COSTS	EXPLANATION for all OTHER COSTS entries
3,000.00	3,000.00									
2,500.00								500.00		
2,200.00					300.00					
1,984.00					216.00					
1,840.00					144.00					
1,690.00							150.00			
1,670.00							20.00			
1,605.00							65.00			
2,469.00			864.00	432.00						
1,929.00					540.00					
1,569.00					360.00					
3,657.00			2,088.00	1,080.00						
3,117.00					540.00					
2,667.00					450.00					
2,307.00					360.00					
2,242.00							65.00			
3,538.00			1,296.00	648.00						
2,782.00					756.00					
2,278.00					504.00					
5,734.00			3,456.00	1,728.00						
4,870.00						864.00				
	3,000.00		7,704.00	3,888.00	4,170.00	864.00	300.00	500.00	0.00	Note: Total each column

CHANGE of INVENTORY

$ spent on INVENTORY	
minus COGS	
equals CHANGE of INVENTORY	

INCOME STATEMENT	Period:	Oct. 2003
REVENUE		7,704.00
COGS		3,888.00
Other Variable Costs (VC)		864.00
CONTRIBUTION MARGIN		2,952.00
FIXED OPERATING COSTS		
Fixed Costs (FC)		300.00
Other Costs (Except taxes on profit) [6]		-
1 TOTAL FIXED OPERATING COSTS		300.00
2 PRE-TAX PROFIT		2,652.00
3 Taxes (on profit) [2] @ 20%		530.40
4 NET PROFIT		2,121.60
5		
6 STARTING BALANCE SHEET	Date:	
7 ASSETS		
8 Cash		-
9 Inventory		-
10 Capital Equipment		-
11 Other Assets		-
12 TOTAL ASSETS		-
13 LIABILITIES		
14 Short-term Liabilities [3]		-
15 Long-term Liabilities		-
16 OWNER'S EQUITY (OE)		-
17 TOTAL LIABILITIES + OE		-
18		
19 ENDING BALANCE SHEET	Date:	
20 ASSETS		
21 Cash		4,870.00
22 Inventory		282.00
23 Capital Equipment		500.00
24 Other Assets		
25 TOTAL ASSETS		
26 LIABILITIES		
27 Short-term Liabilities [3]		530.40
28 Long-term Liabilities		
29 OWNER'S EQUITY (OE)		5,121.60
30 TOTAL LIABILITIES + OE		5,652.00

RET. ON INVESTMENT (ROI)	Period:	
Net Profit ÷ Investment = ROI (Month)		70%
Month ROI x 12 = ROI (Annualized)		848%
RET. ON SALES (ROS) [5]	Period:	
Net Profit ÷ Sales = ROS (Month)		27%

Figure 6-13 Relationship Between Accounting Journal And Financial Statements.

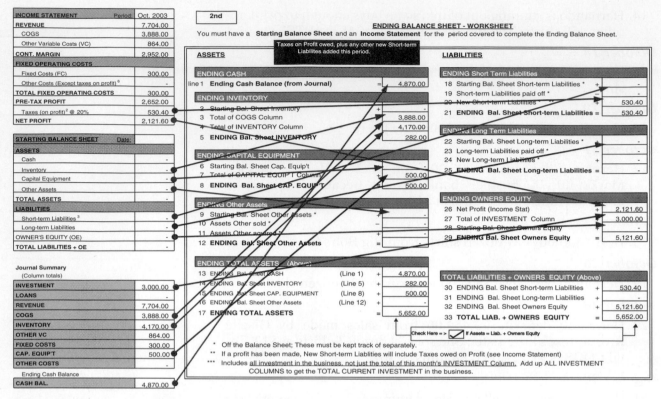

Figure 6-14 Summary ledger with income statement and balance sheet.

»Three Rules for Managing Your Cash

The accounting journal shows how much cash you have on hand. You can be running a profitable business but still be insolvent if your **cash balance** (receipts minus disbursements) becomes negative. In order to avoid getting caught without enough cash to pay your bills, follow these three rules:

1. Collect cash as soon as possible. When you make a sale, try to get paid on the spot.

2. Delay paying bills as long as possible without irritating the supplier. Most bills come with a due date. The phone bill, for instance, is typically due within thirty days. Never pay a bill after the due date, however, without getting permission from the supplier first.

3. Always know your cash balance.

»Keep Your Accounting Current

If you keep your accounting journal every day, running your business will be a lot easier. At the end of each week, you may want to enter the information from your daily journals into a weekly *ledger*. A ledger is a collection of all the accounts of a business, including sales, cash, accounts receivable, and sales tax due. Posting the information from your daily journals to a ledger once a week will give you a good overview of how your business is doing.

By keeping good records on a daily basis, you will be able to prepare monthly income statements and ending balance sheets. These will help you make good decisions for your business. Good accounting practices will help you keep track of your cash, too. An entrepreneur should always know the cash balance! Learn how to keep good records now, and it will become second nature after awhile, like brushing your teeth. You will be way ahead of business owners who never know how much cash they have on hand!

»Chapter Summary

Now that you have studied this chapter you can do the following:

1. Describe the costs of starting a business.

   ■ Start-up investment is the one-time expense of starting a business.

   ■ Cost of goods sold is the cost of selling "one additional unit."

   ■ Operating costs are the costs necessary to operate, not including the cost of goods sold. Operating costs can almost always be divided into seven categories. An easy way to remember these is through the acronym USAIIRD:

      ■ Utilities (gas, electric, telephone)

      ■ Salaries

      ■ Advertising

      ■ Insurance

      ■ Interest

      ■ Rent

      ■ Depreciation

2. Divide your costs into two categories: variable and fixed.

   ■ Variable costs vary (change) with sales. They are broken into two subcategories:

   a. Cost of goods sold, which are the costs associated specifically with each unit of sale, including what follows:

      ■ The cost of materials used to make the product (or deliver the service)

      ■ The cost of labor used to make the product (or deliver the service)

   b. Other variable costs, including the following:

      ■ Commissions

      ■ Shipping and handling charges, etc.

   ■ Fixed costs stay constant whether you sell a lot of units, or very few. Examples of fixed costs include rent, salaries, and insurance.

3. Choose the right insurance policies for your business.

   ■ Insurance protects people and businesses from having property or wealth stolen, lost, or destroyed.

   ■ When buying insurance, choose the policy with the highest deductible you can afford to cover. This will give you the lowest possible premium.

      a. The premium is the monthly payment that pays for the insurance.

      b. The deductible is the portion of expenses that the insuree pays.

4. Set up financial recordkeeping for your business.

   ■ For "cash only" accounting, the only time you make a journal entry is when you have paid or received cash or checks.

   ■ Every time you pay for anything, write it down on the left side of the journal. Each column on the right side of the journal has a heading for a category of income or expense. For each entry on the left side of the journal, make a matching entry on the right side.

5. The accounting journal shows you how much cash you have on hand.

   ■ You can be running a profitable business but still be insolvent if your cash balance (receipts minus disbursements) becomes negative.

   ■ In order to avoid getting caught without enough cash to pay your bills, follow these three rules:

      a. Collect cash as soon as possible. When you make a sale, try to get paid on the spot.

      b. Delay paying bills as long as possible without irritating the supplier. Most bills come with a due date. The phone bill, for instance, is typically due within thirty days. Never pay a bill after the due date, however, without getting permission from the supplier first.

      c. Always know your cash balance.

Key Terms

accounting	inventory cost
allocate	invoice
audit	liability insurance
balance sheet	matching entry
cash balance	moving assembly line
cash flow statement	net profit
cash reserve	overhead
deductible	payback
deduction	premium
depreciation	prototype
fixed cost	receipt
fixed operating cost	reconcile
fraud	start-up investment
income statement	taxes
inflation	transaction
insurance	variable cost

[Entrepreneurship Portfolio]

1. Give an example of a business that you have observed lowering the price of a product. How do you think the business was able to lower the price?

2. Describe the recordkeeping system you intend to set up for your own business. **(Business Plan Practice)**

3. What bank accounts do you intend to set up for your business? What bank will you use? **(Business Plan Practice)**

4. Imagine that you have invented a guitar strap that goes over both shoulders, thereby reducing shoulder strain for the guitarist. This item could be a big seller, but, before you can apply for a patent or convince investors to back you in producing it, you need a prototype. Find at least three manufacturers that could create a prototype for you.

5. For a business you would like to start, estimate what you think the fixed and variable costs would be. Choose a category for each cost from USAIIRD: Utilities, Salaries, Advertising, Interest, Insurance, Rent, and Depreciation. **(Business Plan Practice)**

6. What types of insurance will your business need, and why? What is the highest deductible you feel you can afford? **(Business Plan Practice)** Pick one type of insurance you want to have for your business and find a company online that sells it. Describe the premium, deductible, and payout.

1. Sue, of Sue's Sandwiches, sells sandwiches and soda from a sidewalk cart in a popular park near her home. She sets up her rented cart in the summers to raise money for college. Last month she sold $3,000 worth of product (sandwiches and sodas) to 300 customers. She spent $600 on the sandwich ingredients and buying the sodas wholesale. Her monthly costs are the following: Utilities = $60, Salary = $1500, Advertising = $0, Insurance = $50, Interest = $0, Rent = $300, Depreciation = $0.

   a. What are Sue's variable costs? Explain.

   b. What is Sue's COGS? Explain.

   c. What are her other variable costs? Explain.

   d. What are her fixed costs? Explain.

   e. What is Sue's EOU?

   f. How much cash reserve should she keep in the bank?

2. Mandy is buying an old van from her brother to start her flower-basket delivery service. She planned to buy auto insurance that would pay all her expenses in case she ever got into an accident. She finds that that insurance will cost her $3,000 per year, which is more than she can afford. What do you think Mandy should do?

3. Solve the following problems:

Units Sold	Selling Price	Total Revenue
a. 25	$4.64	$116.00
b. 30	$10.99	_____
c. 12	$1,233.00	_____
d. 75	$545.75	_____
e. 20	$45.03	_____

4. Calculate Total Variable Costs for the same units.

Units Sold	Total Variable Costs per Unit	Total Variable Costs
a. 25	$2.00	$50.00
b. 30	$5.50	_____
c. 12	$620.00	_____
d. 75	$280.00	_____
e. 20	$20.00	_____

5. Calculate Total Contribution Margin for the same items.

Total Revenue	Total Variable Costs	Total Contribution Margin
a. $116	$50	$66
b. _____	_____	_____
c. _____	_____	_____
d. _____	_____	_____
e. _____	_____	_____

6. Calculate Total Profit for the same units.

Total Contribution Margin	Total Fixed Operating Costs	Total Profit
a. $66	$25	$41
b. _____	$600	_____
c. _____	$4,250	_____
d. _____	$1,200	_____
e. _____	$200	_____

7. Calculate Profit per Unit for the same units.

Units Sold	Total Profit	Profit per Unit
a. 25	$41	$1.64
b. 300	_____	_____
c. 120	_____	_____
d. 750	_____	_____
e. 200	_____	_____

8. Some businesses do sell products and services that can injure customers. List three examples and explain how these companies probably use insurance.

Choose one of the companies you listed in "Critical Thinking" and research news stories about it on the Internet. Find out if the company ever had to pay customers who were injured using its products or services. Report your findings to the class.

Miriam Lopez makes funky messenger-style bags and knapsacks and sells them to fashionable boutiques in Manhattan. Below are her business transactions for the first five working days of March 2007. Record these transactions in an accounting journal, create an income statement for the first week of March, and figure her return on investment for the week.

Calculate Miriam's ROI for the week.

1. 3/1/07—Miriam purchases 8 bolts of waterproof canvas cloth from Canal Street Fabrics for $2,000.

2. 3/1/07—A store called The Lab pays its Feb. 20 invoice for $825.04.

3. 3/1/07—Miriam pays the $1,000 monthly rent on her office/workspace.

4. 3/2/07—She buys a used heavy-duty sewing machine for $500. The seller agrees to bill her if she will pay it within 30 days.

5. 3/2/07—She sells 10 bags at a SoHo flea market for $50 each.

6. 3/3/07—Miriam's phone bill was due Feb. 15. To avoid warnings from the phone company, she pays her $120 bill.

7. 3/3/07—Macy's orders 20 of Miriam's bags "on consignment," meaning that the store will only pay if it can sell the bags. If the bags do not sell, the store will return them.

8. 3/4/07—Miriam buys buckles and snaps to make the bags for Macy's for $75.

9. 3/4/07—She decides to hire a publicist to promote her business now that she has a relationship with Macy's. The publicist agrees to work for $250 a week for 6 weeks, with $500 payable in advance to clinch the agreement.

10. 3/5/07—Miriam takes the buyer from The Lab out to lunch: $75.50.

11. 3/5/07—She fills her car's gas tank for $43.29. Since she uses the car almost exclusively for business, she records this as a business expense.

12. 3/5/07—Miriam orders 500 new business cards for $25. She will pay for them when she picks them up next week.

Interview an entrepreneur about insurance policies. Ask how he or she decided what kind of insurance to carry and whether to have large or small deductibles. Present a report on your entrepreneur's insurance plan to the class.

Ask an entrepreneur in your neighborhood to discuss his or her accounting system. Write a one-page essay about the pros and cons of the system and use it to make an oral report to the class.

Exploring Online

Research different accounting software programs online. Choose a program (or programs) for your business and explain why you chose them in a brief essay.

In Your Opinion

Would you rather keep your financial records in an accounting book or on your computer? Why? In each case, how would you protect your records from being lost in a disaster, such as a fire, or, in the case of the computer, a hard-drive crash?

CASE STUDY: The Importance of Cash

Jack Wilson has had a thirty-year career in the building and managing of Web pages with two very well-known Web-based marketing companies. During his career, Jack has been in contact with hundreds of people and companies through projects and industry gatherings. For the past four years and on his own time, Jack has been developing new ways of making it easier for users to maintain and upgrade Web page information. Jack is entering the final stages of writing the software that will provide these benefits and he wants to leave his present position and devote all his time to the project. Jack's employment contract calls for him to honor a noncompete clause for twelve months and he will receive a severance payment of $80,000, which is approximately his annual earnings for the past two years.

The new Web page software will cost about $75,000 in programming fees, and $30,000 in legal fees will be necessary to ready the product for testing and sale. Jack is not experienced in marketing but a consultant that he has met with has predicted that it will take about $30,000 for product packaging and early promotional expenses. The product will probably sell for $2,500 per copy, based on similar types of software. The market for this type of software will be mainly small- to medium-sized businesses that maintain their own Web sites. Jack is aware of a handful of existing software companies whose product line would be a good fit for the type of product he is developing. Some software developers have decided to sell their ideas to larger companies, rather than try to handle the details and expense of launching a product themselves.

Jack has liquid savings of $18,000 and another $90,000 in an IRA account. He owns a home without a mortgage that is worth approximately $150,000. Jack is a conservative person and does not lead a lavish lifestyle. He has worked long and hard on his new product idea and feels as though this is his opportunity to make a contribution to his field and be in charge of his own company. Jack also has the opportunity to provide some consulting services to other programming organizations on a project-by-project basis. This work could bring in fees of $40,000, probably with payment received 6 to 12 months after completion.

Case Study Analysis

1. Does Jack have enough money to start this business? What strategy would you recommend he pursue over the next year?

2. What strategies would you suggest for this entrepreneur to adopt with respect to his use of cash?

3. Is there enough information given for you to make some early suggestions to Jack about pursuing the product on his own versus selling his idea to an established company?

4. What amount of cash reserve for the business should Jack have in his plan?

CASE STUDY: Futrell Party Promotions[4]

The Problem

The telephone rang. Richard Futrell put on his headset and answered, "Good evening, Boston teen hotline. My name is Richard. How can I help you?" The year was 1999. Richard had been working as a hotline counselor at the Mayor's Youth Committee for three years. Every night from 6 to 11 P.M. he took calls from teenagers in the Boston area—advising them on many different issues, such as relationships, family problems, school, and more. Richard had a natural talent for being a good listener. In fact, he listened so well that over time he started noticing some similarities in the types of problems that young people were discussing on the hotline. Specifically, Richard observed that younger teens in the Dorchester and Roxbury communities did not feel safe going out on the weekends in their own neighborhoods. Parents were also worried about the safety of their children and sometimes called to ask whether the Youth Committee ever sponsored teen parties or events. Richard always felt bad telling parents that the Council did not have the funds to organize these types of functions. Richard liked helping people but this was the kind of problem he did not feel he could solve.

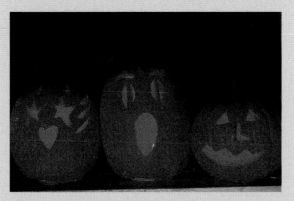

Problems Can Lead to Opportunities

But then, one day in October, Richard came up with an idea:

> *Everybody was asking, "Is there going to be a Halloween party?" But there was not anyone who was throwing a party, so I said, I'll throw*

my own party! I did not know how to DJ, but I had friends who worked as professional DJs. I just contacted everyone I knew who could help out and then made it happen.

Richard decided to use all $700 of his own personal savings to purchase services and supplies for the party. His intention was to earn this money back, and also generate a profit, by charging a $10 admission fee. He thought that $10 was a reasonable price because it was about the same amount that teens would typically spend on a weekend night to go out to a movie or play video games at the arcade. Richard knew that he had to be careful about how he allocated his resources, because $700 start-up investment was not going to get him very far.

Getting Organized

Richard's first step in planning his party was to brainstorm a list of all the things he would need to purchase and arrange for the event. The list he created follows:

Space Rental
DJ
Security
Insurance
Flyers
Food
Party Decorations

He thought this was a pretty good list—the only problem was that he did not know how much each item would cost. Could he pay for all of these goods and services with his limited funds? He was not certain. First, he needed to do some research.

Richard Investigates His Costs

Richard called his friend James who worked as a professional DJ to find out how much he would charge to spin records at the party. James normally charged $200 as a DJ at Boston's hottest clubs, but he agreed to reduce his fee to $100 because he saw that Richard was trying to do something positive for the community.

---

[4] This case is based on a real-life example; however, selected details have been fictionalized. Many thanks to Dr. Steven Spinelli and Alex Hardy from Babson College for granting permission to adapt this case from its original version.

Richard then spoke with another friend who worked as a security guard to ask if he could organize a security squad for the event. The friend agreed to find four additional coworkers who could staff the party for $50 apiece.

Richard needed a large, centrally located venue where he could host the party. He remembered that his friend Janelle had once rented a dance studio in an old, converted factory. The studio would be perfect because it was located in the heart of downtown Boston, near the highway and directly across the street from a subway station. He contacted the studio's owner and negotiated a deal to rent the space for $200 for four hours. This rental fee included insurance, in case there was an accident.

Throughout the planning process, Richard leveraged his personal network to assemble the necessary components for his party. As he explained:

If I had to go out and hire professionals, I wouldn't know them. And the fact that I did not have the money right then to pay full market prices for people's services, . . . but these people trusted me and said, "We believe in what you're doing, so we'll provide our services at a discount."

Richard's final step was to get the word out about the party to teens and parents. He called his friend Zeke, who freelanced as a graphic designer, and offered to pay him $50 to design and print 300 flyers. By this point, Richard had already committed $600 of his savings towards entertainment, space rental, security, and promotional costs. With his remaining $100, he decided to purchase chips, soda, cups, and napkins. He figured that he could recoup his investment by selling these snacks at a modest price.

After he conducted his research, Richard then filled in the actual cost of each item on the list:

Item	Cost
Space Rental and Insurance	$200 (for four hours)
DJ	$100
Security	$250 (5 security guards @ $50/each)
Graphic Design and Flyer Production	$50
Food, Decorations, and Misc. Supplies	$100
TOTAL	**$700**

Richard felt satisfied that he had managed his limited resources effectively. He was finally ready for the party. All he had left to do was decide on what costume to wear!

The Party

On the night of the party, Richard arrived early to set up. Despite weeks of planning, he still felt nervous. He had never done anything like this before. What if no one showed up and he lost all his money? At 9 P.M. the doors opened and by 10 P.M. only 20 people had arrived—Richard realized that, at $10 apiece, those 20 people equaled $200. The room looked empty, no one was on the dance floor, and Richard's nerves were on overdrive. Suddenly, at 10:30, the party filled up quickly and by 11 P.M. Richard was amazed to see that a line of kids was forming outside the door. The studio had a fire-hazard limit of 300 and by 11:30 the party was filled to capacity.

Keeping Good Records

In the end, Richard's party was a great success, both personally and financially. When he sat down to calculate his revenue, he discovered that the party had generated $3,750. Richard tabulated his receipts and created the chart below so that he could see how he had accomplished this.

Item	Selling Price per Unit	Number of Units Sold	Revenue Generated
Admission Tickets	$10.00	300	$3000.00
Chips	.50	300	$150.00
Soda	1.00	600	$600.00
TOTAL SALES REVENUE =			$3750.00

It had taken Richard three long years of careful saving to put away $700 from his part-time job at the hotline, so he was amazed that so much money could be generated in a single evening. As he reflected on the experience, Richard realized:

Even if not many people had come to the Halloween party, it would have been a success because I put something together, and I profited from it. Not only profited financially, but profited as an individual. It was something deeper than just the money. You've got to go into business because it is something you love to do and you want to create that independence. If you do something that you love, you always do your best

Future Possibilities

As he drove home after the party, Richard's mind was reeling. He was thinking about the future and what he wanted to accomplish. Maybe he would use some of the profit he earned to throw an even bigger party, or perhaps start a party-planning business. He was not sure—after all, organizing the party had caused him a lot of stress. Or maybe he would put the money in his bank account so that he could save up for graduate school. He had several possibilities to consider. Richard parked his car, got ready for bed, and resolved to think further about his future plans in the morning.

Case Study Analysis

1. Assume that Richard decides to start a party-planning business:

   a. Come up with two ways he could assess the cost of goods or services sold for this business.

   b. What costs, described in the case, will become part of Richard's operating cost structure?

   c. Make a list of additional items Richard will need to purchase to get his business off the ground. Research the cost of these items.

2. One of the reasons why Richard earned a substantial profit is because he convinced his personal contacts to provide their services at a discounted rate. If Richard decides to grow his party-planning business, do you think that he can continue to use this strategy? Why, or why not?

3. Brainstorm three things Richard might have done differently in planning his party to increase his sales revenue.

4. At the end of the case, Richard describes how he "profited as an individual" from the experience of throwing the Halloween party. What do you think he meant by this? Is it possible to profit from something on a personal level even if you do not necessarily earn a financial profit? Can you think of an example from your own life where this happened? Explain.

Chapter 7

Using an Income Statement to Guide a Business

"The propensity to truck, barter, and exchange one thing for another is common to all men."

—Adam Smith, Scottish economist

Performance Objectives

1. Read an income statement.
2. Calculate return on investment (ROI).
3. Perform a financial ratio analysis of an income statement.
4. Perform "same-size" analysis of an income statement.
5. Use operating ratios to compare your business's performance with industry standards.

Two partners—Gary and Steve—decided to start an Internet cafe in Hoboken, New Jersey. Hoboken has a large community of freelance workers, artists, and other types of people who Gary and Steve thought would patronize their business.

The partners spent a lot of start-up money installing super-fast "T1" lines, and making the cafe look up-to-date. All the furniture was custom-designed for the space, as were the curved, metallic ceiling and wall panels. The partners decided to serve gourmet coffees, cakes, and simple sandwiches.

Because so much money was spent on start-up, the partners tried to cut costs by hiring as staff local kids who would work at minimum wage. It soon became apparent to frustrated customers, however, that the staff could not solve technical problems. Customers who were having trouble printing or accessing documents were often told to wait "until Gary or Steve comes in," which was usually not until late in the afternoon.

Gary and Steve had no previous entrepreneurial experience and had gotten most of the financing from their families. Because they had never learned to prepare an income statement, they had no effective way of keeping track of the money going in and out of the business. Within 14 months, Gary and Steve had to close their venture because they were not covering their operating costs. If they had prepared monthly income statements, they could have seen the problems developing and could have taken action to solve them.

Entrepreneurs use three basic financial statements to track their businesses.[1]

- Income statement
- Cash flow statement
- Balance sheet

---

[1] Special thanks to John Harris for many ideas in this chapter.

Together, these three statements show the health of a business at a glance. In this chapter you will learn how to prepare and use the income statement to guide your business and keep it strong.

»A Score Card for the Entrepreneur

Performance Objective 1.〉 Entrepreneurs use their financial records to prepare monthly income statements and then to prepare one at the end of the fiscal year. An older term for this statement is **profit and loss statement,** but since you cannot have both profit and loss at the same time, most people use "income statement" these days. It shows whether the difference between revenues (sales) and expenses (costs) is a profit or a loss. If sales are greater than costs, the income statement balance will be positive, showing that the business is profitable. If sales are less than costs, the income statement balance will be negative, showing a loss.

The income statement is a "scorecard" for the entrepreneur. If the business is not making a profit, examining the statement can show what may be causing the problem. The owner can then take steps to correct the problem before net losses make the business insolvent. Profit is a reward for making the right choices. The income statement will enable you to determine whether your decisions have kept you on the right track each month. Learning to prepare an income statement is not difficult, and it is a great business tool.

»Parts of an Income Statement

The income statement is composed of the following parts:

1. *Revenue:* Money received from sales of the company's product or service.

2. *COGS (cost of goods sold)/COSS (cost of services sold):* These are the costs of materials used to make the product (or deliver the service) plus the costs of labor used to make the product (or deliver the service). A monthly income statement reports total COGS for a month. Simply multiply the COGS from the EOU by the number of units sold during the month.

3. *Gross Profit:* To calculate gross profit, subtract COGS from revenue.

4. *Other Variable Costs (VC):* Costs that vary with sales.

5. *Calculcate Contribution Margin:* Subtract COGS and Other Variable Costs from Revenue.

6. *Fixed Operating Costs:* Costs of operating a business that do not vary with sales. The most common fixed operating costs are utilities, salaries, advertising, insurance, interest, rent, and depreciation (USAIIRD).

7. *Pre-Tax Profit:* Contribution margin minus fixed operating costs. This is a business's profit after all costs have been de-

ducted, but before taxes have been paid. Pre-tax profit is used to calculate how much tax the business owes.

8. *Taxes:* A business must pay taxes on income it earns. It may have to make quarterly estimated tax payments (for small businesses) or monthly payments if it is a larger business.

9. *Net Profit/(Loss):* This is the business's profit or loss after taxes have been paid.

See Figure 7-1 for an example of an income statement.

Income Statement			
Name of Company		**Time Period:**	
Sales/Revenue:			$ _____
COGS (Cost of Goods Sold)			
Total Materials:	$ _____		
Total Labor:	_____		
Total COGS	$ _____	$ _____	$ _____
Gross Profit			
Other variable costs			_____
Commission:	$ _____		
Packaging:	_____		
Total other variable costs	$ _____	$ _____	_____
Total variable costs (per unit)		$ _____	
Contribution Margin			$ _____
Fixed operating costs (USAIRDO)			
Utilities	$ _____		
Salary	_____		
Advertising	_____		
Insurance	_____		
Interest	_____		
Rent	_____		
Depreciation	_____		
Other	_____		
Total fixed operating costs:	$ _____	⟶	$ _____
Pre-Tax Profit			_____
Taxes			_____
Net Profit			$ _____

*Also called "total cost of sales."

Total Sales/Revenue = Units Sold × Unit Selling Price

Total Cost of Goods or Services Sold = Units Sold × Cost of Goods or Services Sold per Unit

Total Other Variable Costs = Units Sold × Other Variable Costs per Unit

Total Variable Costs = Total Cost of Goods or Services Sold + Total Other Variable Costs

Contribution Margin = Total Sales − Total Variable Costs

Total Fixed Costs = Total of USAIIRDO

Pre-Tax Profit/(Loss) = Contribution Margin − Total Fixed Costs

Taxes = Profit × .20 (Estimated)

Net Profit = Pre-Tax Profit − Taxes

Gross Profit = Sales − COGS

Figure 7-1 Income statement.

[Entrepreneurial Wisdom]

Whenever a number in a financial statement is enclosed in parentheses, it is a negative number. If you see ($100) at the bottom of an income statement, the business had a net loss of $100.

Working on an income statement with a colleague.
(Frank Sileman, Omni-Photo Communications, Inc.)

»A Simple Income Statement

The power of the income statement is that it tells you whether you are fulfilling the old formula of "buying low, selling high, and meeting customer needs." Take a look at the following income statement for a simple business. It will illustrate how the income statement functions.

Let's say that David buys 100 handbags at $10 each and sells them all at $25 each at a flea market, for revenue of $2,500. He gives each customer a little charm to attach to the handbag that costs him 50 cents. He also spends $25 on flyers to advertise that he will be selling Saturday at the flea market, and $500 to rent the booth. The following income statement quickly shows whether or not he is making a profit.

David's Income Statement
Handbag sales at flea market (one time)

Sales:	100 handbags × $25/bag		2,500
Less COGS	100 handbags × $10/bag	1,000	1,000
Gross Profit			1,500
Other Variable Costs	100 charms × $0.05/charm	50	50
Total Variable Costs		1,050	
Contribution Margin			1,450
Fixed Costs			
Rent ($500 to rent booth)		500	
Advertising ($25 for flyers)		25	
Total Fixed Costs		525	525
Pre-Tax Profit			925
Taxes 25%			231
Net Profit			694

The income statement not only shows that David's business is profitable but also shows *how* profitable his business is.

»The Double Bottom Line

You have certainly heard the expression, "What's the bottom line?" It refers to the last line on an income statement, which is the one that shows whether a business is profitable or not.

Another bottom line should be considered, though, aside from whether the business is profitable or not. Is your business achieving its mission? If your dream is to have the business fill a need for your community, is this goal being realized? Are you able to make a profit and operate the business in a way that makes you proud? Business goals that go beyond profit might include the following:

- Being a good citizen by doing business in a way that respects the environment—recycling, minimizing waste, looking into energy sources that do not pollute
- Encouraging local people to invest in the business and become equity owners
- Always dealing honestly with customers and suppliers. Treating everyone you do business with the way you would like to be treated
- Treating employees with respect regarding their health and safety; setting up profit-sharing so they will share in the sucess they help create.

Ideally, you want to have a positive *double* bottom line—you are making a profit so you can stay in business *and* achieve your mission.

»Create an Income Statement from Your Ledger

Your income statement will tell you if you have made or lost money. The numbers you need to put in your income statement come out of your ledger.

By keeping accurate records, your income statement will fall into place and you will easily be able to keep track of how your business is doing.

»Return on Investment

An **investment** is something you put time, energy, or money into because you expect to receive money or satisfaction in return.

When you start your own business, you are investing time and energy into the venture as well as money. You do this because you

❬ 2. **Performance Objective**

[Global Impact]

Accounting Differences between Countries

Businesses in different countries prepare, present, and even name income statements differently. In the United Kingdom, for example, the income statement is called "Group Profit and Loss Account." Areas where global practices differ widely include inventory measurement methods, and ways used to value and depreciate property and equipment. Countries also have different laws regarding when a sale can be recognized as income and included on an income statement.

In the United States, United Kingdom, Denmark, Norway, Belgium, Brazil, and Japan, for instance, income from a long-term contract can only be included on the income statement as each percentage of the contract is completed. If you have done 10 percent of the work, you can show 10 percent of the income on your statement. In Germany, on the other hand, you cannot include any of the income on your statement until the contract has been 100 percent completed.

believe that someday your business will return more than the value of the time, energy, and money you put into it. One way to express this idea mathematically is to calculate the **return on investment (ROI).** This is the net profit of a business divided by the start-up investment. It is expressed as a percentage of the original investment.

》Calculating ROI

Investors think about "wealth" rather than money per se because a business may own things such as equipment or real estate that has value, but is not actual cash. To include everything of value, return on investment measures how much wealth changes over time. ROI is a rate of growth. To measure ROI you have to know three things:

1. *Net profit:* The amount the business has earned beyond what it needs to cover its costs.
2. *Total investment in the business:* This includes Start-Up Investment (the amount of money that was required to get the business started plus additional money invested later).
3. The period of time for which you are calculating ROI. This is typically one month or one year.

$$\text{ROI Formula} = \frac{\text{Net Profit}}{\text{Investment}} = \text{ROI}$$

> ! ROI is normally expressed as a percentage. The ROI formula gives you the answer as a decimal. You can express the decimal to a percentage by multiplying the decimal by 100, and adding the "%" sign.

There is an easy way to remember the ROI formula: *What you made over what you paid, times one hundred.*

Say David wants to figure out what his ROI was for the day at the flea market. To measure his ROI David must know the following:

1. **Net Profit:** His income statement shows this to be $694.
2. **Investment:** David invests $1,000 in handbags and $25 in flyers, $50 for charms, plus $500 to rent a booth at the flea market. Total = $1,575
3. **Time Period:** In this case David is calculating his ROI for one day.

He simply divides his investment into the net profit.

$$\frac{\text{Net Profit (\$694)}}{\text{Investment (\$1,000 + 75 + 50 + \$500)}} = \frac{\$694}{\$1,575} = .4406 \times 100 = 44\%$$

David's ROI was 51 percent for the day. ROI tells you what the rate of return was on your investment in your business.

> ### Biz Facts
>
> If you want to project (forecast) your ROI for a year, you will need to convert monthly ROI to annualized ROI. Convert to projected annual ROI by multiplying by 12 months. Monthly ROI % × 12 months = Projected Annual ROI %

ROI is normally "annualized," or expressed, over a year. If David sells at one flea market per month and earns 51 percent ROI each time, his monthly rate of return will be 51 percent (even though he earns it all in one day). If he keeps this up all year, his annual ROI will be as follows: 44% × 12 = 528%

»An Income Statement for a More Complex Business

The income statement for a more complex business follows the same format, and its goal is still the same—to show how profitable the business is. This income statement includes depreciation, however.

Income Statement for Lola's Custom Draperies, Inc.

March 2005		
Sales:	$85,456	
Cost of goods sold:		
Materials	$11,550	
Labor	$17,810	
Total COGS:	$29,360	
Gross Profit:	$56,096	
Other variable costs:		
Sales commissions	$8,000	
Less total variable costs:	$37,360	($11,550 + $17,810 + $8,000)
Contribution margin:	$48,096	($85,456 − $37,360)
Fixed operating costs:		
Factory rent & utilities	$8,000	
Salaries & administrative	$12,000	
Depreciation	$2,000	
Less/total fixed operating costs:	$22,000	($8,000 + $12,000 + $2,000)
Profit before taxes:	$26,096	($48,096 − $22,000)
Taxes (25%):	$6,524	($26,096 × 0.25)
Net profit/(loss):	$19,572	($26,096 − $6,524)

An income statement can be calculated using computer spreadsheet software, such as Microsoft Excel. (See Figure 7-2.) The page of a spreadsheet is divided into rows and columns. Each row has a number, and each column a letter. The "boxes" created by the rows and columns are called "cells." Each cell is designated by the row and column that intersect in it. For example, the highlighted cell that follows is B2. (Note that the "2" in the row heading and the

(Eyewire Collection, Getty Images—
Photodisc)

Figure 7-2 Microsoft Excel
income statement.

"B" in the column heading are bold.) Also, "B2" appears in the
"name box" just under where the font "Arial" is shown.

Each cell can hold only one kind of data. The three types of
spreadsheet **data** follow:

1. Text—words. Use text for labels and other devices that will
   help people understand the spreadsheet when they read it.

2. Numbers, such as 1, 12, 45, H, 1/2, etc.

3. Formulas—to help calculate numbers automatically.

If you want the spreadsheet to add the numbers 3 and 6, for example, put these numbers in different cells, then use another cell for
a formula that will perform the calculation for you. To write a formula with Excel, put an equal sign "=" in the cell first. This tells the
program that you are writing a formula. In Figure 7-3a you can see
how the formula uses the "names" of the cells containing the numbers 3 and 6. The computer will "go get" the number values from

Figure 7-3 Excel cells.

those cells to do the math and will show the answer in the cell that contains the formula (See Figure 7-3b).

A computer spreadsheet is like a word processor for numbers. When you harness the power of the spreadsheet, math becomes a lot less work and a lot more fun.

»Financial Ratio Analysis

So far, we have only looked at how an income statement can tell you whether or not your business is making a profit. But you can also create **financial ratios** from your income statement that will help you analyze your business further.

〈3. **Performance Objective**

To do this, simply divide sales into each line item and multiply by a hundred. In this way, you are expressing each line item as a percentage, or share, of sales. Expressing each item on the income statement as a percentage of sales makes it easy to see the relationship between items. In the following example, for every dollar of sales, 40 cents was spent on cost of goods sold. The contribution margin per dollar was 60 cents. The net profit, after 30 cents was spent on operating costs and 10 cents on taxes, was 20 cents.

Income statement	Dollars	Math	% of sales
Sales	$10	$10/$10 × 100 =	100%
Less Total COGS	$4	$4/$10 × 100 =	40%
Less Other Variable Costs	$0		
Contribution Margin	$6	$6/$10 × 100 =	60%
Less Fixed Operating Costs	$3	$3/$10 × 100 =	30%
Profit	$3	$3/$10 × 100 =	30%
Taxes	$1	$1/$10 × 100 =	10%
Net Profit/(Loss)	$2	$2/$10 × 100 =	20%

> *Analyzing income statement items as percentages of sales makes clear how costs are affecting net profit.*

Analyzing the income statement in this way makes clear how each item is affecting the business's profit. Examining the income statement makes it easy to experiment with ways to improve your business.

To increase contribution margin, you could see if you could cut the cost of goods sold by 10 percent. The next time you analyze your monthly income statement, you will be able to see if this cost cutting increased the contribution margin and by how much.

≫Same Size Analysis

Performance Objective 4.≫

Financial ratio analysis will also allow you to compare the income statements from different months, or years, more easily, even if the sales are different amounts. The percentages let you compare statements as if they were the "same size." For this reason, financial ratio analysis is sometimes called "same size analysis."

When the ratio of expense/sales is used to express expenses as a percentage of sales, it is called an **operating ratio.** The operating ratio expresses what percentage of sales dollars the expense is using up. You can use operating ratios to compare your expenses with those incurred by other businesses in your industry. If your rent is $2,000 per month and your sales in a given month are $10,000, your operating ratio for rent is 20 percent. Is that high or low for your industry? If it is high, you might want to consider moving to another location.

Relating each element of the income statement to sales in this fashion will help you notice changes in your costs from month to month.

Example: Compare the "same size" income statements shown in Figure 7-4. Rocket Rollerskate did not have as much revenue and did not make as much profit in Feburary as it did in January. The company was able to lower both its COGS and its other variable costs in February, though. Which month was better for Rocket? Can you explain your point of view?

≫Return on Sales

Return on sales (ROS) is the percentage created when sales are divided into net income. This is an important measure of the profitability of the business.

Net Income/Sales = Return On Sales (ROS)

ROS is also called **profit margin.** To express this ratio as a percentage, multiply it by 100 (as you would to express ROI as a percentage).

A high ROS ratio can help a company make money more easily; however, the amount of revenue the company has makes a difference. Size of the sale will also make a difference. Hardware stores sell inexpensive items, so they have to make a higher profit margin on each to make a profit. Auto dealers sell expensive items, so they can make money with a smaller ROS on each car they sell.

Rocket Rollerskate Co. "Same Size"		Date: January, 2008	
Revenue	**100%**		**250,000**
COGS	24%	60,000	60,000
Gross Profit	**76%**		**190,000**
Other Variable Costs	14%	35,000	35,000
Total Variable Costs	38%	95,000	
Contribution Margin	**62%**		**155,000**
Fixed Costs	34%		85,000
Pre-Tax Profit	**28%**		**70,000**
Taxes 20%	5.6%		14,000
Net Profit	**22.4%**		**56,000**

Rocket Rollerskate Co. "Same Size"		Date: February, 2008	
Revenue	**100%**		**225,000**
COGS	20%	45,000	45,000
Gross Profit	**80%**		**180,000**
Other Variable Costs	12%	27,000	27,000
Total Variable Costs	32%	72,000	
Contribution Margin	**68%**		**153,000**
Fixed Costs	38%		85,000
Pre-Tax Profit	**30%**		**68,000**
Taxes 20%	6.0%		13,600
Net Profit	**24.2%**		**54,400**

Figure 7-4 "Same size" income statements.

ROS (Profit Margin) Table

ROS	Margin Range	Typical Product
Very low	2–5%	Very high volume *or* very high price
Low	6–10%	High volume *or* high price
Moderate	11–20%	Moderate volume *and* moderate price
High	20–30%	Low volume *or* low price
Very high	30% and up	Very low volume *or* very low price

»Computerized Financial Statements

Although it is good practice to learn how to create these financial statements and ratio analyses on paper, once you are actually running your business you will probably want to keep these records on your computer. Microsoft Small Business Financial Manager for Office is especially useful because it guides you through analyses that can help you make business decisions by creating "what if" scenarios using Excel spreadsheets.

With this type of software you can also turn your financial information into graphs and pie charts that show at a glance how the business is likely to perform in different scenarios—if a supplier raises prices, for example.

The income statement is the "scorecard" of the business. If your business is successful, your income statements will prove it. Companies typically create income statements to see how they're doing:

- Once a month
- Every three months (quarterly)
- Each year (annually)

Once you have been in business 12 months, you can create a yearly income statement showing yearly net profit.

» Creating Wealth by Selling a Profitable Business

A successful small business can usually be sold for between three and five times its yearly net profit, because the buyer expects the business to continue to generate more profit. If your net profit for one year is $10,000, you should be able to sell your business for at least 3 × $10,000—$30,000.

From the buyer's perspective, this represents a 33 percent annual return on the investment required to buy the business ($10,000/ $30,000 = 33%), which is a very attractive return.

If you are in business for three years, however, and can increase your net profit each year, your business will be worth even more. If your start-up business earns $10,000 in year one, $25,000 in year two, and $60,000 in year three, it could be valued at $180,000 just by applying the "three times" rule of thumb. How a business grows affects its value. A business with increasing yearly net profit will be considered more valuable than a business with earnings that stay the same each year.

[Step Into The Shoes]

Charles Schwab Finds His Market Niche

Charles Schwab opened his own brokerage firm in 1971 when he was 34. Like Jacoby & Meyers with legal services, Schwab uncovered a market niche when he began offering discount pricing for informed investors who were tired of paying hefty commissions to stockbrokers. These investors did not need someone else to do their research and make their decisions and they flocked to take advantage of the cheaper rates. By 1981, Charles Schwab & Company's earnings were $5 million. In 1982, BankAmerica bought the company for $53 million but left Schwab in place as CEO. In the 1990s, Schwab became the leading online discount broker and the fastest growing American company of the decade. Today, Charles Schwab is the nation's largest online brokerage and one of the largest e-commerce businesses in the world.

This is how entrepreneurs create fortunes. They establish a successful business, sell it, and use the resulting wealth to create new enterprises and more wealth. Entrepreneurs also use their wealth to support political, environmental, and social causes. What will you do with your wealth?

»Chapter Summary

Now that you have studied this chapter you can do the following:

1. Read an income statement.
   - An income statement shows whether the difference between revenues (sales) and expenses (costs) is a profit or a loss.
   - If sales are greater than costs, the income statement balance will be positive, showing that the business earned a profit. If sales are less than costs, the balance will be negative, showing a loss.
   - The elements of an income statement follow:
     a. *Revenue*—Money a business makes for selling its products.
     b. *Cost of goods sold*—The cost of goods sold for one unit times the number of units sold. Never disclose your cost of goods sold. You want to keep your profit margin private.
     c. *Gross profit*—Revenue less the cost of the product or service.
     d. *Other variable costs*—Costs that vary with sales.
     e. *Contribution margin*—Sales minus variable costs (cost of goods sold + other variable costs).
     f. *Fixed operating costs*—Items that must be paid to operate a business. These items include utilities, salaries, advertising, insurance, interest, rent, and depreciation (referred to as USAIIRD).
     g. *Profit before taxes*—A business's profit after all costs have been deducted but before paying taxes.
     h. *Taxes*—A business must pay income tax on its profit. (Sales, property and other taxes are business expenses and are not included on this line.)
     i. *Net profit/(loss)*—A business's profit or loss after taxes.
2. Calculate return on investment (ROI).
   - ROI is the net profit of a business divided by the start-up costs, which are the original investment in the business.
   - $\dfrac{\text{Return} - \text{Investment}}{\text{Investment}} \times 100$
3. Perform a financial ratio analysis of an income statement.
   - Expressing each item on the income statement as a percentage of sales makes it easy to see the relationship between items.
   - Financial ratio analysis also allows you to compare the income statements from different months, or years, more easily, even if the sales are different amounts.
   - The percentages let you compare statements as if they were the "same size." For this reason, financial ratio analysis is sometimes called "same size analysis."
     Net Income/Sales = Return On Sales (ROS)

Key Terms

contribution margin
data
financial ratio
gross profit
investment

operating ratio
profit and loss statement
profit margin
return on investment (ROI)
return on sales (ROS)

[Entrepreneurship Portfolio]

Critical Thinking Exercises

1. Repeat the exercise from Key Concept Questions using accounting software. Then run the following "what if" scenarios and create graphs or other visuals showing how each scenario would affect the business's monthly and yearly financial picture:

   a. What if the restaurant finds a paper supplier that is willing to supply paper for only $8,000 in June and $96,000 for the year?

   b. What if sales for June were $250,000 and sales for the year were $2,000,000? (Assuming the company's tax rate is 25 percent, do not forget, that this would change the tax picture, as well.)

   c. What if the owner of this franchise faced start-up costs of $400,000 instead of $300,000? How would that affect the ROI?

2. If you were to open a clothing store, what do you think would be a reasonable operating ratio for the store's rent, and why?

3. When you open your business, which items do you intend to depreciate, and why?

Key Concept Questions

1. Given the following data, on a separate sheet of paper create monthly and yearly income statements for this fast-food restaurant in New York City.

   a. Sales for the month of June were $300,000. Sales for the year were $2,600,000.

   b. The sum of $66,000 was spent on food in June (it was $792,000 for the year). The store spent $9,000 on paper to wrap food items in June and $108,000 for the year.

   c. Taxes for June were $15,000. For the year, taxes were $233,000.

   d. Fixed operating costs for June were $175,000. Operating costs for the year were $1,000,000.

   e. Use Excel (or MS Small Business Financial Manager) to create a graph showing the monthly and yearly income statements for this business.

2. If the owner of this fast-food restaurant invested $300,000 in start-up costs, what was his ROI for the year? (Assume June as average.)

3. Calculate the financial ratios (ROI and ROS) for both the monthly and the yearly income statement. What do the financial ratios tell you about this business?

4. What would the profit before taxes be if the owner finds a paper supplier who only charges $100,000 for the year?

5. What would the profit margin for the year be in that case?

6. Suppose you wanted to raise profits by $5,000 a month. What would you do, and why?

1. Make a spreadsheet on a computer, using text, numbers, and formulas.

2. The formulas for the first three rows (enter data in green cells). Rows are shown in Figure 7-5 to get you started. If you do not have a computer handy, write the formulas on a piece of paper.

Application Exercise

Figure 7-5 Rocket Rollerskate income statement.

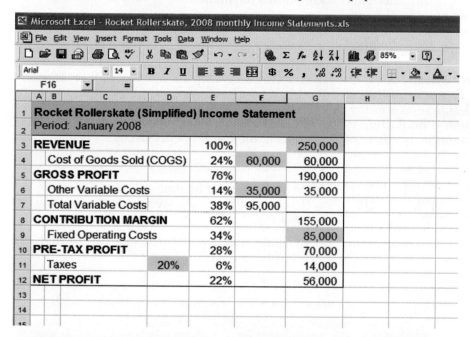

CASE STUDY: Preparing an Income Statement

On June 30, Michael Walsh completed his first year as an independent Web design consultant. The year was full of challenges but Michael managed to bill twelve different companies a total of $173,000 for his services, and he collected all but two invoices, which totaled $7,500. There were three part-time employees who helped with design and data entry. These employees were paid a total of $38,000 for the year and Michael paid himself a salary of $4,200 per month. The employee benefits and payroll taxes were $16,500 for the year. Michael would like to pay himself a year-end bonus of $6,000.

The Web design business is basically labor intensive but Michael invested in a state-of-the-art PC with all the relevant Web design software. This package cost $5,000. The system is hooked up to an Internet via a DSL with a monthly payment of $1,000 for the service. Office expenses were unusually high for the first year, totaling $4,500, and another $1,000 was spent during the year on postage and advertising expenses. For the first six months of the year, Michael worked out of his home. On January 1, the company signed a lease for $1,100 a month and moved into a three-room office suite.

Michael moved a desk, several chairs, and four filing cabinets into the new offices. He also purchased a conference-room table and chairs and an office cubicle for $8,000 from a local office-supply dealer. The office required two new computers, a wireless network, and a phone system; all these items are covered by a three-year lease with payments of $300 per month after a $500 down payment.

In starting the business, Michael and his wife took a home equity loan for $40,000. Michael has the company making the interest-only $500 monthly loan payments. Michael and his wife took a three-day trip to the World Web Design Conference in California, in February. The cost of this trip was $2,500 and Michael met a new client while at the conference. The Walshes file a joint tax return; their average tax rate is 28 percent.

Case Study Analysis

1. Prepare a simple income statement for the first year of Michael's Web design consulting business.

2. Evaluate Michael's performance for his first year in business.

CASE STUDY: Sandra Kendricks, Kickin' It Apparel

Sandra Kendricks, 28, recently started her own fashion label, Kickin' It Apparel, in Los Angeles. After delaying her dream of starting a business for several years, Sandra is elated to be doing what she loves—designing and manufacturing apparel for the urban youth market.

Learning the Ropes

By the time Sandra launched Kickin' It, in 2004, she had already had some first-hand knowledge of the fashion industry. As a college student, Sandra had spent a summer working as an intern at the urban apparel label, FUBU™. Sandra loved the rush of working in New York City's fashion district and discovering the latest trends. When she returned home to California that September, she

knew that she had found her calling. One day she would sit at the helm of her own fashion empire. It was just a matter of time and planning.

A Dream Deferred

After college graduation, Sandra tried to find a job at a design company, but the economy was in recession and no one was hiring entry-level staff. Instead, she found employment as a computer programmer in Silicon Valley. The stuffy, 9 to 5 environment of the software company was an abrupt change from the fast pace she had enjoyed while working at FUBU. Sandra knew that the life of a computer programmer was not for her, but she was happy to be earning money so that she could start paying back her student loans.

In the fall of 2003, Sandra decided to quit her job so that she could fully focus her attention on launching Kickin' It. Over the years, she had saved $20,000 for her start-up investment, but her attempts to organize a business plan had always been undermined by the demands of working 9 to 5. So, one day, after reading about how one of her fellow interns from FUBU had started his own business, she abruptly handed in her resignation. She could not allow life to keep passing her by.

Getting Started: An Opportunity Presents Itself

Sandra used all her savings to purchase basic equipment she would need for her business. The following list shows how she allocated her start-up investment:

Item	Cost
Computer	$2,900
Digital camera	$500
Color printer	$2,000
Sewing machine	$5,000
Sewing supplies (thread, etc.)	$500
Business cards	$100
Scanner	$1,000
Fitting mannequin	$2,000
Cash reserve fund	$6,000
Total Start-up Investment	**$20,000**

After purchasing the supplies, Sandra began to map out her marketing plan. She decided that her first step would be to notify her network of friends and contacts in the fashion world that she was back in the game. She hoped that one of her contacts might connect her with an opportunity.

Opportunity Knocks

In April, Sandra received an e-mail from her fellow FUBU intern, Andre Jones. A friend of Jones's who owned a formal-wear boutique in Beverly Hills wanted to increase her inventory of evening gowns. Prom season was right around the corner, and the boutique owner was anxious to have more dresses in stock. Jones asked Sandra if she could create four fresh designs and have a total of 100 dresses manufactured within the next 30 days.

Jones explained the finances of the deal. The boutique owner would pay Sandra a wholesale price of $150 per dress. For a total order of 100 dresses, Sandra would earn $15,000. She would be paid in two installments: $5,000 up front and the remainder upon completion of the order. Jones asked that Sandra pay him a 5 percent commission in exchange for connecting her to this business opportunity. This meant that, if Sandra earned $15,000, Jones would receive $750, or $7.50 per dress.

Sandra had butterflies in her stomach. She had been out of the industry so long that she did not know if she could make 100 high-end dresses for under $15,000. Was this a good deal? What if she lost money on the job? Even worse, what if she ran out of money and could not complete the order on time—or at all? Despite her uncertainty, Sandra decided to take a leap of faith and embrace the opportunity that had been presented to her.

Getting to Work

Sandra spent the next week scouring the latest fashion magazines and touring department stores to check out the competition's products. After spending many late nights sketching designs and purchasing materials, Sandra was ready to start making her dresses. She quickly realized that she could not do all of the manufacturing herself, so she made arrangements to subcontract the production of 25 dresses to a local seamstress who charged $10/hour for her labor.

Tracking Her Costs

Sandra sat down and calculated her economics of one unit, along with a projected monthly income statement. She wanted to figure out how she could complete the order under budget so that she would earn a profit—even if it was a small one. Here is what she projected:

Economics of Unit for One Dress

Date: April 2004

Unit of Sale: One Dress

Selling Price (Revenue)			**150.00**
Less COGS			
Direct labor $10/hour × 3 hours per dress	30.00		
Materials	35.00		
Total COGS	65.00	65.00	65.00
Gross Profit			**85.00**
Less Other Variable Costs			
Commission 5% of Andre Jones (= 5% of $150)	7.50		
Shipping	3.00		
Total Other Variable Costs	10.50	10.50	10.50
Total Variable Costs (COGS + Other VC)		75.50	
Contribution margin per unit			**74.50**

Kickin' It Apparel

Date: April 2004

Sandra Kendricks

Projected Income Statement – May 2004

Assumption: 100 dresses will be sold in May 2004

Revenue	$150 selling price per dress × 100 units sold			**15,000.00**
Less COGS				
Direct Labor	$30 per dress × 100 units sold	3,000.00		
Materials	$35 per dress × 100 units sold	3,500.00		
Total COGS		6,500.00	6,500.00	6,500.00
Gross Profit				**8,500.00**
Less Other Variable Costs				
Commission	Andre Jones sells 100 dresses × 5%	750.00		
Shipping	$3.00 per dress × 100 dresses	300.00		
Total Other Variable Costs		1,050.00	1,050.00	1,050.00
Total Variable Costs (COGS + Other VC)			7,550.00	
Contribution Margin				**7,450.00**
Less Fixed Costs (USAIIRDO)				
Utilities		100.00		
Salaries		3,000.00		
Advertising		50.00		
Insurance		200.00		
Interest		—		
Rent		—		
Depreciation		200.00		
Other		—		
Total Fixed Costs		3,550.00		3,550.00
Pre-Tax Profit				**3,900.00**
Taxes	20%			780.00
Net profit				**3,120.00**

Sandra Examines Her Costs

After reviewing her calculations, Sandra felt uncertain. She had hoped to earn a higher net profit. It was going to require a lot of time and energy to produce 100 dresses, and $3,120 seemed like a small amount considering how much effort the job would require.

Sandra was also confused about the accuracy of her projections. She had estimated that it would take three hours to manufacture one dress at a direct labor cost of $30 per dress. But what if more time was needed? Then her net profit would shrink even further. Even though Sandra would be producing 75 of the 100 dresses, and therefore did not necessarily have to pay herself in "real cash" for her direct labor, she still needed to account for her labor as an actual cost.

How Should Sandra Get Paid?

In her income statement, Sandra decided to include $3,000.00 in salary costs. She figured that, as president and CEO of Kickin' It, she should be compensated for her time. After all, if she was not managing the company, Kickin' It would not exist as a business. But was $3,000 the right amount? Is this how much her time, skill, and expertise were worth in the marketplace? And $3000 was a hefty fixed cost for her business to pay out each month. She was not sure the company could afford it.

Sandra tried to brainstorm some other possibilities. Perhaps instead of paying herself a monthly salary, she could receive a commission based on her sales revenue. In this scenario, her salary would appear on the income statement as a variable cost, as opposed to a monthly fixed cost. Just as Andre Jones was earning 5 percent of the total sales order, Sandra could allocate 15 percent of Kickin' It's sales to herself as salary. This way, she would not be locked into paying herself a fixed amount each month. Her salary would vary with the total sales.

This strategy seemed like a good plan for Kickin' It, but not necessarily for Sandra. What if Kickin' It did not make any money in a given month, then Sandra would not receive a salary at all. As an employee in Silicon Valley, Sandra had grown accustomed to receiving a set paycheck every two weeks. How could she manage her own personal expenses if she did not know how much money she would be earning from month to month? But if Kickin' It was profitable, did not that mean Sandra would also be making money, since she owned the company? It was all so confusing.

Sandra looked at the clock. It was already close to midnight. It was too late to turn back—she had already made the commitment to complete the order. She brewed a pot of coffee and turned on her sewing machine. She would have to figure out her salary issues later. It was time to get to work.

Case Study Analysis

1. Sandra's total start-up investment is $20,000. However, in calculating this amount, she did not account for the time and labor she invested to get her business off the ground. Suppose Sandra put in 500 hours of "sweat equity" valuing her labor at a rate of $16 per hour. What would her total start-up investment be?

2. The case explains that Sandra is confused about how she should compensate herself for her labor. Assume that she decides to pay herself a 15 percent commission instead of the monthly salary of $3,000. Recalculate her projected monthly income statement based on this scenario.

3. Sandra suspects that she might be underestimating the amount of time needed to manufacture a dress. Sandra estimates that, on average, each dress will require three hours of direct labor at a cost of $10/hour. Assume that in reality it takes five hours to manufacture a single dress. Recalculate the economics of one unit and projected monthly income statement based on this scenario.

4. In the case, Sandra expresses concern that she might not earn enough money to make it worthwhile for her to take on this job. Review her economics of one unit and projected monthly income statement. What might Sandra do differently to increase her net profit?

5. At the end of the case, Sandra surmises that if Kickin' It is a profitable business, then she will also personally earn money from its success. Are Sandra and Kickin' It one and the same entity? Explain your answer.

Chapter 8 | Financing Strategy: Debt or Equity?

"You do not get what you deserve, you get what you negotiate."

—Chester L. Karrass, pioneer of negotiation theory

Performance Objectives

1. Identify sources of capital for financing your business.
2. Explain the relationship between risk and reward.
3. Compare the pros and cons of debt and equity financing.
4. Establish a personal credit history.

To start or expand a business, you will need to raise some money. Raising money for a business is an aspect of **financing,** which is the use and manipulation of money. For entrepreneurs, that means obtaining the money to start and operate a business successfully.

There are two ways to finance a business:

1. Borrow money (debt)
2. Exchange a share of the business for money (equity)

Anita Roddick, owner of The Body Shop, opened her first store in England, in 1976. Within a few months, she was eager to open a second store because the first one was doing so well, but no bank would lend her money. Since borrowing was not an option for Roddick, she turned to equity financing. Her friend Ian McGlinn offered

The Body Shop sells a product roughly every 0.4 seconds to 77 million customers through its stores around the world.
(Rob Crandall, Stock Boston)

Use the ROI formula to calculate McGlinn's return on his investment in Anita Roddick's company.

ROI: _____ %

Performance Objective 1.》

to give her the equivalent of $7,500 in exchange for half the business, which Roddick accepted and used to open her second store.

McGlinn's share of The Body Shop came to be worth over $240 million—a dramatic return on investment! Roddick says she does not regret exchanging half of her (now) multimillion-dollar corporation for $7,500 because, without McGlinn's equity investment, she would not have been able to expand her company.

There are many potential sources of capital for your business. All capital can be classified as either debt or equity. Sources of capital include the following:

- Family and friends (equity or debt)
- Accounts payable (debt)
- "Angels" (equity)
- Banks, credit unions (debt)
- Minority financing sources (equity or debt)
- Small Business Investment Companies (SBICs, debt)

》Family and Friends

Family and friends are obvious sources for loans. But what about offering them equity (ownership), instead? Unless your business is incorporated, you will not have actual stock shares to sell, but you can still offer a piece of the profits in exchange for capital. You might offer 10 percent of the profits, for example, in exchange for the financing you need.

Explain to family and friends that, if they *loan* you money, they will only earn back the amount of the loan plus interest. If they invest capital in exchange for *equity,* on the other hand, they could get back much more than the original amount. Acknowledge that equity is more risky than debt but explain that the potential for reward is much higher. Be careful not to take money from friends and family that they cannot afford to lose should the business fail, however.

》How Often Do Small Businesses Really Fail?

It is a popular, oft-quoted misperception that "Four out of five small firms fail in the first five years of operation." You are likely to hear this from potential investors. According to *The Portable MBA in Entrepreneurship,*[1] however, "this claim has no basis in fact . . .

---

[1] William D. Bygrave and Andrew Zacharkis, eds., *The Portable MBA in Entrepreneurship,* p. 199 (New York: John Wiley & Sons, 1997).

Actually, there is good evidence that more than half—rather than one-fifth—of new small firms survive for eight or more years."

Business failure is defined by Dun & Bradstreet (D&B), which operates the largest commercial credit rating service in the United States, as "business termination with losses to creditors." D&B, which followed 814,000 small firms formed in 1977–78 for eight years, reported that, of the small ventures that were recorded as terminated during their first eight years of operation, only 20 percent to 25 percent actually closed due to bankruptcy. The other 75 percent to 80 percent were reported as terminations, but they were

- Businesses that were sold to new owners
- Businesses that changed—from a flower shop to a general nursery, for example
- Businesses that were closed when the owners retired or moved on to other businesses

The article concludes that the survival rate of the small firm, far from being four out of five, is closer to one out of two. More than half of all new small firms can expect to survive for at least eight years.[2]

A small business is considered a "high-risk, high-return" investment. For the investor willing to accept the risk, a small business can be a great investment opportunity. The return on investment (ROI) of a successful small business can be thousands of percent, but risk of business failure is also high. If your business fails, you and your investors will lose your investments. Your job, when you write your business plan, will be to prove that your business will succeed and that your investors can look forward to a high rate of return.

> *Over half of all new small businesses will survive for at least eight years.*

»Investors Want Their Money to Grow

When you ask a banker or friend for money for your business, you are asking for an investment. You should know, therefore, about some of the other options available to your potential investors. After all, they are only going to put money in your venture if you can convince them that it is a more attractive investment than their other options.

There are three categories of financial investments:

1. *Stocks*—Shares of companies (equity)
2. *Bonds*—Loans to companies or government entities for more than one year
3. *Cash*—Savings accounts, treasury bills, and other investments that can be liquidated (turned into cash) within 24 hours

Real estate, which is land or buildings, is another important investment. All investments involve some risk, which is the possibility that you could lose money. There is an interesting relationship between risk and reward:

> *The greater the potential reward of an investment, the more risky it probably is. High reward = High risk*

[2] E. Lewis Bryan, "Financial Management and Capital Formation in Small Business," *Journal of Small Business Management*, July 1, 1984.

‹2. **Performance Objective**

> ! *If someone offers to sell you an investment by claiming that it is low risk yet offers a high return, be very cautious. It is probably too good to be true.*

This implies the following:

If an investment is not risky, the reward will probably not be high. Low risk = Low reward

»The Time Value of Money

Money grows fastest in investments that offer a **compound** rate of return. A compound rate is one that is calculated with the interest that has already accumulated. The younger you are when you start saving for a goal, such as retirement, the more compounding will help your money grow. Suppose you invest $100 in an investment that pays 10 percent compounded annually. At the end of a year, you will have $110 ($100 plus $10 interest). At the end of the next year, you will have $121 ($110 plus $11 interest). Each year, your money will grow faster because you are earning interest on your interest.

The U.S. government allows you to set up tax-free retirement accounts called IRAs (Individual Retirement Accounts). "Tax-free" means you won't have to pay taxes on your returns as long as you keep the money in the IRA until you retire. If you withdraw it, you will have to pay a *penalty* and that year's income tax.

One type of retirement account, the Roth IRA, can be a good choice for a young person, because it allows a one-time withdrawal of money to buy a house. So, with the Roth, you can save not only for your retirement but for buying a house as well. There is a maximum amount of money you are allowed to invest in an IRA each year. To encourage people to save, the U.S. government has been increasing that limit each year.

Let's look at two individuals who have invested money in IRAs. Let's assume that they both receive 12 percent per year.

Person A: Invests $2,000 a year for 6 years at a rate of return of 12 percent, then stops.

Person B: Spends $2,000 a year for 6 years, then invests $2,000 a year for the next 35 years at a rate of return of 12 percent.

Person A: Invested a total of $12,000: $2,000 per year × 6 years = $12,000.

Person B: Invested a total of $70,000: $2,000 per year × 35 years = $70,000.

The following chart shows how each investment would grow over time.

At "age 62," Person A, who only invested $12,000, has earned nearly as much on the investment as Person B, who invested $70,000.

»The Future Value of Money

The **future value** of money is the amount it will **accrue** (gain) over time through investment. You can determine this easily using a Future Value Chart. Simply look up ten periods at 10 percent on the chart and you will find that $100 invested at 10 percent will grow to

$259 in 10 years. Compound interest—money making money—is the essence of investment.

Future Value of $1 after "N" Periods

Periods	1%	2%	3%	4%	5%	6%	7%	8%	9%	10%	11%	12%
1	1.0100	1.0200	1.0300	1.0400	1.0500	1.0600	1.0700	1.0800	1.0900	1.1000	1.1100	1.1200
2	1.0201	1.0404	1.0609	1.0816	1.1025	1.1236	1.1449	1.1664	1.1881	1.2100	1.2321	1.2544
3	1.0303	1.0612	1.0927	1.1249	1.1576	1.1910	1.2250	1.2597	1.2950	1.3310	1.3676	1.4049
4	1.0406	1.0824	1.1255	1.1699	1.2155	1.2625	1.3108	1.3605	1.4116	1.4641	1.5181	1.5735
5	**1.0510**	**1.1041**	**1.1593**	**1.2167**	**1.2763**	**1.3382**	**1.4026**	**1.4693**	**1.5386**	**1.6105**	**1.6851**	**1.7623**
6	1.0615	1.1261	1.1941	1.2653	1.3401	1.4185	1.5007	1.5869	1.6771	1.7716	1.8704	1.9738
7	1.0721	1.1487	1.2299	1.3159	1.4071	1.5036	1.6058	1.7138	1.8280	1.9487	2.0762	2.2107
8	1.0829	1.1717	1.2668	1.3686	1.4775	1.5939	1.1782	1.8509	1.9926	2.1436	2.3045	2.4760
9	1.0937	1.1951	1.3048	1.4233	1.5513	1.6895	1.8385	1.9990	2.1719	2.3580	2.5580	2.7731
10	1.1046	1.2190	1.3439	1.4802	1.6209	1.7909	1.9672	2.1589	2.3674	2.5937	2.8394	3.1059
11	1.1157	1.2434	1.3842	1.5395	1.7103	1.8983	2.1049	2.3316	2.5084	2.8531	3.1518	3.4786
12	1.1268	1.2682	1.4258	1.6010	1.7959	2.0122	2.2522	2.5182	2.8127	3.1384	2.4985	3.8960
13	1.1381	1.2936	1.4685	1.6651	1.8057	2.1329	2.4098	2.7196	3.0658	3.4523	3.8833	4.3635
14	1.1495	1.3195	1.5126	1.7317	1.9799	2.2609	2.5785	2.9372	3.3417	3.7975	4.3104	4.8871
15	1.1610	1.3459	1.5580	1.8009	2.0789	2.3966	2.7590	3.1722	3.6425	4.1773	4.7846	5.4736

»The Present Value of Money

Another way to look at investing is summed up by the old saying "A bird in the hand is worth two in the bush." You always want to have your money now. If you cannot have it now, you want to be compensated with a return.

Your money is worth more to you when it is in your hand for three reasons.

1. *Inflation*—When prices rise, a dollar tomorrow will buy less than a dollar does today.
2. *Risk*—When you put your money in an investment, there is always some risk of losing it.
3. *Opportunity*—When you put your money in an investment, you are giving up the opportunity to use it for a better investment.

Say a customer promises to pay you, three years from now, $10,000 for designing a Web site. Your next-best opportunity for investment has an ROI of 10 percent.

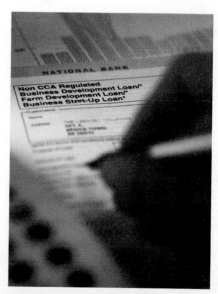

Filling out a loan application.
(Getty Images—Digital Vision)

Present value is the amount an investment is worth discounted back to the present. Look at the Present Value chart (see Figure 8–1) under period 3 (for three years) and 10 percent. The present value of $1.00 at three years and 10 percent is $0.75. The present value of the promise of $10,000, therefore, is $7,500 ($10,000 × 0.75 = $7,500). Your client's promise is worth only $7,500 in the present. Perhaps you should charge interest, because you are essentially providing a $10,000 loan for three years. Anytime you are asked to wait for payment, you should be compensated, because money in your hand now is worth significantly more than money promised for the future.

Biz Facts

When you sell a business, the price reflects more than the nuts and bolts of the operation. You are also selling the future stream of income that the business is expected to generate. This income is reflected in the price of the business, which is its present value. This is why businesses typically sell for several times their annual net income.

	Interest Rate per Year									
Year	1%	2%	3%	4%	5%	6%	7%	8%	9%	10%
1	0.990	0.980	0.971	0.962	0.952	0.943	0.935	0.926	0.917	0.909
2	0.960	0.961	0.943	0.925	0.907	0.890	0.873	0.857	0.842	0.826
3	0.971	0.942	0.915	0.889	0.864	0.840	0.816	0.794	0.772	0.751
4	0.961	0.924	0.886	0.855	0.823	0.792	0.763	0.735	0.708	0.683
5	0.951	0.906	0.863	0.822	0.784	0.747	0.713	0.681	0.650	0.621
6	0.942	0.888	0.837	0.790	0.746	0.705	0.666	0.630	0.596	0.584
7	0.933	0.871	0.813	0.760	0.711	0.665	0.623	0.583	0.547	0.513
8	0.923	0.853	0.789	0.731	0.677	0.627	0.582	0.540	0.502	0.467
9	0.914	0.837	0.766	0.703	0.645	0.592	0.544	0.500	0.460	0.424
10	0.905	0.820	0.744	0.676	0.614	0.558	0.508	0.463	0.422	0.386
11	0.896	0.804	0.722	0.650	0.585	0.527	0.475	0.429	0.388	0.350
12	0.887	0.788	0.701	0.625	0.557	0.497	0.444	0.397	0.356	0.319
13	0.879	0.773	0.681	0.601	0.530	0.469	0.415	0.368	0.326	0.290
14	0.870	0.758	0.661	0.577	0.505	0.442	0.388	0.340	0.299	0.263
15	0.861	0.743	0.642	0.555	0.481	0.417	0.362	0.315	0.275	0.239

Figure 8-1 Net present value chart.

»How You Can Compensate Investors

Now you can understand why investors are only willing to invest in your business if they believe they will receive a healthy return on their investment.

There are two ways you can offer to compensate an investor.

1. **Debt**—You borrow the money and promise to pay it back over a set period of time at a set rate of interest. Corporations sell debt in the form of bonds. You could borrow money from family and friends to finance your business and offer to pay them back with interest.

2. **Equity**—You give up a percentage of ownership in your business for money. The investor receives a percentage of future profits from the business based on the percentage of ownership. Corporations sell equity in the form of stock. You cannot sell stock unless your business is incorporated, but you *can* sell equity. You could offer a percentage of ownership in your business that will entitle the investor to a share of your future profits in exchange for financing.

Basic Business Legal Structures

Sole Proprietorship—Owned by one person, who may also be the only employee. The sole proprietor is personally *liable,* or responsible, for all debt. The sole proprietor keeps all profit from the business. It is easy and inexpensive to register a sole proprietorship at your county courthouse or chamber of commerce. **Example: An artist who makes and sells her own jewelry might choose a sole proprietorship structure.**

Partnership—Ownership is shared by two or more people. The owners are personally liable for all debt and share the profit from the business. Have a lawyer draw up a partnership agreement before registering such a business. **Example: Two friends who start a house-cleaning business together might choose a partnership structure.**

Corporation—An *entity* (legal "person") composed of stockholders who own pieces of the company. Owners are *not* personally liable; the corporation is liable. It is more expensive and complicated to register and run than a sole proprietorship or partnership. **Example: A clothing designer who hopes to sell her clothes to stores internationally might choose to incorporate.**

One disadvantage of corporations is that they pay tax on the profit they earn—and then when investors receive their shares of the profit, they have to pay tax on it again. This is called **double taxation.** A special class of corporations called "S Corporations" are not subject to double taxation, however, and are an appropriate legal structure for some businesses.

Nonprofit Corporation—Also called a 501(c)(3); a corporation whose mission is to improve society in some way. Churches, museums, and charities are all examples of nonprofits. The nonprofit structure is appropriate when you want to provide a service to people who cannot afford it. Nonprofits accept donations (gifts of money) that they must then use to fulfill their mission. **Example: A woman who wants to provide business clothing for women who are trying to find jobs but cannot afford the right clothes might choose a nonprofit structure. She can then accept gifts of clothing and money and use them to fulfill her mission.**

Cooperative—A "co-op" is a business owned and controlled by the customers/members who use its services. Each member has one vote in all decisions, regardless of the number of shares owned. Sometimes small business owners form a co-op, so they can purchase services and supplies together. This helps them get cheaper prices than they could as individuals. **Example: A group of DJs might form a co-op so they can purchase and share equipment and records as a group.**

»Debt Financing: Pros and Cons

Performance Objective   3.»

To finance through debt, the entrepreneur goes to a person or an institution that has money and borrows it, signing a promise to repay the sum with interest. That document is called a promissory note.

Interest is figured by multiplying the principal by the interest rate. The principal is the amount of the loan, not including interest. If $1,200 is borrowed at 10 percent to be paid back over one year, the interest on the loan is $1,200 × .10 = $120. Typically the borrower makes monthly payments until the loan is fully paid.

One advantage of debt is that the lender has no say in the direction of the business as long as the loan payments are made. Another is that the payments are predictable. The disadvantage of debt is that if the loan payments are not made, the lender can force the business into bankruptcy to get the loan back, even if that loan is only a fraction of what the business is worth. The lender can even take the home and possessions of the owner of a sole proprietorship or of a partner in a partnership.

Debt should be carefully considered by the beginning entrepreneur because it often takes time for a new business to show a profit. *The risk of debt is that failure to make loan payments can destroy the business before it gets a chance to prove itself.*

»Equity Financing: Pros and Cons

Equity means that, in return for money, the investor receives a percentage of ownership in the company. For the $1,200 investment discussed earlier, an equity investor might want 10 percent ownership of the company, which would mean 10 percent of the busi-

[Step Into The Shoes]

Donald Trump and Overreliance on Debt

Companies that rely heavily on debt financing are described as highly **leveraged.** Leveraged means financed with debt. This financial strategy works well only when business is very good. When business is slow, debt payments are more difficult to meet.

Reliance solely on debt is dangerous because creditors can force a company into bankruptcy or take over company property. Businesses sometimes find themselves in this position because the business owner was unwilling to give up any control of the company by issuing equity, and therefore relied too heavily on debt financing.

Real estate tycoon Donald Trump made this mistake in the early 1980s. Trump did not want to give up managerial

control by selling stock (equity) when he needed financing. Because of his reputation, banks were willing to lend him a great deal of money. When the economy took a downturn in the late 1980s, however, Trump could not make his loan payments. The banks were able to take several of his most valuable properties. By pruning his real estate holdings and paying off some of his debt, Trump was able to recover and expand his empire during the 1990s.

ness's profits. (This indicates that the business is valued at $12,000.) The investor is hoping that 10 percent of the profits will provide a high rate of return over time on the initial investment of $1,200.

The equity investor assumes greater risk than the debt lender. If the business does not make a profit, neither does the investor. The equity investor cannot force the business into bankruptcy to get back the investment. If creditors force a business into bankruptcy, the creditors get paid off first from the sale of the business's assets. Equity investors have a claim on whatever is left over after the debt investors have been paid.

The equity investor's risk is higher than that of the debt lender, but so is the potential for return. The equity investor could make the investment back many times over if the business prospers. He or she accepts a higher level of risk than the debt lender. The debt lender's risk of losing the investment is lower. So is the debt lender's return.

The advantage of equity financing is that the money does not have to be paid back unless the business is successful. Also, equity investors may offer helpful advice and provide valuable contacts. The disadvantage is that, through giving up ownership, the entrepreneur can lose control of the business to the equity holders, who may attempt to assert some managerial influence to protect their investment.

Debt Financing

Advantages:

- The lender has no say in the future or direction of the business as long as the loan payments are made.

- Loan payments are predictable—they do not change with the fortunes of the business.

- Lenders do not share in the business profits.

[Step Into The Shoes]

Apple's Steve Jobs

Relying too heavily on equity can also be the downfall of a business owner, as the story of Steve Jobs, cofounder of Apple Computer, illustrates. Because Jobs and his partner, Stephen Wozniak, were young men with very little money, debt financing was out of their reach. To raise money, they sold pieces of the company.

By the late 1980s, Apple was very successful—so successful that Jobs was able to hire a prominent PepsiCo executive named John Sculley to take over as Apple's chief executive officer. Unfortunately for Jobs, Sculley eventually set out to convince Apple's board of directors that Jobs was a disruptive influence in the company.

Eventually a vote was taken. The number of votes each shareholder had was proportional to the number of shares he or she owned. Jobs did not own enough of Apple's equity to fight off Sculley's effort to fire him. He was outvoted and thrown out of the company he had started.

Jobs was invited back to lead Apple as interim CEO in 1997, however, and was resoundingly elected as permanent CEO by shareholders in 2000.

Disadvantages:
- If loan payments are not made, the lender can force the business into bankruptcy.
- The lender can even take the home and possessions of the owner of a sole proprietorship or a partner in a partnership to settle a debt.
- Debt payments increase a business's fixed costs, thereby lowering profit.

Equity Financing (Stock, Percentage of Company)

Advantages:
- If the business does not make a profit, the investor does not get paid. The equity investor cannot force the business into bankruptcy in order to get paid.
- The equity investor has an interest in seeing the business succeed and may, therefore, offer helpful advice and valuable contacts.

Disadvantages:
- Through giving up ownership, the entrepreneur can lose control of the business to the equity holders.
- Equity financing is riskier for the investor, so the investor frequently wants both to be able to influence how the company is run and to receive a higher rate of return than a lender.
- The entrepreneur must share profits with other equity investors.

»The Six "C's" of Bank Borrowing

It can be tough for young entrepreneurs to get bank loans, because bankers tend to be conservative lenders. They do not like to lend money unless they are very confident that they will get it back. Bankers operate on the principles of the Six C's:

1. *Collateral*—A banker will want to see you pledge property or assets against the loan that the bank can take and sell if you cannot pay your loan.

2. *Cash Flow*—For a banker to lend you money, your business plan's projected cash flow statements must be convincing enough that the business will generate enough cash to pay off the loan.

3. *Credit History*—One's ability to borrow money is called **credit.** Before a bank will lend you money (or a credit card company grant you a card), it will want to know how you have handled credit in the past. It will contact a **credit reporting agency (CRA)** and get your credit report. These agencies, such as Trans Union and Experian, gather information given to them voluntarily by bankers, suppliers, and other **creditors.**

4. *Capacity*—You will also have to prove to the bank that your business's cash flow will be adequate for you to make your monthly loan payments. You will have to report your projected

income and expenses so the bank can judge your "capacity" to repay the loan.

5. *Commitment*—How much of your own money have you invested in your business? Have you gotten friends or family to invest? The banker wants to see that you are risking your own money, as well.

6. *Conditions*—Finally, a bank will evaluate *conditions;* this is the general economic climate at the time the loan is made. If inflation is on the rise, for example, the bank may be concerned that your earnings will not keep pace with inflation, thus reducing your capacity to repay the loan.

»Establishing a Credit History

If you are a small business owner looking for a loan, a bank will expect you to sign a personal guarantee that you will be responsible for paying it off. In other words, if you fail to repay, the bank will come after not only your business assets, but your personal assets, as well. The bank, therefore, will investigate your personal credit history.

‹4. **Performance Objective**

You may think that you have good credit because you have never borrowed money or used a credit card. Wrong! What you have is "no credit"! To establish credit you must prove that you are capable of making regular payments on a debt.

Typically, most banks will not lend to someone without a credit history, but many department stores will open a **charge account** for someone without a credit history. Charge accounts enable customers to make purchases without paying with cash at the time of purchase. By the end of the month, customers using a charge are expected to pay all or part of the purchase amount. To establish credit, open a charge account, charge a few small purchases and pay for them right away. Never miss a payment or pay later than the due date.

Finally, it is wise to periodically check your credit reports on file with the major credit reporting agencies every six months or so, to make sure they are accurate. For more information, call the following:

■ TransUnion at 1 (800) 916-8800
■ Experian at 1 (888) 397-3742

»Sometimes Credit Reporting Agencies Goof

The CRAs do sometimes make mistakes. You can also have disputes recorded as such, not as bad credit. If you are refusing to pay for your new TV because it does not work, for example, you can contact the CRAs and have the debt designated "disputed," instead of "unpaid."

Keep your credit history spotless—it is virtually impossible to grow a business substantially without using some debt financing.

≫ You Can Avoid Personally Signing for Business Debt

It is difficult to avoid having to personally guarantee a loan for your business, but it is not impossible. Joe Mancuso's book *How to Get a Business Loan Without Signing Your Life Away*[3] provides excellent suggestions, including these:

- Ask. Find out how big a company has to be before the owner does not have to personally guarantee a loan. Find out where your bank draws the line.

- Maybe you cannot get out of the personal guarantee when you sign for the loan. But how about when you have paid off the first third? Or the first half? Ask your banker and continue to bargain once you have shown that you can pay off the loan.

- Get your banker excited about your business. Take her or him to lunch; tell her or him how you have developed a monitor that will reduce the risk of crib deaths. As Mancuso says, "Help the banker be a hero."

- If you cannot get off the guarantee, chip away at it in negotiations. For example, does the guarantee mean the bank can come after your personal assets right away if you miss a payment? Or would the bank have to sue your business first? The latter would be preferable.

≫ Micro-Loan Financing

If you get to the point where you are negotiating a personal guarantee with a bank, you are doing very well. Most young entrepreneurs, however, will not be able to get their initial financing from a bank. If you need a loan, investigate the growing number of micro-loan programs supported by the federal government. A **micro-loan** ranges from $100 to $25,000. The loan is made not based on credit history or collateral but rather on the entrepreneur's character, management ability, and business plan. The money can be used to buy machinery, furniture, inventory, or other supplies for a new business, but may not be used to pay existing debts.

> *The Small Business Administration gives local nonprofits funds to process micro-loan applications.*
> http://www.sba.gov

≫ Line of Credit

Most businesses need to borrow small amounts of cash to pay bills while waiting to receive money from sales. Banks offer a form of debt called a **line of credit** that even small businesses can usually qualify for once they have been in business for at least a year.

---

[3] Joe Mancuso, *How to Get a Business Loan Without Signing Your Life Away* (Upper Saddle River, NJ: Prentice Hall, 1990).

A line of credit is a pre-arranged loan that the business does not have to take until it is needed. The entrepreneur does not have to pay interest unless money is actually borrowed from the line. When the entrepreneur does need cash, all he or she has to do is "draw" on the line of credit, because it has been pre-approved.

A line of credit is a short-term (under one year) loan only. The entrepreneur must replenish the line of credit in full at some point during the business year. The line of credit is not suitable for buying long-term items such as equipment, therefore. It is used only to cover short-term cash crunches.

» Venture Capitalists Seek High ROI

There are many sources for raising capital to start your business. Family, friends, colleagues, and acquaintances might be interested in investing or in making a loan to you. There are also investors and investment companies whose specialty is financing new, high-potential entrepreneurial companies. Because they often provide the initial equity investment, or **venture capital,** to start up a business, they are called **venture capitalists.**

Venture capitalists seek high rates of return. They typically expect to earn six times their money back over a five-year period. That works out to about a 45-percent return on investment. Professional venture capitalists will not usually invest in a company unless its business plan shows it is likely to generate sales of at least $25 million within five years.

Do not waste your time (and to entrepreneurs time is a precious commodity) looking for venture capitalists, unless you are convinced that your business will generate very high returns. The ideal candidates for venture capital are businesses with financial projections that support revenue expectations of over $50 million within five years, growing at 30 to 50 percent per year, with pre-tax profit margins over 20 percent.

» Venture Capitalists Want Equity

If your business plan supports those kinds of numbers, you may be able to interest venture capitalists in your business. Venture capitalists want equity in return for their capital. They are willing to take the higher risk for higher returns. Venture capitalists sometimes seek a majority interest in a business. Someone who holds a majority interest owns more than 50 percent of the business and has, as a result, the final word in management decisions.

To finance the Ford Motor Company, Henry Ford gave up 75 percent of the business for $28,000 in badly needed capital. It took Ford many years to regain control of his company. Still, many small business owners turn to venture capital when they want to grow the business but cannot convince banks to lend them money.

»How Venture Capitalists Reap ROI

Venture capitalists typically reap the return on their equity investments in one of two ways:

1. By selling their percentage share of the business to another investor.
2. By waiting until the company "goes public" (starts selling stock on the open market) and converting their investment into stock. The shares can now be traded on the stock market.

»"Angel" Financing

If your business does not meet the high-flying profit picture that attracts venture capitalists, it might still be of interest to **angels.** Angels are private investors (nonprofessional financing sources) who are typically worth over $1 million and are interested in investing in start-ups for a variety of reasons, from friendship to a desire to support entrepreneurship in a given field. Bill Gates, for example, has bankrolled several biotech start-ups because he is interested in biotechnology.

If your business has good management in place and a solid business plan, you might be able to raise angel financing. This type of investment is typically in the $100,000 to $500,000 range. Angels tend to seek a return of ten times their investment at the end of five years.

The idea is to get one angel in place and have that individual help you find another six to eight coinvestors. The catch is that angels can be very hard to find. Your best bet may be regional venture capital networks, which often also attempt to connect entrepreneurs and angels. Regional networks can be very helpful because angels tend to invest in businesses they can visit frequently. Look for people who are interested in or familiar with your markets and technology. Angels prefer manufacturing, energy, technology, and some service businesses. They tend to avoid retail businesses, which have a higher rate of failure.

»Online Networking

Networking is the exchange of valuable information and contacts among businesspeople. The Internet makes networking easy. You can search for angels—and connect with other entrepreneurs—online. Use search engines such as Google.com, Excite.com, and Yahoo.com, to find such Web sites as the Young Entrepreneurs Organization. Such networking is a great potential source of angel financing.

URLs

Young Entrepreneurs Organization, www.yeo.org

ICR Angel Financing, www.icrnet.com/book/22-sleeve.html

Cloudstart Angel Club, www.cloudstart.com

Try a local or subject-specific online bulletin board, or BBS. Most provide e-mail and Internet access and bring together people with common interests. Like proprietary services, BBSs originally provided proprietary information to subscribers, but now most offer Internet access in addition to hosting message boards and chat rooms.

»Financing for Minorities and Women

If you are African American, Hispanic, Asian, or belong to another minority group, look into Minority Enterprise Small Business Investment Companies (MESBICs). These are private investment firms, chartered by the SBA, that provide debt and equity capital to new small businesses. To find a MESBIC in your community, try Google, Excite, or Yahoo. Enter MESBIC and your state or city.

Minority Business Development Centers (MBDC) are another good resource. You should be able to find a center in your area through MBDA.gov.

The Small Business Administration (SBA.gov) has a special loan program to encourage female entrepreneurs.

> *Minority Business Development Centers;* http://www.mbda.gov *Small Business Administration,* http://www.sba.gov/womeninbusiness

»Youth Financing

If you are an entrepreneur under 25, you may qualify for grants, scholarships, and awards designed to promote youth entrepreneurship. Such sources of start-up capital include the following:

Ernst & Young Entrepreneur of the Year Award—
http://www.ey.com/GLOBAL/content.nsf/International/EGC - Events - EoY
   To qualify for the Ernst & Young award, you must be an owner/manager primarily responsible for the recent performance of a privately held or public company that is at least two years old. Eight to ten award recipients are selected in several industry and special award categories.

Guardian Life Insurance Girls Going Places Scholarship Award—
http://www.guardianlife.com/womens_channel/girls_going_places/ggp_program_agenda.html

National Association for the Self-Employed Future Entrepreneur of the Year Award—
http://benefits.nase.org/show_benefit.asp?Benefit-Scholarship
   The NASE "Future Entrepreneur of the Year" award and scholarship program is the nation's only major program supporting the philosophy of entrepreneurship, rather than a specific profession. The scholarship prize of $12,000 is given to a young man or woman who demonstrates leadership and academic excellence, ingenuity, and entrepreneurial spirit. In addition, NASE awards 22 other young individuals $4,000 scholarships. Since the program's inception, the organization has provided financial assistance of $855,000 to 423 students.

NFIB Free Enterprise Scholars Awards—
http://www.nfibeducationfoundation.org/
Each year the NFIB Education Foundation grants at least 100 NFIB Free Enterprise Scholars Awards nationwide in the amount of $1,000 each. These awards are nonrenewable and are not based on financial need. The awards can be applied to educational expenses at any accredited, nonprofit two- or four-year college, university, or vocational/technical school in the United States. A recipient may transfer from one school to another and retain the award.

NFTE Young Entrepreneur of the Year—
http://www.nfte.com
NFTE graduates can win an all-expenses-paid trip to New York to attend NFTE's annual "Salute to the Entrepreneurial Spirit" Awards Dinner, and a grant of $750 (business plan category) or $1,000 (operational business category) to be applied toward their business or college education.

SBA Young Entrepreneur of the Year Award—
http://www.sba.gov
At National Small Business Week, one outstanding entrepreneur is named to represent each state, the District of Columbia, Puerto Rico, and Guam as the state Small Business Person of the Year. From this group, the national Small Business Person of the Year is chosen.

Youth In Action Awards—
http://www.youthlink.org/us/awards.php
YouthActionNet gives awards to youth leaders and their emerging projects that promote social change and connect youth with local communities. It supports youth-led projects that have clearly defined goals and have potential for growth or further replication. Award recipients will receive $500, which includes funds for a disposable camera to photo-document their project for an online photo gallery. Recipients will also have the opportunity to take part in an online journal and contribute to a booklet of case studies highlighting the

[Global Impact]

The U.S. Encourages Other Nations to Become More Entrepreneurial

We encourage you to think globally when it comes to finding customers, researching the competition—and looking for capital. If you live in the United States, you are probably in the best place to find capital for your business. Europe's share of the venture capital market in 1999 was only 20 percent of $135 billion invested globally. American investors, meanwhile, invested $97.6 billion.

European countries are trying to change that, however. The members of the European Union have set forth an agenda for creating a dynamic, entrepreneurial, knowledge-based economy. Venture capital (called "risk capital" in Europe) was identified as a key factor in achieving this. Other countries and regions are undertaking similar efforts to become more entrepreneurial, which means more investors in these countries will be looking to finance small businesses.

work of young people who are bringing positive change to their communities.

»Bootstrap Financing

Last but not least, there is always **bootstrap financing,** which is finding creative ways to stretch existing capital as far as it can go. If you cannot secure venture or angel financing, do not let it stop you. Many hugely successful businesses have been started for under $10,000 by entrepreneurs who used a variety of techniques to stay afloat, including the following:

- Hiring as few employees as possible. Using temporary service agencies for staffing needs can help cut down on insurance and tax expenditures.
- Leasing rather than buying equipment.
- Getting suppliers to extend your credit terms so you can take longer to pay bills.
- Using personal savings, taking a second mortgage, arranging low-interest loans from friends and relatives.
- Floating accounts payable.
- Working from home, or borrowing office space to save on fixed costs.
- Putting profits back into the business to keep it going.

»Floating Accounts Payable

Float is the term for the time between a payment transaction and when the cash is actually received in someone's account. If a customer buys something from you but does not pay for two weeks, that period is a float. If you receive your phone bill on March 1 but do not pay it until March 20, you have floated your bill for 20 days.

Accounts payable is money a business owes its suppliers. You should always negotiate the best possible payment terms with your suppliers in advance so that your business can use float to have as much cash on hand as possible. This is a form of short-term financing from your own company.

Say you have a bill for $50 due October 15. You also have an opportunity to buy merchandise for $50 that you know you can resell in five days for $100. You could call the supplier and ask if you could pay the bill on October 20. You have just arranged an interest-free loan of $50 for five days.

Always call the creditor and request permission to pay a bill late. Never just skip a payment.

> Brainstorm ways to reduce hirings—using independent contractors, barter, etc.

»Your Business Plan Is the Key to Raising Capital

No matter whom you approach to raise money for your business, you will need a business plan. Venture capitalists and bankers will refuse to see an entrepreneur who does not have one. You may have a brilliant idea, but if it is not set forth in a well-written business plan, no investor will be interested.

A well-written plan shows potential investors that the entrepreneur has carefully thought through the business. All investors—bankers, friends, neighbors, or venture capitalists—crave information. The more information you offer investors about how their money will be used, the more willing they will be to invest in your business. Your plan should be so thoughtful and well written that the only question it raises in an investor's mind is "How much can I invest?"

»Writing a Business Plan Will Save You Time and Money

As you work on your business plan, problems you might not have thought of will be uncovered. Working them out on paper will save you time and money. Before you serve your first customer, you will have answered every question you can. How much should you charge for your product or service? What exactly *is* your product or service? What is one unit? What are your costs? How are you going to market your product or service? How do you plan to sell it?

Such questions can quickly overwhelm you if you start a business without a plan. By the time you have used all the worksheets, however, you will have answers—and you will have a rough draft of a business plan for your business.

A good business plan must include the following:

- Your business idea
- Long- and short-term goals
- Market research
- Marketing plan
- Start-up and operating costs
- Management
- Legal structure
- Time management
- Financing
- Breakeven analysis
- Accounting system
- Projected monthly income statement
- Projected yearly income statement
- Financial ratio analysis
- Balance sheet

Business Plan Competitions

- **NFTE Advanced Entrepreneurship Seminar Business Plan Competition**
- **EBLS Business Plan Competition**—*http://www.medweek.gov*
- **Carrot Capital**—*http://www.carrotcapital.com*
- **2002 JCI Best Business Plan (BBP) in the World Competition**
- **Fleet Youth Entrepreneur of the Year Award for New York City**—*http://ccnyc.neighborhoodlink.com/ccnyc/genpage.html? n_id5660130940*
- **Biz Builder National Business Plan Competition**

»Chapter Summary

Now that you have studied this chapter you can do the following:

1. Identify sources of capital for financing your business.

   - Debt—You borrow the money and promise to pay it back over a set period of time at a set rate of interest. Corporations sell debt in the form of bonds. You could borrow money from family and friends to finance your business.

   - Equity—You give up a percentage of ownership in your business for money. The investor receives a percentage of future profits from the business based on the percentage of ownership. Corporations sell equity in the form of stock. You cannot sell stock unless your business is incorporated, but you *can* sell equity. You could offer ownership and a share of your future profits in exchange for financing.

   - Sources of capital include family and friends, accounts payable, "angels," minority financing sources, bank loans, and credit lines.

2. Explain the relationship between risk and reward.

   - The greater the potential reward of an investment, the more risk it probably has.

     High reward = High risk

   - If an investment is not risky, the reward will probably not be high.

     Low risk = Low reward

3. Compare the pros and cons of debt and equity financing.

   Debt Advantages:

   - The lender has no say in the future or direction of the business as long as the loan payments are made.

   - Loan payments are predictable—they do not change with the fortunes of the business.

   Debt Disadvantages:

   - Debt can be an expensive way to finance a business if interest rates are high.

   - If loan payments are not made, the lender can force the business into bankruptcy.

■ The lender can take the home and possessions of the owner of a sole proprietorship or a partner in a partnership to settle a debt.

■ Loan payments increase fixed costs and decrease profits.

Equity Advantages:

■ If the business does not make a profit, investors do not get paid. The equity investor cannot force the business into bankruptcy in order to retrieve the investment.

■ The equity investor has an interest in seeing the business succeed and may, therefore, offer helpful advice and valuable contacts.

Equity Disadvantages:

■ Through giving up ownership, the entrepreneur can lose control of the business to the equity holders.

■ Equity financing is riskier for the investor, so the investor frequently wants both to be able to influence how the company is run and to receive a higher rate of return than a lender.

■ The entrepreneur will share profits with other equity investors.

4. Establish a personal credit history.

■ To establish credit you must prove that you are capable of making regular payments on a debt.

■ To establish credit, open a charge account, charge a few small purchases, and pay for them right away. Never miss a payment or pay later than the due date.

■ Check your credit reports on file with the credit reporting agencies every six months to make sure they are accurate.

Key Terms

accounts payable	float
accrue	future value
angel	leveraged
bootstrap financing	line of credit
charge account	micro-loan
compound	networking
credit	present value
creditor	real estate
credit reporting agency (CRA)	venture capital
double taxation	venture capitalist
financing	

[Entrepreneurship Portfolio]

Critical Thinking Exercises

1. What type of financing will you seek as start-up capital, and why?

2. What steps could you take to improve your creditworthiness?

3. How would you counter the argument from a potential investor that "most small businesses fail"?

1. Fill in the following table, using the Future Value chart in this chapter, to show the amounts of one invested dollar's growth at the interest rates and time periods given.

Periods	Interest Rate (%)	Future Value of $10
2	5	$11.0250
5	7	_____
10	12	_____
1	1	_____
7	8	_____

2. Fill in the following table, using a Present Value chart, to show the amounts of the net present value of $100 at the interest rates and time periods given.

Periods	Interest Rate (%)	Present Value of $1
2	5	$90.793
5	7	_____
10	12	_____
1	1	_____
7	8	_____

If you currently subscribe to or use an online service, BBS, or ISP, discuss what you like and dislike about the service and why you chose it.

1. Visit Business Owners Idea Café online and use the tool at http://www.businessownersideacafe.com/financing/index.htm to figure out how much capital you will need to get your business off the ground.
2. Visit www.privacyrights.org/fs/fs6-crdt.htm to learn about your rights to financial privacy; then answer the following questions:
   (a) Who has access to your credit reports?
   (b) What information cannot be legally included in your credit reports?
   (c) After how many years is unpaid debt erased from your credit reports?

Find three networking opportunities in your community. Describe how you could take advantage of them for your business.

Visit a local bank and ask about its line of credit. Have the banker explain the terms to you and what a small start-up business would have to show to qualify for the line of credit. Report back to the class.

Are there any angel investors that might be interested in your business? Who are they and how did you find them?

CASE STUDY: Present Value Calculations

Kay is considering investing in a franchise, which will require an initial outlay of $100,000. She has conducted market research and found that her after-tax cash flow from this investment should be about $20,000 a year for the next seven years.

The franchisor stated that she would generate a 20 percent rate of return. She currently has her money in a mutual fund, which has grown at an average rate of 14 percent.

Kay tells the franchisor that, since money has a time value, the actual rate of return according to her calculations would be much less than 20 percent.

Case Study Analysis

1. Do you agree with the franchisor or with Kay?

2. What methods are being used by Kay and the franchisor to calculate the rate of return?

3. Should Kay make this investment? Why or why not?

4. Should Kay speak with other franchise owners? What questions should she ask them?

CASE STUDY: Lee's Ice Cream

As the bell rang and the clock struck 3 P.M., South High School social studies teacher Jimmie Lee raced to the parking lot. It was a sunny afternoon in May—a perfect day to sell ice cream. Four years before, Jimmie had begun selling frozen treats in the spring and summer to children on Cleveland's east side. He had always wanted to be his own boss and driving an ice cream truck seemed like a great idea, because he could operate his business in the afternoons and during the summer months, when school was not in session. It helped that he was one of the most popular teachers at South High. All of Jimmie's students, and their parents, bypassed the other ice cream trucks and waited for Mr. Lee to drive down the block.

Getting Started: Jimmie Does His Research

To get Lee's Ice Cream off the ground, Jimmie had to learn to be creative, resourceful, and patient. When he first came up with his idea, he called his friend Joy Greaves, who had worked in the ice cream business for over 15 years. He wanted to know how much Joy thought it would cost to start his business. Joy estimated that Jimmie would need to invest about $25,000 dollars to purchase the necessary supplies and equipment, which included the following:

Item	Estimated Cost
Ice cream truck	$18,000
Freezer	$3,000
Soft-serve ice cream machine	$2,200
300 portions of soft-serve ice cream, napkins, toppings, and ice cream cones	$200
Insurance—first quarterly payment	$500
Commercial vendor's permit	$100
Electric generator	$1,000
Total Estimated Start-up Investment	$25,000

Can Jimmie Reduce His Start-up Investment?

As a public school teacher, Jimmie did not earn a large salary. He had $7,000 in savings, but, based on Joy's projections, this was not going to get him very far. Initially, Jimmie was discouraged, but then he started to brainstorm. Perhaps he could lower his start-up investment by purchasing used equipment. He wondered whether or not this would pay off in the long run—if this equipment required costly repairs or replacement parts that were no longer being manufactured. He scoured the local classifieds for used trucks, generators, and freezers to see how much he could save. Based on this research, Jimmie calculated a revised start-up investment budget:

Jimmie's Start-up Investment Estimates

Item	Estimated Cost
Used ice cream truck (including freezer)	$10,000
Used soft-serve ice cream machine	$1,500
300 servings of soft-serve ice cream, napkins, toppings, and ice cream cones	$200
Insurance—first quarterly payment	$500
Commercial vendor's permit	$100
Service fees for refurbishing used equipment	$1000
Used electric generator	$700
Total Estimated Start-up Investment	$14,000
Difference between Joy's Start-up Investment Estimates and Jimmie's Estimates	$11,000

If Jimmie purchased the equipment he researched, he would save $11,000. This was a lot of money. He decided it was worth the risk. He hoped that, if he ever did have to pay for repairs, it would cost less than $11,000 and he would still come out ahead.

Financing Strategy

Jimmie felt better knowing that he would only need $14,000 to get his business off the ground. He already had $7,000, which covered half of the projected start-up investment. He wondered how he could raise the rest of the money. A friend suggested that he apply for a bank loan, but, when he inquired at his bank, he was told that the chances of obtaining this type of loan were slim. Jimmie had never run a business before, so the bank was hesitant to invest in him. What other options did he have?

Jimmie decided to pitch his idea for Lee's Ice Cream to his friends and family. Perhaps they would be willing to loan him money if he agreed to pay them back with interest. He asked his brothers and sisters, but they turned him down. They did not think Jimmie was truly serious about his business. Then he called his best friend, Greg Allen, who worked as an auto shop teacher at South High, to see if he had any good ideas. Greg said that he had an old electric generator he would be willing to repair and donate. He even agreed to install it free of charge. Jimmie had planned to pay $700 for a used generator, so this was a great savings. Jimmie was one step closer to achieving his dream.

After hanging up the phone with Greg, Jimmie decided to visit his mother to see if she would be willing to give him a loan. At first Jimmie's mother was resistant, but he took the time to walk her through the business plan he had created. His mother was not totally convinced, but she liked the fact that Jimmie had thoroughly researched his idea. She decided to loan him $3,000. Jimmie promised that he would pay her back at 8 percent interest within a year's time.

Where Is the Money Coming From?

At this point, Jimmie was close to having his funding in place. He made a chart to get a clearer picture of his start-up investment:

Funding Source	Equity	Debt	Gift
Personal Savings	$7,000		
Relatives		$3,000 loan from his mother (to be paid back at 8% interest within one year)	
Friends			
Grants or Gifts			Electric generator ($700 value)
Other			
Subtotal	$7,000	$3,000	$700

Total Equity + Total Debt + Total Gift = Total Financing: $10,700
Difference between Total Start-up Investment and Total Financing = $14,000 − $10,700 = $3,300

Jimmie was so close to having all of his start-up investment capital in place, he could practically taste it. He only needed $3,300. That evening, Greg called to say that he had finished repairing the electric generator and could install it as soon as Jimmie was ready. Jimmie explained that he did not feel comfortable purchasing a truck until he had secured his total start-up investment. "How much do you still have left to raise?" Greg asked. "Only $3,300," Jimmie replied. "Well," if you will "sell me an equity stake in your company," Greg said, "I'll write you a check for $3,300."

To Sell or Not to Sell?

Jimmie was not sure how he felt about this. He really liked the idea of owning his business outright. Did he want to share ownership with someone else, even if it was Greg, his best friend? Also, Jimmie was not sure what percentage of his total equity he should offer Greg in exchange for $3,300. How could he figure out what Lee's Ice Cream was worth if his business had not yet earned a dime? Jimmie thanked Greg for his offer and explained that he needed to think about it overnight. He promised to call him back first thing in the morning.

Case Study Analysis

1. If you were in Jimmie's shoes, would you sell Greg an equity stake in Lee's Ice Cream? Explain. If Jimmie does sell equity for $3,300, what percentage of the business should he offer to Greg?

2. Assume that Jimmie rejects Greg's offer. Brainstorm three other financing strategies for Jimmie to investigate.

3. Examine Jimmie's projected income statement for the period covering May 1 through August 31, 2004 (Chart A). Assume that Jimmie does decide to sell Greg partial ownership in Lee's Ice Cream. Using the projected income statement as a guide, determine what percentage of his total equity Jimmie should offer Greg in exchange for $3,300. Explain your reasoning.

Chart A - Projected Income Statement - Lee's Ice Cream
Period May 1 – Aug 31, 2004

Revenue		36,900.00
COGS	5,000.00	5,000.00
Gross Profit		**31,900.00**
Other Variable Costs	535.00	535.00
Total Variable Costs	5,535.00	
Contribution Margin		**31,365.00**
Fixed Costs		6,000.00
Pre-Tax Profit		**25,365.00**
Taxes	25%	6,341.25
Net Profit		**19,023.75**

4. Jimmie's mother agreed to loan him $3,000 at 8 percent interest. Calculate the total amount Jimmie will owe to his mother.

5. Jimmie will sell his ice cream cones for $2 a piece. Assume the following about Jimmie's cost of goods sold for one ice cream cone:

Soft-serve ice cream:	.20
Ice cream cone:	.05
Napkin:	.02
Topping:	.03

- What is the total COGS for one ice cream cone?
- What is Jimmie's gross profit per unit?

6. Jimmie believes that he can sell an average of 150 ice cream cones per day at $2 per cone. Jimmie operates his business seven days per week between May and August, for a total of 123 days. Calculate the following:

- How many ice cream cones would Jimmie sell in total?
- What would Jimmie's total revenue be?
- What is Jimmie's total COGS?
- Calculate Jimmie's gross profit.
- Assume that Jimmie's total monthly operating costs are $1,500. His business operates for four months of the year. Calculate his total net profit for one year of business operations.

Cash Flow: The Lifeblood of a Business

"If you do your job well, the last thing you have to worry about is money, just as if you live right, you will be happy."

—Edwin Land, founder of Polaroid Corporation

Performance Objectives

1. Use a cash flow statement to guide your business operations.
2. Read a cash flow statement.
3. Manage and forecast cash flows effectively.
4. File appropriate tax returns for your business.
5. Collect sales tax.

David Kendricks, 28, has started his own label, Kickin' Records. He intends to find and produce hip-hop artists from his hometown of Newark, New Jersey.

Dave invested $25,000 in his new business. He saved the money by working at two jobs for five years. Dave set up a Web site from which he'll be able to sell his CDs. He bought an answering machine and created and printed his own stationery and business cards. He is presently spending his time from 8 P.M. until 3 A.M. looking for groups to sign to his recording label.

Dave goes to nightclubs and concerts and is spending about $100 a night on cover charges, transportation, and drinks. He has been finding, however, that the groups at the better clubs and concerts are already signed and have producers. Dave has had no sales because he hasn't produced any CDs yet. After being in business for six months, he's almost $20,000 in debt. Dave's business may go under because he isn't keeping close watch on his cash flow.

(Michael Shay, Creative Eye/MIRA.com)

Cash is the energy that keeps your business flowing, just as electricity keeps the lights burning. Run out of electricity and your lights will go out. Run out of cash and your business will soon be finished. Without cash on hand, you may be unable to pay important bills, even while the income statement says you are earning a profit. If you cannot pay the phone company and your phone gets cut off, it will not matter what the income statement says.

The income statement shows you what's going on with sales. It tells you how much revenue is coming in and how much that revenue is in relation to cost of goods sold and operating costs. The balance sheet is a snapshot of your business. It shows your assets and liabilities and the net worth.[1]

---

[1] Special thanks to John Harris for ideas in this chapter.

»The Income Statement Does Not Show How Much Cash You Really Have

Performance Objective 1.〉 Once you start a business, however, you will notice that sometimes, even when the income statement says you are making a profit, you have no money! This happens because there is often a time lag between making a sale and actually getting paid. If you make a sale and the customer promises to pay you in a week, the sale is posted on the income statement, but you do not actually have the cash yet.

For all the good information and guidance a monthly income statement can provide, you cannot base your business's daily operation by using the income statement alone. You will also need to use a monthly cash flow statement to track the money going in and out of the business. Simply put, **cash flow** is the difference between the money you take in and the money you spend.

Cash is the lifeblood of a business. If you are making sales, but don't have enough cash coming in to cover bills, your business will soon be finished. Without cash on hand, you can find yourself unable to pay important bills—even while the income statement says you are earning a profit. William Stolze, author of *Start Up: An Entrepreneur's Guide to Launching and Managing a New Business* (1994), calls the cash flow statement "by far the most important financial control in a start-up venture."[2]

The **cash flow statement** records inflows and outflows of money as they occur. If a sale is made in June, but the customer does not pay until August, the cash flow statement will not show the sale until August, when the cash "flows" into the business.

[Step into the Shoes]

King C. Gillette Faces a Cash Crunch

King Gillette was a traveling salesman for 28 years. In his spare time, he had tried to come up with a great product. He invented all kinds of gadgets that did not pan out, but, in 1885, when he cut himself shaving with his dull, straight razor, inspiration hit. Gillette thought of a disposable "safety" razor.

Gillette and a partner eventually got financing together and launched their business. The future seemed bright, but soon the company was $12,500 in debt. Even though people were excited about the product, by 1901 "We were backed up to the wall with our creditors lined up in front

waiting for the signal to fire," Gillette wrote later.[3] A cash crunch nearly destroyed a company that now is over 100 years old and makes such items as toothbrushes, as well as razors.

Gillette convinced a Boston investor to put money in the company, and, by the end of 1904, Gillette was producing a quarter million razor sets per year. This is an example of how an angel investor can help.

---

[2] William Stolze, *Start Up: An Entrepreneur's Guide to Launching and Managing a New Business*, p. 96 (Franklin Lakes, NJ: Career Press, 1994).
[3] Russell B. Adams, *King C. Gillette: The Man and His Wonderful Shaving Device* (New York: Little, Brown, 1978).

Can you think of a business that might bring in a lot of cash during part of the year and not much the rest of the time?

_____

_____

»Rules to Keep Cash Flowing

In order to avoid getting caught without enough cash to pay your bills, follow these rules:

1. *Collect cash as soon as possible.* When you make a sale, try to get paid on the spot.
2. *Pay your bills by the due date, not earlier.* You do not have to pay a bill the day it arrives in your mailbox. Look for the "due date." You will need to mail your payment so it arrives by that date.
3. *Check on your cash balance every day.* Always know how much cash you have on hand. One measure of your cash flow, therefore, is the cash balance in your accounting journal.
4. *Lease instead of buying equipment where feasible.*
5. *Avoid buying inventory that does not resell quickly.* Unless it is part of your competitive advantage to offer customers a wide selection, minimize the amount of inventory you stock. Inventory ties up cash—the cash you use to purchase inventory and the cash you spend storing it.

You can calculate your ongoing **cash balance** by subtracting cash disbursements from cash receipts, as you do when balancing your checkbook. Your goal is *never* to have a negative cash balance.

Use your accounting journal to keep track of the money your business receives and spends each day. Keep receipts for every purchase you make. Cash flow will equal the cash receipts less the cash disbursements for a business over a period of time.

»Noncash Expenses Can Distort Your Financial Picture

The income statement can distort your cash picture because it may include **noncash expenses,** such as depreciation. When you depreciate an asset, you are deducting a portion of its cost from your

Biz Facts

You can calculate your ongoing cash balance by subtracting cash disbursements from cash receipts. Your goal is to *never* to have a negative cash balance.

income statement. But you aren't actually spending that cash. You do not pay out money when you record a depreciation expense on your income statement.

Depreciation is a noncash expense because no money actually goes out. If depreciation is deducted from an income statement, therefore, the statement no longer accurately reflects how much cash the business is really holding. The cash flow statement does not include depreciation because it is not actual cash leaving the business.

»The Cyclical Nature of Cash Flow

The entrepreneur needs a cash flow statement to depict the cash position of the business at specified points in time. The cash flow statement records inflows and outflows when they occur.

In addition, cash flow is cyclical for many businesses, meaning that the amount of cash flowing into a business may depend on where the business is in its fiscal year. A flower store will have a lot of cash coming in around Mother's Day and Valentine's Day, for example, but may have very little during the fall. A college campus bookstore will have to spend a lot of cash before school starts to stock up on books, and will have a lot of cash coming in when students arrive to buy books for their classes. This is why keeping one eye on cash flow at all times will be crucial to the survival of your business. The phone company and the bank will not care that you won't have money coming in over the next three months; they will want their regular monthly payments. When you write your business plan, include a **seasonality scenario** describing your expectations for seasonal changes in your cash flow.

»Reading a Cash Flow Statement

Performance Objective 2.〉 On the following page is a simple cash flow statement for a small business. The first section records all sources of income. These are cash inflows, or *receipts* (not to be confused with receipts for purchases). The next section reports cash outflows, or disbursements, that must be made that month—insurance payments, interest payments, cost of goods sold, salaries, and the like.

The last section shows the net change in cash flow. This tells the entrepreneur whether the business had a positive or negative cash flow that month. You can have all the sales in the world and still go out of business if you do not have enough cash flowing in to cover your monthly cash outflows. The cash flow statement is essentially the business's budget.

The Cash Flow Equation

Cash Flow = Cash Receipts − Cash Disbursements

Here is an example of a cash flow statement. Inflows and outflows of cash are divided into three categories:

1. *Operation*—Money used to run the business
2. *Investment*—Money going into and out of investments in the business, such as equipment, vehicles, or real estate
3. *Financing*—Money used to finance the business (debt and equity)

Cash Flow Statement for Lola's Custom Draperies, Inc., March 2006

Cash Flow from Operating:

Cash Inflows:

Sales	$65,400	
Added Noncash Expenses	2,000	
Total Cash Inflows	**$67,400**	

Cash Outflows:

Variable Costs		
COGS	$29,360	
Other VC (Sales Commissions)	6,540	
Fixed Costs		
Factory Rent & Utilities	8,000	
Sales & Administrative	12,000	
Part-Time Tech Support Salary	1,000	
Taxes	2,875	($11,500 × .25)
Total cash used in operating activities	**$59,775**	
Net Cash Flow from Operating	**$7,625**	($67,400 − $59,775)

Cash Flow Out from Investing:

Purchase of Equipment	6,000	
Net Cash Flow from Investing	**$6,000**	

Cash Flow from Financing:

Loans	25,000	
Gifts	0	
Equity Investment	0	
Net Cash Flow In from Financing	**$25,000**	
Net Increase (Decrease) in Cash	**$25,000**	
Cash, Beginning:	0	
Cash, End:	**$26,625**	

Daniel Crow, an employee in the receiving department of REI's Distribution Center in Sumner, Washington, sorts products during an October inventory.
(Dean J. Koepfler, AP Wide World Photos)

»Forecasting Cash Flow

Performance Objective 3.›

As you get your business off the ground, you will need to prepare monthly cash flow projections to make sure there is enough money coming in to pay the bills. As with other financial statements, you will want to learn how to keep cash flow projections on your computer.

There are two steps to forecasting cash flow receipts:

1. Project your cash receipts from all possible sources. *Remember*, orders are not cash receipts because you cannot guarantee that every order will become cash. Some may be canceled and some customers may not pay. Cash receipts are checks that you are sure are going to clear, or credit card orders that have been phoned in, or cash itself.

2. Subtract expenses you expect to have from these projected cash receipts. Cash expenses are *only* those expenses you will actually have to pay during the projected time period.

How can you be sure that these projections will be accurate? You cannot be completely sure, but you should create them anyway, and review and update them constantly as you receive new information.

[Global Impact]

Cash Flow Statements Are Not Required in Every Country

In the United States, corporations are required by law to present cash flow statements. In some countries, however, companies are not required to present either a statement of cash flow or a statement of fund flow. This is the case in Germany, Italy, and Denmark. In Germany, many large companies voluntarily provide either a cash flow or funds flow statement. The United Kingdom does require cash flow statements, but only for large companies. The international trend, however, is moving toward the U.S. practice of requiring cash flow statements, as governments recognize that income statements do not reveal a company's true cash position and can mislead investors.

»Risking Your Cash on Inventory

As discussed previously, the entrepreneur takes a risk every time he or she spends cash. If you buy inventory, for example, you take the risk that no one will buy it at a price that will give you a profit.

There are two other risks with inventory: storage costs and **pilferage.** You will have to make sure you can sell the inventory at a price that will include the costs of storing it, and cover pilfering—the stealing of inventory by employees or customers. Barneys, the famous New York clothing store, had a 7 percent pilferage rate, which helped drive it out of business (although it made a comeback later).

There is also the danger that you will invest in inventory based on the expectation of receiving cash from the customers who owe you money (accounts receivable). However, a percentage of these receivables will probably never be collected, and if you aren't keeping track of your cash flow statement, you could get caught in a squeeze between your suppliers—who want you to pay for inventory you've purchased—and customers who haven't yet paid you for what they bought. Here is the catch: If you cannot pay your creditors, you could lose ownership of your business. That's what happened to Donald Trump and the Taj Mahal, in Atlantic City. He couldn't pay his loans so he had to turn over 80 percent ownership in the casino to the banks.

»Credit Squeeze

Credit is the ability to buy something without spending actual cash at the time of purchase. Once you have established a relationship with a supplier, he or she may be willing to let you buy on credit. If you own a store, you might be able to buy Christmas ornaments from your supplier in October and promise to pay for them in 60 days, after your Christmas sales.

If you aren't using a cash flow statement to keep track of your cash, however, you could get caught in the squeeze discussed previously, between your suppliers and your customers. Your suppliers might not extend you credit in the future. If you get into a position where you cannot pay your suppliers back at all, you could be forced to sell the business.

»The Burn Rate

It is normal to have a negative cash flow for the first few months of your cash flow projections, when you start your business. You are likely to spend more than you earn in the beginning stages. Businesses, such as biotechnology companies, that spend a lot on research and development (R&D) can have a negative cash flow, or **burn rate,** of as much as $1 million per month!

You will want to have a good enough business plan so that investors will include money to pay the first few month's bills.

Since a new company will probably spend more money than it earns while it is getting off the ground the question is this: For how long can you afford to lose cash?

The answer will depend on two things:

1. The amount of capital invested in the business.
2. The amount of revenue being earned.

Together, Capital Invested + Revenue = Cash on Hand

The rate at which your company will need to spend capital to cover overhead costs before beginning to generate a positive cash flow is called the burn rate. The burn rate is typically expressed in terms of cash spent per month. A burn rate of $10,000 per month means that the company is spending that amount monthly to cover rent and other operating expenses. If the company has, say, $20,000 in cash and is making $2,000 a month in sales, how long could it hold out?

Cash on Hand/Negative Cash Outflow per Month = Number of Months before Cash Runs Out

»Working Capital: How Much Cash Does the Company Have to Grow?

Once a business is operational, an entrepreneur must keep an eye on **working capital,** which is current assets minus current liabilities.

Current Assets − Current Liabilities = Working Capital

Working capital tells you how much cash the company would have if it paid all its short-term debt tomorrow with the cash it has on hand. What's left over is cash the company can use free and clear to build the business, fund its growth, and produce value for its shareholders.

All other things being equal, a company with positive working capital will always outperform a company with negative working capital. The latter cannot spend as aggressively to bring a product to market as a company that has positive working capital can. In addition, if a company runs out of working capital and still has bills to pay and products to develop, it may not be able to stay afloat.

»Cash and Taxes

Performance Objective 4.) Once your business begins making a profit, you will have to pay taxes—and that will also have an impact on your cash flow. Self-employed people, such as sole proprietors, by definition, do not have Social Security tax taken out of their income by employers. They must pay their own **self-employment tax.**

If you have net income from self-employment of over $400 a year, you are required to pay 15.3 percent of that income to Social Security as self-employment tax. The tax form you will use is called the Schedule SE. These taxes must be paid quarterly, so you will need to be putting aside cash in order to make the payments.

The federal government is financed primarily by personal and corporate income taxes. States usually raise money from **sales tax** on goods (not services). Most states also levy an income tax. City and other local governments are supported primarily by taxes on property.

Sole proprietors also pay income tax on the profit earned by their businesses. You must file an income tax return if you are single and under 65 years old and your income for the year was more than $5,550. Income taxes fund the federal government's operations and the many services it provides. You must make estimated tax payments to the IRS quarterly.

»Filing Tax Returns

Both income tax and self-employment tax returns must be filed (mailed) to the Internal Revenue Service (IRS) by midnight on April 15 of each year. If you file late, you may have to pay penalties and interest.

Failure to file tax returns at all can lead the IRS to charge penalties and, in extreme cases, even put someone in jail for tax evasion.

A basic form is the 1040 U.S. Individual Tax Return, and Schedule C—Profit or Loss from Business. Self-employment tax is filed using the Schedule SE. Tax forms are usually available at your local post office or bank. Forms can also be ordered from the IRS by calling 1-800-829-3676, or by visiting the IRS online www.irs.gov. and downloading any form you need.

The tax code is very complex. The IRS offers booklets and telephone service to help answer questions. Help with the 1040 form is available from 1-800-424-1040. You can also go to the IRS office in your town and meet with an agent who will guide you through the forms for free. It is important to get new forms and booklets each year, as rules, rates, and forms change from one year to the next. You should have the tax forms for your business prepared by a certified public accountant (CPA) or by a tax preparation service, such as H & R Block.

»Collecting Sales Tax

〈5. Performance Objective

If you sell products or services to the public, you will have to charge state sales tax and then turn in (quarterly) the taxes you collected to the state. Apply to your state's department of taxation for the necessary forms. In New York State, for example, entrepreneurs use the New York State and Local Sales and Use Tax Return to report quarterly sales tax. Some states only charge tax on products; some charge tax on products and services.

»Two ID Numbers You Will Need to Obtain

The legal structure you choose for your business will affect how you handle your taxes. But certain administrative tasks will be the same for all legal structures, and include the following:

■ Obtaining a federal identification number for the business— this is basically a Social Security number for the company that you can use to identify your business in all interactions with the federal government.

■ Obtaining a sales and use tax registration number from the state—you will be required by wholesalers to present this number to prove that you are buying items for resale and are therefore exempt from sales tax.

Corporations, LLCs, and limited partnerships must, in addition, file an annual report with the state government, along with a tax return, and pay an annual fee. The report must state the business address, and include the officers, directors, managers, and general partners.

»Tax Issues for Different Legal Structures

Each legal structure has tax advantages and disadvantages.

■ *Sole Proprietorship*—All profit earned by a sole proprietorship belongs to the owner and affects his/her tax liability. The business does not pay taxes on profit separately.

■ *Partnership*—Since a partnership is not a separate entity, the tax issues are basically the same as they are for the sole proprietorship, except that profits and losses are shared among the partners, who report them on their income tax returns.

■ *Limited Partnership*—This is treated in the same way as a partnership, except that a limited partner can use any losses as a tax shelter without being exposed to personal liability. This can be an incentive for family and friend investors looking for tax shelters.

■ *Corporation (Subchapter C)*—A corporation's profits are taxed whether or not any share of the profits is distributed to owners. Owners must also pay income tax on any profit they receive. This "double taxation" is a disadvantage of C-Corporations.

■ *Subchapter S Corporation*—Small companies can use this structure to avoid double taxation. The S-Corp does not pay tax on profits. The profit is taxed only once, as owner income. This structure requires all partners to take profits and losses in proportion to their ownership, so it does not offer the tax shelter possibility that a Limited Partnership does.

■ *Limited Liability Corporation*—This structure can offer both a tax shelter to some partners and a more creative allocation of profit and losses.

Finally, note that dividends paid by a business to stockholders are not tax deductible, but interest payments made to creditors are. This can be an incentive to raise capital via borrowing, depending on the tax issues your business faces.

» Make Tax Time Easier by Keeping Good Records

The tax code is widely viewed as excessively complicated and confusing, but your tax preparer will have an easier time of it if you have been keeping good records throughout the year. You will have to determine your net income (gross income minus expenses). If you have kept track of income and expenses in your ledger, this should not be too difficult.

Mistakes on your tax return could cause the IRS to *audit* you. That means the IRS would send an agent to your business to examine your ledgers and receipts and invoices to make sure your taxes were filed correctly. This is another excellent reason to keep good records and file all invoices and receipts, whether or not you use an accountant for tax preparation.

Several excellent software packages are available to help you prepare your tax return, but remember, the IRS likes paper. You must still keep all your receipts and other paper records for at least six years after you file a return.

Do not confuse accounting with taxation. Your accounting software generates financial records but you will still need tax software, like Turbo Tax (ChipSoft Inc.), to prepare your tax returns. Some accounting software, such as Quicken, allows you to export your financial information into your tax program.

If you do prepare your own tax returns on a computer, it is still a good idea to have a professional tax preparer review them. Your accountant is familar with changes to the tax code and can be a valuable consultant on tax-related matters. An accountant usually won't charge you to answer questions throughout the year, if he or she prepares your annual tax return.

URLs

TurboTax, *www.turbotax.com*
Quicken, *www.quicken.com*

» Tax Forms for the Entrepreneur

- The **1040EZ** is the simplest tax form to complete. However, as soon as you begin making business income—more than $400 in a calendar year—you will be required to pay taxes, and possibly file a Schedule SE (see below). It will be a good idea to call the IRS and explain your situation. A representative will be happy to let you know which forms you will need to file. Live telephone assistance is available from 7 A.M. to 10 P.M. your local time (Alaska and Hawaii follow Pacific times)—for individuals: 1-800-829-1040; for businesses: 1-800-829-4933. Once you know the forms you will need, you might want to seek professional tax advice, as suggested on the following page.

- Self-Employment Tax (**Schedule SE**)—This form is used to calculate self-employment tax due on self-employment income.

If you earned over $400 during the year, you must file a Schedule SE and pay self-employment tax.

■ Profit or Loss from Business (**Schedule C**)—In addition to self-employment tax, you will also pay income tax on your entrepreneurial income. You will file that income using Schedule C: Profit or Loss from Business.

One of the best business investments you can make is to hire a top-notch small business tax accountant or attorney as a consultant. Run your tax returns by this advisor each year, or have an expert prepare them, and you will minimize your chances of run-ins with the IRS.

≫As a Taxpayer, You Can Ask Questions

Tax forms and laws are confusing and change frequently. People do not agree on who should pay taxes and what government programs and services taxes should support. As a taxpayer you have the right to ask these questions:

■ Where are my tax dollars going?

■ Are my tax dollars supporting services that will benefit me and my community?

■ Am I paying taxes to support services that could be better supplied by private industry than by the government?

■ Are the tax rates fair?

Taxpayers demand answers to these questions from the politicians who represent them in city councils, state legislatures, and the United States Congress. One of the most important jobs politicians do each year is figure government budgets and then determine how much to tax people to finance them. They also pass laws to change the tax code.

Many business owners argue that the tax laws are so complicated and the rates are so high that people are afraid to start new businesses. Excessively high tax rates can damage business formation by discouraging entrepreneurs. Some people argue that many of the services government provides—such as the postal service or garbage collection—could be supplied more efficiently by private industry.

≫Chapter Summary

Now that you have studied this chapter you can do the following:

1. Use a cash flow statement to guide your business operations.

■ Cash flow is the difference between the money you take in and the money you disburse.

■ Without cash on hand, you can find yourself unable to pay important bills, even while the income statement says you are earning a profit.

2. Read a cash flow statement.

   ■ The first section of the cash flow statement records all sources of income that come into the business.

   ■ The next section reports cash outflows (disbursements) that must be made that month

   ■ The last section shows the net change in cash flow.

3. Manage and forecast cash flows effectively.

   ■ *Collect cash as soon as possible.* When you make a sale, try to get paid on the spot.

   ■ *Pay your bills by the due date, not earlier.* You do not have to pay a bill the day it arrives in your mailbox. Look for the "due date." You will need to mail your payment so it arrives by that date but not before.

   ■ *Check on your cash balance every day.*

4. Project your cash receipts from all possible sources. Subtract expenses you expect to have from these projected cash receipts.

5. File appropriate tax returns for your business.

   ■ Both income tax and self-employment tax returns must be filed (mailed to the IRS) by midnight on April 15 of each year.

   ■ Income tax is filed using the basic 1040 U.S. Individual Tax Return, and Schedule C—Profit or Loss from Business. Self-employment tax is filed using the Schedule SE.

6. Collect sales tax.

   ■ If you sell products or services to the public, you will have to charge your customers applicable sales tax and then turn it in to the state quarterly.

   ■ Apply to your state's department of taxation for the necessary forms.

Key Terms

burn rate	pilferage
cash balance	sales tax
cash flow	seasonality scenario
cash flow statement	self-employment tax
credit	working capital
noncash expenses	

[Entrepreneurship Portfolio]

1. Describe what you think the seasonality scenario would be for one year for a business you would like to start. Explain how you think the cash flow will be affected during the course of the year.

2. Imagine you are the owner of an upscale clothing store, like Barneys in Manhattan, which was driven out of business by a 7 percent

Critical Thinking Exercises

pilferage rate. What creative solutions could you come up with to reduce pilferage?

3. What are three rules for managing your cash?

4. Calculate the projected burn rate for your business. **(Business Plan Practice)**

5. Which tax forms will you have to fill out for your business? **(Business Plan Practice)**

   1040 U.S. Individual Tax Return _____

   Schedule C, Profit or Loss from Business _____

   Schedule SE, Self-Employment Tax _____

   Quarterly Sales and Use Tax Return _____

6. Figure out how much income tax each of the following individuals owes. The marginal tax rates are structured as follows:

   ■ Income up to $42,350 is taxed at 15 percent.

   ■ Income between $42,350 and $61,400 is taxed at 28 percent.

   ■ Income between $61,401 and $128,100 is taxed at 31 percent.

   The different rates apply to different portions of one's income.

Taxable Income	Tax Due
Jim: $42,000	_____
Michael: $98,750	_____
Susan: $24,000	_____
Kate: $100,520	_____

Key Concept Questions

1. Create a cumulative cash flow graph for a business with the following monthly cash balances:

January:	$40,000
February:	$25,000
March:	$13,000
April:	$5,000
May:	$12,000
June:	$2,000
July:	0
August:	0
September:	$1,500
October:	$8,500
November:	$12,000
December:	$21,000

2. Discuss methods of reducing pre-tax profit in order to reduce taxes for a corporation, a limited partnership, and a sole proprietorship.

3. What is a public service that you think could be provided more efficiently by private business? Why?

4. Which laws—such as minimum wage and age requirements, health and safety regulations, or antidiscrimation laws—will affect your business? **(Business Plan Practice)**

5. Calculate working capital for Angelina's company. Describe how her level of working capital might affect her business decisions.

Angelina's Jewelry Co. (Problem A) 7/30/06

ASSETS

Current Assets		
Cash	10,000	
Inventory	10,000	
Other Current Assets (Securities)	10,000	
	30,000	
Total Current Assets		30,000
Long-term Assets		70,000
TOTAL ASSETS		100,000

LIABILITIES

Short-term Liabilities		
Accounts Payable (AP)	10,000	
Short-term Loans	5,000	
Total Short-term Liabilities	15,000	15,000
Total Long-term Liabilities		15,000
OWNER'S EQUITY		70,000
TOTAL LIABILITIES + OE		100,000

Create a projected cash flow statement for your business for one year. **(Business Plan Practice)**

Application Exercise

Print the tax documents list available at http://www.ideacafe.com/bizforms/tax.html and highlight the forms you think you will need.

Exploring Online

CASE STUDY: Ed's Auto Parts

Ed Hernandez worked in auto parts stores for most of his life. After working with a large corporation for more than ten years, he decided to open his own business to serve both the auto repair shops and the general public. Because of his experience in the industry, he was well known by many of the proprietors of auto repair shops and also residents of his community. In the first year of business, the company grossed $290,000 and had a net profit before tax of $8,000.

Although his retail customers paid with cash or credit card, Ed offered the auto repair shops 30 days' credit. This was necessary in order to be competitive with other parts stores in the area. The increasing level of accounts receivable placed a great strain on the company cash flow, and, because of the lack of cash, Ed found it difficult to replace the inventory as quickly as it sold. When the business first opened, the inventory level was $65,000 and the accounts receivable was zero; however, by the end of the first year, accounts receivable was $25,000 and the inventory had dropped to $50,000. Ed's Auto Parts did not have a problem with bad debts; in fact, almost all his customers paid within 30 days, and only a few took 45 to 60 days. However, the normal 30-day credit was enough delay to cause cash problems.

Ed was concerned that the drop in inventory could result in lost sales if the customers could not get the parts they needed. He might also lose the repair shops as customers if the inventory shortages occurred frequently. Ed decided to ask his bank for a loan of $25,000. He planned to use $15,000 to restock inventory to its original level; the remaining $10,000 would be used as working capital.

Case Study Analysis

1. In addition to the bank loan, what could Ed do to try to collect his receivables faster?

2. Consider the request for $25,000. Is this the optimum amount?

3. Does the cash flow problem indicate that Ed is a poor manager? What could he have done differently, if anything?

CASE STUDY: Excelsior-Henderson Motorcycles

In 1993, brothers Dave and Dan Hanlon, along with Dan's wife Jennie, announced their plans to launch a motorcycle company called Excelsior-Henderson in their hometown of Belle Plain, Minnesota. The trio shared a passion for motorcycle riding and they wanted to turn their hobby into a business. Locals were thrilled that Excelsior-Henderson would provide badly needed jobs to people in the area. Skeptics questioned whether the Hanlons could successfully compete with big name brands like Harley Davidson, manufactured in neighboring Wisconsin, which dominated (over 80 percent) of the motorcycle market.

The Hanlons felt that they were ready for the challenge. In Dave's words, "Everybody in the industry who heard about us said: 'This has never been done. It cannot be done. And it will not be done.' And it was that kind of attitude that made us very, very tough." Their goal from the outset was to corner a small niche—1.5 percent—of the upscale motorcycle cruiser market. High-end leisure

cruiser bikes account for over 50 percent of all motorcycle revenue. Riders like them because their engines rev loud and slow, they feature a lot of flashy chrome, and their wide saddles make them comfortable to ride.

None of the partners had prior business ownership experience—let alone experience designing and manufacturing motorcycles. At heart, they were motorcycle riders who were passionate about bikes. During the time of Excelsior-Henderson's start-up, Jennie was working as a fashion model and her husband Dave was employed as a middle manager for a truck-leasing company. With degrees in business and accounting, along with past work experience as a mechanic, Dan was probably the most qualified of the three. But what the partners lacked in hands-on experience they believed they could make up for with hard work, passion, and commitment.

To raise funds for their start-up investment, the Hanlons reached out to their personal network of family, friends, and local investors. Within two years, they had secured $600,000 in financing. In 1996, the state of Minnesota provided them with a $7 million dollar business development loan. They even convinced Governor Anne Clarkson to pose atop one of their motorcycles at a photo op in St. Paul, the state capital. It looked as if the Hanlons were on their way.

In 1997, the Hanlons decided to put out an "IPO" (Initial Public Offering) so that they could sell equity in their company in exchange for cash flow that would help them to build the business. Shares of Excelsior-Henderson were introduced on the NASDAQ at a price of $7.50. Dan Hanlon felt that the company was proceeding too quickly with taking the company public. Excelsior-Henderson was operating with a negative cash flow and Hanlon had wanted to wait until the financial position had improved before it sold shares in the open market. However, a local newspaper had obtained a copy of Excelsior-Henderson's business plan, which outlined its intention to go public at some point. Once the story ran—against the company's wishes—the partners felt pressured to move ahead with the IPO sooner than they had intended.

All told, the IPO brought close to $100 million into Excelsior-Henderson's coffers. However, the Hanlons did not succeed in translating these resources into a profitable company. Excelsior-Henderson's stock price peaked at $10.50 in 1999 but then plummeted to below $3. Things were not looking good for the Hanlons.

Why did Excelsior-Henderson fail despite the company's success in designing and producing a quality product? One factor was the company's production costs. It had intended to manufacture at a cost of $9,000 per motorcycle. But, in reality, the company was spending between $10,000 and $14,000 to produce each bike.

The company also failed to meet its sales targets. In 1999, the Hanlons set out to sell 4,000 motorcycles. By the end of their fiscal year, they reported 1,800 units sold. They fell short of their sales target by over 50 percent. During the life span of their business, the Hanlons devoted seven years to designing their product and building their manufacturing plant. But by the time they were up and running, they had gone through a good percentage of their start-up investment. All told, they were only manufacturing motorcycles for eight months before they were forced to file for Chapter 11 bankruptcy protection.

According to Don Brown, an independent motorcycle analyst with DJB Associates LLC, in Irvine, California, "It takes about $150 million these days to field a new motorcycle of that type. They probably overestimated the market, and they probably did not do enough research to determine the styling and performance elements and the price point that would stand the best chance."

Excelsior-Henderson was rescued from bankruptcy when a Florida-based investment firm, under the name of "EH Partners," decided to acquire the failing company in 1999. The terms of the agreement stipulated that the Hanlons would remain with the company, but in nonexecutive positions. However, within a year, EH Partners had defaulted on its payments to creditors and ultimately filed for bankruptcy protection in its own right. Despite the company's difficulties, some locals hoped that Excelsior-Henderson would rise from the ashes. But Dan Hanlon no longer shared this dream: "Let [Excelsior-Henderson] have its peace," he said. "There is nothing left to restart. Let's be real about it."

Case Study Analysis

1. Excelsior-Henderson raised $100 million in debt and equity investment and yet it still went bankrupt. List three ways that the company could have better managed its cash flow.

2. The case mentions that Dan Hanlon was reluctant to issue an IPO while Excelsior-Henderson was still operating with a negative cash flow. IPOs are a way for companies to generate revenue by selling equity. Explain Hanlon's position. Why did he want to wait until the company was more financially stable before taking it public?

3. Why do you think that "EH Partners" decided to buy Excelsior-Henderson? What would EH Partners have to gain from purchasing a failed company?

4. Excelsior-Henderson succeeded in creating a quality product but this did not save it from failure. Explain some of the mistakes that the Hanlons made. What should they have done differently?

5. Excelsior-Henderson was a company that received a lot of media coverage. The Hanlons estimate that between 1993 and 1999 they averaged a story per day in both local and regional outlets. Explain why this media coverage may have both helped and hurt this entrepreneurial venture.

CASE SOURCES

Terry Fielder and Tony Kennedy, "An Unbelievable Mess" *Minneapolis-St. Paul Star Tribune*, December 7, 2001.

"Bank Sues Excelsior Henderson Motorcycles for Loan Repayment," Associated Press, April 7, 2001.

"Former head of Rollerblade now running Excelsior Henderson," Associated Press, October 11, 2000.

Jim McCraw, "3 Biker Entrepreneurs Take on Mighty Harley," *The New York Times*, August 20, 1999.

Unit 3   BUSINESS PLAN PRACTICE

At the end of each unit, you will have an opportunity to work on your own business plan. Please go to the Business Plan Worksheet Template section for Unit Three on the BizBuilder CD now to develop the following segments of your plan:

Fixed Costs

1. List and describe your monthly fixed costs.
2. Add a cash reserve that covers three months of fixed costs.

Insurance

What types of insurance will your business need, and why? What is the highest deductible you feel you can afford?

Recordkeeping

1. Describe your recordkeeping system.
2. List any bank accounts you will open for your business.
3. Will you accept personal checks from customers? Credit cards? Will you offer charge accounts or customer credit?

Projected Income Statement

1. Complete a monthly projected budget and one-year income statement for your business.

2. Use your projected one-year income statement to calculate:

   Projected ROI for one year: _____%

   Projected ROS for one year: _____ %

   Projected Payback for one year: _____%

Cash Flow

1. Create a projected cash flow statement for your business for one year.
2. Calculate the burn rate for your business.

Taxation

1. What tax forms will you have to fill out for your business?

   1040 U.S. Individual Tax Return _____

   Schedule C, Profit or Loss from Business _____

   Schedule SE, Self-Employment Tax _____

   Quarterly Sales and Use Tax Return _____

Small Business and Government

Which laws—such as minimum wage and age requirements, health and safety regulations, or anti-discrimination laws—will affect your business?

Financing Strategy

1. List the items you will need to buy to start your business.
2. Add up the costs to get your total start-up capital.
3. Add a cash reserve of one half your total start-up capital.
4. List the sources of financing for your start-up capital. Identify whether each source is equity, debt, or a gift. Indicate the amount and type for each source.
5. What is your debt ratio? What is your debt-to-equity ratio?
6. What is your "payback" period? In other words, how long will it take you to earn enough profit to cover start-up capital?

Raising Capital

1. Describe financing sources that might be willing to invest in your business in exchange for equity.

   Friends and family _____
   "Angels" _____
   MESBICs_____
   Other _____

2. Describe any debt financing you intend to pursue.
3. Do you plan to use bootstrap financing? Explain.

Venture Capital

1. Do you plan to pursue venture capital? Why, or why not?
2. List potential sources of venture capital.

UNIT FOUR

Operating a Small Business Effectively

Chapter 10 | Choosing Legal Structures and Distribution Channels

"Remember that time is money."

—Benjamin Franklin, American statesman, inventor, and writer

Performance Objectives

1. Describe the four basic types of business.
2. Develop a production-distribution chain for your business.
3. Draft contracts and use them to build your business.
4. Protect your intellectual property.
5. Choose a legal structure for your business.

Steve Jobs and Stephen Wozniak were in their early twenties in California when Jobs sold his Volkswagen mini-bus, and Wozniak his Hewlett-Packard calculator to raise $1,300 to start Apple Computer. They built the computers themselves in a garage.

Jobs and Wozniak made sales calls to every computer store in the area with their one sample computer and convinced a small store in Mountain View to order 50. The store agreed to pay Apple $548 for each machine.

Jobs and Wozniak had one month to build the 50 computers, but they did not have the money to buy parts. Using the order, though, the partners found a parts supplier that was willing to give them $25,000 worth of parts on 30 days credit. They started building the computers. By the end of the month, they had built 100, and delivered 50 to the store in Mountain View. They paid the supplier back for the parts on the twenty-ninth day. In the first six months of 2004, Apple sold almost $4 billion worth of computers, iPods, software, and related products. Steve Jobs is CEO, at an annual compensation that adds up to over $70 million.

Your business, no matter how humble its beginnings, probably has the potential to grow into a multimillion-dollar business, so it is important that you think through every step of its development. How you organize your business—the legal structure you choose, the relationships with suppliers you develop, the managers you hire—will have a tremendous impact on your ability to grow.

Apple President John Sculley (center) and co-founders Steve Jobs (left) and Stephen Wozniak (right) unveil the Apple IIc in 1984. (Corbis/Bettmann)

»The Four Basic Business Types

All businesses, large or small, can be divided into four basic types:

1. Manufacturing
2. Wholesale
3. Retail
4. Service

⟨1. Performance Objective

»Manufacturing: Makes Products

A manufacturing business is one that makes a tangible product. A manufacturer rarely sells its products directly to the consumer. It typically sells large quantities of its product to wholesalers. Some examples of manufacturing businesses are the following:

- Automobile maker
- Sporting goods manufacturer
- Book publisher

»Wholesale: Buys Products from Manufacturer and Sells to Retailer

A wholesale business buys products from manufacturers in bulk and sells smaller quantities to retailers from warehouses. Some wholesalers also have store outlets, but they do not sell to consumers. If you see a store with a sign that reads "To the Trade Only," it is a wholesaler. A wholesaler is sometimes called the "middleman," because wholesalers operate between manufacturers and retailers.

»Buying from a Wholesaler

One very simple way to start a business is to buy products in bulk from a wholesaler and resell them one piece at a time to customers. You could buy a dozen watches for $240 ($20 apiece) from a wholesaler, for example, and sell them at a flea market for $40 each.

A wholesaler is not legally allowed to sell to you unless you have a sales tax identification number. This shows that you intend to pay sales tax when you resell any item you purchase. Visit the Department of Revenue Web site for your state to apply for a sales tax ID number.

If you live in a city, there will probably be wholesale outlets you can visit in person. Find them by looking through your local phone company's *Business to Business Guide.* Libraries usually carry these directories. If you live in a small town or rural area without wholesale suppliers, pick the nearest large city and look in its *Business to Business Guide.* You can call wholesalers whose products interest you and order goods through the mail. You can also look up wholesalers by industry or location in the *American Wholesalers and Distributors Directory.* Your library should have a copy.

Another way to locate wholesalers is to contact the following:

Manufacturers' Agents National Association
One Spectrum Pointe, Suite 150
Lake Forest, CA 92630
1-877-626-2776

To reach your customers sometimes takes more than one language! A bilingual store sign from Chinatown, New York City. (Jeff Greenburg, Omni-Photo Communications, Inc.)

In addition, most major product lines (sporting goods, candy manufacturers, etc.) have trade associations—many of which are located in Washington, DC. These organizations will be happy to tell you about wholesalers in your area.

»Retail: Buys Products from Wholesaler and Sells to Consumer

A retail business buys from a wholesaler and sells directly to the consumer. Retailers operate stores that are open to the public. Examples of retail businesses are the following:

- Clothing store
- Book store
- Newspaper stand

»Service: Sells Time, Skills, or Expertise

The fourth type of business is a service business. A service business provides intangibles, such as time, skills, or expertise in exchange for a fee. Examples of service businesses are the following:

- Travel agency
- Law office
- Car washing
- Software development
- Business consulting

The previous examples are retail service businesses because they sell directly to the end consumer. There are also service businesses that serve wholesale or manufacturing customers.

»The Production-Distribution Chain

The consumer is the final link in a chain that extends from the manufacturer to the wholesaler to the retailer. When a consumer buys a pair of athletic shoes in a sporting goods store, for example, the chain would be as follows:

Performance Objective 2.»

1. Manufacturer produces a great quantity of a particular athletic shoe.
2. Wholesaler buys a large number of these shoes from the manufacturer.
3. Retailer buys a much smaller number of these shoes to stock a store.
4. Consumer walks into the retailer's store and buys one pair of shoes.

»Each Link Marks Up the Price

At every link in the chain, the price of a product is increased to cover expenses and to generate profit. These increases in price are called markups. At each step along the chain the price of a product is "marked up."

The markup is largely dictated by the competition. If the competition marks up its products 10 percent, for example, you will probably go out of business if you mark up yours by 20 percent—consumers will gravitate to the lower prices quickly.

When consumers purchase a product from a retail store, they are paying the retailer's **gross profit margin**—the markup from the price the retailer paid the wholesaler to the price the retailer is charging the customer. This markup, also called **gross profit per unit,** is used to cover operating costs as well as to provide a profit to the entrepreneur.

"Buy low, sell high" is an old business saying. If you are able to purchase a product at a relatively low wholesale price, and customers are willing to pay a retail price that includes a relatively high markup, you will have a profitable business.

Biz Facts

The expression "I can get it for you wholesale" means the person making the offer can get the item at the wholesaler's price, that is, without the retailer's markup. The tradition of bargaining in certain societies is carried on with the knowledge that the seller has marked up his cost. The bargainers are really negotiating the seller's profit margin.

If an athletic shoe store buys a sneaker from the wholesaler for $20 and sells it for $45, the retailer's markup is $25. This $25 markup is also called the gross profit per unit.

Retail Price − Wholesale Cost = Gross Profit
$45   − $20   = $25

»A Typical Markup

The manufacturer and retailer typically double the cost (or "keystone") to determine a selling price. A wholesaler usually marks up by about 20 percent to figure the selling price, since the wholesaler is only providing a service (stocking the manufacturer's product) for the retailer. If the wholesaler were to charge too high a price, the retailer might try to buy directly from the manufacturer and "eliminate the middleman."

Here is how a dollar of manufacturing cost gets marked up:

Manufacturer
$1.00 Manufacturer's Cost
$2.00 Manufacturer's Price

(*Wholesaler*
    $2.00 Wholesaler's Cost
    $2.40 Wholesaler's Price

    (*Retailer*
        $2.40 Retailer's Cost
        $4.80 Retailer's Price

        (*Consumer*
            $4.80 Consumer's Cost

There can be other links in this chain besides the four we have discussed. A manufacturer may have to buy raw materials or manufactured parts to make the product. There may be other middlemen, such as agents, brokers, or other wholesalers, between manufacturer and wholesaler or between wholesaler and retailer.

Using the markups described above, calculate the price at each link in the distribution chain for a blouse that cost the manufacturer $4.75 to make:

Manufacturer's cost: $_____

Manufacturer's price: $_____

Wholesale cost: $_____

Wholesaler's price: $_____

Retail cost: $_____

Retailer's price: $_____

»Percentage Markups

Because most entrepreneurs sell many items at different prices with different wholesale costs, it would be time-consuming to try to figure an acceptable markup for each item. Instead, retailers use percentage markups. Every item in a gift shop, for example, could be marked up 50 percent.

$$\text{Wholesale Cost} \times \text{Markup \%} = \text{Markup}$$

If you know the markup and wholesale cost of an item, you can figure the markup percentage using this formula:

$$\frac{\text{Markup}}{\text{Wholesale Cost}} \times 100 = \text{Markup \%}$$

Let's say the gift shop buys cards for $2 each from the wholesaler and sell them for $3 each.

$$\text{Markup} = \$3.00 - \$2.00 = \$1.00$$

If the gift shop owner finds, while doing her monthly income statement, that she is not generating enough profit, she can raise her markup percentage slightly to try to increase revenue. Or she can try to find a cheaper wholesale supplier to lower her costs.

»Use Search Engines to Find Wholesalers

Wholesale buying can be facilitated by using the Internet because many online businesses are trying to offer goods at low prices by cutting out the middleman. You may find Internet sites from which you could purchase products to resell at a profit.

The Web can be an overwhelming place, but search engines (also called "portals") make it easy to find the information you need among the millions of sites. Popular search engines include Google, Yahoo!, Lycos, Excite, Net Search, and WebCrawler.

Search engines continuously search the Web for new pages, storing the URLs for new pages in a database that searchers can access. To conduct a search, type in a keyword or phrase and the search engine will go through its database for pages containing that word or phrase.

It is virtually impossible for any one search engine to store URLs for every new page that crops up on the Net, so, if you do not find what you're looking for using one search engine, try another one.

»Markdowns and Discounts

Entrepreneurs also mark down prices to reduce inventory. You might want to reduce inventory for the following reasons:

- It is getting expensive to store it.
- The seasons are changing and you need to make room for new merchandise.
- Some items are just not selling at the current price.

A letter of agreement puts an oral understanding in writing, in the form of a business letter. The other party must respond to it in writing, either agreeing with it or suggesting changes.

Fax Contracts

Contracts are often sent via fax machines, which scan and transmit exact copies of anything on a printed page, including handwritten signatures. You can set up your computer to send faxes through a modem. A modem translates signals from your computer into a form that can be sent over ordinary telephone lines.

As more and more people own fax machines and use modems to get online, the opportunities to promote your business expand. Instead of mailing coupons to prospective customers, for instance, why not fax them? If you have a modem hooked up to your computer and fax machine, you can save time by programming your computer to fax your coupon to a list of fax numbers. The computer will automatically send your fax to the numbers on the list, leaving you free to do something else.

Breach of Contract

A contract is broken, or "breached," when a **signatory,** a person who signed the contract, fails to fulfill it. The person injured by the signatory's failure to comply with the contract may then sue for **breach of contract.**

For a contract to be breached, it must first be "legally binding." Most states require that all signatories be 18 years of age and that the contract represent an "exchange of value." If a contract is breached, a **lawsuit** must be brought by the injured party within the state's **statute of limitations,** which limits the time period within which legal action may be taken.

A lawsuit is an attempt to recover a right or claim through legal action. Because lawyers are expensive and court cases time-consuming, lawsuits should be avoided whenever possible. Other options are **small claims court** and **arbitration.**

Small Claims Court

Conflicts involving less than a certain sum of money, which varies by state law, can usually be resolved in a small claims court. In New York State, claims for $2,500 or less can be settled in this manner. In small claims court, each person is allowed to represent him- or herself before a court official. The official hears each side's arguments and makes a decision that is legally binding.

Arbitration

Sometimes contracts specify that conflicts may be settled in arbitration, instead of in court. In such cases an arbitrator—someone both sides agree to trust—is chosen to act as judge. The parties agree to abide by the arbitrator's decision.

A Contract Is No Substitute for Trust

A contract is not a substitute for understanding and communication. If you do not like or trust someone, having a contract will not improve the relationship. It could lead, instead, to a lawsuit. Never sign a contract with someone you do not get along with or trust.

A good reason never to sign a contract with such a person is that you might need to renegotiate the contract at some point. Running a small business is challenging and unpredictable. Say you make jewelry and you get credit from your silver supplier so you can fill a large order. If the store decides not to buy the necklaces, how will you pay back the supplier? If you have a friendly relationship, you may be able to discuss your situation and negotiate a longer term for the contract.

»Why Manufacturing Is Unique

Although entrepreneurs have successfully started all types of businesses, manufacturing companies offer some unique advantages for start-ups. Manufacturers can do the following:

1. Build products that do not exist yet
2. Fine-tune the design and features of the product in ways that "resale" businesses cannot
3. Get a patent on product designs to block competitors

There are disadvantages to starting a manufacturing business, however, including these caveats:

1. It can cost a lot to set up and maintain a manufacturing company. Manufacturing equipment can be expensive and so can the costs of purchasing (or leasing) a suitable manufacturing plant.
2. It can also be costly to hire and train workers to do the work.
3. Manufacturers have to pay to make the product first, but must then wait for the product to sell before getting their money back. The more processes that are needed, the more costly it can be to become a manufacturing company.

»The Idea-to-Product Process

A manufacturer can make every piece of its own product or have parts made by subcontractors. Many companies make the most important or complex parts of their products, but subcontract minor parts. Manufacturers like Ford and General Motors rely on other companies for parts that go into their cars. Many companies do the final assembly, regardless of who makes the parts.

»Job Shops[1]

Some manufacturing companies do not actually make a "final" product. Instead, these job shops, or "jobbers," are subcontractors for other manufacturers. They use their manufacturing plant and equipment to make parts or even entire products for other companies. Job shops usually work with drawings and specifications provided by the product's manufacturer. They usually get work by submitting and winning a bid. Job shops are useful to manufacturers because they are often able to achieve the following:

- Make a part less expensively
- Deliver a part more quickly
- Maintain and provide specialized equipment, so the major manufacturers do not have to purchase or maintain it themselves
- Offer manufacturing facilities to companies that do not have their own

[1]Many of the ideas in this chapter were developed by John Harris.

It does not matter whether a company makes its own product or has parts or all of it made by subcontractors. What counts is that the manufacturer controls the design, formula, or specifications of how the product is to be made.

The manufacturer controls the design of the product and provides the following:

- Drawings and Specifications—Diagrams and renderings tell others how to make the product and its parts. This includes written information about the materials, dimensions, *tolerances* (range of acceptable size variation), and parts to be used. These drawings will help you and others visualize what will be made. Sketches are okay at first, but complete and accurate drawings should be made later.

- Parts and Materials List—This list includes all of the materials and separate parts you will need to make the product. You must figure out where to get everything and how much it will cost.

- Prototype—Make a working sample of the product. This is called a **prototype.** Making a prototype lets you test the product to see if it works correctly. You may also find ways to improve the product or make it more cheaply while constructing the prototype. Because you are only making one (or a few), prototypes will cost a lot more than the actual product will when you make it in larger quantities.

> *When calling suppliers, ask for "OEM pricing." Many companies have better prices for Original Equipment Manufacturers.*

Whether you do it yourself or have others do it for you, manufacturing involves **tooling** and **setup costs.** Manufacturers must estimate what these costs will be before starting to manufacture the product.

- Tooling costs are required to make or adapt the equipment for your product. These costs are also called "one-time" costs because you pay for them when you set up the first time, but not again for additional orders. Manufacturers usually do not include these expenses in their "cost-each" of the product. Not all products have significant tooling costs.

- Setup costs have to be paid each time you make a batch, or a "lot," of the product. This covers the effort of getting ready to make the product each time. The larger the quantity produced, the smaller the setup costs will be per item manufactured. Almost all products have setup costs.

Biz Facts

To find a company to make your prototype, look in the *Thomas Register,* which is a giant catalog listing almost all the manufacturing companies in the United States. (It has about 25 volumes, each about 4 inches thick.) There are national and also regional versions of the *Thomas Register.* You can find a copy in most public libraries, or you can use Thomas online at the following:

http://www.thomasregister.com/ (national catalog)
http://www.thomasregional.com/ (regional versions)

[Step Into The Shoes]

Louis Temple Invents the Harpoon . . . and Dies Poor

Obtaining a patent can mean the difference between earning millions and living in poverty, as the case of Louis Temple illustrates. Temple was an African American living in New Bedford, Massachusetts, in the nineteenth century. In those days, whales were hunted for the rich oil derived from their blubber (fat). The oil was used for lighting lamps and making candles. New Bedford was the capital of the whaling industry.

Whales were hunted with spears called *harpoons.* Temple, a blacksmith, invented a "toggle" harpoon, which had a moveable head that prevented the whale from slipping free. Temple gave prototypes of the harpoon to several New Bedford ship captains to try on their whale-hunting voyages.

Whaling voyages took about two years. By the time the ships returned and reported the harpoon's great success,

Temple's invention had become public domain. Although he made some money from selling the harpoons he made in his blacksmith shop, it was nothing like the fortune he would have earned if he had patented his invention in time.

Temple was injured in a fall in his fifties and became unable to work. He and his family slipped into poverty, and when he died, at 54, everything he owned had to be sold to pay his debts. If his toggle harpoon had been patented, Temple and his family would have been extremely wealthy. How will you protect *your* intellectual property so you can profit from it?

≫ Public Domain

If an invention is put into use by the inventor for more than one year without obtaining a patent, the invention is considered to be in the **public domain.** This means that a patent will no longer be granted—anyone may use the invention without paying the inventor.

≫ When Filing a Patent Is Necessary

Performance Objective 4.≻

A patent cannot be obtained on a mere idea or suggestion. An invention should be fully developed and actually work before you can seek patent protection. You will have to prepare detailed drawings showing exactly how it works.

You do not need to obtain a patent unless you

- Have invented a product that you intend to market yourself or sell to a manufacturer
- Believe that someone else could successfully sell the product by copying your invention

The average patent takes at least two years to obtain. A patent search has to be undertaken, to make certain that the idea is new. Getting a patent is a complex legal process. Before starting it, see a registered patent agent or an attorney.

A patent application must include the following:

1. An in-depth description of the invention
2. A drawing of the invention (if appropriate)
3. A completed "Declaration for Patent Application"
4. A notarized statement from the inventor to the effect that he or she is the original inventor of the subject of the application

The filing fee typically ranges from $345 to $690.

Patent & Trademark Office
2900 Crystal Drive
Arlington, VA 22202
(703) 305–8600

> **!** *Do not go to the trouble and expense of obtaining a patent unless your invention is unique and you intend to use it commercially.*

»Manufacturing Tips

1. You may be able to make part or all of your product in your house or apartment; however, most cities and towns have zoning laws that limit what you can do in a residential area. If your business involves backing up tractor-trailer loads of steel, you will probably have to seek a location in a commercial area.
2. If manufacturing your product requires expensive equipment, consider working with a job shop that can make it for you. You can use one job shop, or many, depending on the item. Even if your product is complicated, you may be able to buy the parts but do the final assembly yourself. As we have pointed out, even large manufacturers often manufacture in this way. You can find job shops in the *Thomas Register*.
3. People who work in job shops know how to make things efficiently. They are seldom asked for design advice, though, because that's "engineer's work." See if you can get your jobber to help you improve your design and make it affordable. If you're lucky, he or she may not even charge you.

> **!** *If people go out of their way to help you, you should go out of your way to give them business. Relationships with subcontractors can make or break a small manufacturing business.*

[Global Impact]

Finding Foreign Partners

Big corporations often have gone overseas, where costs are lower. Changes in technology have made it easier than ever for small companies to do this, too. UPS, Fed Ex, and others are all competing for your international shipping business. You can also ship larger products by boat. Ocean freight is slower but much less expensive. Finding an overseas manufacturing partner could turn your manufacturing idea into a profitable business.

The following resources can help you find foreign partners:

1. The CIA Factbook, at http://www.cia.gov/cia/publications/factbook/ includes facts such as the following:
   - How much the average worker earns per year
   - How much education people have
   - What languages are spoken
2. Locate foreign companies on foreign search engines. Find "International Search Engines," or "(your country of interest) Search Engines," to get connected.
3. Every foreign country has a U.S. embassy in Washington, D.C. Each is all interested in making business connections in America.

»Just-in-Time Manufacturing

Although it is cheaper to manufacture products overseas, many American companies are taking advantage of new manufacturing methods to stay competitive. Just in time (JIT) manufacturing was developed in Japanese factories, but it is also very effective for the small entrepreneur.

JIT manufacturers ignore traditional concepts, like increasing the size of lots to take advantage of mass production methods. Instead, JIT focuses on making the smallest amount of product possible, but doing it quickly and efficiently. Goals of JIT manufacturing include the following:

1. Running the smallest lots (batches) possible
2. Reducing setup time and cost to the bare minimum
3. Scheduling production so that products are finished "just in time" to be shipped
4. Staying flexible to make the widest range of products, with the smallest setup and changeover costs

Companies often have a lot of money tied up in inventory, but if the inventory goes out of style, or is made obsolete by new technology, it may not sell. Losses such as these cost manufacturing businesses many millions each year. JIT is efficient because it does not waste raw materials, labor, shipping, and warehousing costs to make products that might never be sold.

»The Four Parts of a Business

Every business, no matter what type, is composed of four parts. Large businesses (corporations) employ experts who oversee these different operations. An entrepreneur, though, might initially have to handle all four parts alone. The parts are the following:

1. *Production*—Making or obtaining the product.
2. *Financing*—Securing and efficiently using money to develop the business.

A small, youth-owned company in New York makes skateboards. It has six styles, each of which uses a different wooden body. These bodies must be glued to waterproof plywood, then steamed and bent to form the correct shape. The outside contour of the body is cut out with a band saw. The owners do this after school in their high school's Tech Ed room. They can make the bodies themselves or pay other students to do it. Every skateboard style uses the same wheel assemblies and fasteners obtained from a wholesaler online.

The teenagers have signed a contract with a Madison Avenue marketing firm to create designs based on players from the NBA all-star team. The kids have to pay a royalty of $2 for every skateboard they manufacture, whether they sell it or not.

How could you apply JIT concepts to this business?

_____

_____

_____

3. *Marketing*—Developing strategies for getting the consumer interested in the product or service.

4. *Customer Service*—Maintaining and servicing a product (or service) once it has been sold—the act of keeping customers happy and loyal. (Customer service should not be confused with a service business.)

Business Legal Structures

After you pick the kind of business you want to be in, you will know where you fit into the production-distribution chain and you will be able to research markups, markdowns, and discounts in your industry so that you can be competitive. Next, you will have to choose a legal structure.

⟨**5.** **Performance Objective**

There are three basic legal business structures:

1. Sole proprietorship
2. Partnership
3. Corporation

First, let's look at sole proprietorships and partnerships.

Sole Proprietorship

A **sole proprietorship** is owned by one person, who also may be the sole employee. The owner receives all the business profits, but is also responsible for all the losses. Most student businesses are sole proprietorships.

The sole proprietor is personally **liable,** or responsible, for any lawsuits that arise from accidents, faulty merchandise, unpaid bills, or other business problems. This means the winner of a lawsuit against a sole proprietor can collect money not only from the business but can ask a court to force the owner to sell private possessions. The owner could lose his or her house or car, for example.

There are two kinds of liability:

■ Liability for debt
■ Liability for causing injury or death to others

A young person starting a business should only sell products or services that are highly unlikely to hurt anyone, in order to avoid lawsuits.

Advantages of Sole Proprietorship

■ It is relatively easy to start. Registration does not require much paperwork and is less expensive than for a partnership or corporation.
■ The business owner pays personal income tax on the business's earnings.
■ There are fewer government regulations than for the other forms of business.
■ Sole proprietors can make quick decisions and act without interference from others.
■ A sole proprietor keeps all the profits from the business.

Disadvantages of a Sole Proprietorship

- It can be difficult to raise enough money by oneself to start or expand the business.
- A sole proprietor must often put in long hours, often working six or even seven days a week, but there is no one to share the responsibilities and efforts.
- There is no way to limit personal legal liability from lawsuits related to the business.
- There is often no one to offer encouragement or feedback.
- The odds of failure are high, usually because of a lack of financing or business expertise.

»How to Register a Sole Proprietorship

It is easy and inexpensive to register a sole proprietorship. When you do, you will have a real business!

- If you do not register your business, you may be fined or even prosecuted by the IRS or other government agencies.
- If you are not registered, you cannot use the court system or bring a lawsuit.
- Banks like to see business ownership the way employers like to see that you have had previous work experience. If your business is not registered, banks will not even *consider* loaning you money.
- You can add having operated a registered business to your resume.

Steps to Registering:

1. Choose a name for your business.
2. Fill out a "Doing Business As" (DBA) form with the name of the business and your name, so the state will know the name of the person who owns the business.
3. An official may then conduct a name search to make sure the name you have chosen is not already being used. You may even be asked to help research the records yourself.
4. After the name of your business has been established, you will fill out a registration form and pay the required fee.
5. You may be asked to take the form to a **notary** to have it notarized and bring it back to the registration office. A notary is a person who has been given the authority by the state to witness the signing of documents. You will have to show the notary identification so he or she knows who is signing the registration form. A notary usually charges a fee of around a dollar.

»Licenses, Permits, and Certificates

Once registered, you will need to research local regulations that may apply to your business at the chamber of commerce.

Zoning regulations often prohibit certain types of businesses from operating in specified areas. There may be other regulations, too, such as restrictions on obtaining a liquor license for a bar or restaurant. If your business involves food, you will need to comply with safety and health regulations and probably obtain certain **permits.**

Contact the county courthouse or your local chamber of commerce to find out which licenses and permits are necessary.

- *Permit*—An official document that gives you the right to carry on a specific activity, such as holding an outdoor concert.
- *License*—An official document that gives you the right to engage in an activity for as long as the license is valid. A driver's license gives you the right to operate a motor vehicle.
- *Certificate*—Official document that proves something. A DBA, for example, proves that your business is registered as a sole proprietorship.

»Other Regulations

If you hire employees to work for you, there will be federal, state, and city regulations that come into effect. If you are the owner and only employee, however, those laws will not affect you (with the important exception of paying federal income tax on your profits).

»Sales Tax Identification Number

Every business, regardless of its size, must obtain a sales tax identification number and collect the appropriate taxes on all retail sales.

Collecting sales tax from businesses is one way government pays for paved roads, street lights, police and fire departments—all of which make it easier for businesses to operate.

To find out which sales taxes are required in your locality, consult your phone book for your state's sales tax office, or other relevant government office.

It is extremely important to follow all federal, state, and local regulations, and to pay all applicable personal and business taxes. As your business expands, your records and dealings must be completely honest and legal.

»Partnership

A **partnership** consists of two or more owners who make the decisions for the business together and share the profits and losses. As in a sole proprietorship, the owners face unlimited liability in any lawsuits. This means that *each* partner can be held responsible for paying debts or judgments.

The exception is the **limited partnership.** The limited partners have no say in the daily operation of the business and have, as a result, limited liability. Even so, there must still be at least one "general partner" who is liable for all partnership debts.

Partners bring different strengths and skills to a business. This can help the venture grow and succeed. In addition, partners can support and advise each other. On the other hand, partnership disagreements can become quite unpleasant and destroy the partnership, the friendship, and the business.

Despite the advantages of partnerships, we suggest being very cautious about entering into one, even with a good friend or relative. A lawyer should be consulted and a Partnership Agreement drawn up that carefully defines the responsibilities of each partner.

» Corporation

There are several types of **corporations,** but each is considered a legal "person" or "entity" composed of stockholders under one common name. So-called "C Corporations" issue stock. The shareholders who purchase the stock then elect a board of directors who manage the company.

The corporate legal structure offers two key advantages:

1. Corporations may issue stock to raise money. Essentially, the company sells pieces of itself to stockholders, who then become owners of the company.

2. The corporation offers limited liability. Unlike sole proprietorships and partnerships, the owners of a corporation cannot have their personal assets taken to pay business lawsuit settlements or debts. Only the assets of the corporation can be used to pay corporate debts. Most lenders will not lend money to a small, closely held corporation, however, unless the owners personally guarantee the debt—in which case the owners do become personally liable and can have their personal property confiscated to pay it.

The main disadvantage of corporations is that corporate income is taxed twice. First, the corporation must pay corporate income tax on its earnings. Then, when the corporation distributes its earnings as dividends to stockholders, they must include those dividends as personal income on their tax returns. A corporation is owned by its stockholders.

Shares of stock represent a percentage of ownership of a corporation. If privately held, the shares are owned by only a few people. In a "public" corporation, such as Ford or IBM, the company's stock is offered for sale to the general public and anyone may purchase it at the market price. Stockholders are paid dividends when the company's profits are good. Dividends are part of the stockholders' return on their investment in the company.

> **!** *When the abbreviation Inc. (for Incorporated), Corp. (for Corporation), or Ltd. (for Limited) appears after a company's name, it means it has been legally incorporated.*

» Types of Corporations

1. *C Corporation* Most big companies, and many smaller ones, are C Corporations. They sell ownership as shares of stock. Stockholders may vote on important company decisions. To

Advantages of Corporations

- Limited legal liability: the personal assets of the officers or stockholders cannot be used to pay corporate debts.
- Money can be raised through the issuing of stock.
- Ownership can be transferred easily, because the new owner does not personally absorb the corporation's debts.

Disadvantages of Corporations

- Corporations are often more heavily taxed than sole proprietorships or partnerships. Their profits are taxed twice: first, as the income of the corporation, and again as dividends to stockholders, who must include such dividends as personal income on their tax returns.
- The founder of a corporation (the original entrepreneur) can lose control to the stockholders and board of directors if he or she no longer owns more than half the stock. This happened to Steve Jobs, the cofounder of Apple Computer, who was eventually fired by the company (though eventually rehired).
- It is more expensive to start a corporation.

Corporations are subject to many government regulations.

raise capital, the C Corporation can sell more stock, or obtain loans from banks or investors.

Examples: Microsoft, General Motors

2. **Subchapter S Corporation** This type of corporation limits the number of stockholders to 75. It offers most of the limited-liability protection of the corporation, but Subchapter S corporate income is only taxed once—as the personal income of the owners.

Examples: Auto mechanic shop, print shop, graphic design firm

3. **Professional Corporation** Doctors, lawyers, architects, and other professionals can also incorporate themselves. The initials PC (Professional Corporation) after a doctor or lawyer's name means the individual has incorporated his or her practice, or belongs to a practice with others in the same profession. Professional corporations are subject to special rules.

Examples: Medical clinic, law office

4. **Nonprofit Corporation** A nonprofit corporation is set up with a specific mission to improve society. Churches, museums, charitable foundations, and trade associations are examples of nonprofit corporations. Nonprofit corporations are *tax-exempt*. They do not pay taxes on their income because the income is being used to help society. On the other hand, though, nonprofits may not sell stock or pay dividends. No one owns a nonprofit corporation.

Examples: National Foundation for Teaching Entrepreneurship, Bill and Melinda Gates Foundation

5. **Limited Liability Company (LLC)** The limited liability company (LLC) combines the best features of partnerships and corporations and is an excellent choice for many small businesses, especially one whose owners want to protect its assets from lawsuits.

With an LLC, income is taxed only once, as the personal income of the partners, but the partners receive the protection of their personal assets from lawsuits, as in the structure of a C Corporation. In addition, many of the restrictions regarding number and type of shareholders that apply to the Subchapter S Corporation do not apply to LLCs, making them even more attractive.

Examples: Skateboard shop, consulting firm

To compare these legal structures, please see Figure 10–1.

» Electronic Storefront (Web site)

No matter what type of business you have, opening an electronic storefront could introduce it to customers all over the world. An electronic storefront is a place online that customers can visit to view your catalog, price lists, and other information.

You will need to decide if you want to put your store up with an online service or by yourself. An online service would typically build your storefront for you, and include promotion and advertisements as part of the deal, to help make its subscribers aware of your store. On the other hand, if you put a site up yourself, you would have more control over what it looks like and where it is located, and your potential customers would not be limited to the subscribers to a particular online service.

One of the most cost-efficient ways to set up an electronic storefront is to hire a consultant to help you design it and choose which server to use.

URLs

StoreFront, *www.storefront.net*

MonsterCommerce, *www.monstercommerce.com*

» Tips for Entrepreneurs Who Want to Start Not-for-Profit Organizations

There are huge markets where people have needs—for food, shelter, education, and more—but cannot afford to meet them.

In the United States, there is the 501(c)(3) not-for-profit corporation to help address this situation. Technically speaking, a 501(c)(3) is a tax-exempt legal structure that can receive charitable donations from individuals, businesses, the government, and philanthropic foundations. Examples of well-known nonprofit corporations include the Boys and Girls Clubs, the YMCA, and the Sierra Club. People who donate money to not-for-profits benefit from their generosity by being able to deduct these contributions from their taxable income.

In the United States, close to one million organizations qualified for 501(c)(3) status in 2003, compared with 600,000 in 1993. Charitable donations rose from $148.4 billion in 1993 to $240.7 billion ten years later.[2] While competition for resources has increased,

---

[2] Jessica Stannard-Friel, *MBAs at the Crossroads of Corporate and Nonprofit America*, 12/03/04. From "On Philanthropy" Web site, *www.onphilanthropy.com*.

COMPARISON OF LEGAL STRUCTURES

	Sole Proprietorship	General or Limited Partnership	C Corporation	Subchapter S Corporation	Nonprofit Corporation	Limited Liability Company
Ownership	The proprietor	The partners	The stockholders	The stockholders	No one	The members
Liability	Unlimited	Limited in most cases	Limited	Limited	Limited	Limited
Taxation Issues	Individual* (lowest rate)	Individual* (lowest rate)	Corporate rate; "double taxation"	Individual* (lowest rate)	None	Individual* (lowest rate)
How profits are distributed	Proprietor receives all	Partners receive profits according to partnership agreement	Earnings paid to stockholders as dividends in proportion to the number of shares owned	Earnings paid to stockholders as dividends in proportion to the number of shares owned	Surplus cannot be distributed	Same as partnership
Voting on policy	Not necessary	The partners	Common voting stockholders	Common voting stockholders	The board of directors/trustees agreement	Per agreed-on operating procedure
Life of legal structure	Terminates on death of owner	Terminates on death of partner	Unlimited	Unlimited	Unlimited through trustees	Variable
Capitalization	Difficult	Easier than sole proprietorship	Excellent—ownership is sold as shares of stock	Good—same as partnership	Difficult because there is no ownership to sell as stock	Same as partnership

*When the double taxation of corporations is taken into account.

Figure 10-1 Comparison of legal structures.

more resources are now available to support the growth of organizations that choose to incorporate as nonprofits.

Like any business, a not-for-profit needs to generate revenue to cover its expenses. It needs to identify a target market and figure out how it will deliver its products and services. Some key differences and considerations exist, however, and you should be aware of them before you choose this legal structure:

1. ***No one can own a not-for-profit organization.*** A nonprofit cannot be bought and sold like other businesses. If you decided to dissolve a not-for-profit, you would not be able to sell it for your own financial gain. Nor can you issue stock to raise money. Not-for-profits are great vehicles for improving society; they are not effective as tools for creating wealth.

2. ***Not-for-profits are mission-driven.*** Before you can go into business as a nonprofit, you need to be crystal clear about your organization's mission. What problem(s) are you trying to solve? Is there a market of donors who will contribute money to your cause?

3. ***Define your unit of change.*** In a for-profit business, the return on investment is calculated by looking at the corporation's financial returns. Not-for-profit entrepreneurs need to think about their ROI a little differently. Not-for-profits do not exist to make money, so the ultimate measure of success will not be financial. Your ROI will be based on how much it will cost you to provide your services, and what level of change you brought about as a result of this investment.

4. ***Figure out how you will evaluate your success.*** As a not-for-profit entrepreneur, you will need to set goals regarding the changes you intend to manifest in society. How many homeless people will you feed? How many students will graduate as a result of your dropout prevention program? These goals must tie back to your costs. How much does it cost to provide these services? Given these costs, how many units of change did your organization achieve? How can you prove that your organization brought about these changes?

5. ***Analyze your financing strategy.*** Not-for-profit corporations have access to a large revenue stream that other business structures cannot tap. Not-for-profits generate revenue through grants, gifts, and earned income.

»Chapter Summary

Now that you have studied this chapter you can do the following:

1. Describe the four basic types of business.

   ▨ A manufacturing business makes a tangible product. A manufacturer rarely sells its products directly to the consumer. It typically sells large quantities of a product to wholesalers.

   ▨ A wholesale business buys products from manufacturers in bulk and sells smaller quantities to retailers from warehouses.

- ■ A retail business buys from a wholesaler and sells directly to the consumer. Retailers operate stores that are open to the public.

- ■ A service business provides intangibles such as time, skills, or expertise in exchange for a fee.

2. Develop a production-distribution chain for your business.

   - ■ At every link in the chain, the price of a product is increased to cover expenses and to generate profit for that link. These increases in price are called markups.

   - ■ The manufacturer and retailer typically double their cost (keystone) to determine a selling price. The wholesaler usually increases its cost by approximately 20 percent to figure a selling price, since the wholesaler is only providing a service (stocking the manufacturer's product) for the retailer.

   - ■ Markup Formulas:

     Wholesale Cost $\times$ Markup % = Markup

     $$\frac{Markup}{Wholesale\ Cost} \times 100 = Markup\ \%$$

3. Draft contracts and use them to build your business.

   - ■ A contract is a formal, written agreement between two or more parties.

   - ■ The relationships between the links in a production-distribution chain are defined by contracts.

   - ■ Never sign a contract without having an attorney examine it for you.

   - ■ Never sign a contract that you have not read yourself from top to bottom, even if your lawyer tells you it is all right.

4. Protect your intellectual property.

   - ■ Your thoughts and creations are your intellectual property.

   - ■ Patents protect inventions; copyrights protect works of art.

5. Choose a legal structure for your business.

   - ■ A sole proprietorship is owned by one person who also may be the sole employee.

   - ■ A partnership consists of two or more owners who make the decisions for the business together and share the profits and losses.

   - ■ A corporation is a legal "person" (entity) composed of stockholders under a common name.

   - ■ A Subchapter S corporation limits the number of stockholders to 75. It offers most of the limited liability protection of the corporation, but Subchapter-S corporate income is only taxed once—as the personal income of the owners.

   - ■ A nonprofit corporation is set up with a specific mission to improve society. Churches, museums, charitable foundations, and trade associations are examples of nonprofit corporations. Nonprofit corporations are *tax-exempt*.

   - ■ A limited liability company (LLC) combines the best features of partnerships and corporations and is an excellent choice for many small businesses.

Key Terms

arbitration
breach of contract
certificate
contract
contingency
corporation
draft
gross profit margin
gross profit per unit
lawsuit
letter of agreement
liable
license

limited partnership
notary
partnership
permit
prototype
public domain
setup costs
signatory
small claims court
sole proprietorship
statute of limitations
tooling costs

[Entrepreneurship Portfolio]

Critical Thinking Exercises

1. Production-Distribution Chain **(Business Plan Practice)**
   a. How do you plan to distribute your product to your target market?
   b. Use the following chart to show the production-distribution channel for your own business and the markups at each point in the chain.

   Manufacturer

   Name:_____

   Contact information: _____

   Markup: $_____

   Markup percentage: %_____

   Wholesaler

   Name:_____

   Contact information: _____

   Markup: $_____

   Markup percentage: %_____

   c. What is the estimated delivery time between when you place an order with your supplier and when you will have the product available for your customers?

2. A manufacturer makes a line of woman's handbags. This company offers 6,000 different styles of handbags in its catalog. It sells almost 25,000 handbags per year, but it is not known which style is going to sell from one week to the next.

   The company has a JIT system and a mass production system to make the same line of handbags. Both manufacturing systems work well, and both cost about the same to operate. The JIT system can make up to 100 handbags a day; however, it is very flexible. If necessary, it can produce 100 completely different styles in a single day of operation.

   The mass production system takes half a day to set up and can make 1,000 handbags—all the same style—in the second half of the day. It is 10 times as fast as the JIT system.

Raw materials cost $4 per handbag and are the same whichever system is used to do the work. The company likes to order enough materials to make 2,000 handbags. That's usually enough to cover a month of orders.

The company has discovered a trick to run more than one style of handbag with the mass production system. If it sets up in the morning and runs just one handbag until noon, it can use the afternoon to change over to a different style and still have time to run another handbag before closing at 5:00. This gives it two handbags produced in one day, if necessary.

The average day—100 handbags, each of a different style are ordered	Mass Production System: using the "regular method"	Mass Production System: using the "2 setups" trick	JIT System
Units shipped	1	2	100
Percentage of orders for the day filled	1%	2%	100%
Amount of unsold inventory created	999	0	0
Raw materials available for future work	1,000 units / $4,000 value	1,998 units / $7,992 value	1,900 units / $ 7,600 value

    a. Which system is more efficient? Why?

    b. If the company could only keep one of these manufacturing systems, which one do you think it should keep? Explain.

3. What can happen to an entrepreneur who is personally liable for the business? How can you protect yourself from personal liability? Say your friend wants to start a business making custom skateboards. Write a memo to your friend explaining the risks involved and ways to protect him- or herself.

4. Choose a partner in class and make a list of the technology each of you can personally access. Brainstorm how you might combine your technological resources to create a successful business. Describe in detail how the partnership would work. For example, would the person contributing more technology have a larger share of the business, or would profits and expenses be split equally? Draw up a partnership agreement that specifies each partner's duties and how much money and time each will invest in the business.

5. Which legal structure will you choose for your business? **(Business Plan Practice)**

    Sole proprietorship _____

    Partnership _____

    Limited partnership _____

    C corporation _____

    Subchapter S _____

    Limited liability corporation _____

    Not-for-profit corporation _____

    a. Why did you choose this structure?

    b. Who will be the partners or stockholders for your company?

    c. Describe the steps you will take to register your business.

6. If your business is incorporated, what percentage of your company is owned by one share of stock? Is your corporation's stock publicly or privately held? **(Business Plan Practice)**

7. Examine the labels on the shoes and clothing you are wearing today. Which items were made in foreign countries? How many dollars per hour do you think the people earned who made these articles of clothing? Why do you think the company that manufactured these items had them made abroad?

Key Concept Questions

1. What is the most important contract you will need to run your business? Describe any additional contracts you have or plan to secure. **(Business Plan Practice)**

2. Negotiate and write a letter of agreement between you and a fellow student. You could agree to become business partners, for example, or to supply a product or service for the other person's business.

3. Find a lawyer who might be willing to help you with your business. Try asking your parents, relatives who are in business, or storeowners in your community. The Small Business Administration sometimes offers free or low-cost legal services to entrepreneurs. **(Business Plan Practice)**

4. Use your local telephone company's *Business to Business Guide* or *The American Wholesalers and Distributors Directory* to locate wholesalers you could visit or from whom you could order products for resale.

5. Is a DBA a certificate, a permit, or a license? Explain.

6. Which government identification number must you have before you can sell a product or service? Why? **(Business Plan Practice)**

7. What is the purpose of having a form notarized?

8. What does your signature at the bottom of a contract mean in a court of law? What two things should you do before signing a contract?

Application Exercises

1. Calculate the following markups and markup percentages.

Item	Retail Price	Wholesale Cost	Markup	Markup%
Watch	$85.00	$40.00	_____	_____
Car	$25,499.00	$12,250.00	_____	_____
Sunglasses	$112.99	$42.00	_____	_____
Sneakers	$53.69	$18.00	_____	_____
Computer	$1200.00	$800.00	_____	_____
Discman	$117.00	$60.00	_____	_____

2. Assume you are a contractor and you have been hired to build a house. Your direct labor costs are $45,000. Your materials will cost $55,000. What do you think you should charge for the job? Explain your reasoning.

For the business you plan to start, research licensing regulations in your area and describe how they will affect your operation.

Exploring Your Community

1. Where will you purchase the products you plan to sell, or the products you plan to use to manufacture the products you will be selling?

2. Have you applied for a sales tax ID number?

3. What are the zoning laws in your location? Does your business comply?

4. What nonprofit business could you start to help your community? Answer the questions below to describe it (**Business Plan Practice):**

   (a) What is the name of your nonprofit?

   (b) What problem(s) are you are trying to solve?

   (c) Describe the mission of your organization.

   (d) Describe the programs and services you plan to create.

5. How will your organization achieve the changes you intend to bring about?

6. What is the unit of change (per person, animal, house, etc.)?

7. How will you measure these changes?

8. Who are your competitors?

9. How much will it cost you to deliver a unit of service?

10. What sources of funding will you seek?

CASE STUDY: How to Organize

Sam Jones, Mary Adams, and Larry Brown have been talking about starting their own business for several years. Sam is an electronics repairman, Mary is a partner in a large law firm, and Larry is an excellent salesperson. Sam and Larry will work in the business on an equal basis.

It will cost $100,000 to start this business. Sam has no money, Mary has $60,000, and Larry has $40,000. Sam has contacts with three organizations that appear willing to buy services from the new company for a minimum of two years. Each customer would buy approximately $50,000 of services per year. The service to be provided is brand new to the waste disposal field and was developed by Larry and Sam over the past three years. Mary has been their advisor on legal and design-protection issues and she has not charged any fees with respect to the development of the concept or the business. Since the service is new,

there is some concern about the amount of liability that would be necessary. One of the primary tasks of the new company will be to build a service center that will require financing a building, probably with a bank loan. Sam and Mary have excellent credit ratings, but Larry has accumulated some credit problems relating to a failed housing development some four years before. Several of Sam and Larry's colleagues have followed their plans for the new waste disposal service and have expressed an interest in investing some money.

Case Study Analysis

1. What information about forms of organization does the group need?

2. What form of organization would you recommend to the group and why?

CASE STUDY: Magnetic Poetry

Dave Kapell, founder of the innovative company Magnetic Poetry, Inc., should be thankful that he has allergies. Kapell heads a wildly successful $7 million dollar Minnesota-based business that designs and markets theme-based poetry kits, each containing 470 words on magnetic strips that people typically affix to their refrigerators and rearrange creatively. But, ten years ago, Kapell was a struggling cabdriver and aspiring musician who liked to write songs by cutting out words from newspapers and magazines. He would spend hours arranging the cutouts on metal cookie trays until he had "written" a song. But after one too many allergy attacks, Kapell decided to glue his paper cutouts to magnets so that his songs wouldn't blow away each time he was overcome by the urge to sneeze.

Whenever his friends came over to visit, they would play with the word magnets on Kapell's refrigerator. In 1993, a friend suggested that he experiment with selling his magnets at a local crafts fair. Kapell got to work and laboriously produced one hundred of his magnetic word kits using a typewriter, a magnet sheet, laminate coating, and scissors. Much to his surprise, he sold all of the kits within three hours. He knew that he was on to something.

Kapell realized that he couldn't tackle the manufacturing of his word kits on his own and decided to hire some friends to help him. For $10 an hour, along with free pizza and beer, his friends created several hundred new kits. According to Kapell, "That was the start of about three years of absolute cranking, keeping up with demand."[3]

As word continued to spread about his product, he realized that he needed to upgrade his manufacturing process. He and his friends were losing sleep by staying up all night trying to fulfill orders on time. Kapell decided to invest $5,000 in sales revenue to hire a local graphic design firm to produce 1,000 prototype kits. He continued to use this same supplier, but became increasingly frustrated when his orders were placed at the end of the list whenever bigger clients wanted their products made.

Kapell realized that he needed to have more control over his manufacturing. He decided to start a second business, separate from Magnetic Poetry, called U.S. Magnetix, which was solely dedicated to printing and producing flexible magnetic products. Kapell put up $100,000 from his cash flow to cover the basic equipment costs for launching U.S. Magnetix. This initial investment bought him a 40 percent stake in the business. He now had the means of production in place to turn orders around in three days' time. Magnetic Poetry was ready to go to the next level.

During the start-up phase of his business, Dave chose to operate Magnetic Poetry as a sole proprietorship. Initially, this legal structure worked well. All he had to do to make his business "official" was go down to the local county courthouse and file a "Doing Business As" form and he was up and running. Yet, as his company grew, Dave's lawyer advised him to register his business as a Subchapter S corporation. Under this new legal structure, Dave would not be personally liable in the event that Magnetic Poetry was sued or went bankrupt.

The next problem Kapell needed to solve was how to best distribute his product. He had developed an ingenious, one-of-a-kind idea and had been successful in selling it locally at crafts fairs. But how could he increase his distribution network? He began to investigate how he could sell Magnetic Poetry kits wholesale to other retailers. Kapell approached Pam Jones, who managed a museum gift shop in Minneapolis. She liked

---

[3] Alyson Ward, "Still Drawn to the Tiles: Magnetic Poetry strong after 10 Years on Market." *Contra Costa Times*, September 22, 2003.

Kapell's poetry kits but was unimpressed with his no-frills cardboard packaging. So Kapell got to work and repackaged his kits in clear-plastic boxes. Jones liked what she saw and bought several dozen kits at a wholesale price of $9.50 each. Within a day, she had sold a dozen kits at a retail price of $20.

In 1996, Magnetic Poetry took a major leap forward with its distribution when it sealed a deal with the national book retailer Barnes & Noble. In celebration of National Poetry Month, the book store announced that it would sell Magnetic Poetry kits at all of its retail chains throughout the United States. Up until this point, Kapell had primarily been distributing his product to independent bookstores and specialty gift shops. The Barnes & Noble deal connected Kapell's company to a powerful distribution channel. Soon customers in such locations as Texas and New Mexico were snapping up Magnetic Poetry kits off the shelves. Then Kapell started producing kits in foreign languages. His distribution network now includes international retailers in France, Spain, Germany, and Italy.

Over the last ten years, Magnetic Poetry has grown from a local business that was essentially started by accident into a $7-million enterprise with worldwide reach. Kapell's company has been credited with inspiring scores of people to find their "inner poet," or overcome writer's block.

In 2001, Kapell decided to sell his 40 percent stake in his second company, U.S. Magnetix, so that he could fully focus his energies on developing new products and marketing ideas for Magnetic Poetry. While he no longer owns the manufacturing arm of his business, he still serves as one of U.S. Magnetix's biggest customers, responsible for generating 15 percent of its annual revenue. Kapell believes that Magnetic Poetry is poised for continued growth. While his youthful dream was to become the next David Bowie, Kapell seems to have found his niche as an entrepreneur.

Case Study Analysis

1. Magnetic Poetry kits are currently sold in bookstores, specialty gift shops, and online. Brainstorm three additional distribution outlets for this product.

2. Assume the following about Magnetic Poetry's cost structure: The wholesale price for one Original Magnetic Poetry Kit is $9.50. The retail price is $20. It costs the company as follows:

$2.50 to manufacture one Original Magnetic Poetry Kit

.50 to package it

.50 for shipping and handling

$1.00 of variable costs per kit

a. Calculate the contribution margin.

b. Assume that Magnetic Poetry has monthly fixed costs of $20,000. How many kits would the company need to sell in order to break even?

c. Calculate the markup percentage for the following:
   ● Manufacturer → Retailer
   ● Retailer → Consumer

3. Do you think it was a good idea for Kapell to sell his 40 percent ownership shares of U.S. Magnetix? What are some things he needs to consider now that he no longer has an ownership stake in the manufacturing arm of his business?

4. As Magnetic Poetry evolved from a start-up into a thriving business, Dave made the decision to change his legal structure from a sole proprietorship into a Subchapter S corporation. What are the advantages and disadvantages of each of these legal structures? Why do you think that Dave's advisors encouraged him to change his legal structure?

5. Go online and visit Magnetic Poetry's Web site at *www.magneticpoetry.com*. What other products has this company developed? How do these products connect to Kapell's original concept?

CASE SOURCES

www.magneticpoetry.com.

Paul Levy, "Magnetic Poetry Proves Attractive," *Minneapolis–St. Paul Star Tribune*. Friday, December 28, 2001.

Tim Gihring, Associated Press writer, "Poetry to the People: Mantra of Magnetic Poetry Kit Maker," South Coast *Today.com* (an edition of *The Standard Times*). May 20, 1996.

Monte Hanson, "A Magnetic Partnership," *Finance and Commerce*. December 29, 2001. *http://www. finance-commerce. com/recent_articles/011229.htm.*

Alyson Ward, "Still Drawn to the Tiles: Magnetic Poetry Strong after 10 Years on Market." Posted on September 22, 2003.

Knight Ridder Newspapers, *http://www.contraco-statimes.com/mld/cctimes/6831510.htm?1c.*

Chapter 11 | Effective Leadership: Managing Resources and Employees

> # "Give a man a fish and you feed him for a day. Teach a man to fish and you feed him for a lifetime."

—Lao Tzu, founder of Taoism

Performance Objectives

1. Explain what makes someone an effective leader.
2. Research the laws and tax issues affecting employees.
3. Recruit, manage, and motivate your employees.
4. Describe the tasks handled by corporate managers.
5. Make sure your business is run in an ethical manner.

Madam C. J. Walker was born Sarah Breedlove to poor Louisiana farmers in 1867. Her parents died when she was a child, and she was reared in poverty by her married sister. Despite her difficult beginnings, Madam Walker became the first self-made American female millionaire and one of the first African-American millionaires.

Madam Walker worked for 18 years as a washerwoman in St. Louis, but, when she was 38, she mixed up in her washtubs some soaps and shampoos especially for African-American skin and hair. At first she sold her products door to door, but she soon began to train a group of "agent-operators." Walker taught her agents her sales methods and the manufacturing of her products.

At the peak of her career, Walker employed about 2,000 agents. One of her great marketing strategies was to organize her agents into clubs that promoted social and charitable causes. She offered cash prizes to the clubs that did the greatest amount of charitable and educational work in the African-American community. She also encouraged her agents to open beauty salons and other businesses. Not only did Madam Walker's methods foreshadow the emphasis we see today on socially responsible entrepreneurship, but she also left behind a rich legacy of black female entrepreneurial leadership.

Madam C. J. Walker—America's first female self-made millionaire. (Courtesy of the Library of Congress)

» Leadership Comes from Self-Esteem

A leader is someone who has the confidence and energy to do things on his or her own. Leadership comes from self-esteem. If you believe in yourself, you can do things with confidence and you will inspire confidence in others. Develop a positive attitude and you will become a leader. Great leaders are optimists—they have trained themselves to think positively, no matter what.

Running a business requires leadership. One day you may have employees who will look to you for leadership.

»Manage Your Time Wisely

Leaders learn how to manage their hours so they can get more done in less time. One of the most important things you can do when you start your first business is to learn how to manage your time more efficiently. Getting more done in less time is the name of the game.

You may not have employees to manage yet but you could probably manage yourself better. Here is a tool called the PERT chart (**P**rogram **E**valuation and **R**eview **T**echnique) that you can use when you feel overwhelmed by the many things you need to do when starting up your first business. As your business grows, you can use the PERT concept to manage more complex tasks.

Sample PERT Chart

Task	Week 1	Week 2	Week 3	Week 4	Week 5	Week 6
Befriend banker	X	X	X	X	X	X
Order letterhead		X				
Select location	X					
Register business	X					
Bulk mail permit			X			
Select ad agency	X					
Meet with lawyer				X		
Meet with accountant				X		
Vendor statement					X	
Utilities deposits					X	
Promotional material					X	
Phone system			X	X	X	
Web site designed						X
Database set up						X
Network computers						X

»How Will You Pay Yourself?

Before you hire employees for your business, figure out how to pay your first employee—yourself! Once your business is breaking even, decide how you want to distribute the profit. The decision you make will affect your financial recordkeeping, so think it through. Your choices are the following:

1. Pay yourself a **commission**—a percentage of every sale. It is treated as a variable operating cost, because it fluctuates with sales.

2. Pay yourself a **salary,** which is a fixed amount of money paid at a set time. You could choose to receive your salary once a week or once a month. A salary is a fixed operating cost, because it does not change with sales.

3. If you have a service or manufacturing business, you could pay yourself an hourly wage. An hourly wage is considered a cost of goods sold, because it is factored into the cost of the product or service.

4. Pay yourself a **dividend**—a share of the company's profits.

Entrepreneurs who do not pay themselves regularly tend to overstate their return on investment, because they have not taken their pay out of the net profit and treated that pay as a cost. This can also increase the amount of tax the business will owe. Anything that reduces the net profit reduces the tax on net profit. Of course, you will have to pay income tax on the money you pay yourself, but generally you will come out ahead if you treat some of your business profit as self-payment.

Another reason to pay yourself is that it enables you to be honest about whether or not the business is really worth your time. Could you be making more money working for someone else? Is the best choice to keep working for yourself? Thinking entrepreneurially includes a realistic consideration of whether you would be happier *not* running a business.

»Adding Employees to the Mix

As the business grows, you may have to hire employees. At first, these might just be friends or family members helping out with deliveries or boxing up shipments. But eventually you will need to hire "real" employees. Once you do, you will have to become aware of the laws and tax issues affecting hiring. These include the following:

⟨2. **Performance Objective**

- *Payroll Taxes.* If you hire employees, you will have to deduct **payroll tax** from their earnings. Your accountant can advise you in more detail when you get to this point. For now, it is important that you know you will be responsible for contributing to Social Security on their behalf.

- *Fair Labor Standards Act.* The **Fair Labor Standards Act,** passed in 1938, requires you to pay employees at least minimum wage. It also prohibits you from hiring anyone under 16 years of age full time.

- *Equal Pay Act of 1963.* The **Equal Pay Act** requires employers to pay men and women the same amount for the same work.

- *Antidiscrimination Laws.* Laws that protect employees against discrimination on the basis of age, race, religion, national origin, or because of color, gender, or physical disabilities are called **antidiscrimination laws.**

»Hiring Employees

Performance Objective 3. ›

Hiring employees is also called **recruitment.** Perhaps the most important thing you can do is to bring other capable, motivated people into your business. In the bestseller *Good to Great*, management expert Jim Collins says great leaders "get the right people on the bus—sometimes even before a company decides exactly what business it will be in."[1]

Here are some ways to bring employees into your business:

■ Bring people in as partners. Partners share the risks and rewards of the venture and will co-own the business with you.

■ Hire experts to work on specific tasks on a contract or hourly basis. For example, you might hire a professional accountant to work one day per month on your recordkeeping.

■ Hire someone as a full-time, permanent employee. The most common way to do this is an "at will" arrangement. Typically the "at will" employment relationship continues for an indefinite amount of time, but can be ended by either party in writing with, say, two weeks notice.

There are specific steps in the recruiting process:

1. *Defining the job.* Think about what you need this employee to do and what kind of skills you will need.
2. *Posting the job.* Will you place an ad in a newspaper? Put up want-ad posters?
3. *Screening resumés.* A resumé is a one-page summary of a person's education and work experience. When you post the opportunity, ask for people who want the job to mail or fax their resumés.
4. *Interviewing candidates.* Use the resumés to choose several people to interview. Beforehand, prepare the questions you want to ask about the individual's skills and ambitions.
5. *Checking references.* Ask the candidates who interest you to provide at least two references from previous employers or other professional people who can tell you about their character.
6. *Negotiating salary.* You and the candidate you choose will have to negotiate how much you intend to pay, and any benefits the job includes, such as health insurance.
7. *Hiring.* Once you decide to hire someone, you will have paperwork to fill out to start creating paychecks.
8. *Orientation.* This is the process of introducing the employee into the company and teaching him or her about the job.

»Office Intranet

Once your business has grown to the point where you have employees, you will want to create an "intranet"—a communication network for your team. Microsoft Office is an example of the software that will allow you to create an intranet where all members of

Businesswomen conferring.
(Color Day Production/10154548/Getty Images)

---

[1] Jim Collins, *Good to Great: Why Some Companies Make the Leap . . . and Some Don't,* p. 13 (New York: Collin, 2001)..

your team can view documents or hold discussions. It includes a feature that automatically notifies members of the team when a member updates a document.

URLs

Intranets.com, *www.intranets.com*

Intranet Reference Site, *www.intrack.com/intranet*

» Growing Your Team

Ways to find talented employees include the following:

- *Campus Recruiting.* Companies from all industries visit college campuses every year to meet and hire recent graduates into full-time roles. Established companies in banking, consulting, accounting, consumer products, technology, health care, and others are all big recruiters on college and graduate school campuses.
- *Staffing and Recruiting.* Companies plan and hire according to staffing plans and budgets, and typically use a combination of internal recruiters (employees of the company), outside recruiters (agencies or contingency firms), and Internet job-board postings.

Finding great employees has become much easier with the advent of online job-listing services such as Career Builder and Monster.com.

- *Executive Search.* When companies need to hire a senior executive, the CEO, the board of directors, or the director of human resources will engage in an "executive search." These top job openings are often not advertised, and the process is often managed by an outside search firm.

» Getting the Best Out of Your Employees

When you do hire people, treat them fairly and with respect. This approach will get you the best results. Many companies make their employees part owners by giving shares that entitle them to a portion of the company profits. Wouldn't you work harder if you knew your efforts would make a difference in your wallet?

Follow these guidelines and you should be a terrific boss:

1. Get the right people. Putting the right people in the right job is at least half the battle. This means getting to know each employee's strengths and weaknesses.
2. Provide a fair salary and good working conditions.
3. Share your vision for the company.
4. Give employees incentives to work hard—start a profit-sharing plan, for example.
5. Give them control over their work.
6. Give them definite responsibilities and areas of control.

»Encourage Your Employees to Be Socially Responsible

Back in the early 1900s, Madam Walker motivated her employees by encouraging them to get involved in helping their communities. There are many ways that entrepreneurs can use their businesses to help their communities and contribute to society. By being an entrepreneur, you already make an important contribution by providing goods and services to consumers in your area who need them. You can also use your business to support social issues that are important to you. By running your business in a way that is consistent with your ethics and core values, you will develop a **socially responsible business.**

Ways to make your business socially responsible include the following:

- Recycle paper, glass, or plastic.
- Donate a portion of profits to a charity.
- Refuse animal testing of products.
- Offer employees incentives to volunteer in the community.
- Establish a safe and healthy workplace.

> **!** *To get more ideas on how to make your business socially responsible, check out Standards of Corporate Responsibility at http://www.svn.org/initiatives/standards.html.*

»Corporate Management— Building a Team

Performance Objective 4. As a small business grows, it will reach a point where the entrepreneur and a few employees cannot handle operations efficiently. At that stage, the business will need **management.** Management is the art of planning and organizing a business so it can meet its goals.

Many successful entrepreneurs are creative people who tend to get bored with the everyday details of running a business. The wisest entrepreneurs recognize this about themselves and hire managers to run the business.

[Global Impact]

One Person Really Can Make a Difference

Anita Roddick, who founded The Body Shop, is a good example of an entrepreneur who has used her company as a force for social change. Her first big campaign came in 1985. Roddick let Greenpeace, an environmental preservation group, put up posters in Body Shop stores to educate people about the dumping of hazardous waste into the North Sea.

In the 1990s, fifteen political prisoners were released due to the volume of letters that Body Shop customers wrote. Another Body Shop campaign raised public awareness about the destruction of the Brazilian rain forest.

While traveling in Brazil, Roddick met with some of the tribal leaders in the Amazon region to figure out how the forest could produce income without cutting down trees. The Body Shop began buying Brazil-nut oil and beads from some of the tribes. This helped tribe members establish their own small businesses without destroying the rain forest. Roddick believes that helping poor people start their own business ventures is an effective way to address the negative effects that poverty can have on people's lives.

Figure 11-1 Management organizational chart.

An entrepreneur with a growing corporation can raise capital by selling stock. The entrepreneur can use some of the capital raised to hire managers to organize the business. This will free the entrepreneur to spend less time managing and more time thinking up new business ideas.

A management organizational chart for a small business might look like Figure 11-1.

What Do Managers Do?

Business professor Nathan Himmelstein of Rutgers University breaks management into ten functions, using the acronym POLDSCCRIM.

1. ***Planning***—Managers perform three types of planning: strategic, tactical, and operational.

   (a) *Strategic plans* are 3 to 5 year overall strategies for achieving a business's long-term growth, sales, and positioning goals.

   (b) *Tactical plans* are the short-term implementation that make strategic goals happen. Tactical plans are for one year or less and have very specific objectives.

   (c) *Operational plans* are short-term methods for achieving tactical goals. These include budgets, regulations, and schedules for day-to-day operation of the business.

2. ***Organizing***—This function includes everything from hiring people to buying/leasing equipment and resources. It includes setting up an organizational chart and defining each person's responsibilities.

3. ***Leading***—This function is about the style in which you and your managers lead the company. There are basically three leadership styles.[2]

   • Power-oriented—Managers who use this style tightly control the business operations and do not welcome suggestions from employees or share authority and responsibility with them. It is most effective in large operations or in situations where employees are inexperienced or are dealing with a crisis.

---

[2] Kathleen Allen, *Entrepreneurship and Small Business Management* (Blacklick, Ohio: Glencoe/McGraw-Hill, 1994).

- Routine-oriented—Managers using this style tend to focus on keeping day-to-day operations running smoothly and delegate responsibilities to employees. This style works best in large or mid-sized companies that have established operational systems that do not require much tweaking to be effective.

- Achievement-oriented—These managers are very open to employee input, are willing to share authority and responsibility, and are focused on achieving long-term goals. This style is the most appropriate for a small business, although sometimes you will have to take on the other styles to deal with a crisis or to stabilize operations.

4. *Directing*—After you and your managers have made your plans and organized your employees and resources, it is time to direct and motivate employees to perform the work that will move the company toward its strategic goals.

5. *Staffing*—This function involves managing the people in the company by making sure they are being placed in the positions that best use their skills and experience. It includes employee training and development, setting up pay and benefits packages, recruiting, and screening.

6. *Controlling*—This step involves measuring the business's performance and trying to figure out how to improve it. Is the business adhering to its budget? Are products achieving the level of quality set as a goal? How about customer service? If there are differences between what was planned and what the company actually achieved, controlling will require corrective action to align plans and actions.

7. *Coordinating*—This is the task of blending all management efforts into a unified system. Coordinating includes creating in-house communications phone and e-mail systems and teaching everyone to use them, scheduling regular meetings and updates, and generally making sure all managers are using appropriate styles and are working toward the same goals.

8. *Representing*—Managers represent a company to its people and its people to the company; they also represent the company to the outside world. Managers need to dress and behave in a way that accurately reflects the company culture.

9. *Innovating*—Managers should always be innovating—developing new ways to meet strategic, tactical, and operational goals. The entrepreneur may be the guiding creative force behind the company, but managers should also be creative problem solvers.

10. *Motivating*—Managers should realize that every decision they make will affect employee motivation and morale positively or negatively. Even a manager's assumptions about the employees will affect them. If a manager assumes that people need to be pushed to work, for example, and treats the employees that way, he/she will incur resentment. A manager who assumes that employees want to do their best and embrace responsibil-

ity will be more successful. Some ways managers can motivate include involving employees in decisions, providing meaningful work, recognizing outstanding contributions, evaluating performance, and rewarding achievement.[3]

»The Entrepreneur Sets the Tone for the Company

⟨ 5. **Performance Objective**

No matter whom you hire to manage your company, you still set the tone for how the company operates. Are you disorganized and chaotic? Chances are your company will have the same problem. Are you honest and straightforward? This will encourage your managers and employees to behave similarly.

Ethics are standards and rules that help one determine right from wrong. The Golden Rule "Do unto others as you would have others do unto you"—is a well-known ethic. A behavior may be legal and still not be ethical. For example, it is not illegal to be rude to your customers and employees, but it is unethical (and not very smart).

Ethical business behavior is not only moral, but it also makes good business sense. Have you ever bought something from a store and felt you were cheated? How did you react? Did you ever go back to that store again? Probably not. You may have even told your friends about the experience. The store lost more than just one customer.

»Managerial Styles That Work

As your business grows, it will develop its own "culture." Companies like Wal-Mart and Home Depot spend significant amounts to create a work environment that inspires and motivates employees. How you or your managers treat the employees of your business will have a profound effect on the culture. Adopt the best managerial style for your company and maintain it consistently. According to expert Daniel Goleman, the main styles and their advantages and drawbacks are the following:[4]

1. *Coercive Style*—To coerce someone means to pressure him or her into doing what you want. This commanding approach can be effective in a disaster scenario or with problem employees who need a forceful manager. In most situations, though, a coercive leadership style hurts employee morale and diminishes the flexibility and effectiveness of the business. Employees stop thinking and acting for themselves.

2. *Authoritative Style*—An authoritative leader takes a "come with me" approach, stating the overall goal but giving employees freedom to figure out how best to achieve it. This works

---

[3] Allen, *Entrepreneurship*.

[4] Daniel Goleman, "Leadership That Gets Results" *Harvard Business Review*, March–April 2000.

well if the leader is an expert, but is not so good if he/she is not but is leading people (a team of scientists, for example) who are.

3. *Affiliative Style*—This is a "people come first" method that is effective when the business is in the team-building stage. It can fail when employees are lost and need direction.

4. *Democratic Style*—This style gives employees a strong voice in how the company is run. This can build morale and work if employees are capable of handling responsibility. It can result, however, in endless meetings and confused employees who feel leaderless.

5. *Pacesetting Style*—This type of leader sets very high perform-ance standards for himself or herself and challenges employ-ees to meet them, too. This can be very good when employees are also self-motivated but can overwhelm those who are not so committed to the business.

6. *Coaching Style*—This style focuses on helping each employee to grow through training and support. This can be a good ap-proach for starting and growing a business, but may not work with employees who have been with the business for a while and may be resistant to change.

The key lies in not choosing one strategy that is "best," but in be-ing aware of all of them and consciously choosing the one that is most effective for your company at any given time. Outstanding leaders use a collection of leadership styles, applying them in the right measure at the right time.

»Ethical Employer/Employee Relationships

It is important to treat your employees well, too. Aside from the fact that it is morally right to treat people ethically, it is in your best in-terest to do so. As the entrepreneur, your values will set the ethical tone for your company. If you think it is okay to be rude or cheat a customer, your employees will not only copy your behavior, but they also will probably try to cheat you!

Employees who feel used by their employers will not do their best work. The most successful companies are those in which the em-ployees' interests correspond with what is best for the company.

Many large businesses offer their employees company stock at a discount, or give generous bonuses at the end of the year, based on how well the company does. In this way, the employees know that they will profit from the company's success. This will motivate them to care about the company for which they work.

»Corporate Ethical Scandals

The issue of business ethics exploded in 2002, when several huge corporations were found to have published inaccurate financial statements. These false numbers made the companies look so good that they were some of the most highly recommended stock picks on Wall Street.

Top executives at Enron, WorldCom-MCI, Tyco, Global Crossing, and other large firms had inflated their companies' earnings so they could pocket fat bonuses, while misleading shareholders. When the truth came out, public confidence in the stock market plummeted, along with stock prices. Investors lost millions.

One of the companies, the energy giant Enron, had strongly encouraged its own employees to invest most or all of their retirement savings in company stock—even while top executives knew the worth of the stock was based on false numbers. These employees had their life savings wiped out by the unethical behavior of these executives.

Enron collapsed and thousands of employees lost their jobs and saw their pension funds reduced to nothing. Tyco was split into four different companies. Its CEO was forced to resign when it was learned that he had used company money to buy an $18 million apartment in Manhattan and furnish it with expensive artwork.

The scandals of 2002 were a failure of **corporate governance,** meaning that these companies did not have rules and safeguards in place to ensure that executives behaved legally and ethically. Even at this early stage in developing your business, you must think about how you will guarantee that your business remains both ethical and legal as it grows.

1. ***Never Just Take Company Profits to Pay Yourself***—That's a bad habit that can eventually lead to the behavior that brought down the CEO of Tyco—he thought of the company's money as his money, and this ultimately destroyed his career. Do not treat your business earnings as your personal income. Instead, decide on a wage or salary you will pay yourself and always document this, expenses, and other financial records and statements.

2. ***Keep Accurate Records***—As your business grows, have your records checked once a year by a reputable accountant. By the time your company becomes a multimillion-dollar corporation, you will have established a reputation for honest financial reporting.

3. ***Use Financial Controls***—Once you have employees, use simple financial controls such as the following:

   (a) Always have two people open the mail, so no one can steal checks.

   (b) Arrange for yourself and one other person to be required to sign all checks sent out by the business. Using a double signature like this will assure that no one person can use the company checks for personal expenses.

4. ***Create an Advisory Board***—Ask businesspeople you respect and other community leaders to be on your advisory board— a group of people who will advise you on how to run your business. Choose people with strong ethics, and listen to what they say.

»Firing and Laying Off Employees

Sometimes you hire someone and it just does not work out. Can you fire that person? Yes, but protect yourself by documenting the reasons. You can be sued if an employee proves he or she was fired for no good reason. You cannot just fire someone because you do not like the person; you will need to prove that this employee violated company ethics or was not performing the job well.

1. Protect your company from wrongful-termination lawsuits by conducting regular employee performance reviews. Have each employee read and sign his/her review. (See Figure 11-2.)

2. If an employee is violating rules, give notification in writing (and keep a copy for your records). If things still do not improve and you have to let the employee go, you will have proof that there were problems with his/her performance.

Objective #1: _____

    Observed Achievements: _____

Objective #2: _____

    Observed Achievements: _____

Objective #3: _____

    Observed Achievements: _____

Manager Feedback Only:

General Comments: _____

Employee Strengths: _____

Areas for Improvement: _____

Employee Overall Rating (based on numerical scale below): _____

Rating Key:
1. **Outstanding:** Extraordinary performance well beyond the expectations or requirements of the position.
2. **Above Satisfactory:** Excels beyond the basic requirements of the position.
3. **Satisfactory:** Meets requirements of the position. Displays the work of a fully competent employee.
4. **Needs Improvement:** At times, performs at a level that is below that of a competent employee. Improvement is necessary.
5. **Unsatisfactory:** Performance is consistently below the standards set for this position. The employee has clearly failed to complete certain tasks that have been deemed critical to the position. A continued rating at this level may result in the demotion or termination of the employee.

Date: _____

Employee's Signature: _____

Manager's Signature: _____

Figure 11-2 Sample employee performance plan and appraisal.

Sometimes you might have to lay off employees. They may have performed their jobs well, but you either do not need their skills anymore or cannot afford to continue to employ them. To prevent legal complications, offer employees **severance,** pay which is a continued salary for a limited time, and make serious efforts to help them find new employment.

»Human Resources

Human resources (also called HR, Human Capital, or Personnel) is the department of a company that hires, trains, and develops employees.

For a business just starting out, it may not be practical to have a director of human resources. Instead, the entrepreneur will handle these tasks. Rarely does a company hire a separate human resources professional until it has 20 or more employees.

Once a company starts to build momentum and grows beyond several hundred employees, it will need to closely manage key human resources disciplines. For large companies, each of the following areas might represent one or more full-time jobs within the HR department.

Compensation and Payroll

- How are employees paid? How much of the compensation is salary? How much is performance based? Which employees receive stock in the company and in what amounts and under what terms? How does compensation tie into the overall finances of the business? How does the company's compensation program compare to the pay of similar employees at competing companies? HR executives work closely with finance managers to answer these questions about compensation and to set company policy accordingly.

Benefits

- Today's full-time employees expect an array of benefits as part of their compensation. The basics include health insurance for the employee and his or her family, life insurance, vacation and sick time, and retirement savings plans. HR usually leads the process of selecting the benefits programs that the company makes available to employees on a subsidized basis.

Biz Facts

Many companies staff their human resources organizations using a ratio of one HR executive per 50 to 200 employees.

Organizational Development

- Organizational Structure—The HR department will help the founder, CEO, and board of directors analyze the pros and cons of various possibilities, establish the appropriate organizational structure, and help manage transitions that need to be made from one framework to another.

- Employee Retention—Sometimes paying people well to do their jobs is not enough to prevent them from being lured away to work for a competitor. HR develops employee retention programs that help build morale, create mentoring opportunities, and provide training and other benefits to keep employees excited about staying. Why? Because it is very expensive to recruit and train new employees.

- Succession Planning—When you promote your sales manager to vice president of sales, who will fill the vacancy? The HR department will work with managers to fill the position.

Training and Development

- Even senior executives require ongoing training from time to time. HR managers develop employee training in-house, and may also use outside training providers for specific situations. Some businesses help companies train their sales teams. Major universities, like Harvard, offer executive education curriculums through special programs.

Labor Law and HR Compliance

The United States has well-developed laws to protect the rights of workers and employees. Everyone involved in hiring, firing, and managing people needs to be aware of both the letter and the spirit of these laws, which are typically translated into policies by the HR and legal teams at a company. For example, laws forbid companies from hiring or promoting on the basis of age or race. It is illegal for employers to ask candidates how old they are, or where they are from during the interview process. Companies can expose themselves to enormous liability if they do not properly manage the process of hiring, rewarding, and terminating employees.

Human Resources Strategy

Strategic HR departments will also dedicate resources to identifying ways to maximize the productivity and effectiveness of the overall organization through its HR practices.

- *Diversity*—Many leading companies, with Avon Products as a good example, have found that, by creating a more diverse workforce in terms of gender and ethnic diversity, they better represent and understand their diverse customer base. This translates into increased business and greater customer loyalty. Avon is known for having a diverse workforce, from the

CEO down to the sales representative level, and has linked its employee diversity strategy with its marketing, using the tagline "The Company for Women."

■ ***Benchmarking***—For companies to be competitive, they must understand their own employee base, but they must also understand the skills and motivations of the employees of the companies with which they compete. Benchmarking is a process that lets companies put their highest-performing employees in context with those of their competitors. As an entrepreneur, you will want to ensure that your employees' skills keep pace with those of your competitors.

■ ***Retention***—As noted earlier, it is paramount for companies to hang on to the employees who drive the business. HR strategy puts much focus on programs and benefits that keep employees engaged and motivated to fulfill the company's mission.

Could You Start an HR Business?

Many companies, large and small, are dedicated to providing human resources services to corporate clients. Here is how some leading firms got started: Adecco provides staffing services to 250,000 clients around the world. It started in 1957 when Henri-Ferdinand Lavanchy, an accountant at the time, decided to start a recruiting company because a client asked him to help fill a job. In 1969, Lester Korn and Richard Ferry started a recruitment firm. Today, with over $300 million in revenue, Korn/Ferry International specializes in helping clients hire top executives, including CEOs. When companies have thousands of employees, the task of getting paychecks out twice a month can be daunting. Payroll provider Automatic Data Processing cuts checks for over 30 million people on behalf of its clients. ADP was started by Henry Taub in 1949, when he was 22. The company had eight clients and had $2,000 in revenue in its first year.

》Chapter Summary

Now that you have studied this chapter you can do the following:

1. Explain what makes someone an effective leader.

   ■ A leader is someone who has the confidence and energy to do things on his or her own.

   ■ Leadership comes from self-esteem. If you believe in yourself, you can do things with confidence and you will inspire confidence in others.

   ■ Leaders learn how to manage their time so they can get more done in less time.

2. Research the laws and tax issues affecting employees.

   ■ Payroll taxes. If you hire people, you will have to deduct payroll taxes from their earnings.

- Fair Labor Standards Act. This law, passed in 1938, requires you to pay employees at least minimum wage. It also prohibits you from hiring anyone under the age of 16 full time.
- Equal Pay Act of 1963. This law requires employers to pay men and women the same amount for the same work.
- Antidiscrimination laws. These are other laws that protect people against discrimination on the basis of age, race, religion, national origin, or because of color, gender, or physical disabilities.

3. Recruit, manage, and motivate your employees.

- Hiring employees is also called recruitment.
- Bring people in as partners. Partners share the risks and rewards of the venture and will co-own the business with you.
- Hire experts to work on specific tasks on a contractual or hourly basis. For example, you might hire a professional accountant to work one day per month on your recordkeeping.
- Hire someone as a full-time, permanent employee. The most common way to do this is with an "at will" arrangement.

4. Describe the tasks handled by corporate managers.

- Planning
- Organizing
- Leading
- Directing
- Staffing
- Controlling
- Coordinating
- Representing
- Innovating
- Motivating

5. Make sure your business is run in an ethical manner.

- Never just take company profits to pay yourself.
- Keep accurate records.
- Use financial controls.
- Create an advisory board.

Key Terms

antidiscrimination laws
commission
corporate governance
dividend
Equal Pay Act
ethics
Fair Labor Standards Act

human resources
management
payroll tax
recruitment
salary
severance
socially responsible business

[Entrepreneurship Portfolio]

Critical Thinking Exercises

1. Describe three leaders you admire. What characteristics do you most admire about them, and why?

2. Explain how you could find five additional hours in your weekly schedule to manage your business. Create a weekly time-management schedule for yourself.

3. Fill out a PERT chart for your business. **(Business Plan Practice)**

4. Will you be hiring employees? If so, name them and describe their qualifications, their salaries, and how they will help your business.

5. Provide contact information for your accountant, attorney, banker, and insurance agent.

6. What are your policies toward employees? How do you plan to make your business a positive and rewarding place to work?

7. Describe the corporate governance plan for your company. It should include five policies (rules) that will be the backbone of your company's ethics. **(Business Plan Practice)**

8. Provide information for each of your mentors or advisors. If there is a board of advisors, list each and describe his/her commitment to the board. **(Business Plan Practice)**

Key Concept Questions

1. How old does someone have to be before he or she can work full time?

2. What is one kind of tax employers have to pay for employees?

3. Can you fire an employee if you have an argument about religion?

4. How does incorporating help an entrepreneur put management into place?

Application Exercises

1. What qualities and qualifications will you look for in employees for your business? List five and explain why they are the most important to you.

2. What would push you to fire an employee? List five qualities or failures that you feel would justify firing an employee from your business. Describe also how you would plan to handle the firing.

3. Choose three ways you plan to run a socially responsible business, such as: **(Business Plan Practice)**

- Recycling paper, glass, or plastic
- Donating a portion of profits to a charity
- No animal testing of products
- Offering employees incentives to volunteer in the community
- Establishing a safe and healthy workplace
- Other

Exploring Online

Choose a corporation that has been involved in an ethical scandal and research it online. Relate this story in a class presentation. Describe the lessons you have learned as an entrepreneur from researching this event. Hint: Try entering "corporate" and "scandal" into a search engine.

In Your Opinion

Discuss with a group: Should an employer be able to fire an employee if the latter is often ill? Before the discussion, prepare by searching the Internet to determine what legal issues may be involved.

CASE STUDY: Leading Whistle Laundry

Angela Saenz is the manager of one of eighteen Whistle Laundry & Dry Cleaners. She has had the opportunity to attend a variety of leadership seminars and workshops over the past six years while she has managed the store. She has also encouraged her two supervisors, Uri and Horace, to attend some of the seminars with her. Uri is enthusiastic about the opportunity, but Horace thinks it is a waste of time. Uri thinks the investment of making people happy at their jobs is well worth the effort. Horace feels cleaners have a job to do and his employees should just do it or go elsewhere. Both Uri and Horace speak a second language, which they find helpful in supervising many of their non-English-speaking employees.

Angela thinks that possibly she needs to consider sending Horace to a different type of seminar than she and Uri usually attend. While reading the local newspaper, she noticed that there were two seminars coming up in the next couple of weeks. One was a Situational Supervisory Skills seminar offered by a team of leadership experts. The other was a Task-Centered vs. People-Oriented Leadership seminar.

In the meantime, Angela has been looking at another seminar flyer she has received. This upcoming program was on developing traits needed by every successful leader—charismatic leadership for men and women, and participatory leadership in a diverse and competitive marketplace.

Case Study Analysis

1. What might Angela and her supervisors learn from these different seminars?

2. Do you think Angela, Uri, and Horace are effective leaders?

CASE STUDY: Malden Mills

In 1906, a Hungarian immigrant named Henry Feuerstein built a textile mill, Malden Mills, on the outskirts of Boston. Over the years, the business was passed down to Henry's grandson Aaron. During the 1980s, Malden Mills invented a unique fabric called Polartec, lightweight, warm, and durable, a "fleece," made from recycled plastics. Malden Mills used Polartec to manufacture jackets, vests, and other outerwear products. In 1999, *Time* recognized Polartec as one of the top inventions of the century.

In the meantime, many manufacturing businesses had relocated overseas or to Mexico, where labor and production costs were cheaper. But Malden Mills bucked this trend and kept its operations firmly planted in Massachusetts. President Aaron Feuerstein had been raised by his father and grandfather to value his workers and to treat them with respect. As Feuerstein explained: "We have a mission of responsibility to both shareholders and our top asset: our employees. We're not prepared to skip town for cost savings."

The Fire

In December 1995, coincidentally on Aaron's birthday, a devastating fire broke out at the Malden Mills plant. Within hours, most of the factory had burned to the ground. The 3,000 employees feared that their jobs had been destroyed along with the fire. But, within a day, Feuerstein announced that "it was not the end" and that he would rebuild the factory buildings exactly where they had stood. He also vowed to use the insurance money from the fire to continue paying his employees with full benefits until the plant was back in business.

"We Will Rebuild"

It took Feuerstein months to rebuild and it cost millions of dollars to fulfill the promise he had made to his employees. Business-minded skeptics questioned Feuerstein's decision. It would have been cheaper to cash out of the business altogether or rebuild the plant in Asia. How could he justify paying people who weren't doing any work? Because Malden Mills was a privately owned family business, Feuerstein did not need to seek approval for his plans from shareholders or board members. He called all his own shots.

He also never second-guessed himself. "I consider our workers an asset, not an expense," explained Feuerstein. "I have a responsibility to the workers, both blue-collar and white-collar. I have an equal responsibility to the community. It would have been unconscionable to put 3,000 people on the streets and deliver a deathblow to the cities of Lawrence and Methuen. Maybe on paper our company is worth less to Wall Street, but I can tell you it is worth more."

Corporate Hero

Feuerstein's gestures of corporate goodwill earned him praise from employees, customers, and the public at large. The media ran countless stories on him, President Clinton invited him to Washington as an honored guest, and he was awarded twelve honorary degrees from educational institutions. People who heard the story on TV wrote him fan letters and sent in donations totaling $10,000. His employees cheered him and worked doubly hard to get the business back off the ground. "Before the fire, that plant produced 130,000 yards a week," Feuerstein said. "A few weeks after the fire, it was up to 230,000 yards. Our people became very creative. They were willing to work 25 hours a day."

An Uphill Battle

In the wake of the fire, Malden Mills struggled to regain its profitability. Despite the hard work and dedication of its employees, the company was losing money. Feuerstein had secured $100 million in bank loans to finance the rebuilding of the plant and he was struggling to pay back his creditors. In 2001, Feuerstein reluctantly filed for Chapter 11 bankruptcy protection. Naysayers questioned whether Feuerstein was a case study in nice guys finishing last. Feuerstein disagreed: "I do not attribute our financial problems to our employees. We got ourselves overleveraged after the fire and weren't aggressive or creative enough in marketing. We're going to emerge successfully from this. You will see: The future will be great."

Phoenix Rising

In 2003, Malden Mills landed a $19 million contract with the U.S. Department of Defense to manufacture high-performance apparel for the military. Feuerstein's goodwill was recognized by political leaders and this helped the company secure this pivotal government contract. Within weeks, Malden Mills announced that it had rebounded and was no longer facing bankruptcy.

Restructuring

Malden Mills is a very different company than it was ten years ago. In the aftermath of its Chapter 11 filing, the company was restructured and it now has a corporate board. Because it assumed tremendous debt to rebuild after the fire, the company's stock is now held by different creditors. This means that Feuerstein no longer owns his business outright—his creditors do. Feuerstein is trying to obtain a new loan with the U.S. Import/Export Bank so that he can raise the capital to repay his creditors and resume direct control over the business. So while the company is now more financially stable, its future still remains uncertain.

Case Study Analysis

1. List the pros and cons of Feuerstein's decision to spend $25 million to pay his employees in the aftermath of the fire. In what ways did this decision both benefit and harm Malden Mills?

2. Imagine a scenario where you are the president of Malden Mills. What do you think you would have done after the fire? Write a paragraph describing your action plan.

3. Write a paragraph describing Feuerstein's philosophy of human resource management.

4. Before the fire, Malden Mills was a privately held company, owned by Feuerstein. After the fire, Feuerstein had to borrow money from different creditors in order to rebuild his business. Please answer the following:

   ■ What is the difference between a privately owned company and one that is publicly owned?

   ■ What was Feuerstein able to do when he had private ownership over Malden Mills that he couldn't do once he sold equity to creditors?

   ■ What are the costs and benefits of debt financing?

5. Many would describe Feuerstein as an ethical businessperson. Explain why he developed this reputation.

6. Brainstorm three concrete ways that Feuerstein's reputation as a benevolent leader has helped his company.

CASE SOURCES

Articles and press releases featured on the Malden Mills Web site. See *http://www.polartec.com/about/corporate.php*.

Unit 4   BUSINESS PLAN PRACTICE

At the end of each unit, you will have an opportunity to work on your own business plan. Please go to the Business Plan Worksheet Template section for Unit 4 on the BizBuilder CD now to develop the following segments of your plan:

Legal Structure

1. What is your business legal structure?

   Sole Proprietorship _____

   Partnership _____

   Limited Partnership _____

   C Corporation _____

   Subchapter S _____

   Limited Liability Corporation _____

   Not-for-Profit Corporation? _____

. Why did you choose this legal structure?
3. Who will be the partners or stockholders for your company?
   a. If your business is incorporated, describe what percentage of your company is owned by one share of stock.
   b. Is your corporation's stock publicly or privately held?
4. Have you registered your business?

Manufacturing

1. What are the zoning laws in your area? Does your business comply?
2. Do you intend to manufacture your product? If so, describe the manufacturing process you will use. If not, describe how your product is being manufactured.

Buying Wholesale

1. Where are you purchasing the products you plan to sell, or the parts you plan to use to manufacture the products you will sell?
2. Have you applied for a sales tax ID number?

Production-Distribution Chain

1. How do you plan to distribute your product to your target market?
2. Use the following chart to show the production-distribution chain for your own business, and the markups at each point along the way.

   Manufacturer
   Name:_____
   Contact Information: _____
   Markup: $_____
   Markup Percentage: %_____

   Wholesaler
   Name:_____
   Contact Information: _____
   Markup: $_____
   Markup Percentage: %_____

3. What is the estimated delivery time between when you place an order with your supplier and when you will have the product available for your customers?

Contracts

1. What is the most important contract you will need to run your business?
2. Describe any additional contracts you have or plan to secure.
3. Who is your attorney?

Human Resources

1. Fill out a PERT chart for your business.
2. Will you be hiring employees? If so, describe what their qualifications should be, what you intend to pay them, and how they will help your business.
3. Provide contact information for your accountant, attorney, banker, and insurance agent.
4. What will your policies be toward employees? How do you plan to make your business a positive and rewarding place to work?
5. Create an organizational chart for your business.

Ethical Business Behavior

1. Describe the corporate governance plan for your business. It should include five policies (rules) that will be the backbone of your company's ethics.
2. Provide information on each of your mentors or advisors. If there is a board of advisors, list each member and describe their personal commitments to the board.

Socially Responsible Business

Choose three ways you plan to run a socially responsible business, such as:

■ Recycling paper, glass, or plastic
■ Donating a portion of profits to a charity
■ No animal testing of products
■ Offering employees incentives to volunteer in the community
■ Establishing a safe and healthy workplace
■ Other

Financial Statements for Portland Freelancer's Cafe

Start-up Investment	
Start-up Costs	
Soundproof Quiet Room	15,000
Laser Printers	7,000
High-Speed Internet Access Setup	10,000
Workstations	20,000
Supplies/Equipment	25,000
Furniture	8,000
Fixtures	5,000
Cash Reserves	10,000
Total Start-up Investments	**100,000**

Economics of One Unit (EOU)			
Unit of Sale: Computer/Internet Services (average per customer)			
Average Sale Total (Revenue)			**4.00**
Less COGS			
Computer time	–		
Printer materials	0.25		
Total COGS	0.25	0.25	0.25
Gross Profit			**3.75**
Less Other Variable Costs			
Commission 5% to manager	0.20		
Total Other Variable Costs	0.20	0.20	0.20
Total Variable Costs (COGS + Other VC)		0.45	
Contribution Margin			**3.55**

Economics of One Unit (EOU)			
Unit of Sale: Food and Beverage Sales (average per customer)			
Average Sale Total (Revenue)			**2.00**
Less COGS			
Food	0.80		
Beverage	0.20		
Total COGS	1.00	1.00	1.00
Gross Profit			**1.00**
Less Other Variable Costs			
Commission 5% to manager	0.10		
Total Other Variable Costs	0.10	0.10	0.10
Total Variable Costs (COGS + Other VC)		1.10	
Contribution Margin			**0.90**

Figure 12-10 Start-up investment and economics of one unit.

Portland Feelancer's Café
INCOME STATEMENT
for the year ending 12/31/2003

		Jan	Feb	Mar	Apr	May	Jun	Jul	Aug	Sep	Oct	Nov	Dec	Year
No. Units sold- Computer Services		1,500	1,000	600	550	550	500	500	450	450	450	400	400	7,350
No. Units sold- Food and Beverage		4,500	4,750	5,000	5,100	5,200	5,300	5,400	5,500	5,600	5,700	5,800	6,000	63,850
Revenue														
Computer Service Fees		6,000	4,000	2,400	2,200	2,200	2,000	2,000	1,800	1,800	1,800	1,600	1,600	29,400
Food and Beverage Sales		9,000	9,500	10,000	10,200	10,400	10,600	10,800	11,000	11,200	11,400	11,600	12,000	127,700
Total Revenue		**15,000**	**13,500**	**12,400**	**12,400**	**12,600**	**12,600**	**12,800**	**12,800**	**13,000**	**13,200**	**13,200**	**13,600**	**157,100**
Less COGS														
Printer Matls (paper, ink)		375	250	150	138	138	125	125	113	113	113	100	100	1,838
Food		3,600	3,800	4,000	4,080	4,160	4,240	4,320	4,400	4,480	4,560	4,640	4,800	51,080
Beverages		900	950	1,000	1,020	1,040	1,060	1,080	1,100	1,120	1,140	1,160	1,200	12,770
Total COGS		4,875	5,000	5,150	5,238	5,338	5,425	5,525	5,613	5,713	5,813	5,900	6,100	65,688
Gross Profit		**10,125**	**8,500**	**7,250**	**7,163**	**7,263**	**7,175**	**7,275**	**7,188**	**7,288**	**7,388**	**7,300**	**7,500**	**91,413**
Less Other Variable Costs														
Commission, Computer	5%	300	200	120	110	110	100	100	90	90	90	80	80	1,470
Commission, Food/Bev.	5%	450	475	500	510	520	530	540	550	560	570	580	600	6,385
Total Other Variable Costs		750	675	620	620	630	630	640	640	650	660	660	680	7,855
Total Var. Costs (COGS + Other VC)		5,625	5,675	5,770	5,858	5,968	6,055	6,165	6,253	6,363	6,473	6,560	6,780	73,543
Contribution Margin		**9,375**	**7,825**	**6,630**	**6,543**	**6,633**	**6,545**	**6,635**	**6,548**	**6,638**	**6,728**	**6,640**	**6,820**	**83,558**

Less Fixed Costs (USAIIRDO)

Utilities													
Electricity	150	150	150	150	150	150	150	150	150	150	150	150	1,800
Gas	250	250	250	250	250	250	250	250	250	250	250	250	3,000
Water	100	100	100	100	100	100	100	100	100	100	100	100	1,200
Telephone	75	75	75	75	75	75	75	75	75	75	75	75	900
High Speed Internet	425	425	425	425	425	425	425	425	425	425	425	425	5,100
Wireless Internet service	30	30	30	30	30	30	30	30	30	30	30	30	360
Total Utilities	1,030	1,030	1,030	1,030	1,030	1,030	1,030	1,030	1,030	1,030	1,030	1,030	12,360
Salaries													
Amy & Steve salary	1,000	1,000	1,000	1,000	1,000	1,000	1,000	1,000	1,000	1,000	1,000	1,000	12,000
Tech Support (Part time)	1,000	1,000	1,000	1,000	1,000	1,000	1,000	1,000	1,000	1,000	1,000	1,000	12,000
Total Salaries	2,000	2,000	2,000	2,000	2,000	2,000	2,000	2,000	2,000	2,000	2,000	2,000	24,000
Advertising	1,000	1,000	1,000	1,000	1,000	1,000	1,000	1,000	1,000	1,000	1,000	1,000	12,000
Insurance	500	500	500	500	500	500	500	500	500	500	500	500	6,000
Interest	1,469	1,469	1,469	1,469	1,469	1,469	1,469	1,469	1,469	1,469	1,469	1,469	17,628
Rent	1,000	1,000	1,000	1,000	1,000	1,000	1,000	1,000	1,000	1,000	1,000	1,000	12,000
Depreciation	1,333	1,333	1,333	1,333	1,333	1,333	1,333	1,333	1,333	1,333	1,333	1,333	15,996
Other	-	-	-	-	-	-	-	-	-	-	-	-	-
Total Fixed Costs	8,332	8,332	8,332	8,332	8,332	8,332	8,332	8,332	8,332	8,332	8,332	8,332	99,984
Pre-Tax Profit	1,043	(507)	(1,702)	(1,790)	(1,700)	(1,787)	(1,697)	(1,785)	(1,695)	(1,605)	(1,692)	(1,512)	(16,427)
Taxes 20%	208.60	(507)	(1,702)	(1,790)	(1,700)	(1,787)	(1,697)	(1,785)	(1,695)	(1,605)	(1,692)	(1,512)	(16,427)
Net Profit	834	(507)	(1,702)	(1,790)	(1,700)	(1,787)	(1,697)	(1,785)	(1,695)	(1,605)	(1,692)	(1,512)	(16,427)

* Remember Revenue minus COGS Equals Gross Profit minus Other Variable Costs equals Contribution Margin.

Figure 12-11 2003 Income statement.

CASH FLOW STATEMENT
for the year ending 12/31/2003

	Jan	Feb	Mar	Apr	May	Jun	Jul	Aug	Sep	Oct	Nov	Dec	Year
Number of Units—Computer Services	1,500	1,000	600	550	550	500	500	450	450	450	400	400	7,350
Number of Units—Food & Beverage Sales	4,500	4,750	5,000	5,100	5,200	5,300	5,400	5,500	5,600	5,700	5,800	6,000	63,850
Cash Flow from Operating:													
Cash Inflows:													
Computer Usage Fees	$ 6,000	$ 4,000	$ 2,400	$ 2,200	$ 2,200	$ 2,000	$ 2,000	$ 1,800	$ 1,800	$ 1,800	$ 1,600	$ 1,600	$29,400
Food and Beverage Sales	$ 9,000	$ 9,500	$10,000	$10,200	$10,400	$10,600	$10,800	$11,000	$11,200	$11,400	$11,600	$12,000	$127,700
Total Cash Inflows	$ 15,000	$13,500	$12,400	$12,400	$12,600	$12,600	$12,800	$12,800	$13,000	$13,200	$13,200	$13,600	$157,100
Cash Outflows:													
Variable Costs													
COGS	$ 4,875	$ 5,000	$ 5,150	$ 5,238	$ 5,338	$ 5,425	$ 5,525	$ 5,613	$ 5,713	$ 5,813	$ 5,900	$ 6,100	$65,688
Other Variable Costs	$ 750	$ 675	$ 620	$ 620	$ 630	$ 630	$ 640	$ 640	$ 650	$ 660	$ 660	$ 680	$7,855
Utilities													
Electricity, Gas, Water, Telephone	$ 500	$ 500	$ 500	$ 500	$ 500	$ 500	$ 500	$ 500	$ 500	$ 500	$ 500	$ 500	$6,000
High-Speed Internet Access	$ 500	$ 500	$ 500	$ 500	$ 500	$ 500	$ 500	$ 500	$ 500	$ 500	$ 500	$ 500	$6,000
Wireless Internet	$ 30	$ 30	$ 30	$ 30	$ 30	$ 30	$ 30	$ 30	$ 30	$ 30	$ 30	$ 30	$360
Salaries													
Part-Time Tech Support Salary	$ 1,000	$ 1,000	$ 1,000	$ 1,000	$ 1,000	$ 1,000	$ 1,000	$ 1,000	$ 1,000	$ 1,000	$ 1,000	$ 1,000	$ 12,000
Amy and Steve's Salary	$ 1,000	$ 1,000	$ 1,000	$ 1,000	$ 1,000	$ 1,000	$ 1,000	$ 1,000	$ 1,000	$ 1,000	$ 1,000	$ 1,000	$ 12,000
Advertising	$ 1,000	$ 1,000	$ 1,000	$ 1,000	$ 1,000	$ 1,000	$ 1,000	$ 1,000	$ 1,000	$ 1,000	$ 1,000	$ 1,000	$ 12,000
Insurance	$ 500	$ 500	$ 500	$ 500	$ 500	$ 500	$ 500	$ 500	$ 500	$ 500	$ 500	$ 500	$ 6,000
Interest Expense	$ 1,469	$ 1,469	$ 1,469	$ 1,469	$ 1,469	$ 1,469	$ 1,469	$ 1,469	$ 1,469	$ 1,469	$ 1,469	$ 1,469	$ 17,623
Rent	$ 1,000	$ 1,001	$ 1,002	$ 1,003	$ 1,004	$ 1,005	$ 1,006	$ 1,007	$ 1,008	$ 1,009	$ 1,010	$ 1,011	$ 12,000
Total Cash Used in Operating Activities	$ 12,624	$12,675	$12,771	$12,859	$12,970	$13,059	$13,170	$13,258	$13,369	$13,480	$13,569	$13,790	$157,526
Net Cash Flow from Operating	$ 2,376	$ 825	($ 371)	($ 459)	($ 370)	($ 459)	($ 370)	($ 458)	($ 369)	($ 280)	($ 369)	($ 190)	($ 426)

Cash Flow Out from Investing:

	1	2	3	4	5	6	7	8	9	10	11	12	Total
Cash Flow Out from Investing:													
Soundproof Quiet Room	$ 15,000	$ 0	$ 0	$ 0	$ 0	$ 0	$ 0	$ 0	$ 0	$ 0	$ 0	$ 0	$ 15,000
Laser Printers	$ 7,000	$ 0	$ 0	$ 0	$ 0	$ 0	$ 0	$ 0	$ 0	$ 0	$ 0	$ 0	$ 7,000
High-Speed Internet Access													
Setup	$ 10,000	$ 0	$ 0	$ 0	$ 0	$ 0	$ 0	$ 0	$ 0	$ 0	$ 0	$ 0	$ 10,000
Workstations	$ 20,000	$ 0	$ 0	$ 0	$ 0	$ 0	$ 0	$ 0	$ 0	$ 0	$ 0	$ 0	$ 20,000
Supplies/Equipment	$ 25,000	$ 0	$ 0	$ 0	$ 0	$ 0	$ 0	$ 0	$ 0	$ 0	$ 0	$ 0	$ 25,000
Furniture	$ 8,000	$ 0	$ 0	$ 0	$ 0	$ 0	$ 0	$ 0	$ 0	$ 0	$ 0	$ 0	$ 8,000
Fixtures	$ 5,000	$ 0	$ 0	$ 0	$ 0	$ 0	$ 0	$ 0	$ 0	$ 0	$ 0	$ 0	$ 5,000
Net Cash Flow Out from Investing	$ 90,000	$ 0	$ 0	$ 0	$ 0	$ 0	$ 0	$ 0	$ 0	$ 0	$ 0	$ 0	$ 90,000
Financing:													
Cash Received from Uncle (12% APR)	$ 50,000	$ 0	$ 0	$ 0	$ 0	$ 0	$ 0	$ 0	$ 0	$ 0	$ 0	$ 0	$ 50,000
Cash Received from Brother	$ 20,000	$ 0	$ 0	$ 0	$ 0	$ 0	$ 0	$ 0	$ 0	$ 0	$ 0	$ 0	$ 20,000
Cash Received from Mother	$ 10,000	$ 0	$ 0	$ 0	$ 0	$ 0	$ 0	$ 0	$ 0	$ 0	$ 0	$ 0	$ 10,000
Cash Received from Personal Savings	$ 20,000	$ 0	$ 0	$ 0	$ 0	$ 0	$ 0	$ 0	$ 0	$ 0	$ 0	$ 0	$ 20,000
Net Cash Flow In from Financing	$ 100,000	$ 0	$ 0	$ 0	$ 0	$ 0	$ 0	$ 0	$ 0	$ 0	$ 0	$ 0	$ 100,000
Net Increase (Decrease) in Cash	$ 12,376	$ 825	($ 371)	($ 459)	($ 370)	($ 459)	($ 458)	($ 369)	($ 369)	($ 280)	($ 190)	($ 190)	$ 9,574
Cash, Beginning:	$ 10,000	$ 22,376	$ 23,202	$ 22,831	$ 22,372	$ 22,002	$ 21,543	$ 21,174	$ 20,716	$ 20,346	$ 20,066	$ 19,698	$ 10,000
Cash, End:	$ 22,376	$ 23,202	$ 22,831	$ 22,372	$ 22,002	$ 21,543	$ 21,174	$ 20,716	$ 20,346	$ 20,066	$ 19,698	$ 19,508	$ 19,574

Figure 12-12 2003 Cash flow statement.

BALANCE SHEET for the year ending 12/31/2003		
	Opening	**Closing**
ASSETS		
Current Assets:		
Cash	$110,000	$19,574
Accounts Receivable	0	0
Total Current Assets	**$110,000**	**$19,574**
Fixed Assets (Property and Equipment):		
Soundproof Quiet Room	$ 15,000	$15,000
Laser Printers	2,000	2,000
Workstations	30,000	30,000
Supplies/Equipment	25,000	25,000
Furniture	3,000	3,000
Fixtures	5,000	5,000
Total Property and Equipment	**$ 80,000**	**$80,000**
Less Accumulated Depreciation	**$ 0**	**$16,000**
Total Property and Equipment (net)	**$ 80,000**	**$64,000**
Total Assets	**$190,000**	**$83,574**
LIABILITIES AND OWNER'S EQUITY		
Current Liabilities:		
Accounts Payable	$ 0	$ 0
Total Current Liabilities	**$ 0**	**$ 0**
Long-Term Liability (Uncle's Loan)	**$ 50,000**	**$32,377**
Total Liabilities	**$ 50,000**	**$32,377**
Owner's Equity	**$140,000**	**$51,198**
Amy	40%	40%
Steve	40%	40%
Steve's Brother	20%	20%
Total Liabilities and Owner's Equity	**$190,000**	**$83,574**

Figure 12-13 2003 balance sheet.

Case Study Analysis

1. Evaluate the economics of one unit analysis that Amy and Steve conducted and then answer the following questions:

    a. Amy and Steve assume that, for every $6 in sales, $4 will come from selling computer-related services. Calculate what percentage of their total sales revenue per unit this $4 represents.

    b. For every $2 in food and beverage sales, Amy and Steve assume that their COGS per unit will be $1. Calculate the markup percentage.

    c. For every $4 in computer services sales, Amy and Steve assume that their COGS per unit will be 25 cents. Calculate the markup percentage.

2. List three things that Amy and Steve should consider doing to adapt to the changes in their environment now that their customers no longer want to pay for Internet services and expect the café to provide free wireless connections.

3. Evaluate Amy and Steve's income statement for their first month of operations:

    a. Is the café operating at a profit or a loss?

    b. How many units above or below breakeven were sold?

4. Amy and Steve decided to take on a $50,000 loan to finance their start-up investment. Each month they are paying $1,469 in interest charges. Look at their total monthly fixed costs. What percentage of their total monthly fixed costs does this $1,469 represent?

5. What is the debt-to-equity ratio of the Portland Freelancer's Café?

6. Look at each section of the café's cash flow statement. Write a memo highlighting three insights you have about why this business is not succeeding based on what you see in its cash flow statement.

7. Review the café's balance sheet. Explain why the net value of the café's property and equipment has decreased from $80,000 in month one to $64,000 at year-end.

"All businesses were launched by entrepreneurs and all were once small."

—Nat Shulman, family business owner and columnist

Performance Objectives

1. Describe the benefits of focusing a brand.
2. Describe how businesses use licensing to profit from their brands.
3. Explain why profits follow quality.
4. Explain how a business can be franchised.
5. Discuss five ways to harvest a business.

Liz Claiborne is a hugely successful entrepreneur who never graduated from high school. Claiborne was born in Belgium to American parents in 1929. Women were not expected to work in those days, so education was not considered so important for them. When she fell in love with fashion and wanted to become a designer, her family was strongly against it.

Claiborne was determined, though, and at twenty-one she applied for a job on Seventh Avenue in New York City's garment district. She got employment as a sketcher, model, and "pick-up-pins girl"—and an opportunity to observe her market from the inside. What she observed was that women were starting to go to work but few designers were making clothes for them to wear to their jobs. Here was an opportunity to become a designer and make clothes that women really needed. She founded Liz Claiborne, Inc., which today is a billion-dollar corporation that provides quality affordable clothing for working women.

One entrepreneur can create a business that grows from a small sole proprietorship to an international conglomerate. Once the business has a name that stands for something attractive to consumers, the name itself becomes valuable.

Liz Claiborne, Inc. sells clothes all over the world, and also **licenses** its name to other companies—"renting" the right to use the Claiborne name to sell products that reflect the Claiborne vision. The licensee pays a fee for the license and may also pay royalties on sales to the licensor.

In 2004, for example, Liz Claiborne announced that it would license its name to the Eastman Group (the licensee) to make men's shoes under the Claiborne label.

"Licensing our brands is a key aspect of our growth strategy, enabling us to extend Claiborne's presence in the market," said Barbara Friedman, president of Licensing in a press release. "We are pleased to be teaming with Eastman Group on our Claiborne footwear collection. Their innovative product design and expertise in manufacturing will help us offer superior product and value to the Claiborne customer. The addition of footwear to the Claiborne product mix furthers our goal of making a complete lifestyle statement."[1]

Max Mizrahi, president of Eastman Group, stated: "This is a great opportunity for us to partner with a classic American brand with a reputation for fashion and superb quality. We anticipate that our footwear expertise, coupled with Claiborne's reputation, will open many doors with retailers and make an impact immediately."[2]

Fashion designers and celebrities have made millions by licensing their famous names for perfume, athletic shoes, and other products. Licensing is also subject to fewer government regulations than franchising.

»Focus Your Brand

Performance Objective 1.»

A **brand** is a name, term, sign, logo, design, or combination of these that identifies the products or services of a company and differentiates them from those of competitors. The brand represents the company's promise to consistently deliver a specific set of benefits to customers. Customers who buy Liz Claiborne clothes, for example, expect classic clothing suitable for the workplace. They have come to trust the brand to meet their needs.

Businesses do better when customers know what to expect from a brand, according to an influential book by marketing expert Al Ries.[3] He argues that, in industry after industry, the narrowly focused companies are the big winners. He contends that too many managers are hooked on growth for its own sake and develop misguided expansion that dilutes the strength of a company's brand.

Many companies have taken popular brands, such as Adidas athletic shoes, and applied them with disastrous results to products like Adidas cologne. It did not work to apply a brand associated with sneakers to cologne! Bic, known for its pens, branched into pantyhose and had a similar failure.

Using an established brand to promote different kinds of products is called **line extension.** It can work if the brand is strong and the new product the brand is being applied to is similar to the original. Kraft General Foods successfully applied the Jell-O brand name to a line of puddings, after Jell-O had been established as the preeminent gelatin dessert.

A clearly focused brand can go a long way—the Hard Rock Hotel and Casino, Las Vegas.
(Wesley R. Hitt, Creative Eye/MIRA.com)

List some brands you trust, and explain why you trust them.

_____

_____

[1] "Liz Claiborne Inc. Announces Licensing Agreement with Eastman Group. *PR Newswire,* July 1, 2004.
[2] Ibid.
[3] Al Ries. *Focus: The Future of Your Company Depends on It* (New York, New York: Harper Business, 1996).

[Step Into The Shoes]

Fixing General Motors by Focusing the Brand

This is what Alfred Sloan did when he took over General Motors in 1921. At that time the product line was a melange of overlapping price ranges:

Chevrolet: $795 to $2,075

Oakland: $1,395 to $2,065

Oldsmobile: $1,445 to $3,300

Scripps-Booth: $1,545 to $2,295

Sheridan: $1,685

Buick: $1,795 to $3,295

Cadillac: $3,790 to $5,690

Sloan replaced this with a single-focus strategy with multiple steps. A customer could move up the "automobile ladder" as his or her finances improved.

- Chevrolet: $450 to $600
- Pontiac: $600 to $900
- Oldsmobile: $900 to $1,200
- Buick: $1,200 to $1,700
- Cadillac: 2,000 to $3,700

It took ten years for General Motors to surpass Ford using this strategy but once it did it could not be stopped. It held close to 50 percent of the American market for over half a century.

»Diversification Comes with a Price

To a budding entrepreneur or a seasoned executive, **diversification,** or spreading the brand out among many products, can look like the way to get more market share. Ries argues that diversification comes with a price. "It unfocuses the company and leads to loss of power."[4] Focus, in contrast, attracts exactly the right employees to a company and reinforces its strength in the marketplace.

The best way to launch new product lines, Ries suggests, is to give them their own names, price ranges, and identities.

»When Licensing Can Be Effective

Similarly, licensing can damage your brand if not handled carefully. Licensing is only effective when the licensor is confident that the company name will not be tarnished by how the licensee uses it. If Coca-Cola licensed its name to a T-shirt maker, there would not be much the T-shirt maker could do to tarnish the reputation of Coca-Cola. Coca-Cola would get free advertising, as well as royalties. A **royalty** is a percentage of the revenue generated by the sale of each unit.

❬2. Performance Objective

Coca-Cola would not license its name to a soft drink manufacturer, however, because a licensing agreement would not guarantee that the manufacturer would make a product of the same quality as Coca-Cola's. If Coca-Cola did want to expand in this fashion, it would be better served by creating a **franchise.**

---

[4] Ibid., p. 273.

A franchise is a business that markets a product or service in the exact manner prescribed by the person who developed the business. As an entrepreneur, you could develop a concept and a business operation that could be reproduced and sold to other entrepreneurs. They buy the right to run the business exactly the way that you instructed and pay you a royalty, or share of the profits.

»How a McDonald's Franchise Works

Let's look at how franchises can grow a business. McDonald's is an example of a franchise operation. McDonald's was developed by Ray Kroc, who had persuaded the McDonald brothers to let him become the franchising agent for their highly successful hamburger restaurant in San Bernardino, California, in 1955. Kroc's great insight was to realize that the franchisees—the people who bought McDonald's franchises—needed extensive training and support in order to make the food taste like the food from the original restaurant. Kroc timed everything. McDonald's franchisees are taught exactly how many minutes to fry potatoes and when to turn a burger. They are also taught precisely how to greet customers and handle orders.

A McDonald's franchisee is an entrepreneur. The franchisee owns the restaurant, but agrees to market the food under the McDonald's name and trademark in the exact fashion developed by Kroc. This is spelled out in the franchise agreement. In return, the franchisee knows he or she is investing in a proven, successful business concept. The franchisee also benefits from use of the McDonald's trademark, and from management training, marketing, national advertising, and promotional assistance provided by the parent company. McDonald's, as franchisor, receives a franchise fee and royalties.

Although franchising has been around in the United States since the Singer Sewing Machine Company first used it in the 1850s, its popularity has exploded in recent years. Over 4,000 companies offer franchises. The number of individual franchises grew to nearly half a million between 1977 and 1987.

Women and minorities have been especially drawn to franchises as a way to enter the business world. Recognizing this, Burger King, Pizza Hut, Taco Bell, Kentucky Fried Chicken, and Baskin-Robbins all offer special financing and other incentives to recruit minority franchise owners. Other franchise programs have focused with great success on recruiting women.

»Royalty Fees

Through franchising, Ray Kroc turned a simple idea—the fast production of inexpensive hamburgers—into an internationally recognized symbol of American enterprise. Today, franchising accounts for more than $800 billion in annual sales in a wide variety of industries.

A Pizza Hut franchise in Los Angeles.
(Bill Aron, PhotoEdit)

The following are fees, start-up costs, and royalty fees for some popular franchises:[5]

Franchise	Franchise Fee	Start-up Costs	Royalty Fee
McDonald's	$45,000	$489,000–$1.5 million	12.5%
Arby's Inc.	$25,000–$37,500	$333,000–$2 million	4%
General Nutrition Franchising, Inc.	$30,000	$132,000–$182,000	6%

»Profits Follow Quality

〈 3. Performance Objective

Kroc and other successful franchise developers made delivering consistent quality to the customer their top priority. This ensures that a hamburger at a Wendy's in San Francisco tastes the same as one served at a Wendy's in New York.

For many years, American entrepreneurs focused on short-term profits, not so much on quality. In the early 1950s, however, an American economist, W. Edwards Deming, argued that companies should focus on making quality products instead of on maximizing profits—and that profit would flow from that focus. His revolutionary concept was ignored by American business, so he went to Japan, which was rebuilding after the devastation of World War II.

In those days, Japan was notorious for the poor quality of its manufactured products. The phrase "Made in Japan" was jokingly used to refer to anything poorly made. Deming gave a series of lectures in Japan, though, that the Japanese took to heart. They began focusing on quality and soon proved that Deming's theory that profits follow quality was correct. The high quality of Japanese cars and stereos won over customers worldwide.

American entrepreneurs and corporate executives traveled to Japan to study why the Japanese had become so successful. They brought Deming's ideas back home, where they finally began to be adopted.

As you develop your business, it will be the consistent quality of your product or service that will lead to profit. If you can develop a way to deliver quality consistently, you will have a business concept that can eventually be franchised.

»Do Your Homework before You Get Involved with a Franchise

Before you get involved in either franchising your business or becoming a franchisee, consult with a franchise attorney and do extensive research. Some eager franchisees have been burned by franchisors who open too many franchises in an area or who fail to honor the franchise contract. Before investing in a franchise, talk to

---

[5] Numbers may not be up-to-date.

other franchisees of the same company. Are they happy with their sales? With the level of support, training, and advertising provided by the franchisor? Get the answers to all your questions before you agree to become a franchisee.

»The Franchise Agreement

Performance Objective 4.》 The franchise agreement is the contract between the franchisor and franchisee. The contract establishes the standards that assure uniformity of product and service throughout the franchise chain.
Included in the franchise agreement are the following:

- The term of the agreement or length of time the franchisor and franchisee agree to work together.
- Standards of quality and performance.
- An agreement on royalties—Usually a percentage of the franchise's sales paid to the franchisor.
- "Non-compete clauses" stating that, for instance, if you own a McDonald's, you cannot own a Blimpies.
- Territories—Franchisees are usually assigned territories in which they can do business. Within the assigned territory no other franchisee from that company will be allowed to compete.

Benefits of Franchising

Franchisor

- Growth of minimal capital investment.
- Lower marketing and promotional costs.
- Royalties.

Franchisee

- Ownership of a business with less risk than is involved in starting a business alone.
- Help with management and training.
- Advertising—The franchise chain can afford television ads, etc., that the small-business owner could not finance alone.

Drawbacks of Franchising

Franchisor

- The franchisee may disregard the training and fail to operate the business properly, tarnishing the reputation of the franchise.
- It can be difficult to find qualified or trustworthy franchisees.
- Franchisees who do not experience success may try to sue the franchisor.
- There are many federal and state regulations in franchising.

Franchisee

- Giving up control—Much of the franchise's operations are dictated by the franchisor.
- Franchisor may fail to deliver promised training and support.
- Franchisor may engage in poor business practices that affect earnings or image of franchise.

[Global Impact: Franchising Worldwide]

Want to be an international mogul? Check out these sites:

International Franchising Opportunities—www.franchiseintl.com

World Franchising—www.worldfranchising.com

International Franchising's directory lists over 1,000 North American franchises that train and support franchisees over-seas. It also provides contact information for consultants and attorneys specializing in international franchising. World Franchising lists the top 100 franchises worldwide, as well as the top 50 franchises with under 50 operating units.

»Think Big from the Start

It is important that you are aware of the possibilities offered by franchising and licensing from the moment you start your business. This way you will be motivated to keep your business organized and to try to develop a foolproof operational system. After all, some day hundreds, or even thousands, of entrepreneurs might be eager to buy that system from you!

Franchising and licensing are called **replication** strategies, be-cause they are ways to obtain money from a business you created by letting others copy, or replicate, it.

Another method of obtaining money from your business is to **harvest** it. Harvesting means the business has been sold, taken pub-lic, or merged with a larger company. Harvesting differs from repli-cation in that the entrepreneur is no longer involved once the business is harvested, but walks away with a chunk of the business's value as cash or stock.

In William Petty's article on harvesting,[6] he quotes Steve Covey, author of *The Seven Habits of Highly Effective People*, who says a key to being effective in life is "beginning with the end in mind." To that Petty adds, "If the entrepreneur's goal with the venture is only to provide a living, then the exit or harvest strategy is of no concern. But if the goal is to create value for the owners and the other stake-holders in the company, a harvest strategy is absolutely mandatory."

The harvest strategy is important not only to the entrepreneur but also to investors, as it tells them how their investment will even-tually be turned into cash or stock.

Not every business can be harvested. Some are loaded with debt or have not created a product or service of lasting value. The entre-preneur can only leave such a business via **liquidation** (selling all its assets) or bankruptcy.

> To take a business public means to arrange to sell its stock in the stock market. The first offering of a business's stock is called an **IPO,** short for Initial Public Offering.

»When to Harvest Your Business

Petty recommends that the entrepreneur be sensitive to the fact that offers to buy one's business, take it public, or merge it with a bigger company will come and go throughout the life of the firm. Although you want to be aware of all opportunities, it usually requires at least ten years to build a company worth harvesting.

---

[6] William Petty, "Harvesting" *The Portable MBA in Entrepreneurship,* 2nd ed. William D. Bygrave, Editor (New York, New York: Bygrave, Wiley, 1997).

»The Net Present Value of Money

The **net present value** of money is the value to you today of something that you hope to get in the future. The price of a stock today, for example, represents what the market thinks that stock will be worth in the future. The price is really the stock's net present value.

All purchases, in fact, are based on net present value. Ultimately the price of something is its net present value.

A business that is profitable and is likely to be profitable in the future can be sold for a sum that represents its net present value today. This is net present value in action. Most wealth is created by buying and selling assets that have a future value.

»How to Value a Business

There are many ways to estimate the net present value of a business. Value, after all, is subjective, meaning it is subject to a person's opinion or preferences. One person might be willing to pay a higher price for a business than another would. The first buyer has a more optimistic opinion of the business's future, or may simply want it more than the other buyer does.

Here are some methods entrepreneurs use to estimate the value of a business:

1. Compare it with similar businesses. If you are looking to sell your dry-cleaning business, check out how much other dry-cleaning stores in your area are bringing in when they are sold.

2. In most industries, there are one or two key benchmarks used to help value a business. For gas stations, it might be barrels of gas sold per week; for a dry-cleaner, it might be the number of shirts cleaned per week.

3. Look at a multiple of net earnings. One rule of thumb says a business can sell for around three times its annual net earnings. If the business earns $100,000 net profit per year, for example, it could be expected to sell for $300,000.

The valuation of companies is part art and part science, and its ultimate goal is to arrive at a **fair market value,** which according to the IRS, is "The price at which property would change hands between a willing buyer and willing seller, neither under any compulsion to buy or sell and both having reasonable knowledge of the relevant facts."[7]

»The Science of Valuation

There are three primary methods that buyers and sellers use:

1. Book Value
2. Future Earnings
3. Market-Based Value

In practice, these three methods are often used concurrently, and all provide unique and helpful perspectives on the value of a com-

---

[7] Andrea Hock, "When a Business Is Family-Owned; Determining Value Is Art Not Science," *New York Journal*, May 29, 2001, p. 3.

pany. Furthermore, there are many variations on each method. Below is a more in-depth description of each.

> ***Book Value (Net Worth = Assets − Liabilities):*** One of the most common methods for computing a company's valuation, the **book value** method looks at a company as assets minus liabilities. This method is the most common one used for valuing companies, and also the simplest.

> ***Future Earnings:*** This method uses a company's estimated future earnings as the main determinant of its value. It is most useful for companies that are growing quickly. In these cases, past earnings are not an accurate reflection of true value. This method of valuation must take into account the time value of money as well as the rate of return.

> ***Market-Based (Value = P/E Ratio × Estimated Future Net Earnings):*** In the market-based approach, the value of the company is based on the price/earnings (P/E) ratio of comparable public companies. The P/E ratio is determined by dividing a company's stock price by its earnings per share. This method is effective because of its simplicity, but may be lacking when there are no similar public companies to compare the business with.

Despite the sophistication of these three techniques, all of them are ultimately only estimates. Each business will have unique characteristics and special circumstances. In the end, it will be the entrepreneur's job to use negotiation to get the highest price possible.

»Sell Online

Once you do decide to sell your business, or pursue another exit strategy, use the Internet to maximize your prospects. If you decide to sell, you can list your business with databases such as BizBuySell.com, which sends registered users who might want to buy your business e-mails alerting them that you want to sell.

»Harvesting Options[8]

Harvesting options for exiting a business fall into five categories:

1. ***Increase the Free Cash Flows***—For the first seven to ten years of the business, you will want to reinvest as much profit as possible into the business in order to grow. Once you are ready to exit, however, you can begin reducing investment and taking cash out as dividends. This strategy will require investing only the amount of cash needed to keep the business effective in its current target markets, without attempting to move into new ones.

   ⟨5. **Performance Objective**

   Advantages
   - You can retain ownership of the firm with this strategy.
   - You do not have to seek a buyer.

---

[8]Special thanks to Jeff Timmons.

Disadvantages

- You will need a good accountant to help avoid major taxes.
- It can take a long time to execute this exit strategy.

2. *Management Buy-out (MBO)*—In this strategy, the entrepreneur sells the firm to the managers, who raise the money to buy it via personal savings and debt.

Advantages

- If the business has value, the managers usually do want to buy it.
- The entrepreneur has the emotional satisfaction of selling to people he knows and has trained.

Disadvantages

- If the managers use primarily debt to buy the company, they may not be able to actually pay off the deal.
- If the final payment to the entrepreneur depends on the company's earnings during the last few quarters, the managers may have an incentive to attempt to lower the company's profits.

3. *Employee Stock Ownership Plan (ESOP)*—This strategy both provides an employee retirement plan and allows the entrepreneur and partners to sell their stock and exit the company. The firm establishes a plan that allows employees to buy company stock as part of their retirement plan; when the owners are ready to exit, the ESOP borrows money and uses the cash to buy their stock. As the loan is paid off, the stock is added to the employee benefit fund.

Advantages

- The ESOP has some special tax advantages, among them: the company can deduct both the principal and interest payments on the loan, and the dividends paid on any stock held in the ESOP are considered a tax-deductible expense.

Disadvantages

- This is not a good strategy if the entrepreneur does not want the employees to have control of the company. The ESOP must extend to all employees and requires the entrepreneur to open up the company's books.

4. *Merging or Being Acquired*—Selling the company to another company can be an exciting exit strategy for an entrepreneur who would like to see his or her creation have an opportunity to grow significantly by using another company's funds.

Advantages

- This strategy can finance growth that the company could not achieve on its own; the entrepreneur can either exit the company at the time of the merger or acquisition or be part of the growth and exit later.

Disadvantages

- This can be an emotionally draining strategy with a lot of ups and downs during negotiations; the sale can take over a year to finalize.

5. ***Initial Public Offering (IPO)***—"Going public" means to sell stock in your company in the stock market. It requires choosing an investment banker to develop the IPO, making sales presentations to brokers and institutional investors (the "roadshow") nationally and perhaps internationally, and, finally, offering your stock on the market and holding your breath as you watch its price rise or fall.

Advantages

- If your business is "hot," this can be a very profitable way to harvest it. The market may place a large premium on your company's value.

Disadvantages

- An IPO is a very exciting, but very stressful and all-consuming, way to harvest a company, and it requires a lot of work from the entrepreneur, but, ultimately, it is the market that will determine the outcome.

This overview of harvesting strategies should help you plan the final stage of your relationship with the company you are starting to create now.

»Investors Will Care about Your Exit Strategy, Too

The exit (harvesting) strategy is important not only to the entrepreneur but also to investors. They will want to know how they will one day get the return on their investment. Your business plan should tell them, by including an exit strategy.

In the business plan, spell out for investors how and when they should be able to get the return on their investment. The entrepreneur will need to show financial data that indicate in about how many years the investors could cash out.

Many entrepreneurs think it is enough to simply tell investors that eventually the business will go public and the investors' share of the business will be worth "a lot of money." Of the thousands of new ventures launched every year in the United States, however, only a small percentage actually ever go public. Yet, according to David Newton, in *entrepreneur.com* (January 15, 2001), over 70 percent of all formal business plans presented to angel investors and venture capitalists name "going public" as the primary exit strategy. Most estimate that going public will happen within just four years from the launch date.

»Exit Strategy Options

Simply claiming that your business will "go public" one day will probably get a skeptical reaction from your potential investors. Investors understand that you cannot guarantee an exit strategy, but you can show that you understand that for most small businesses going public is a fantasy. Show that you understand exit strategies by thinking through these four basic possibilities. Choose the one that you think best describes what could happen for your business.

1. ***Acquisition***–Do you believe that you could create a business that someone will want to buy (*acquire*) one day? Your exit strategy could be that you intend to create a business that will be valuable for one of your suppliers, or a major competitor, to buy. The plan is that the purchase price will pay you and your equity investors more money than you put into the business. A fair sale price, based on the business's annual net profit, should allow the original investors to realize a good return on their investment. As we have said, a common rule of thumb says that a small business is worth three times its annual net profit.

2. ***Earn Out***–To use an earn-out strategy, you will need projected cash flow statements that show the business eventually genereating a strong positive cash flow. At that point, you can start offering to buy out your investors' shares at a price greater than they paid for them. The purchase price usually rises over time.

3. ***Debt-Equity Exchange***–If your investors will be lending you money, you can offer to eventually trade equity for portions of the debt. This will slowly reduce the interest due over time (as the face value of the loan decreases). In this way, you can decide at what pace—and at what price—to reduce your debt.

4. ***Merger***–This strategy is similar to that of acquisition, but, with a **merger,** two companies join together to share their strengths. One company might have an extensive customer base, while the other might have a distribution channel the first company needs. Or perhaps each company is doing well in separate markets, and a merger would open up these complementary markets to each other's products or services. Regardless, cash will change hands, and original investors can make their shares available for sale to complete the merger.

» Chapter Summary

Now that you have studied this chapter you can do the following:

1. Describe the benefits of focusing a brand.

   ■ A brand is a name, term, sign, logo, design, or combination of these that identifies the products or services of a company and differentiates them from those of competitors.

   ■ Businesses do better when customers know what to expect from a brand.

2. Explain why profits follow quality.

   ■ In the early 1950s, an American economist named W. Edwards Deming argued that companies should focus on making quality products instead of on maximizing profits—and that profit would flow from that focus.

■ The Japanese took to Deming's theories and soon proved them to be correct.

3. Explain how a business can be franchised.

■ A franchise is a business that markets a product or service in the exact manner prescribed by the person who developed the business.

■ As an entrepreneur you could develop a concept and a business operation that can be reproduced and sold to other entrepreneurs. They buy the right to run the business exactly the way that you instruct and pay you a royalty, or share of the profits.

4. Describe how businesses use licensing to profit from their brands.

■ The licensee pays a fee for the license and may also pay royalties on sales to the licensor.

■ Licensing is only effective when the licensor is confident that his or her company name will not be tarnished by how the licensee uses it.

5. Discuss five ways to harvest a business.

■ Increase the free cash flows—Once you are ready to exit, you can begin reducing reinvestment and collecting revenue as cash.

■ Management buy-out (MBO)—The entrepreneur sells the firm to the managers, who raise the money to buy the firm via personal savings and debt.

■ Employee stock ownership plan (ESOP)—This provides an employee retirement plan and allows the entrepreneur and partners to sell their stock to the employees and exit the company.

■ Merging or being acquired—Selling the business to another company.

■ Initial public offering (IPO)—"Going public" means to sell stock in your company in the stock market.

Key Terms

book value	license
brand	line extension
diversification	liquidation
fair market value	merger
franchise	net present value
harvesting	replication
IPO	royalty

[Entrepreneurship Portfolio]

1. What did Ray Kroc do with his franchise that was unique?

2. Describe the differences between a licensing agreement and a franchising agreement.

3. Give an example of a business that could lead to licensing agreements and a business that could be franchised.

Critical Thinking Exercises

4. Do you plan to franchise your business or license any of your products? Explain. **(Business Plan Practice)**

5. Describe the exit strategy you plan to use to harvest your business. Why do you think this exit strategy will be attractive to potential investors? **(Business Plan Practice)**

Key Concept Questions

1. Describe a brand that you think is losing its focus. Explain what you think the company's managers are doing wrong and how you could improve the situation.

2. Choose one of the harvesting strategies described in the chapter and research it in depth. Write a one-page report to present to the class.

Application Exercise

1. For each franchise in the chart below, calculate how much you would owe the franchisor in royalties if you made $1 million in sales.

Franchise	Franchise Fee	Start-up Costs	Royalty Fee
McDonald's	$45,000	$489,000–$1.5 million	12.5%
Arby's Inc.	$25,000–$37,500	$333,000–$2 million	4%
General Nutrition Franchising Inc.	$30,000	$132,000–$182,000	6%
Tastee-Freez	$5,000	$39,000	4%

Exploring Online

The American Association of Franchisees and Dealers (AAFD) is a national trade association that represents the rights and interests of franchisees and independent dealers across the country. Visit this association online at http://www.aafd.org to learn more about franchisees and the valuable resources available.

1. Search the site for the article, "AAFD Road Map to Selecting a Franchise." Read the section called "8 Things to Look for in a Franchise." For each of the eight tips in the article, write a one-sentence summary.

2. Find a franchise online you might be interested in owning. Answer the following:
   (a) What is the franchise? What does it sell?
   (b) Why are you interested in owning it?
   (c) What is the franchise fee?
   (d) What are the start-up costs?
   (e) What is the royalty fee?
   (f) Describe the training the franchisor offers to franchisees.
   (g) Describe the marketing the franchisor provides for franchisees.

3. Find a business online you might be interested in buying. Describe how much you would bid to buy the business and explain your valuation method.

CASE STUDY: Buying a Franchise

Toni and Ray Smith have been exploring the possibility of buying a franchise with their life savings. The couple has each worked for several large corporations over the past twenty years, primarily in the marketing and customer services areas. Both Toni and Ray have MBAs from a large Midwestern university.

After two years of study, the couple has narrowed their franchise choices to two. The first choice is an established, well-known fast-food franchise. This opportunity is available immediately in their hometown. The funds needed for the initial franchise fee deposit, land and building costs, and start-up expense is right at the maximum of their budget, but they are very impressed with the track record of this company and the business forecast for the next seven years. Although neither Toni nor Ray has any retail or food service experience, they are moderately optimistic about their ability to take on this business. The franchise company does not predict that there will be any additional franchise units available in their state for the next ten years.

Their other franchise opportunity is a fairly new concept in the staffing field, concentrating on the need for financial and legal services for medium-sized businesses that want to outsource these functions. The concept has additional appeal because Toni and Ray feel strongly that, if outsourcing must occur, it should be handled domestically. The franchise cost, fees, and start-up expenses are modest and there is a possibility that they could acquire the rights for additional franchises in their state for a one-time fee. This fee would entitle them to either open new franchises or sell the rights to new franchises in the area.

Toni and Ray are committed to working for themselves and they believe that franchising offers them a way to buy into successful concepts. Their plan is to make sufficient money to support a good lifestyle and to reap the rewards of not only an income-producing venture but also a scenario that will accumulate significant wealth for them in the future.

Case Study Analysis

1. Which franchise option presents a better opportunity for harvesting a significant amount of cash?

2. Which franchise option presents a better opportunity for replicating the product?

3. What advantages does franchising offer over other entrepreneurial options?

CASE STUDY: Ben & Jerry's

In 1978, when Ben Cohen and Jerry Greenfield decided to start selling homemade ice cream out of a converted gas station in Burlington, Vermont, they never imagined that "Ben & Jerry's" would eventually grow into an international premium ice cream brand. Twenty years later, the business had evolved from a homespun Vermont-based scoop shop into a multimillion dollar company with worldwide franchises in locations ranging from Boston to Tokyo to Paris. This ice cream upstart became famous for churning out offbeat flavors like Bovinity Divinity, Chubby Hubby, and Cherry Garcia, and for its colorful marketing campaigns.

For instance, when Ben & Jerry's decided to hire a new CEO in 1994, it held a "Yo, I'm your CEO!" contest and invited customers to submit application essays for the job. In 1999, to commemorate its twenty-first anniversary, the company launched a "Coast-to-Coast Free Cone Day" and gave out 550,000 cones to happy customers.

A Commitment to Social Responsibility

Cohen and Greenfield rejected a profits-driven bottom line approach to managing their business. Instead, they chose to invest in socially responsible causes and business practices that did not always earn maximum profits, but, rather, gave something back to society and helped the environment. For example, they established an executive policy of contributing 7.5 percent of the company's pre-tax earnings to charity. In 1991, they paid out half a million dollars to help offset losses suffered by local Vermont milk suppliers during a time of intense price fluctuation in the dairy industry. They also spent many years perfecting the production of an "Eco-Pint" ice cream container made from unbleached paperboard and nontoxic color dyes. These kinds of corporate good works earned Ben & Jerry's a #1 ranking for corporate social responsibility in a national poll conducted by Harris Interactive in 1999.

Unhappy Shareholders

By 2000, Ben & Jerry's was a publicly owned company traded on the NASDAQ and was generating over $200 million dollars in annual sales, with a net income of $3.3 million. But their shareholders weren't happy. The stock price had been stagnant for many years and, in 1997, slipped as low as $12 a share. By 2000, the stock had climbed to $20 but some shareholders still wanted to earn a better return. One persistent challenge faced by the company was that it did not own its own distribution channels. As a result, it paid a high operating cost to get its products to market. Rumors began to circulate in the media that a large corporation might want to purchase the folksy company.

Takeover

By the end of the year, negotiations were underway between Ben & Jerry's corporate board and Unilever, a $52 billion European-based consumer goods firm. Overnight, as word spread about the impending sale, grassroots "Save Ben & Jerry's" protest campaigns sprouted all over the United States. Loyal consumers who valued the company's commitment to social responsibility feared that a larger corporate entity would not continue to support causes like saving the rain forests or employing homeless people. Many opposed the sale, including Ben Cohen and Jerry Greenfield themselves, who unsuccessfully tried to execute a counter-deal with a venture capital firm that would have taken the company private. Vermont politicians weighed in and broadcast their view that the company should preserve its independence. After all, Ben & Jerry's had created many jobs in Vermont and the company's policy of buying Vermont-only milk had been a major boon for local farmers. But, despite these collective protests, the company was bought by Unilever in 2000 for $326 million or $43.60 per share.

How did this happen? According to corporate charter law, company boards are mandated to prioritize shareholders' interests when making decisions that impact the bottom line. In the case of Ben & Jerry's, Unilever was offering to pay more than double the company's current $21/share stock price. The board felt that this was an offer it couldn't refuse.

An Uncertain Future

Under the terms of the deal, both Ben and Jerry remained employees of the company, earning annual salaries of $200,000 each. A new CEO was hired by Unilever to manage the company's operations. Unilever promised that it would continue Ben & Jerry's commitment to social responsibility, but many were skeptical about this. Several months after Unilever took the helm, Ben Cohen commented to *The New York Times* that "What Ben & Jerry's used to be is one of these smaller 'social values led' businesses. What Ben & Jerry's is in the process of becoming is an entity inside a larger business, trying to infuse those values into that business. We expect that it will be a long and winding road."[9]

Case Study Analysis

1. Why do you think Unilever was willing to purchase Ben & Jerry's for more than double the company's stock price? Why was Ben & Jerry's an attractive investment? *(Remember: When Ben & Jerry's was sold, its stock price was $21/share. Unilever purchased shares at $43.60).*

2. One of the ways that entrepreneurs earn money is by starting businesses and then selling them. When the sale went through, Jerry Greenfield sold his 900,000 shares in the company at 43.60 and Ben Cohen got the same price for his 220,000.

   a. How much did Ben and Jerry earn respectively from the sale?

   b. When they started their company, in 1978, Ben and Jerry each invested $6,000. Calculate the return on investment for each.

3. Review the different harvesting strategies described in the chapter. What strategy did Ben & Jerry's use? What are the pros and cons of this strategy?

4. Go online and conduct research on Ben & Jerry's. Is the company more profitable now under the leadership of Unilever? Does it still contribute a percentage of its profits to charity? Identify three ways the company has changed since it was sold.

5. Explain why the sale of Ben & Jerry's occurred, even though the company's founders did not want this to happen.

CASE SOURCES

www.benandjerrys.com.

The New York Times. "Investment Group Makes Bid for Ben & Jerry's," by Constance Hays. Section C; page 1; Column 2; Business/Financial Desk. February 10, 2000.

---

[9] Constance Hays, "Ben and Jerry's Deal Takes on Slightly New Flavor," *The New York Times*, May 2, 2002.

"Money is better than poverty, if only for financial reasons."

—Woody Allen, American comic and filmmaker

Performance Objectives

1. Describe how compound interest works.
2. Find your investment risk tolerance.
3. Explain how diversification protects an investment portfolio.
4. Describe how mutual funds provide diversification.
5. Design an investment portfolio to meet your financial goals.

When John D. Rockefeller was still a teenager (back in the mid-nineteenth century), he lent $50 to a neighboring farmer. A year later the farmer paid him back the $50 plus $3.50 interest. Around the same time, Rockefeller had made $1.12 for thirty hours of back-breaking work hoeing potatoes for another neighbor. "From that time on," he said in his biography, "I was determined to make money work for me." Rockefeller built a great fortune on that insight.[2]

Money grows on its own through wise investments.[3] You are not doing physical labor but mental labor, when you invest, by deciding on the best place to put your money.

Starting and operating a successful small business is a fine achievement. What you do with your earnings, however, will determine whether you have a secure financial future or whether you will always be struggling to get by.

The key to being able to buy a car and a home, put your children through college, and retire comfortably is saving money and investing it. Whether you have an entrepreneurial career or not, always think like an entrepreneur when it comes to the money you earn. Learn how to invest your money so it will earn more money. Even if you work for others, you will still be working for yourself—and you should put your money to work for you!

»Always Save 10 Percent of Your Income

When you earn money, what do you do with it? If you're like most people, you use it to pay bills and buy things. Here is an idea: Pay yourself first. Get into the good habit of automatically saving

---

[1] This chapter will recapitulate some of the topics and concepts discussed in earlier chapters.

[2] Allan Nevins, *Study in Power: John D. Rockefeller, Industrialist and Philanthropist,* (Norwalk, CT: Easton Press, 1989).

[3] Some ideas in this chapter are drawn from material created in partnership with the Merrill Lynch Financial Literacy Program, *Investing Pays Off.*

> If you begin saving 10 percent of your income this month, how much money will you have saved in twelve months?
>
> $_____

10 percent of your income, and you will have taken the first step toward building wealth.

If you do not make very much money, this may sound hard, or even impossible. Try it, though, and you will discover ways to get by without that 10 percent. Let's say you plan to pay yourself $800 from your small business this month. Without even thinking about it, put $80 into your savings account. You will still have $720 to use for bills and purchases.

Make saving 10 percent a habit and pretty soon you will not even miss the money you save. And, before you know it, you will have a nice sum in the bank.

»Make Your Money Work for You

Performance Objective 1.›

If you invest $100 at 10 percent interest for one year, you will have $110 at the end of that period. If you let the accumulating interest and the original $100 remain in this investment for ten years, it will grow to $259. The interest is compounding. **Compound interest** is interest added to the interest that you already earned. Money making money like this is the essence of investment.

Too often, the concept of compounding interest is misunderstood. People tend to think that, if you invest $1.00 at 10 percent over five years, it will end up at $1.50. The actual amount would be $1.61.

»How Inflation Affects Investments

As we have noted, the value of bonds is affected by **inflation.** When prices rise, money isn't worth as much. A $100 bond bought today will only pay the bondholder $100 at maturity. The bond offers no protection against inflation because, no matter what happens to the value of a dollar, the bond will still only be redeemable for $100. When investors hear economic news that makes them worry about inflation, therefore, bond prices usually decline. No investor wants to pay $100 for a bond that may only be worth $70 at maturity.

»Future Value of an Annuity

An annuity is a sum of money that is paid or invested annually. You can use a future value table to calculate the **future value** of a sum that you invested. Use the following table to answer questions like this one: "If, beginning one year from now, I can invest $3,000 a year for a period of 30 years, and I expect to earn 10 percent compound interest during this time, how much will I have at the end of 30 years?"

Start with the percentage (10%), and read down to the number of periods (30). There you will find the factor (164.4940). Multiply the annual annuity ($3,000) by this factor (164.4940) to determine the amount of money you will have at the end of 30 years.

$3,000 × 164.4940 = $493,482.

You will have $493,482 at the end of 30 years if you put $3,000 into this investment each year.

n / i	3%	5%	7%	10%	12%	15%	20%
1	1.0000	1.0000	1.0000	1.0000	1.0000	1.0000	1.0000
2	2.0300	2.0500	2.0700	2.1000	2.1200	2.1500	2.2000
3	3.0909	3.1525	3.2149	3.3100	3.3744	3.4725	3.6400
4	4.1836	4.3101	4.4399	4.6410	4.7793	4.9934	5.3680
5	5.3091	5.5256	5.7507	6.1051	6.3528	6.7424	7.4416
10	11.4639	12.5779	13.8164	15.9374	17.5487	20.3037	25.9587
15	18.5989	21.5786	25.1290	31.7725	37.2797	47.5804	72.0351
20	26.8704	33.0660	40.9955	57.2750	72.0524	102.4436	186.6880
25	36.4593	47.7271	63.2490	98.3471	133.3339	212.7930	471.9811
30	47.5754	66.4388	94.4608	164.4940	241.3327	434.7451	1181.8816
40	75.4013	120.7998	199.6351	442.5926	1358.2300	1779.0903	7343.8578
50	112.7969	209.3480	406.5289	1163.9085	2400.0182	7217.7163	45497.1908

»The Risk-Reward Relationship

There are three types of financial investments (assets): stocks, bonds, and cash. **Real estate,** which comprises land and buildings, is another important investment.

All investments involve some risk, which is the possibility that you could lose money. Remember, there is an interesting relationship between risk and reward:

The greater the potential reward of an investment, the more risky it will probably be.

High Reward = High Risk

This implies that:

If an investment carries little risk, the reward will probably be low.

Low Risk = Low Reward

The digital ticker tape displays stock quotes at the New York Stock Exchange, New York City.
(Robert Brenner, PhotoEdit)

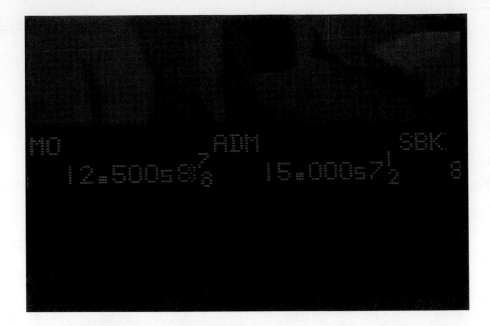

»Time and Liquidity Affect Investment Risk

Factors that affect investment risk include time and liquidity.

Time. The longer someone has your money, the greater the chance that your investment could somehow be lost. The longer you have to wait for the payback on your investment, the greater the return should be.

Liquidity. Liquidity refers to the ease of getting cash in and out of an investment. How "liquid" is it? Can you get your money out in twenty-four hours? Or do you have to commit to keeping it in for a longer period? More time equals more risk; therefore, less liquid investments are riskier, and they should offer higher returns.

»How Much Risk Can *You* Tolerate?

One more factor must be considered when deciding on the risk and potential reward an investment offers: How do *you* feel about risk?

Everyone has a different tolerance for risk. Some people love to skydive. Others do not even like roller coasters. People who like to skydive are not *better;* they are just different.

Similarly, there is no "right" level of tolerance for investment risk. Some people prefer safe investments that offer lower rates of return, because they are not very risky. Some people prefer to take greater risks with their money, in the hope of earning higher returns.

What's important is that you know how *you* feel about risk—before you make a single decision. You will want to buy investments that let you sleep. If you stay awake at night worrying about an investment, then it was too risky for you.

Take this survey to find your investment risk tolerance level.[4]

Remember, it is not "better" to have a higher or lower tolerance for risk. All that matters is that you know your own risk tolerance so you can choose investments that are right for you!

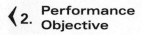

2. **Performance Objective**

Category I: Thinking about Risk

1. I'd be willing to earn less on my investments in order to receive a rate of return I can count on.

2. I'm much more concerned with getting solid, consistent results on my investments than possibly higher returns that are risky.

3. If my investments fluctuate (change value) in year-by-year returns, I can handle It, If It means I mlght get higher total returns in the long run.

4. Keeping risk very low is more important for me than taking a chance in order to achieve high investment returns.

5. I am willing to accept some risk in order to get my investments to grow.

6. The final result is more important than how I got there. If I have to risk a bad year to meet my goal, that's okay.

Category II: Thinking about the Future

1. When it comes to my future, I like to play it safe. I don't want to lose any of the money—capital—I invest.

2. I would prefer investments that earn income now. That's more important than keeping all my capital.

3. I'm interested in preserving my capital, but I can handle some decrease in its value to increase the income I'm earning on my investments right now.

Category III: Thinking about My Capital

1. I am not much of a gambler. I'm more concerned with preserving the value of my capital than in going into riskier investments that may increase in value later on.

2. Growth of my capital in the future is as important as preserving its present value.

3. I am more concerned with providing greater future growth than playing it safe now and preserving my current assets.

Category IV: Thinking about ROI

Given the choice of the following three investments, I would choose:

1. Investment 1: 100 percent chance of a 5 percent rate of return per year over the next five years.

2. Investment 2: 75 percent chance of a 10 percent rate of return per year, or 25 percent chance of a 4 percent rate of return per year over the next five years.

3. Investment 3: 50 percent chance of a 20 percent rate of return per year, or 50 percent chance of a 5 percent loss per year over the next five years.

Your Score: Add up the numbers next to your checkmarks. Find your risk level below.

Point Total	Risk Level
3–6	**Low risk tolerance**
7–10	**Medium risk tolerance**
11–15	**High risk tolerance**

---

[4] From the Merrill Lynch's *Investing Pays Off.*

(Gary Buss, Getty Images, Inc.—Taxi)

»Choosing Investments: Stocks, Bonds, or Cash?

Once you have saved some money and have determined your risk tolerance, you are ready to invest. You can choose from three types of investments:

- **Stocks** represent equity shares of a company. If you own stock in a business, you own a piece of it, however small. Stocks may pay dividends, which are a share of the company's profits. Stocks can be traded (bought and sold) on the stock market. Stocks tend to be more risky (and potentially more rewarding) investments than bonds or cash.
- **Bonds** are interest-bearing loans. Corporations use bonds to borrow money that they agree to pay back on a specific date. Bonds pay interest. When the bond comes due, the money paid for the bond will be returned. Bonds can also be traded—on the bond market. Bonds are more risky than cash, but less risky (typically) than stocks.
- **Cash** investments can be turned into cash within twenty-four hours. They have low rates of interest because the risk of losing the investment is low. Stocks and bonds can also be turned into cash by selling them, but sometimes the price you can get will be lower than what you paid. That's one reason stocks and bonds are riskier than cash investments.

Your savings account is an example of a cash investment. There is almost no risk that you will lose your money, so a savings account typically pays a very low interest rate. Treasury bills are another cash investment. Treasury bills are short-term loans made to the U.S. government. The government pays you a fairly low interest rate and guarantees that you will get your money back. Both the risk and the return are low. Treasury bills can be sold on the market for cash within twenty-four hours.

»Keep an Emergency Fund in Cash

Before you invest in stocks and bonds, make sure you have enough cash saved to cover your personal expenses (food, clothes, rent, transportation, etc.) for at least three months. This will be your emergency fund. It will prevent you from having to sell off your other investments in the event that some emergency prevents you

Biz Facts

Treasury bills are called "bills" instead of "bonds" because they mature, or come due, in less than a year. The U.S. government also sells Treasury bonds, which have longer maturities—from one to ten years, or longer.

[Global Impact]

World News Affects Investments

Investments can be affected by world events. If war breaks out, for example, stock prices usually fall. When there is uncertainty, people tend to move their money into cash and other low risk, highly liquid investments, even if it means taking a loss. Bad news often drives the stock market down.

A stock's price may change in reaction to news about the company that issued it, economic news, political changes, or world events. Because stock prices change in reaction to information, they are considered to be **volatile** investments. This means they can change frequently and somewhat unpredictably.

from being able to earn money for a while. Keep your emergency fund in a savings account, or in other investments that can be turned into cash within a day.

»Diversification

〈3. Performance Objective

Protect yourself from volatility by spreading your money out over different types of investment (diversifying). It is the opposite of "putting all your eggs in one basket."

If you have $10,000 and you put it all in the stock of one company, you will lose all your money if that company goes out of business. It is wiser to diversify—buy smaller amounts of many different stocks. When you own $1,000 each of 10 stocks, if one company fails and its stock becomes worthless, you will only lose $1,000.

Because the stock market and the bond market tend to behave differently, it is also good to own both stocks and bonds. That way, when the stock market goes down, your bonds may go up, and vice versa.

»The Stock Market Goes Up over Time

Although stocks can be volatile over short periods, over time the ups tend to cancel out the downs. The stock market has historically averaged annual returns of around 11 percent. This is a much higher return than less risky investments such as Treasury bills. A good rule of thumb is to only invest money in stocks that you can keep invested for over ten years. This lets time work for you to cancel the volatility associated with the stock market.

»Mutual Funds: Diversification You Can Afford

〈4. Performance Objective

If you plan to invest in stocks, you should own at least 25 in different industries to spread out the risk. Unless you have the money and the knowledge to pick individual stocks, consider investing in

mutual funds. A mutual fund is a company that collects money from many different investors. The fund's managers then choose stocks for the investors. You (and all the other investors) are letting the mutual fund's managers use your money to pick the investments he or she thinks will best maximize the ROI of the fund as a whole.

When you buy into a mutual fund you are buying shares in that fund, which probably owns hundreds of stocks (or bonds). You own these investments, too, even if you only invest a hundred dollars. There are many kinds of stock mutual funds. Some invest only in certain industries, such as aerospace technology or precious metals. Others invest widely in the stock market as a whole to spread out risk.

»Index Funds

Most mutual funds charge management fees for investing your money. Some funds, however, are not managed because they are designed to buy and hold stocks in the same proportions as an index—such as the S&P 500—which is an index created by Standard & Poor's that tracks 500 stocks. With these **index funds,** more of your money goes toward the actual investment, because you are not paying management fees.

»Creating Your Portfolio

Performance Objective 5.〉 A collection of investments is called a **portfolio.** The investments you choose to put in your portfolio will depend on the following:

1. Your investment goals
2. Your risk tolerance
3. The amount of time you have to reach your goals

Let's say you are 18, you have medium risk tolerance, and your goal is to buy a house by 28. You have 10 years to reach this goal. You are comfortable with some risk and have enough time (10 years) to consider investing in stocks. You have $3,000 to invest and you decide to put $1,500 in a stock mutual fund and $1,500 in a bond mutual fund. Your portfolio is shown in Figure 14-1.

Actually, you should also have an emergency fund, in cash. Here is what your portfolio would look like if you had $1,000 in cash (see Figure 14-2).

When you invest, choose stocks, bonds, and cash according to percentages that you set as goals. Pick a monthly amount you can

Figure 14-1 Investment portfolio with zero cash.

Current Cash Value		Investment Mix	
Stocks:	$1500	Stocks:	50%
Bonds:	$1500	Bonds:	50%
Cash:	$ 0	Cash:	0%
Total:	$3000	Total:	100%

Current Cash Value		Investment Mix	
Stocks:	$1500	Stocks:	37.5%
Bonds:	$1500	Bonds:	37.5%
Cash:	$1000	Cash:	25%
Total:	$4000	Total:	100%

Figure 14-2 Investment portfolio with $1,000 cash.

afford and start building your portfolio. Let's say you can afford $200 per month and you've already got your emergency fund set aside. If you decide to invest 50 percent in stocks and 50 percent in bonds, you would invest $100 every month in each.

»Rebalance Your Portfolio Once a Year

Let's say you have a portfolio invested 70 percent in stocks, 20 percent in bonds, and 10 percent in cash. What if this year your bond investments do well and your stocks do not? Before you know it, your portfolio could be 50 percent in stocks, 40 percent in bonds, and 10 percent in cash.

You will need to rebalance your portfolio because you are now overinvested in bonds. Even though the bonds are doing well, you should sell some and buy stocks instead, until you return to your 70/20/10 percent balance.

Once a year, say on your birthday, check to see if your portfolio needs to be rebalanced.

»Chapter Summary

Now that you have studied this chapter you can do the following:

1. Describe how compound interest works.
   - Compound interest is the money you earn on interest that you already earned.
2. Find your investment risk tolerance.
   - Everyone has a different tolerance for investment risk.
   - There is no "right" level of tolerance. Some people prefer safe investments that offer lower rates of return because they are not risky. Some prefer to take greater risks with their money, in the hope of earning higher returns.
3. Explain how diversification protects an investment portfolio.
   - Protect yourself from volatility by spreading your money out (diversifying) over different types of investment.
   - Because the stock and bond markets tend to behave differently, it is also good to diversify by owning both stocks and bonds.
4. Describe how mutual funds provide diversification.
   - A mutual fund is a company that collects money from many different investors. The fund's managers then choose investments.

- When you buy into a mutual fund you are buying shares in that fund, which probably owns hundreds of stocks (or bonds). You own these investments, too, even if you only invest a small amount.

5. Design an investment portfolio to meet your financial goals.

- A collection of investments is called a portfolio.
- The investments you choose to put in your portfolio will depend on the following:
  a. Your investment goals
  b. Your risk tolerance
  c. The amount of time you have to reach your investment goals

Key Terms

compound interest	mutual fund
future value	portfolio
index fund	real estate
inflation	volatile

[Entrepreneurship Portfolio]

Critical Thinking Exercises

1. How much are you currently saving and investing each month? How could you increase that amount by paying yourself first? Describe how you plan to cut your expenses to increase the amount of money you can save to invest.

2. Describe your risk tolerance and the types of investments you think are in line with it.

3. I plan to save _____ percent of my net income to achieve personal financial goals.
   a. My primary financial goal is _____.
   b. My investment risk tolerance is _____.
   c. I will invest my savings as follows:

Current Cash Value	**Investment Mix**
Stocks $_____	Stocks _____%
Bonds $_____	Bonds _____%
Cash $_____	Cash _____%

(Business Plan Practice)

4. How would you invest in order to buy a home? You will need a *down payment*. The down payment will secure a *mortgage,* which is a loan from a bank to purchase a home. The down payment is usually 10 percent of the price. So, with a down payment saved of $15,000, you could probably buy a $150,000 home.

5. I have _____ years to save for my first home.

6. I can invest for my home in (circle the answer that applies) the following:

   a. stocks (I have more than 10 years to invest for this goal)

   b. bonds (I have fewer than 10 years to invest for this goal)

7. **I plan to save a down payment of \$_____ so that I can buy my first home at age _____ for \$_____.**

---

1. Using the Future Value Table, figure the net gain (or loss) of the following investments:

   a. \$500 invested at 3 percent for 1 year

   b. \$100 invested at 7 percent for 7 years

   c. \$2,000 invested at 10 percent for 5 years

2. Describe how inflation affects bond prices. How would inflation affect stock prices? What is your own projection regarding inflation for the next 10 years?

3. Pretend you have \$10,000 to invest. How would you choose to invest it? If you could choose from the possibilities below, how much would you put into each? In other words, how would you diversify your money? Create your own portfolio but remember, the total has to add up to \$10,000.

   Savings account (historically, a 2 to 3 percent ROI)

   \$_____

   "Blue Chip" stock (a high-quality stock with an ROI of 10 percent over the last 10 years)

   \$_____

   New computer company's stock (ROI over the last six months of 25 percent)

   \$_____

   Mutual fund that invests in a wide variety of stocks (ROI over last 10 years of 11 percent)

   \$_____

   S&P Index mutual fund (ROI over last 10 years of 11 percent)

   \$_____

   Bonds that pay 6 percent interest and return the principal after 20 years

   \$_____

   Total invested: \$_____

Key Concept Questions

4. Describe your portfolio.

Current Cash Value		**Investment Mix**	
Stocks	$_____	Stocks	_____%
Bonds	$_____	Bonds	_____%
Cash	$_____	Cash	_____%

5. Choose an imaginary amount to invest in this portfolio every year.

Each year I will invest the following:
$_____ in stocks
$_____ in bonds
$_____ in cash

6. **Rebalancing:** I will rebalance my portfolio once a year on this date: _____

7. Calculate the value of your portfolio 20 years from now without further investment. To do this you will need to create a weighted-average ROI for your portfolio, because each segment may have a different ROI. Use this formula:

(ROI on Investment A × Weight of Investment A) +

(ROI on Investment B × Weight of Investment B) +

(ROI on Investment C × Weight of Investment C) =

Weighted Average ROI of Investments

Example:

A: S&P Index Mutual Fund	50% of portfolio	Expected ROI 11%
B: Bond Fund	20% of portfolio	Expected ROI 12%
C: Savings Bonds	20% of portfolio	Expected ROI 6%
D: Money Market Fund	10% of portfolio	Expected ROI 4%

Math: Remember "%" means "out of 100," so to express a percentage as a number, divide it by 100. So 50% becomes .50 (50/100 = .50) and 100% becomes 1.00, etc.

$(.50 \times .11) + (.20 \times .12) + (.20 \times .06) + (.10 \times .04) =$

$(.0555) + (.024) + (.012) + (.004) = .0955$ or 9.55%

The weighted average annual return for this portfolio is 9.55%.

To find the future value of your portfolio, look up your weighted average return in the Future Value N-Chart.

Application Exercises

1. Use a Future Value chart to find the future value of the amount you plan to invest each year.

2. Calculate the total future value of your portfolio by adding the future value to the future value of the annuity.

The S&P 500 is a widely diversified group of 500 stocks that are fol-lowed by an established company called Standard & Poor's. The S&P 500 is drawn from many industries. It is so well diversified that it pretty much indicates the condition of the stock market as a whole. For this exercise, find the S&P 500 online. Now choose one stock to follow. Find a site online that reports its daily stock price. Follow both the stock and the S&P 500 for one week and fill in the following:

Exploring Online

Your Stock   **The S&P 500**

Day 1 Closing Price $_____ $_____

Day 2 Closing Price $_____   _____ % change $_____   _____

Day 3 Closing Price $_____   _____ % change $_____   _____

Day 4 Closing Price $_____   _____ % change $_____   _____

Day 5 Closing Price $_____   _____ % change $_____   _____

  a. Which did better (increased more in value) for the week, your stock or the S&P 500?

  b. What were some factors in the news this week that might have af-fected your stock? What might have affected the S&P 500?

  c. For this one week, was diversification a good strategy or not? Explain.

  d. What would your ROI for the week be if you had invested $10,000 in the stock? What would it be for the S&P 500?

Hint: Take your five-day closing price and subtract it from your day-one closing price, then divide it by your day-one closing price and multiply it by 100. This will give you the percentage of increase/decrease.

CASE STUDY: Money to Invest

Sarah Mix is a single, 30-year-old business owner who has $500 a month to invest. This money is in excess of the contribution to her company pension plan. Sarah hears that many of her friends are in-vesting in mutual funds. Her grandfather, Grandpa Russ, invested in the stock market and lost every-thing. He advises her to invest only in bonds. Her uncle Bill thinks that she should invest in stock mutual funds, but only in conservatively managed firms that invest in U.S. blue-chip stocks. Sarah notes that her Grandpa is 70 years old and that her uncle is 55. Her friend, Jane, who is also 30, said she only invests in small, capital-growth funds.

Sarah's investment goals are to provide a long-term savings that might be used for retirement or possible business investment. She is an avid reader of business journals and is very interested in new business opportunities. Sarah understands the theory of risk and return and considers herself a moderate risk taker.

Case Study Analysis

1. What would you advise Sarah to invest in?

2. Why do you think these people have different investment strategies?

3. What other investment options would you suggest to Sarah, and why?

CASE STUDY: Warren Buffett and Berkshire Hathaway

Every spring, some 14,000 people make an annual pilgrimage to Omaha, Nebraska, to seek investment advice from a septuagenarian named Warren Buffet. These pilgrims are all shareholders in a publicly traded company, Berkshire Hathaway, that Buffett launched in 1951 with $500,000. His biggest supporters like to call him "the Oracle of Omaha" or the "Forrest Gump of Finance." Berkshire Hathaway has come to be valued at over $42 billion dollars and Buffett is widely admired on Wall Street as a living legend.

Berkshire Hathaway

Unlike other businesses that manufacture a product or provide a service, Berkshire Hathaway is a "holding company" for all Buffett's investments. Some of the companies in his "portfolio" include American Express, General Electric, and Coca-Cola. For example, Berkshire Hathaway owns an 18 percent stake in *The Washington Post* and an 8 percent stake in Coca-Cola.

Berkshire Hathaway has generated an astounding 23 percent in average compound interest for its shareholders. If you were lucky enough to purchase one single share of Berkshire Hathaway "A" stock in 1969, at $9 a share, today that share would be worth $88,000.

Buffett as a Role Model

You would never know it by looking at him, but Buffett is one of the most successful investors in modern history. He likes to snack on Cracker Jacks and Cherry Coke and still lives in the modest home he purchased for $43,000 over 50 years ago. While other CEOs at his level receive multi-million dollar compensation packages, Buffett has opted to pay himself a comparatively modest salary of $100,000. Ninety-nine percent of Buffett's wealth comes from his investment income. In 1998, he single-handedly purchased 20 percent of the world's silver supply!

Buffett has emerged in recent years as a role model for ethical business behavior. In his annual letter to Berkshire Hathaway shareholders in 2003, he wrote, "In judging whether corporate America is serious about reforming itself, CEO pay remains the acid test . . . to date, the results aren't encouraging . . . CEOs have often amassed riches while their shareholders have experienced disasters."

Value Investing

So what has been the secret of Buffett's success? The answer lies in a strategy called "value investing." Buffett likes to selectively purchase shares in companies that have strong brands, healthy cash flow, and a solid management structure. "Our only strategy is to look for businesses we understand, with economics and managements we like, and which we can buy at a reasonable price."

Buffett likes to invest in companies that lie within something he calls his "circle of competence." In other words, he likes to put his money behind businesses he can see and understand, and that have a paper trail of successful earnings. He believes that if you do your research properly, you can find good stocks that are selling for less than what they are actually worth, or will be worth more in the future than they are today.

In part, Buffett's success has been built around his conviction that, over time, the market will correct itself and the stock's price will rise. When this happens, the investor makes a profit. Buffett has been so talented at picking these kinds of undervalued companies that he has consistently earned a phenomenal return on investment (ROI).

Long-Term Investing

While day traders might buy and sell their stocks in a matter of minutes, Buffett likes to hold on to his investments indefinitely. He refers to his approach as the "Rip Van Winkle effect." When making an investment decision, Buffett projects into the future. He studies a company's balance sheet to assess its earnings potential. He needs to be convinced that in 10 to 20 years the company will be generating a significantly higher net profit than it is today.

Because of his long-term vision, some consider Buffett to be a traditional investor. During the Internet stock boom of the late 1990s, Buffett refused to get on the dot-com bandwagon. While other Wall Street analysts were trumpeting the benefits of purchasing such stocks, Buffett preferred to stick with his tried and true method. Buffett came out on top when many Internet stocks crashed in 2001. "We have never found one technology company where we think we know enough about how it will look in ten years to make a rational valuation decision. If we cannot value it, we will not buy it."

Buffett's Beginnings

Buffett was first introduced to the world of money management by his father. Buffett Senior worked as a stockbroker in downtown Omaha and then later became a U.S. Congressman. As a boy, Buffett Junior operated several paper routes, from which he saved $6,000. In college, he started several entrepreneurial ventures, including a pinball rental company and a used-golf-ball business. By age 11, Buffett had already made his first stock purchase. He bought three shares of a company called Cities Services Preferred, at $38 share. By the time he sold his shares, the stock was trading at $40. The stock later went on to appreciate and peaked at $200 per share. This experience taught Buffett about the benefits of holding on to promising stocks.

Succession Plan?

Today, the biggest concern among Berkshire Hathaway's shareholders is what will happen when Buffett no longer runs the company. While he has no immediate plans to retire, the day will eventually come when he will have to pass the torch. Buffett insists that money does not drive him to get up in the morning; he simply loves what he does: "I enjoy money as a by-product," he says. "I would do what I do if I had to pay to do it every day. Some people play golf all day, or the piano if they're good at it . . . I wanted to have enough money so that I could do what I wanted to do, and by the time I was 30, I did. But I always wanted to be free to do what I liked to do."

Case Study Analysis

1. Write a paragraph describing Buffett's investment philosophy.

2. Go online and look up the current share price for Berkshire Hathaway's "A" stock. (Hint: The stock code is "BRK.A.") Assume that you purchased ten shares of stock for $88,000 in July 2004. Calculate the following:

   a. Your profit/(loss) for this investment
   b. Your return on investment, or ROI (what you made/what you paid × 100)

3. Typically, when an investment risk is high, an investor will either win big or lose big. Do you think that this principle applies to Warren Buffett and Berkshire Hathaway? Is Buffett a "risk-taking" investor? Why, or why not? Explain your answer.

4. Buffet chooses to pay himself a salary of $100,000. While this may seem like a lot of money to most people, consider the fact that Berkshire Hathaway is worth $42 billion! And $100,000 is less than 3 percent of this sum.

   a. Why do you think Buffet keeps his salary so low?
   b. How does this strategy benefit Buffett personally, as well as Berkshire Hathaway's shareholders?

5. Entrepreneurs can get paid in five different ways:

   ■ Annual salary
   ■ Wages on direct work (per hour or per unit of sale)
   ■ Dividends/draw on equity
   ■ Appreciation of resale value (rise in stock price)
   ■ Sales commission

   How does Buffett get paid? Which of the payment strategies listed above does he use?

CASE SOURCES

"Conquering Wall St. With Common Sense." *The Sunday Independent.* August, 15, 1999.

Andy Serwer, Reporter Associate Julia Boorstin, "The Oracle of Everything: Warren Buffett Has Been Right about the Stock Market, Rotten Accounting, CEO Greed, and Corporate Governance. The Rest of Us Are Just Catching On." *Fortune*, November 11, 2002, p. 68.

David Milstead, "Warren's World: Shareholders Flock to Omaha for the 'Woodstock of Capitalism' and Wisdom from their Financial Guru." *Rocky Mountain News*, May 11, 2002.

Unit 5 BUSINESS PLAN PRACTICE

At the end of each unit, you have had the opportunity to work on your business plan. Please go to the Business Plan Worksheet Template section for Unit 5 on the BizBuilder CD now to develop the following segments of your plan:

Your Balance Sheet

1. Create a Projected Balance Sheet for your business for one year. **(Business Plan Practice)**
2. Create a pie chart showing your current assets, long-term assets, current liabilities, and long-term liabilities. **(Business Plan Practice)**
3. What is your debt ratio?
4. What is your debt-to-equity ratio?

Franchising and Licensing

1. Do you plan to franchise your business, or license any of your products? Explain.

Stocks

1. If your business is incorporated, describe what percentage of your company is owned by one share of stock.
2. Is your corporation's stock publicly or privately held?

Bonds

1. Do you intend to use debt to finance your business? Explain.
2. Do you plan to ever issue bonds to finance your business?

Exit Strategy

1. My exit strategy is _____
   _____
2. I think this strategy would be attractive to my potential investors because _____
   _____
   _____

Financial Planning

1. I plan to save _____ percent of my net income to achieve personal financial goals.
2. My primary financial goal is _____.
3. My risk tolerance for investment is _____.
4. I will invest my savings as follows:

Current Cash Value	Investment Mix
Stocks $_____	Stocks _____%
Bonds $_____	Bonds _____%
Cash $_____	Cash _____%

5. My weighted-average ROI is: _____
6. Using the Rule of 72, the number of years it will take my portfolio to double is _____ years.

Appendix 1 | 100 Business Ideas

What kind of business would you like to start? To jump-start your imagination, look through the following 100 possibilities. We've grouped them so you can find your own interests, hobbies, or skills and see what kind of ventures people with similar interests have started.

Of course, many business ideas fall into more than one category. Writing skills would be needed in "desktop publishing," "writing a cookbook," and "translation," for example. Consider what your friends, family, and neighbors want and need. They are your primary market. In addition, choose a business in which you think you would have a competitive advantage.

You will find the ideas divided into categories. To help you narrow your choice, we've designed the chart below. Read the descriptions on the left and check Yes or No. Where you've answered Yes, look under those headings for suggested businesses that may interest you.

Do You Like To	Yes	No	Look Under These Headings
Work with your hands?			ART, BAKING, CLEANING, COOKING, CRAFTS, GARDENING
Play with animals?			ANIMALS, BIRDS, FISH
Work alone?			COLLECTING, COMPUTERS, INTERNET, WOODWORKING, WRITING
Work with others?			ADVERTISING, CHILDREN, DRIVING, PEOPLE
Speak other languages?			BILINGUAL TEACHING
Teach people?			BICYCLES, DANCING, MUSIC, TEACHING
Work with machines?			BICYCLES, COMPUTERS, DRIVING
Be creative?			ART, CRAFTS, DANCING, HOLIDAYS, MUSIC, PAINTING, SILKSCREENING, WOODWORKING, WRITING

Do You Like To	Yes	No	Look Under These Headings
Entertain people?			ENTERTAINMENT, DANCING, MUSIC
Use computers?			COMPUTERS, INTERNET
Use cameras?			PHOTOGRAPHY, VIDEO
Buy clothes?			CLOTHING, SILKSCREENING
Cook?			BAKING, COOKING

»Advertising/Publicity

Are you interested in a career in advertising or publicity? These businesses will give you great experience!

Design flyers and posters—Help a local business create its brand!

Distribute flyers, posters, and brochures—Do stores in your neighborhood need people to hand out flyers? These can be distributed on the street, put on car windshields, or given out at social functions. You could offer this service to shopkeepers on a regular basis. (Just make sure you find out where it is legal to put up posters!)

Publicist—Get hired to write press releases. Help artists, musicians, or entrepreneurs get publicity by sending out releases, e-mailing, and calling local newspapers and radio stations.

Image consultant—Help businesses and entertainers market themselves to young people—like you! Daniel Green (20) and Lukus Eichmann (19) of Saddlelite offer their services as image consultants to celebrities who want to find out how to attract younger fans.

»Animals

Do you love animals? Read books to learn how to care for them. Ask a neighborhood veterinarian to be your mentor.

Cat sitter—Get hired to care for cats while their owners are out of town. Be sure to have the owner write down the cat's food and water needs, and an emergency number for the vet.

Dog walker—Take three or four neighborhood dogs at a time out for their walks and make money providing a (very) necessary service for your busy neighbors. Don't forget the pooper scooper!

Pet grooming—Give a dog a bath today!

Pet bowls—Create personalized doggie bowls by painting each dog's name on the bowl in nontoxic paint.

»Art

Almost any artistic talent can be turned into a business. What can you create that someone else might want?

Artist—Offices decorate with art and so do family members and friends. Create a portfolio of photos of your artwork that you can carry with you to show customers.

Art gallery—Have talented friends? Show their work in your home or at a youth center or other public space. You can take a commission for every piece you sell.

Calligraphy—Learn *calligraphy,* the art of handwriting, in an elegant or unusual style. Calligraphy is in demand for wedding invitations, menus, birth announcements, etc. You can also hand-letter poems or lyrics on fine paper, frame them, and sell them.

Pottery—A hobby like pottery can quickly become a successful business. Sell your pottery at trade fairs. You can put pictures of it online, too. Offer to create special pieces to customers' specifications.

»Baking

Some ideas for selling cakes, cookies, brownies, bread, and other products you can bake at home include the following:

Fresh-baked bread for people in need—Set up a nonprofit business that delivers baked goods to people who are too old or sick to bake or to leave their homes to buy fresh bread. You could take donations from people and businesses in your neighborhood and even apply for grants for your business, because it is helping society.

Bake sales—Hold a bake sale at a flea market, at your church, in your backyard, or at school. (Be sure to get permission.)

Cookie delivery business—Sign families up for your weekly cookie deliveries. You can deliver a batch of a different type of homemade cookie each week.

»Bicycles

Just about any skill you have can be turned into a business if you can find a way to fill a consumer need. Can you ride a bike? Here are some ideas.

Bicycle repair—Learn to repair flat tires, slipped chains, and worn brakes. You could run a special each spring when people get their bikes out of storage for the warm weather.

Messenger service—Have wheels, will deliver! In New York City, businesses depend on the bike messengers who deliver important documents all over town. Perhaps you could provide a similar service in your area.

Bike design—A graduate of this course, Jame MacNeil, started Bulldog Bikes, a company that designs and manufactures BMX bikes for urban streets. Bulldog Bikes even has its own teams! (www.bulldogbikes.com)

»Birds

Are you interested in learning about the birds in your area? Do you have a pet bird? Here are some "bird-brained" ideas:

Birdcage service—Offer to clean cages regularly and stock them with food and water. Bird owners can enjoy their pets while you maintain the cages. How do you find bird owners in your area? Try posting flyers at pet stores.

Bird-watching guide—If you teach yourself about the birds in your region, you can organize bird-watching trips to local parks. You can also hire yourself out as a bird guide to people who organize camping trips or hikes.

Raising birds for sale—Popular breeds, like parakeets and finches, are not difficult to raise. Find a mentor to advise you, like a local veterinarian or pet shop owner.

»Books

Book selling—Start a business selling books, concentrating on those you like to read yourself. Once you start making money, you can buy in quantity to get lower prices. Although the larger publishers will only give a discount for sizable orders, smaller publishers might be willing to sell you quantities at a discount.

Used book selling—An even cheaper way to get into the book-selling business is to collect used books from friends and family (go through your bookshelf and get rid of books you do not want anymore, too). Set up a table at a flea market or on the street and start selling! (Check local laws before you set up a table on the street.)

Write a book—Another entrepreneurship student, Michael Simmons, has written *The Student Success Manifesto*, which he sells on his campus at New York University and online at www.successmanifesto.com. What could you write? A novel? A children's book? A book of advice for other students?

»Children

Do you like kids? Are you reliable and responsible? There are a lot of businesses you can create that involve children. Whenever you work with a child, get a letter of reference from the parent so that other parents will know they can trust you.

Babysitting service—Before parents leave their children in your care, make sure they give you cell-phone numbers and/or phone numbers where they can be reached, the number of the nearest relative, and the number for the child's doctor. Be sure to ask about bedtimes, food allergies, television and Internet restrictions, and whether the parents want you to answer the phone. Then have fun with the kids!

Mother's helper—A mother's helper keeps children occupied so busy mothers can relax or devote their attention to something else. The mother will still be in the house, but you will take care of the children. This is a safe way to get some babysitting experience.

Teach activities—Teach your specialty (such as crafts, cooking, or exercise) to children one or two afternoons a week, or just have a special playtime with puppets, storytelling, or other activities.

Children's stories—Create a "storytime" at your house for children in the neighborhood. Parents can drop off their children for an hour or two to have you read to them. You could also make tapes of your readings and sell them.

»Cleaning

Are you a neatnik? Turn your love of cleanliness into a business!

Car washing—Car washing can be a steady source of income if you put some effort into it. Consider working with a team of friends and advertise speedy service for busy people. Learn to wax and detail cars so you can also offer these services.

House/office cleaning—Houses and offices need to be cleaned. Many people and business owners do not have time to clean and would be happy to hire you.

Laundry and ironing—Do you have access to a good washer and dryer? Doing laundry (like dog-walking and house cleaning) is a chore many people cannot find time to do. Laundry and ironing could be combined with another service, such as child care.

»Clothing

If you have a passion for clothes, there are many businesses you could start. You can sell old fashions, create new ones, or bring the latest trends to the people in your market.

Clothing design—Create your own line and start out selling to local stores. Two of our graduates sold their "skinny jeans" to top stores in New York and Los Angeles.

Vintage clothing—After 20 years or so, fashions often become popular again. Do your parents or other relatives have old clothes they'd like to get rid of? Collect them and start selling "vintage" clothing!

Buying wholesale for resale—A student who took this course, traveled regularly from her neighborhood to the wholesale district in the nearest city, where she bought trendy fashions that were not yet in the stores in her area. Back home, she resold the clothes in her own store.

»Collecting

If you collect baseball cards, sports caps, comics, or other items that are inexpensive now but could gain value in the future, consider a collecting business. You can visit collector fairs to buy and sell your items. Collect things that you genuinely like, because you will have them for a while.

Vinyl records—DJs are always looking for new sounds, so you never know what someone might pay for an old record you bought at a garage sale for 50 cents. Check out *Goldmine* and *Record Collector* magazines for helpful info.

Comics—If you have, say, only $200, you might be able to make more money buying and selling comic books than you could buying and selling stock! Use software like Comic Collector to catalog your collection. *Overstreet Comic Price Review* is another good resource.

»Computers

Computer repair/software installation—Are you the one your friends (or your parents!) call when they have computer trouble? Become a computer consultant and sell your expertise.

Word-processing service—Are you a fast and accurate typist? If you can type well, there are many services you could offer, such as typing papers for other students or typing a manuscript for a busy author.

Desktop publishing—You will need access to a computer, laser printer, and a good word-processing program. You will also need design skills. With these resources, you can create newsletters, menus, and programs, and create and maintain mailing lists.

Web site design—If you are computer literate and comfortable on the Internet, assist others in designing their "home pages" on the World Wide Web. Dreamweaver software makes it easy to design Web sites without having to learn HTML.

Graphic arts—Learn how to use programs like Adobe Photoshop and Quark and you can provide graphic arts services, including photo retouching, and the creation of flyers, posters, brochures, and other promotional materials.

»Cooking

If you love to cook, you can provide products, services, or both! Let your creativity soar, but always with the customer in mind. What kind of food do the people in your market like? What is difficult to find?

Catering—A catering business can supply whole menus for parties and other occasions.

Pasta—Create a line of fresh pasta and sauces.

Organic baby food—Parents want their babies to eat healthy, too.

Cookbook—Do you come from a family in which a lot of great recipes have been handed down over the years? Put together a cookbook!

»Crafts

Do you like to make jewelry, leather goods, or other handicrafts? Sell your own work and, perhaps, for a percentage, creations by your friends, as well.

Jewelry-making—Start with inexpensive supplies, like wire and beads. Maybe one day you will work in gold and diamonds!

Greeting-card design—You can create beautiful greeting cards with rubber stamps, ink, and small silkscreens. If you have a good sense of humor, this is a great place to use it.

Handbags—Decorate vintage handbags or make your own out of felt, fabric, or leather.

Candle-making—A crafts store has everything you will need to make decorative candles. You can buy wax or melt down old candles and crayons. Try using empty milk cartons as molds.

»Dancing

Dance lessons—Even if you are a beginner, you probably know enough to teach young children.

Hip-hop dance troupe—If you have friends who are also talented dancers, why not get a group together and offer your services to local hip-hop groups?

»Driving

Do you like to drive? If you start a business using a car or van, make sure you have up-to-date insurance. Do not borrow a car from a parent or friend for your business without being sure you are covered by the insurance policy.

Errand service—Offer to run errands and make deliveries for small businesspeople and others who do not have the time to do so. Make yourself indispensable and you will soon have a growing business.

Meal delivery—Are there restaurants in your area that do not offer delivery because they do not want to pay for their own staff? You could offer to make deliveries for three or more restaurants so that they can share the cost.

Messenger service—Do you enjoy running around? Try a messenger/small-package delivery service. It is a business with low start-up costs. The service can expand rapidly as you build a reputation for reliability.

»Entertainment

Are you a natural performer who enjoys being in front of an audience? Do you know any magic tricks or have theater experience?

Clown—If you love making kids laugh, become a clown and you will be in demand for birthday parties around town.

Magician—Is there a magic club at your school where you could learn tricks? You can also learn from books and practice on your friends. As a magician, you can entertain at birthday parties and other events.

Party DJ—A DJ plays records at parties. You will need one or two turntables and lots of records. Some DJs form record pools so they can share their records and equipment. Local record labels might give you free records to promote their artists.

Balloon decorating—Learn how to make balloon animals and how to tie balloons together to make party decorations!

»Fish

If fish are a hobby of yours, why not turn it into income?

Aquarium care—You will need to know how to care for both fresh and saltwater tanks. Offer your services to local businesses and restaurants, as well as to individuals.

Fishing—If you live in an area that has good fishing, become a fishing guide. You can organize day trips to nearby lakes and rivers.

»Gardening

Chores like mowing the lawn are a lot more fun when you're getting paid. Almost anything you do around the house can be turned into a business.

Fresh herbs and flowers—Is there a room in your house or apartment that gets a lot of sunlight? You can grow fresh herbs and flowers and supply them to restaurants. This can be a good "second" business because plants do not have to be watched every minute of the day.

Yardwork—Do you like working outdoors? From the street, you can often spot lawns and gardens that are not being kept up by their owners as well as they should be. You could also shovel snow in the winter.

Plant care—Offices could hire you to come in once a week to water, clean, and fertilize their plants. As more and more people work outside the home, there is more demand for household plant care, too.

Window boxes—Fill wooden window boxes with flowers. You can make and decorate the boxes yourself.

»Hair

Do you love to make your friends' hair look great? Before you start a business styling or cutting hair, check local regulations for necessary permits.

»Holidays

Are you one of those people who gets excited about holidays? Holidays are business opportunities.

Gift baskets—Every holiday is an opportunity to create a different gift basket that you can sell for a profit. You can also offer a custom service and make baskets based on the special interests of the people receiving them.

Seasonal sales—Do you have spare time during the holidays? Try selling seasonal specialties, such as Christmas decorations or Valentine's Day candy, which have short but intense sales seasons. If you are willing to put in the time, you can make a lot of money in a relatively short period.

»Internet

People come up with creative new businesses using the Internet every day. What will you invent?

Genealogy—Researching genealogy, which is the history of someone's ancestors, is easy online (but you will have to subscribe to some basic sites to access the genealogical information). Teach yourself how to create family trees. Every family is a potential customer.

Web site—If you come up with a popular idea for a Web site, you can sell advertising space. Got a great comic character? You could create some fun Quicktime movies. How about electronic greeting cards? What could you put online that other people would want to see?

EBay auctions—Learn how to bid on EBay and you could offer your services to people who have things to sell but do not have the time or skill.

»Music

Do you play music? Or just love being around it? Either way, there are a lot of businesses you could start.

Band—Start a rock band and get hired to play at parties, weddings, and corporate events.

Music lessons—Do you play an instrument well enough to teach someone else? Even if you have only intermediate knowledge, you could probably teach beginners.

Stickers and buttons—Rock and rap artists need stickers and buttons imprinted with their logos for promotion. So do stores and sports teams. Why not save them the trouble of contracting with a sticker or button manufacturer? If you establish a relationship with a manufacturer yourself, you can get a good price because you will be bringing that company new business. Turn that price advantage into profit.

String quartet—Do you play in the band or orchestra at school? Get some friends together and start a string quartet to get hired for store openings, weddings, parties, etc.

»Painting

Are you good with a brush? Advertise your services on grocery store bulletin boards and with flyers at hardware stores.

Housepainting—You will need to learn about types of paint and how to "cut," so your lines look clean. See if you can find someone experienced who is willing to teach you the basics.

Furniture—Old furniture can be made to look like new with a nice coat of paint. Shop flea markets for bargains you can refinish and sell, or offer refinishing services.

Signage—If you can paint lettering well, you can create signs for local businesses.

»People

Are you a "people person"? Try a business that involves getting people together or getting them up!

Dating newsletter—Are you a natural matchmaker? Start an e-mail dating newsletter.

Wake-up service—Are you an early riser? Start a wake-up service for your fellow students.

»Photography

Have you ever thought about a career in photography? Get experience and earn money at the same time.

Wedding photography—If you are a skilled photographer, offer to shoot a couple of weddings for free to build your portfolio. Be aware that wedding photography has to be very professional.

Photo journalist—Local newspapers often buy photos of events and parties from freelance photographers.

»Sales

In this course, you will learn how to go to a wholesale district and buy items in quantity at a discount that you can then sell at retail prices. You can sell almost anything: candy, perfume, headbands, jewelry, ties, watches, etc.

»Silkscreening

Silkscreening is easy and cheap. All you need are a silkscreen, ink, a "wedge" to press the ink through the screen, and something to silkscreen.

T-shirts—Bands need T-shirts silkscreened with their logos. So do sports teams.

Creative clothing—You can also silkscreen pants, shorts, skirts, and dresses with your own cool designs.

»Teaching

Are you always explaining school assignments to your friends? Do you like helping people understand things?

Tutoring—Do you know one of your school subjects well enough to teach other students? Giving lessons (tutoring) requires patience, but you will discover the rewards and satisfaction of teaching.

Lessons—Anything you can do, from playing guitar to making clothes, you can teach.

»Translating

Are you bilingual? Did you grow up speaking another language? Put your language skills to good use!

Translation—Translate ads, flyers, signs, etc., for local shopkeepers who want to reach customers who speak different languages.

Teach English—Teach English as a second language to people in the community who need help.

Teach your second language—Teach your language to people who speak only English.

»Video

Do you have a good camera or camcorder?

Videotape events—People like to have their weddings, birthdays, parties, and other events videotaped. You will need samples of your work to show to prospective clients.

Videotape concerts—Bands like to have their shows videotaped so they can see how to improve their performance. You will have to be of legal age, however, to enter a club that serves alcohol.

Digital moviemaking—With digital video, anyone with a camera can make a movie without the expense of buying the film that made moviemaking so expensive. Check out Michael Dean's *$30 Film School* (Muska & Lipman Books).

»Woodworking

Woodworking skills can be used to create many types of businesses.

Carpentry—If you are skilled at carpentry, sell your services. You can build cabinets, shelves, and help renovate homes.

Birdcages—One student who finished this course started a successful business by building birdcages out of wood in his uncle's garage.

Decorative carving—If you are artistically talented, try learning scrollwork, which is decorative carving in wood for screens or furniture.

Board games—Create interesting versions of board games, such as chess or checkers.

»Writing

Are you a talented writer?

Pennysaver newspaper—Get local businesses to buy ads in your newspaper that customers can cut out and use as coupons. You can write stories about businesses and people in the community, as well.

Fanzine—A *fanzine* is a magazine written specifically for fans of just about anything, from a genre of music to pop stars.

Poetry for special occasions—How about composing poetry for special occasions, like birthdays and graduations? Sell poetry personalized with names, dates, and photos, or lace hand-kerchiefs embroidered with poetry that guests receive as gifts.

Appendix 2 | Sample Student Business Plan

Your Business Idea

1. Describe your business idea. What is the name of your business?

   I plan to start a business called "Oldies but Goodies DJ Service." Customers will hire me to DJ at special events including family reunions, retirement parties, birthdays, and anniversary celebrations. Oldies but Goodies will specialize in playing R & B and Motown-era music from the 1950s, and 60s. My business will cater to older customers who enjoy this genre of music. I will deliver my DJ services directly to my clients. When I am hired to play at a party, I will transport all of my equipment and music to the event.

2. Explain how your business idea will satisfy a consumer need.

   Many DJs focus on playing the latest, most cutting-edge tracks, but older customers do not value this feature. I will be satisfying my customers' need to hear the music they enjoy most. Oldies but Goodies will offer its customers a fun-filled, nostalgic musical experience that they can share with their friends and relatives.

3. Provide contact information for each owner.

   **Wanda Maynard or "DJ Wanda-May"
   134 Peach Tree Drive
   Atlanta, Georgia 30301
   404–382–9940**

4. Provide contact information for each owner.

   This is not applicable to my business.

5. If there is more than one owner, describe how the business ownership will be shared.

   I am the sole owner of Oldies but Goodies DJ Service.

Economics of One Unit

6. Do you intend to pay yourself a salary, wage, dividend, or commission? Explain.

   I will pay myself a dividend, an hourly wage, *and* a commission.

   Dividend: I plan to allocate 10 to 15 percent of my yearly net profit as dividend income for myself. This

means that I will pay myself a percentage of my business's net profits as personal income. I will invest my remaining profit back into Oldies but Goodies so that my business can continue to grow.

Wage: It will cost Oldies but Goodies $15 per hour in direct labor costs to deliver its hands-on DJ services to customers. This direct labor cost will be paid to me since I plan to serve as the company's sole DJ. As my business grows, I will consider hiring other DJs as subcontractors. When this happens, the direct labor fee will be paid to my subcontractors, and not to me.

Commission: Each time Oldies but Goodies secures a job, I will pay myself a 5 percent commission, based on my per-unit retail price. If I charge customers a minimum price of $150 for three hours, my commission will amount to $7.50. If a customer hires me for six hours of service, my total commission will be $15.

7. What type of business are you starting?

    I am starting a service business.

8. Calculate the Economics of One Unit for your business.

One Unit = Three Hours of hands-on service (minimum of one hour for setup/cleanup, and two hours of "real-time" DJ service)	
Selling Price per Unit =	$150.00
− COSS per Unit	
Direct Labor (@ $15.00 per hour)	$45.00
− Other Variable Costs	
Commission @ 5%	$7.50
TOTAL Variable Costs per Unit	$70.00
Gross Profit per Unit	$ 97.50

My EOU: I decided to charge my customers a minimum service unit of $150.00. This unit covers three hours of service, including setup and cleanup. If my customers want to hire Oldies but Goodies for more than three hours, I will charge them $150.00 plus $50 for each additional hour. Building my EOU around a three-hour service unit will help me to build a strong foundation for my business.

Evaluating Your Business Idea

9. What resources and skills do you (and the other owners) have that will help make your business successful?

    My business resources include the following:

    • **My large record and CD collection of R & B and Motown-era music.**

    • **My DJ equipment (I already own high-quality turntables).**

- **My car—I will need a car to transport my equipment to events where I will be performing my services.**
- **My network of friends, family, and personal contacts in the radio industry here in Atlanta.**

My business skills include the following:

- **I am very knowledgeable about Motown-era music.**
- **I have excellent organizational skills.**
- **I like interacting with different kinds of people.**
- **I have been practicing my DJ skills as a hobby for the last ten years.**

10. Perform a SWOT analysis of your business.

Strengths	My knowledge of 1950s and 1960s music combined with my extensive record collection will enable me to deliver a high-end musical experience to my customers.
Weaknesses	I have never run my own business before. I will be competing with people who have more experience than I do. I expect to make mistakes but also learn from my mistakes.
Opportunities	There is a growing senior citizen population in the Atlanta metro area. Members of my target market are choosing to retire here. These potential customers have occasions to celebrate such as birthdays and anniversaries. This will create opportunity for my business.
Threats	The Internet allows people to pay to download music very easily. My potential customers might choose to burn CDs with their favorite tunes instead of hiring a DJ to perform. On the other hand, hiring a DJ creates a more festive environment at parties. The DJ can interact with people and create positive energy.

Your Goals

Business Goals:

11. What are your short-term business goals? (less than one year)

- **Save $3,000 towards my start-up investment.**
- **Purchase high-end amplifier and speakers with my start-up capital.**
- **Secure at least 15 DJ "gigs" by year-end.**
- **Earn a yearly net profit of $12,000.**
- **Establish relationships with the human resource managers at three major corporations in Atlanta. One of my market segments consists of corporations. I want them to hire Oldies but Goodies to DJ at employee retirement parties and corporate holiday events.**
- **Establish relationships with managers at at least two different Atlanta-area retirement complexes. I want these managers to use Oldies but Goodies for special events.**

12. What are your long-term business goals? (from one to five years)

- **Have 75 percent of my available DJ time booked consistently.**
- **Increase my sales revenue by at least 20% each year.**
- **Serve as a guest DJ on Atlanta's "oldies" radio station to increase my name recognition.**
- **Hire one or two subcontractors to deliver DJ services. This will enable me to grow my business.**

Personal Goals:

13. What is your career goal? What do you plan to invest to achieve this goal?

Within the next ten years, I want to assume the position of chief financial officer at a major record label. After I gain at least five years of experience as a CFO, I plan to start my own record label here in Atlanta.

14. How much education will you need for your career?

I will need to complete a bachelor's degree in accounting. Afterwards I plan to work for two years for a top-tier accounting firm in New York City. I will then go to graduate school for two years to earn my master's in business administration. I plan to seek internships in the music industry while I attend business school so I can learn more about the industry.

Technology

15. Identify which technological tools you plan to use for your business, and why.

Tool	Function
Cell Phone	• Sales calls
	• Customer care and communciation
Computer and Printer	• Design promotional flyers and business cards
	• Billing and recordkeeping
	• Printing invoices and contracts
	• Burn CDs
E-mail and Internet	• Customer care and communication
	• Web site to promote my business
	• Download new music
DJ Equipment:	• These are the tools of my trade! I cannot deliver my services without this equipment.
Headphones	
Turntables (2)	

Tool	Function
CD player	
Amplifier	
Speakers	

16. Write a memo explaining how you plan to get access to the technology you need.

   I already own most of the equipment needed. I bought a high-end turntable system last year along with a new computer and printer. The most costly items I still need to purchase are an amplifier and speakers. I plan to conduct thorough research online before I buy this equipment. I will also visit different audio supply stores to learn more about the latest models. I am willing to pay more for quality but also want to ensure that I negotiate a competitive price.

Core Beliefs

17. Describe three core beliefs you will use to run your company.

   • **Listen to my customers and identify their needs and preferences.**
   • **Be flexible.**
   • **The road to excellence is paved with discipline and a continuous commitment to quality.**

Supply and Demand

18. What factors influence the demand for your product or service?

   Price: My customers tend to be fickle about money. Older people may be living on fixed incomes. My pricing scheme needs to be perceived as a good value.

19. What factors influence the supply for your product or service?

   My time: I can only be in one place at a given time! Party events typically occur on the weekends. I may find that customers will want to hire Oldies but Goodies at conflicting times. If this kind of situation happens often enough, I will consider subcontracting to other DJs sooner rather than later.

20. How do you plan to protect your product/trademark/logo? (Check one, and explain.)

   _____ patent   ___x___ logo
   _____ copyright
   _____ trademark

   Explain: **I plan to create a logo for Oldies but Goodies and will have this trademarked.**

Competitive Advantage

21. Describe your competitive advantage.

    My competitive advantages include the following:

    • **Other DJs cannot provide the same selection that I will offer. For example, I have built a collection of over 1,000 R & B and Motown-era recordings. At least 100 of my recordings are extremely rare; only a few other collectors in the world own them.**

    • **Based on my market research, only one other DJ service in the Atlanta metro area specializes in this musical genre.**

    • **Other Competitive Advantages?**

Competitor	Weakness	Strengths
DJ Shay	DJ Shay has been playing oldies music at parties for years. Customers complain that he has lost his creative edge. He plays the same tracks over and over again. His reputation has suffered.	DJ Shay hosts a radio show on WRBX that features Motown-era recordings. He has excellent name recognition in Atlanta.
Internet—CD burning	While people can pay legally to download music themselves, playing a CD is not the same as hiring a live DJ. A DJ can stir the crowd and positively influence the energy at a party.	Burning a CD gives the customer total control over the music at an event. It also costs less money than hiring a DJ. It is legal.
Party in a Box Productions	Party in a Box specializes in providing "all music for all occasions." It owns a basic collection of oldies but their selection is limited.	This company has an established reputation in Atlanta, Their prices are very affordable.

International Opportunities

22. Are there customers for your business in other countries? How do you plan to reach them?

    People in countries all over the world appreciate '50s and '60s music. In the short term, I plan to focus my efforts on servicing customers in the Atlanta-metro area only. As my business grows, I will consider expanding to DJ at specialty parties in other locations.

23. Describe any international competitors you have found who may be able to access your customers. How do you intend to compete?

    I do not expect international competitors to pose a threat to my business. My target customer values personal relationships; for small local events, seniors tend to hire people they know and trust.

Fixed Costs

24. List and describe your monthly fixed costs.

Fixed Cost	Amount	Description
Utilities	$100.00	Electricity, Internet, and phone costs
Salaries	$0	I do not plan to pay myself a salary.
Advertising	$150.00	Average monthly costs for business cards, classified ads, promo cards, flyers, and radio ads
Insurance	$75.00	General Business Liability Insurance monthly charge
Interest	$0	I will have no interest because my business is not being financed with debt.
Rent	$100.00	Monthly cost to keep my records and equipment at a secure storage facility
Depreciation	$200.00	Monthly cost for the depreciation of my DJ equipment
Unexpected	$75.00	There are always unexpected costs in business. I am budgeting for the unexpected at an average rate of $75 per month.
TOTAL	$700.00	

Insurance

25. What types of insurance will your business need, and why? What is the highest deductible you feel you can afford?

    I will purchase small business owner's insurance. This insurance plan will protect me in the event that my equipment is stolen or damaged for reasons beyond my control. My insurance plan costs $75 per month and my deductible is $3,000.00.

Recordkeeping

26. Describe your recordkeeping system.

    I will create a computer database to track my client and billing records. I also plan to create a backup paper filing system so that I have hard copies of all my

documents. My recordkeeping system will include the following:

Filing Category	Function
Music Research and Library	To maintain my competitive advantage, I will continue to track down rare Motown-era recordings. I plan to catalog my collection carefully so I know exactly what I own.
Paid Invoices	I will keep copies of all checks and credit card receipts attached to client invoices.
Accounts Receivable	I will file bills I owe to suppliers such as the phone company and my Internet service provider.
Accounts Payable	I will keep track of invoices for payments owed to me by clients.
Marketing Materials	I will keep samples of flyers, business cards, logo designs, and promotional cards.
Prospective Clients	I plan to collect information about potential clients who may be interested in hiring Oldies but Goodies.

27. List any bank accounts you will open for your business.

I will open checking, savings, and line of credit accounts at Liberty Mutual. The checking account will permit me to write checks to suppliers using my business name. I can earn a small amount of interest by depositing my sales revenue into a savings account. My line of credit will cover me in the event that I owe money to suppliers and do not have the cash flow to fully cover my outstanding balances in the short term. I plan to pay my line of credit loans back in full each month.

28. Will you accept personal checks from customers? Credit cards? Will you offer charge accounts or customer credit?

I plan to accept personal checks, credit cards, and cash. My payment policy will require customers to pay a 25 percent deposit when they sign a service contract with me. For example, if a customer hires me to perform five hours of service at an hourly rate of $50, and the fee totals $250.00, then the client must pay me $62.50 (25% of $250.00) up front. I think it is important to require the customer to make this kind of investment. People will take my service more seriously once they have made a financial commitment.

Projected Income Statement

29. Complete a monthly projected budget and one-year income statement for your business.

Monthly Income Statement—September	Unit Price	# of Units	Total
Total Units Sold (one unit = three hours of service; includes setup and cleanup time) =	$150.00	20	$3,000.00
Less Variable Costs			
COSS			
— Direct Labor ($15 per hour at 3 hours):	$45.00	20	$900.00
— Commission (@ 5%)	5% of $150.00 = $7.50	20	$150.00
TOTAL Variable Costs			$1,050.00
Gross Profit (contribution margin)			$1,950.00
Less Fixed Costs			
— Utilities	$100		
— Salaries	$0		
— Advertising	$150		
— Insurance	$75		
— Interest	$0		
— Rent	$100		
— Depreciation	$200		
— Unexpected	$75		
TOTAL Fixed Costs	$700		$700.00
Profit before Tax			$1,250.00
Tax @20% (*estimated)			$ 250.00
Net Profit			$1,000.00

Yearly Income Statement	Unit Price	# of Units	Total
Total Units Sold = 240	$150.00	240	$36,000
Less Variable Costs			
COSS			
— Direct Labor:	$45.00	240	$10,800
— Commission	5 % of $150.00	240	$1800

Yearly Income Statement	Unit Price	# of Units	Total
TOTAL Variable Costs			$12,600
Gross Profit (contribution margin)			$23,400
Less Fixed Costs	Monthly Fixed		Yearly Fixed
— Utilities	$100		$1,200
— Salaries	$0		$0
— Advertising	$150		$1,800
— Insurance	$75		$900
— Interest	$0		$0
— Rent	$100		$1,200
— Depreciation	$200		$2,400
— Unexpected	$75		$900
TOTAL Fixed Costs	$700		$8,400
Profit before Tax			$15,000
Tax @20% (*estimated)			$3,000
Net Profit			$12,000

Financing Strategy

30. List the items you will need to buy to start your business.

Item	Quantity	Cost
Equipment		
Computer (includes CD burner)	1	$650.00 (in kind)
Cell Phone	1	$80.00 (in kind)
Printer	1	$75.00 (in kind)
Turntables and Mixer	1	$2,000.00 (in kind)
Headphones	2	$100.00
CD Player	1	$100.00 (in kind)
Additional Records for My Collection	Multiple	$150.00
Blank CD Stock	25 CDs at $1 each	$25.00
Speakers	2	$500.00
Protective Cases for Records	5 at $30 each	$150.00
Amplifier	1	$550.00

Item	Quantity	Cost
Other Costs		
Promotional Cards	300	@.05/each = $15.00
Legal Fees	1 day	$500.00
Business Cards	200	$35.00
Start-up Investment—TOTAL		$5,000.00
Start-up Investment—Cash Expenditure*		$2,000.00*

*The total value of my start-up investment is $5,000. However, I already own $3,000 worth of equipment. I plan to give Oldies but Goodies this equipment donation as a gift. Therefore, my actual cash expenditures towards my start-up investment will be approximately $2,000.00

31. Add up the items to get your total start-up capital.

    $5,000

    Add a cash reserve that covers three months of fixed costs.

    Fixed Costs = $700/month × 3 = $2,100 + $5,000 = $7,100 Rounded to $7,000.

32. List the sources of financing for your start-up capital. Identify whether each source is equity, debt, or a gift. Indicate the amount and type for each source.

Funding Source	Equity	Debt	Gift
Myself	$3,100.00 (100% equity)		$3,000 worth of equipment
Julius Maynard (father)			$1,000.00
Subtotal	$3,000.00	$0	$4,000.00
TOTAL START-UP INVESTMENT	$7,000.00		

33. What is your debt ratio? What is your debt-to-equity ratio?

    My debt ratio is 0. My debt-to-equity ratio is 0:100. I have zero debt and 100 percent equity in my business.

34. What is your payback period? In other words, how long will it take you to earn enough profit to cover start-up capital?

    Start-up Investment = $7,000

    Yearly projected net profit = $12,000

    Payback = .58 years ($7,000/$12,000)

    My payback is a little more than half a year, or 7 months.

35. Use your projected one-year income statement to calculate the following:

    Projected ROI for one year: _____**171**_____%

    Projected ROS for one year: _____**33**_____%

36. Describe any suppliers with whom you will have to negotiate.

    I conduct business on a weekly basis with Vintage Recordings, a used-record store in downtown Atlanta. As a frequent and reliable customer, I plan to negotiate with the store owner for discounts. I also want to negotiate to see if the owner will post my business and promo cards in the store so that I can raise the profile of Oldies but Goodies.

Raising Capital

37. Describe financing sources that might be willing to invest in your business in exchange for equity.

    Friends and family:

    My father has pledged a gift of $1,000.00

    Angels:

    Not applicable

    MESBICs:

    Not applicable

    Other:

    Not applicable

38. Describe any debt financing you intend to pursue.

    I do not plan to finance my business with debt at this time. I will establish a line of credit to cover me in case I need to make payments while I am waiting to be paid by my clients.

39. Do you plan to use bootstrap financing? Explain.

    I want to purchase the best quality equipment for my business so I do not plan to bootstrap around my equipment purchases. I may barter for other services such as my business cards and promotional materials. For example, I could offer my DJ services to a graphic designer in exchange for a logo or business card prototype.

Venture Capital

40. Do you plan to pursue venture capital? Why, or why not?

    I do not plan to seek venture capital at this time. My start-up investment is modest so I will not require venture financing to launch my business. I may investigate venture financing later on, as my business grows, if I find that I need a large sum of cash to purchase equipment or other assets.

41. List potential sources of venture capital.

    This is not yet applicable to my business.

Competitive Strategy

42. Use the following charts to define your business, analyze your competitive advantage, and determine your tactics.

Business Definition Question	Response
1. *The Offer:* What products and services will be sold by the business?	1. DJ services specializing in Motown-era music
2. *Target Market:* Which consumer segment will the business focus on?	2. Customers ages 50–85 who live in Atlanta
3. *Production Capability:* How will that offer be produced and delivered to those customers?	3. My DJ services will be delivered directly by me using my albums, CDs, and audio equipment.

Competitive Advantage Question	Competitive Difference (USP)
1. *The Offer:* What will be better and different about the products and services that will be sold by the business?	1. I can offer customers a wide variety of recordings, including a large selection of rare recordings. I will also provide my own high-end equipment.
2. *Target Market:* What customers should be the focus of the business, to make it as successful as possible?	2. Older customers who were fans of R and B and Motown music during the 50s and 60s
3. *Production and Delivery Capability:* What will be better or different about the way that offer is produced and delivered to those customers?	3. My DJ equipment is state of the art. Customers can request that I play particular artists. I can customize my lineup of songs to suit my customers' preferences.

Tactical Question	Issues	Solutions
1. *Sales Plan:* Where and how will you sell to your customers?	How to identify prospects and convert them to sales.	I plan to pitch my services to individuals, companies, and nonprofit organizations that employ and/or offer special program services to people from their fifties into their eighties.
2. *Market Communications:* How will you communicate with your customers, and make them aware of your business offer?	How to make customers aware of your offer; how to attract them to the business.	I will use a combination of direct sales, paid advertising, and word of mouth.
3. *Operating Plan:* How will you manage your internal operations?	How to make the business go, and determine who will perform the tasks.	During my first year of operations I will be wearing many hats! I plan to manage all aspects of my business and will use my board of advisors when I need guidance.

Tactical Question	Issues	Solutions
4. *Budget:* How do you plan to manage your revenues and expenses?	What are the sources of revenue; what are the items that have to be purchased?	My revenue will come from providing my services to customers. Before I can launch my business, I will need to purchase some additional equipment such as an amplifier and speakers.

43. Describe your strategy for outperforming the competition.

I will provide a high-quality personalized service. I will promote the fact that I offer the widest and best selection of R & B and Motown-era music.

44. What tactics will you use to carry out this strategy?

I will continue to enrich my music library. I will talk in depth with my customers prior to the event to learn how I can adapt my services to best meet their needs.

45. Write a mission statement for your business in fewer than three sentences that clearly states your competitive advantage, strategy, and tactics.

Oldies but Goodies DJ Service's mission is to offer its customers the best selection of popular and rare recordings from the R & B and Motown-era. We will enhance the life of every party we service by listening to our customers and playing the music that they like best. At Oldies and Goodies we will give 110 percent to make sure that every party is a hit.

Marketing Step One: Consumer Analysis

46. Describe your market research methods (surveys, focus groups, general research, statistical research).

I plan to conduct market research with three different market segments:

- **Individuals**
- **Managers at local senior programs and retirement centers**
- **Human resource managers at local businesses**

My market research methods will include focus groups and surveys. I will also conduct research online.

47. Describe your target consumer:

Age: **50–85**

Gender: **Both**

Income: **$45,000 per year and up**

Marketing Step Two: Market Analysis

48. Research your industry and display the results in a one-page report that includes pie charts and bar or line graphs. Describe your target market within the industry.

   According to the American Disc Jockey Assocation, there are an estimated 60,000 DJs employed in the United States alone. DJs earn between $600 to $1,000 for a four- to five-hour event. DJs typically deliver their services in private homes, catering halls, schools, and outdoor settings.

   According to *The Los Angeles Times*, DJs work three days per week for eight to twelve hours a day on average. DJ services are in higher demand during the December holidays when many people like to throw parties. April through September is also an active period because the majority of weddings take place during this time. It is not uncommon for DJs to book several events on a single weekend to accommodate more business. Weekends are when DJ services are in the highest demand.

   (Sources: American Disc Jockey Association—www.adja.org and *Los Angeles Times*, August 2, 1993, Monday, Orange County Edition, Business; Part D; Page 5; Column 3: Inside Job: Occupation: Mobile Disc Jockey, researched by Janice L. Jones / *Los Angeles Times*).

49. How large is your potential market? Roughly how many consumers are in your market segment?

   According to the 2000 U.S. Census, 400,000 people live in the Atlanta metro area. Of this total, approximately 115,000 are between the ages of 50 and 85. I am assuming that at least 5 percent of this market segment— approximately 6,000 people—will be potential customers for my business.

50. Will you analyze your market segment by location, population, personality, or behavior?

   I will assess my market segment based on location and population. My business will focus on serving a particular demographic located in a particular geographic area (metro-area Atlanta).

51. Explain how your marketing plan targets your market segment.

   I plan to target individuals as well as companies and organizations that service my market segment. For example, there is a total of 50 senior centers and private retirement communities in Atlanta.

52. What percentage of the market do you feel you need to capture for your business to be profitable?

   In order to achieve the goals I outlined in my yearly projected income statement, I would only need to reach 4 percent of the market.

> **Here is my rationale: Target market = 6,000 people.**
> **Projected total units sold = 240. 240 = 4 percent of 6,000.**

53. Who are the potential customers you plan to approach in the first two months of business?

   I want to approach the managers of local senior centers and retirement communities. Each of these places organizes fun events for its participants. I want them to hire me for parties and other special occasions. I will also use my personal network of friends and family to promote my business through word of mouth.

Marketing Step Three: The Marketing Mix

54. Explain why your product will meet a consumer need.

   There are people who want to hear the genre of music that I specialize in when they throw parties or attend social events.

55. Describe your pricing strategy.

   My minimum service unit includes three hours of direct service time for a retail price of $150. If customers want to hire me for more than three hours, they will pay an additional $50 per hour. I wanted to set up my pricing so that each "gig" is worth my time and effort.

56. How do you intend to market your product or service? Complete the marketing chart below:

Methods	Description	Target Market	Amount to Be Spent
Billboards			
Brochures	Simple brochure that highlights the benefits and features of my business	Individual customers, corporations, and senior centers	
Business cards	Basic business cards I can distribute to potential customers		
Catalog			
Demonstration		Individual customers, corporations, and senior centers	
Direct mail			
E-mail/fax			
Flyers	Simple flyers to post in senior centers, record stores, local supermarket, etc.	Individual customers	

Methods	Description	Target Market	Amount to Be Spent
Free gifts			
Online store			
Phone calls			
Posters			
Promo items			
Sales calls	I can make direct sales calls to promote my business	Personal friends and contacts	
Samples	I will make a sample CD to give to my potential customers	Individual customers, corporations, and senior centers	
Special events	I can perform my DJ services at local charity events	Individual customers, corporations, and senior centers	
Web site			
TOTAL			

57. How do you plan to promote your business?

I plan to sell my services directly to customers. As my business grows I will build a Web site so that customers can learn more about my services online. Using paid advertising, promotional cards, and business cards will also help to raise the profile of my business.

58. What is your business slogan? Do you have a logo for your business? How do you intend to protect it?

Slogan: "Oldies but Goodies—We play your favorite hits from back in the day." I will have my slogan copyrighted with the help of my lawyer.

59. Where do you intend to advertise?

I will advertise in my local newspaper and my local radio station.

60. How do you plan to get publicity for your business?

I can offer my DJ services for free at local charity events. I will also consider throwing an annual dance party for seniors in my community.

61. How will your business help others? List all organizations to which you plan to contribute. (Your contribution may be time, money, your product, or something else.)

I will offer DJ classes to young people at my local YMCA. I plan to donate at least 5 percent of my net profits to local charities each year.

62. Do you intend to publicize your philanthropy? Why, or why not? If you do, explain how you will work philanthropy into your marketing.

I plan to highlight my business's contributions to the community in my promotional materials and when I meet with customers directly. I want my customers to feel good about supporting a business that gives back to our community.

63. Write a sample press release for your business.

FOR IMMEDIATE RELEASE ATLANTA, GEORGIA SEPTEMBER 1, 2006

Atlanta Student Launches "Oldies but Goodies" DJ Service

Today, 21-year-old Macomb County Community College student Wanda Maynard—or DJ Wanda-May as she likes to call herself—announced the launch of her first entrepreneurial venture, "Oldies but Goodies DJ Service." Ms. Maynard has been a lifelong collector of R & B and Motown-era music. With Oldies but Goodies she plans to offer her customers a wide variety of over 1,500 vintage recordings to choose from, including rare and hard-to-find tracks. Ms. Maynard aims to bring a nostalgic musical experience to the older customers who make up her target market. "I started my business so that I could offer a great service to people like my grandfather. He loves R & B and Motown. This is what he listened to as a youth. His friends love this music too. I wanted to create opportunities for older folks to share this special music together at parties and special events."

Ms. Maynard plans to run her business on the weekends and the evenings. Oldies but Goodies intends to deliver its services at retirement parties, holiday festivals, anniversary parties, and birthday celebrations. According to Ms. Maynard, "Older people do not want to hear the latest dance tracks. They're looking for a DJ to take them 'back in the day.' I can offer them this experience."

During Ms. Maynard's days, she likes to devote herself to earning top marks in her accounting classes. She plans to use her business as a vehicle for "giving back" to the Atlanta community where she grew up. In the spring, Ms. Maynard will offer a free DJ workshop to teens at the local YMCA and she will deliver her services at local charity events later this year. "I see Oldies but Goodies as my first step in an exciting career focused around entrepreneurship. Ultimately I want to start my own record label here in Atlanta. But before I reach that goal, I plan to earn my MBA and work for established

companies in the music and accounting industries. I am excited to get started. I have so much more to do and learn."

Marketing Mix Chart

64. Describe the marketing mix for your business.

Marketing Mix	Description
Product	**DJ service specializing in R&B and Motown-era music**
Price	**$150 for three hours of service; $50 for every additional hour**
Place	**We bring our services to the customer**
Promotion	**Promo cards, business cards, press releases, radio ads**
Philanthropy	**Offering in kind DJ services at local events, teaching DJ classes at the YMCA, contributing money to local charities**

Marketing Step Four: Breakeven Analysis

65. Perform a breakeven analysis of your business:

Monthly Fixed Costs = $700.00

Gross Profit (Contribution Margin) per Unit = $97.50

700/97.5 = approximately 7 units of service per month must be sold in order for my business to break even

Sales and Customer Service

66. Describe the features and benefits of the product (or service) your business will focus on selling.

The features of my service include the following:

- **My extensive music collection.**
- **New, high-quality equipment.**
- **Personalized service.**
- **My DJ skills—I know how to spin the tracks and I can get people on the dance floor.**

67. Choose three ways you plan to sell your product or service. Describe why you have chosen these three methods and why you think they will work.

- **Direct Sales: My business will be catering to local customers and local events. If people trust me and know that I provide a good service at an excellent value, I believe that they will hire me, so long as there is a need.**

- **Word of Mouth: As my reputation grows, the "buzz" about Oldies but Goodies will spread and potential customers can learn about my business through informal channels.**
- **Radio Advertising: I can reach fellow R&B and Motown music lovers when I pay for on-air advertising that will be broadcast on Atlanta's local oldies station.**

68. Write a one-minute sales pitch for your product (or service).

   Oldies but Goodies DJ Service plays your favorite Motown-era hits from the 1950s and '60s. We have a music library that features over 1,000 LPs and 500 CDs, including rare recordings. DJ Wanda May knows how to get the party started and she will make sure that *everybody* gets on the dance floor. With our top-of-the-line equipment and premiere DJ skills, we will make sure that your next party is a hit.

69. Describe five sales prospects you intend to pitch.

Sales Prospect	Description
Terrance Small	My grandfather's best friend. He plans to throw a big party for his fiftieth wedding anniversary in June.
Elaine Cartwright	Human Resources manager at a local law firm and family friend. She is responsible for coordinating employee retirement events.
Anthony DeSouza	Community Coordinator—Peach Grove Retirement Complex. Mr. DeSouza organizes a big summer bash for seniors each year on the fourth of July.
Tanya Spalding	Program Director—Senior Center—YMCA. Ms. Spalding coordinates social and educational activities for local seniors.
Marcella Robinson	Friend of the family. Ms. Robinson organizes several local charity events each year.

70. List three ways you intend to provide superior customer service.

   I will interview each customer prior to the event to get very specific information about his or her needs.

   I will write down customers' needs and preferences to make sure I have an accurate record.

   I plan to follow up with each customer within three days after the event to make sure they were satisfied with my services. I want them to give me feedback about how I can improve.

71. How will you keep your customer database? Which five questions will you ask every customer to fill out your database?

    I will use an electronic database program. Five questions I plan to ask every customer include the following:

    - **Who are your favorite performers from the R&B or Motown era?**
    - **What is your favorite song?**
    - **What artists do you *not* want me to play?**
    - **What is the occasion that is being celebrated?**
    - **Do you have any special requests or needs?**

Legal Structure

72. What is your business legal structure?

    Sole Proprietorship _____

    Partnership _____

    Limited Partnership _____

    C Corporation _____

    Subchapter S _____

    Limited Liability Corporation ____✓____

    Not-for-Profit Corporation _____

73. Why did you choose this legal structure?

    The LLC legal structure will protect me and my personal assets in the unlikely event that Oldies but Goodies is sued or goes bankrupt.

74. Who will the partners or stockholders for your company be?

    I am the primary shareholder. I own a 100 percent equity stake in my business.

    (a) If your business is incorporated, describe what percentage of your company is owned by one share of stock.

    1/100

    (b) Is your corporation's stock publicly or privately held?
    All of my shares are privately held by me, the president and owner of Oldies but Goodies.

75. Have you registered your business?

    Yes.

76. Have you applied for a sales-tax identification number?

    Yes.

Manufacturing

77. What are the zoning laws in your area? Does your business comply?

    This is not relevant to my business.

78. Do you intend to manufacture your product? If so, describe the manufacturing process you will use. If not, describe how your product will be manufactured.

I am not manufacturing a product. Oldies but Goodies is a service business.

Buying Wholesale

79. Where are you purchasing the products you plan to sell, or the parts you plan to use to manufacture the products you will sell?

I am selling a service. In order to deliver my service I need to own and maintain high-quality DJ equipment, along with a wide selection of recordings. I will continue to purchase recordings to add to my musical library from multiple sources such as used-record stores and the Internet. I plan to purchase the electronic equipment I do not already own from a knowledgeable supplier who can offer me a good price.

80. Have you applied for a sales tax ID number?

Yes.

Production-Distribution Chain

81. How do you plan to distribute your product to your target market?

I will deliver my DJ services directly to my customers. I will provide equipment, including turntables, speakers, and an amplifier.

82. Use this chart to show the production-distribution chain for your own business, and the markups at each point in the chain.

My business sells its services directly to the retail customer. It costs me $45 in direct labor per unit to provide my service and I charge customers $150.

Service

Name: _____

Oldies but Goodies DJ Service

Contact information:
Wanda Maynard or "DJ Wanda-May"

134 Peach Tree Drive

Atlanta, Georgia 30301

404–382–9940

Selling Price: **$150.00**

Markup: $ _____ **$97.50** _____

Markup Percentage: % _____ **65** _____

Retailer

Name:_____

Contact information: _____

Markup: $_____

Markup Percentage: %_____

83. What is the estimated delivery time between when you place an order with your supplier and when you will have the product available for your customers?

I can deliver my service to customers upon request. I plan to own all of the necessary equipment and already possess the skills to offer a quality DJ experience to my target market. The only constraint will be my schedule.

Contracts

84. What is the most important contract you will need to run your business?

    All of my customers will need to sign a service contract. This will protect me in case an event is cancelled or postponed. Upon signature of the service contract, I will require customers to pay Oldies but Goodies a 25 percent deposit of the total charge. The remainder will be due at the event. The service contract also explains my cancellation policy.

85. Describe any additional contracts you have, or plan to secure.

    None

86. Who is your attorney?

    My attorney is Darius Greaves, J.D. He owns his own law practice in downtown Atlanta and works with many entrepreneurs in my community.

Human Resources

87. Fill out a PERT Chart for your business.

Task	Week One	Week Two	Week Three	Week Four	Week Five	Week Six	Week Seven	Week Eight
Make flyers and business cards	X	X						
Create demo CD					X	X		
Make sales call to local senior center								X
Research speaker and amplifier models online			X	X	X			
Research information about local retirement communities in Atlanta					X	X	X	
Call 10 of my grandparents' friends and tell them that Oldies but Goodies is open for business!								X
Have lunch with Marcella Robinson—find out about her next charity event						X		
Open accounts with Liberty Mutual and meet with my banker					X			
Research the cost of on-air advertising with WXPI			X					
Call my brother's friend, DJ Deluxe in Philadelphia, to get insider's advice about managing my business	X							
Meet with my banker, accountant, and lawyer			X	X				

88. Will you be hiring employees? If so, describe what their qualifications should be, what you intend to pay them, and how they will help your business.

I plan to hire subcontractors after I complete my first year of business operations. Using subcontractors will help me to grow my business. Oldies but Goodies can take on additional clients and build our brand. My subcontractors will need to possess outstanding DJ skills and people skills. They must provide their own top-of-the-line equipment. I will pay my subcontractors an hourly wage of $15.00 plus a sales commission of 5 percent of the total service fee.

89. Provide contact information for your accountant, attorney, banker, and insurance agent.

Accountant: Joan Sikes, CPA. 404–247–1020

Attorney: Darius Greaves, J.D. 404–465–9800

Banker: Don Flowers, Liberty Mutual. 404–504–1222

Insurance Agent: Lionel Hastings. 404–782–4000

90. What are your policies toward employees? How do you plan to make your business a positive and rewarding place to work?

I want to motivate my subcontractors to provide an excellent service to customers. I will reward my subcontractors by offering quarterly recognition awards.

91. Create an organizational chart for your business.

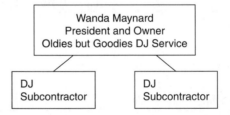

Quality

92. How do you intend to deliver a high-quality product (service) to your customers? Describe the quality-control procedure for your business.

I plan to take excellent care of my equipment. I will get my equipment serviced every three months. My albums are the "jewels" of my business and many of them are 40 to 50 years old. I will take excellent care of these "jewels" by storing them properly and putting albums away immediately after I use them. Interpersonally, even if I am having a bad day, I will put all of that aside to offer my customers a fun-filled party experience. I will triple-check my equipment to make sure that everything works properly before the party starts.

When I hire subcontractors, I will need to develop a thorough quality assurance plan that covers equipment, music, and customer service. I will reward my subcontractors with bonuses when they perform a job well.

Ethical Business Behavior

93. Describe the corporate governance plan for your company. It should include five policies (rules) that will be the backbone of your company's ethics.

    - **Pay suppliers and taxes on time.**
    - **Keep financial records accurate and up-to-date.**
    - **Give back to my community.**
    - **Treat all customers equally.**
    - **Do my best to meet customers' needs and be honest when I cannot deliver what a customer wants.**

94. Provide information for each of your mentors or advisors. If there is a board of advisors, list each member and describe his or her commitment to the board.

    I do not have a formal corporate board. However, I have assembled a collection of supporters whom I can call upon for advice:

    > **Ron D'Angelou: General Manager, WKBX. Music advisor**

    > **Sandra Jackson: Owner, Soul for Real Records. Local entrepreneur. Mentor**

    > **Juan Hernandez: Director of Adult and Senior Programs, YMCA. Mentor**

    > **Alison Markman: Account Manager, Coca-Cola. Financial advisor**

Socially Responsible Business

95. Choose three ways you plan to run a socially responsible business.

    Recycling paper, glass, or plastic ____✓____

    Donating a portion of profits to a charity ____✓____

    No animal testing of products _____

    Offering employees incentives to volunteer in the community _____

    Establishing a safe and healthy workplace _____

    Other ____✓____

    Whenever possible, I will choose to buy my products and equipment from locally owned businesses so that I support other entrepreneurs in my community.

Cash Flow

96. Create a projected cash flow statement for your business for one year.

CASH FLOW STATEMENT
for the year ending 12/31/2003

	Jan	Feb	Mar	Apr	May	Jun	Jul	Aug	Sep	Oct	Nov	Dec	
Number of Units—Computer Services	1,500	1,000	600	550	550	500	500	450	450	450	400	400	7,350
Number of Units—													
Food & Beverage Sales	4,500	4,750	5,000	5,100	5,200	5,300	5,400	5,500	5,600	5,700	5,800	6,000	63,850
Cash Flow from Operating:													
Cash Inflows:													
Computer usage fees	$ 6,000	$ 4,000	$ 2,400	$ 2,200	$ 2,200	$ 2,000	$ 2,000	$ 1,800	$ 1,800	$ 1,800	$ 1,600	$ 1,600	$29,400
Food and beverage sales	9,000	9,500	10,000	10,200	10,400	10,600	10,800	11,000	11,200	11,400	11,600	12,000	$127,700
Total Cash Inflows	$ 15,000	$13,500	$12,400	$12,400	$12,600	$12,600	$12,800	$12,800	$13,000	$13,200	$13,200	$13,600	$157,100
Cash Outflows:													
Variable Costs													
COGS	$ 4,875	$ 5,000	$ 5,150	$ 5,238	$ 5,338	$ 5,425	$ 5,525	$ 5,613	$ 5,713	$ 5,813	$ 5,900	$ 6,100	$ 65,688
Other Variable Costs	$ 750	$ 675	$ 620	$ 620	$ 630	$ 630	$ 640	$ 640	$ 650	$ 660	$ 660	$ 680	$ 7,855
Utilities													
Electricity, Gas, Water, Telephone	$ 500	$ 500	$ 500	$ 500	$ 500	$ 500	$ 500	$ 500	$ 500	$ 500	$ 500	$ 500	$ 6,000
High Speed Internet Access	$ 500	$ 500	$ 500	$ 500	$ 500	$ 500	$ 500	$ 500	$ 500	$ 500	$ 500	$ 500	$ 6,000
Wireless Internet	$ 30	$ 30	$ 30	$ 30	$ 30	$ 30	$ 30	$ 30	$ 30	$ 30	$ 30	$ 30	360
Salaries													
Part-Time Tech Support Salary	$ 1,000	$ 1,000	$ 1,000	$ 1,000	$ 1,000	$ 1,000	$ 1,000	$ 1,000	$ 1,000	$ 1,000	$ 1,000	$ 1,000	$ 12,000
Amy and Steve's Salary	1,000	1,000	1,000	1,000	1,000	1,000	1,000	1,000	1,000	1,000	1,000	1,000	$ 12,000
Advertising	1,000	1,000	1,000	1,000	1,000	1,000	1,000	1,000	1,000	1,000	1,000	1,000	$ 12,000
Insurance	500	500	500	500	500	500	500	500	500	500	500	500	6,000
Interest Expense	1,469	1,469	1,469	1,469	1,469	1,469	1,469	1,469	1,469	1,469	1,469	1,469	17,623
Rent	1,000	1,001	1,002	1,003	1,004	1,005	1,006	1,007	1,008	1,009	1,010	1,011	12,000
Total cash used in operating activities	$ 12,624	$12,675	$12,771	$12,859	$12,970	$13,059	$13,170	$13,258	$13,369	$13,480	$13,569	$13,790	$157,526
Net Cash Flow From Operating	$ 2,376	$ 825	($371)	($459)	($370)	($459)	($370)	($458)	($369)	($280)	($369)	($190)	($426)

Cash Flow Out from Investing:													
Sound Proof Quiet Room	$ 15,000	$0	$0	$0	$0	$0	$0	$0	$0	$0	$0	$0	$ 15,000
Laser Printers	$ 7,000	$0	$0	$0	$0	$0	$0	$0	$0	$0	$0	$0	$ 7,000
High Speed Internet Access Setup	$ 10,000	$0	$0	$0	$0	$0	$0	$0	$0	$0	$0	$0	$ 10,000
Workstations	$ 20,000	$0	$0	$0	$0	$0	$0	$0	$0	$0	$0	$0	$ 20,000
Supplies/Equipment	$ 25,000	$0	$0	$0	$0	$0	$0	$0	$0	$0	$0	$0	$ 25,000
Furniture	$ 8,000	$0	$0	$0	$0	$0	$0	$0	$0	$0	$0	$0	$ 8,000
Fixtures	$ 5,000	$0	$0	$0	$0	$0	$0	$0	$0	$0	$0	$0	$ 5,000
Net Cash Flow Out from Investing	$ 90,000	$0	$0	$0	$0	$0	$0	$0	$0	$0	$0	$0	$ 90,000
Financing:													
Cash received from uncle (12% APR)	$ 50,000	$0	$0	$0	$0	$0	$0	$0	$0	$0	$0	$0	$ 50,000
Cash received from brother	$ 20,000	$0	$0	$0	$0	$0	$0	$0	$0	$0	$0	$0	$ 20,000
Cash received from mother	$ 10,000	$0	$0	$0	$0	$0	$0	$0	$0	$0	$0	$0	$ 10,000
Cash received from personal savings	$ 20,000	$0	$0	$0	$0	$0	$0	$0	$0	$0	$0	$0	$ 20,000
Net Cash Flow In from Financing	$100,000	$0	$0	$0	$0	$0	$0	$0	$0	$0	$0	$0	$100,000
Net Increase (Decrease) in Cash	$ 12,376	$ 825	($371)	($459)	($370)	($459)	($370)	($458)	($369)	($280)	($369)	($190)	9,574
Cash, Beginning:	$ 10,000	$22,376	$23,202	$22,831	$22,372	$22,002	$21,543	$21,174	$20,716	$20,346	$20,066	$19,698	$ 10,000
Cash, End:	$ 22,376	$23,202	$22,831	$22,372	$22,002	$21,543	$21,174	$20,716	$20,346	$20,066	$19,698	$19,508	$ 19,57

97. Calculate the burn rate for your business.

My burn rate is zero because I do not have a negative cash flow.

Intellectual Property

98. Describe any intellectual property you are developing for your business.

My intellectual property will be limited. I plan to create flyers and brochures. As my business grows I will pay a graphic designer to build a Web site for Oldies but Goodies.

99. How do you intend to protect your intellectual property? Explain why it qualifies for this protection.

I plan to have all of my written materials copyrighted. This will prevent other people from using what I have written without my permission.

Taxation

100. Which tax forms will you have to fill out for your business?

1040 U.S. Individual Tax Return ____✓____

Schedule C, Profit or Loss from Business ____✓____

Schedule SE, Self-Employment Tax ____✓____

Quarterly Sales and Use Tax Return ____✓____

Small Business and Government

101. Which laws—such as minimum wage and age requirements, health and safety regulations, or antidiscrimation laws—will affect your business?

Under the advice of my lawyer and accountant, I plan to obey all relevant employment laws.

Building Good Personal and Business Credit

102. My personal credit history is

Bad _____

Good _____

Not yet established ____✓____

103. Describe how you plan to establish good personal credit.

I will pay all of my personal bills on time. After I graduate I will owe debt for my student loans. I plan to pay my student loan balance off within five years of graduation.

104. My business credit history is

Bad _____

Good _____

Not yet established ____✓____

105. Describe how you plan to establish good business credit.

I will pay all of my business bills and suppliers on time. If Oldies but Goodies needs to use its line of credit

account, I will make sure to pay off the balance in full by the end of the month.

Your Balance Sheet

106. Create a Projected Balance Sheet for your business for one year.

Balance Sheet

	Opening	Closing
Assets		
Current Assets:		
Cash	$4,000	$16,375
Accounts Receivable	0	$0
Total Current Assets	**$4,000**	**$16,375**
Fixed Assets (Property and Equipment):		
Headphones	$100	$100
Additional Records for my collection	$150	$150
Blank CD Stock	$25	$25
Speakers	$500	$500
Protective Cases for Records	$150	$150
Amplifier	$550	$550
Total Property and Equipment	**$1,475**	**$1,475**
Less Accumulated Depreciation	**$0**	**$295**
Total Property and Equipment (Net)	**$1,475**	**$1,180**
Total Assets	**$5,475**	**$17,555**
LIABILITIES AND OWNER'S EQUITY		
Current Liabilities:		
Accounts Payable	$0	$0
Total Current Liabilities	**$0**	**$0**
Long-term Liability (Uncle Loan)	**$0**	**$0**
Total Liabilities	**$0**	**$0**
Owner's Equity	**$5,475**	**$17,555**
Total Liabilities and Owner's Equity	**$5,475**	**$17,555**

Franchising and Licensing

107. Do you plan to franchise your business, or license any of your products? Explain.

If my business succeeds, I will consider licensing the Oldies but Goodies brand name to other DJ services. Licensees will need to agree to Oldies but Goodies'

standards of musical genre, selection, and service excellence.

Exit Strategy

108. My exit strategy is

    to sell my business name and equipment to another entrepreneur who shares my love of music from the period and has outstanding DJ skills.

109. I think this exit strategy will be attractive to my potential investors because

    it will be easier to build upon an existing brand name than to start a new business.

110. For how much would you be willing to sell your business in three years? How will you calculate its value?

    If I achieve my goals of growing my business by 20 percent each year, this means that my sales revenue in year three will be about $52,000. I would attempt to sell my business for $150,000, or three times this amount.

Financial Planning

I plan to save at least 10 percent of my net income to achieve personal financial goals.

My primary financial goal is to save money for a down payment on a house and to pay off my college loans within the next five years.

My investment risk tolerance is medium-high. I am young (in my twenties) so even if my investments do not perform well in the short term, over the long run I expect to earn a healthy profit.

111. I will invest my savings as follows:

Current Cash Value	Investment Mix	Expected % ROI
Stocks $2,000	Stocks 40%	Stocks 8%
Bonds $2,000	Bonds 40%	Bonds 6%
Cash $1,000	Cash 20%	Cash 2%

112. My weighted average ROI is: **6%**

    $(.08 \times .40) + (.06 \times .40) + (.02 \times .20) = .032 + .024 + .004 = .06 = 6\%$

113. Using the Rule of 72, the number of years it will take my portfolio to double in value is: **72/6 = 12 years.**

Appendix 3 | Advanced Business Plan

Congratulations! If you've made it this far, you have given yourself a thorough education in entrepreneurship and you will have made progress toward writing a business plan that will impress potential investors and lenders.

At this point, you will probably want to revamp your business plan to reflect all that you have learned. Worksheets similar to the ones you have completed at the end of each unit are on the BizBuilders CD-ROM. Use them to create and print a hard copy of a professional-looking BizBuilders Business Plan. As you'll see below, the worksheets include all the business plan exercises from the book, as well as a projected balance sheet, financial ratios, and exit strategy planning. These features will make your plan a better roadmap for running your business and will make it more attractive to investors.

The BizBuilders CD-ROM also includes a PowerPoint template you can utilize to create a Business Plan Presentation. With a PowerPoint Business Plan Presentation, you can quickly show investors the highlights of your plan.

The BizBuilders Business Plan includes a section for students wishing to start a not-for-profit business. If you are starting a nonprofit, please fill out this section and adjust your business plan accordingly.

Business Pro software is also included with this book to give you another option for preparing your business plan. Explore Business Pro to see if it's a better fit for your business plan. Both the BizBuilders CD and the Business Pro CD can help you write a professional business plan.

» BizBuilder Business Plan Worksheet Questions

(See BizBuilder CD-ROM to fill in worksheets and create your business plan.)

Your Business Idea

1. Describe your business idea. What is the name of your business?
2. Explain how your business idea will satisfy a consumer need.
3. Provide contact information for each owner.
4. If there is more than owner, describe how the business ownership will be shared.

Economics of One Unit

5. Do you intend to pay yourself a salary, wage, dividend, or commission? Explain.
6. What type of business are you starting?
7. Calculate the "economics of one unit" for your business.

Evaluating Your Business Idea

8. What resources and skills do you (and the other owners) have that will help make your business successful?
9. Perform a SWOT analysis of your business.

Your Goals

Business Goals

1. What are your short-term business goals? (less than one year)
2. What are your long-term business goals? (from one to five years)

Technology

3. Identify which technological tools you plan to use for your business, and explain why.
4. Write a memo detailing how you plan to get access to the technology you need.

Core Beliefs

1. Describe three core beliefs you will use to run your company.

Supply and Demand

2. What factors influence the demand for your product or service?
3. What factors influence the supply for your product or service?

Competitive Advantage

4. What type of business are you starting—manufacturing, wholesale, retail, or service?
5. Describe your competitive advantage.
6. Find three competitors and describe them:

Competitor	Weaknesses	Strengths

International Opportunities

1. Are there customers for your business in other countries? How do you plan to reach them? **(Business Plan Practice)**
2. Describe any international competitors you have found who may be able to access your customers. How do you intend to compete? **(Business Plan Practice)**

Fixed Costs

3. List and describe your monthly fixed costs.

4. Add a cash reserve that covers three months of fixed costs.

Insurance

What types of insurance will your business need, and why? What is the highest deductible you feel you can afford?

Recordkeeping

1. Describe your recordkeeping system.

2. List any bank accounts you will open for your business.

3. Will you accept personal checks from customers? Credit cards? Will you offer charge accounts or customer credit?

Projected Income Statement

1. Complete a monthly projected budget and one-year income statement for your business.

2. Use your projected one-year income statement to calculate the following:

   Projected ROI for one year: _____%

   Projected ROS for one year: _____%

   Projected Payback for one year: _____%

Financing Strategy

1. List the items you will need to buy to start your business.

2. Add up the items to get your total start-up capital.

3. Add a cash reserve of one-half your total start-up capital.

4. List the sources of financing for your start-up capital. Identify each source as equity, debt, or gift. Indicate the amount and type for each source.

5. What is your debt ratio? What is your debt-to-equity ratio? Add a cash reserve of one-half your total start-up capital.

6. What is your payback period? In other words, how long will it take you to earn enough profit to cover start-up capital?

Raising Capital

1. Describe financing sources that might be willing to invest in your business in exchange for equity.

   Friends and family _____

   "Angels" _____

   MESBICs _____

   Other _____

2. Describe any debt financing you intend to pursue.

3. Do you plan to use bootstrap financing? Explain.

Venture Capital

1. Do you plan to pursue venture capital? Why, or why not?
2. List potential sources of venture capital.

Competitive Strategy

Use the following charts to define your business, analyze your competitive advantage, and determine your tactics.

1. Describe your strategy for outperforming the competition.
2. What tactics will you use to carry out this strategy?
3. Write a mission statement for your business in two sentences that clearly states your competitive advantage, strategy, and tactics.

Business Definition Question	Response
1. *The Offer:* What products and services will be sold by the business?	1.
2. *Target Market:* Which consumer segment will the business focus on?	2.
3. *Production Capability:* How will that offer be produced and delivered to those customers?	3.

Competitive Advantage Question	Competitive Difference
1. *The Offer:* What will be better and different about the products and services that will be sold by the business?	1.
2. *Target Market:* What customers should be the focus of the business, to make it as successful as possible?	2.
3. *Production and Delivery Capability:* What will be better or different about the way that offer is produced and delivered to those customers?	3.

Tactical Question	Issue	Solution
1. *Sales Plan:* Where and how will you sell to your customers?	How to identify prospects and convert them to sales.	
2. *Market Communications:* How will you communicate with your customers and make them aware of your business offer?	How to make customers aware of your offer; how to attract them to the business.	

Tactical Question	Issue	Solution
3. *Operating Plan:* How will you manage your internal operations?	How to make the business go and determine who will perform the tasks.	
4. *Budget:* How do you plan to manage your revenues and expenses?	What are the sources of revenue? What are the items that have to be purchased?	

Marketing Step One: Consumer Analysis

1. Describe your market research methods (surveys, focus groups, general research, statistical research).
2. Describe your target consumer:

   Age: _____

   Gender: _____

   Income: _____

   Other: _____

Marketing Step Two: Market Analysis

1. How large is your potential market?
2. Will you analyze your market segment by location, population, personality, or behavior?
3. Use your market analysis method to describe your market segment. Roughly how many consumers are in your market segment?
4. Explain how your marketing plan targets your market segment.
5. What percentage of the market do you feel you need to capture for your business to be profitable?
6. Who are the potential customers you plan to approach in the first two months of business?
7. Write a positioning statement for your business.
8. Where is your product/service in the product life cycle?

Marketing Step Three: The Marketing Mix

1. Explain how your product will meet a consumer need.
2. Describe your pricing strategy.
3. Where do you intend to sell your product? Describe the advantages and disadvantages of your location(s).
4. How do you plan to promote your business?
   (a) What is your business slogan? Do you have a logo for your business? How do you intend to protect it?
   (b) Where do you intend to advertise?
   (c) How do you plan to get publicity for your business?

Promotions	Door-to-Door	Online	Street	Store/Office	Other
800 number					
Billboards					
Brochures					
Business cards					
Catalog					
Demonstration					
Direct mail					
E-mail/fax					
Flyers					
Free gifts					
Online store					
Phone calls					
Posters					
Promo items					
Sales calls					
Samples					
Special events					
Web site					

5. How will your business help others? List all the organizations to which you plan to contribute. (Your contribution may be time, money, your product, or something else.)

6. Do you intend to publicize your philanthropy? Why, or why not? If you do, explain how you will work your philanthropy into your marketing.

» Marketing Mix Chart

My Market Segment: _____

Marketing Mix	Decision	Explanation
Product		
Price		
Place		
Promotion		
Philanthropy		

Marketing Step Four: Breakeven Analysis

Use Excel or Lotus 1-2-3 to create a spreadsheet projecting the marketing expenses for your business for six months. Use this data to perform a breakeven analysis of your marketing plan.

Sales and Customer Service

1. Describe the features and benefits of the product (or service) your business will focus on selling.
2. Choose three ways you plan to sell your product or service. Describe why you have chosen these three methods and why you think they will work.
3. Write a one-minute sales pitch for your product (or service).
4. Describe five sales prospects you intend to pitch.
5. Show examples of marketing materials you intend to use to sell.
6. List three ways you intend to provide superior customer service.
7. How will you keep your customer database? What five questions will you ask every customer for your database?

Legal Structure

1. What is your business's legal structure?
   Sole proprietorship _____
   Partnership _____
   Limited Partnership _____
   C Corporation _____
   Subchapter S _____
   Limited Liability Corporation _____
   Not-for-Profit Corporation _____
2. Why did you choose this legal structure?
3. Have you registered your business?
4. Have you applied for a sales-tax identification number?

» Manufacturing

1. What are the zoning laws in your area? Does your business comply?
2. Do you intend to manufacture your product? If so, describe the manufacturing process you will use. If not, describe how your product is manufactured.

Buying Wholesale

1. Where are you purchasing the products you plan to sell, or the parts you will use to manufacture those products?

2. Have you applied for a sales tax ID number?

Production-Distribution Chain

1. How do you plan to distribute your product to your target market?

2. Fill in the following to show the production-distribution channel for your business, and the markups along the chain.

    Manufacturer

    Name: _____

    Contact information: _____

    Markup: $ _____

    Markup percentage: _____%

    Wholesaler

    Name: _____

    Contact information: _____

    Markup: $ _____

    Markup percentage: _____ %

    Retailer (you)

    Markup: $ _____

    Markup percentage: _____ %

3. What is the estimated delivery time between when you place an order with your supplier and when you will have the product available for your customers?

Contracts

1. What is the most important contract you will need to run your business?

2. Describe any additional contracts you have or plan to secure.

3. Who is your attorney?

Human Resources

1. Fill out a PERT chart for your business.

2. Will you be hiring employees? If so, describe what their qualifications should be, what you intend to pay them, and how they will help your business.

3. Provide contact information for your accountant, attorney, banker, and insurance agent.

4. What will your policies toward employees be? How will you make your business a positive and rewarding place to work?

5. Create an organizational chart for your business.

Ethical Business Behavior

1. Describe the corporate governance plan for your company. It should include five policies (rules) that will be the backbone of your company's ethics.

2. Provide information for each of your mentors or advisors. If there is a board of advisors, list each member and describe his/her commitment to the board.

Socially Responsible Business

1. Choose three ways you plan to run a socially responsible business.

   Recycling paper, glass, or plastic _____

   Donating a portion of profits to a charity _____

   No animal testing of products _____

   Offering employees incentives to volunteer in the community _____

   Establishing a safe and healthy workplace _____

   Other _____

   _____

Cash Flow

1. Create a projected cash flow statement for your business for one year.

2. Calculate the burn rate for your business.

Taxation

What tax forms will you have to fill out for your business?
   1040 U.S. Individual Tax Return _____
   Schedule C, Profit or Loss from Business _____
   Schedule SE, Self-Employment Tax _____
   Quarterly Sales and Use Tax Return _____

Small Business and Government

What laws—such as minimum wage and age requirements, health and safety regulations, or antidiscrimination laws—will affect your business?

Your Balance Sheet

1. Create a Projected Balance Sheet for your business for one year. **(Business Plan Practice)**

2. Create a pie chart showing your current assets, long-term assets, current liabilities, and long-term liabilities. **(Business Plan Practice)**

3. What is your debt ratio?

4. What is your debt-to-equity ratio?

Franchising and Licensing

Do you plan to franchise your business, or license any of your products? Explain.

Stocks

1. Who will be the partners or stockholders for your company?
2. If your business is incorporated, describe what percentage of the company is owned by one share of stock.
3. Is your corporation's stock publicly or privately held?

Bonds

1. Do you intend to use debt to finance your business? Explain. (Refer to Raising Capital Section.)
2. Do you plan to issue bonds to finance your business at some point in the future?

Exit Strategy

1. My exit strategy is _____
   _____

2. I think this strategy would be attractive to my potential investors because_____
   _____

Financial Planning

1. I plan to save _____ percent of my net income to achieve personal financial goals.
2. My primary financial goal is _____.
3. My investment risk tolerance is _____.
4. I will invest my savings as follows:

Current Cash Value	Investment Mix
Stocks $_____	Stocks_____%
Bonds $_____	Bonds_____%
Cash $_____	Cash_____%

5. My weighted average ROI is_____
6. Using the Rule of 72, the number of years it will take my portfolio to double is _____.

If you are starting a not-for-profit business:

1. What is the name of your nonprofit?
2. What problem(s) are you trying to solve?
3. Describe the mission of your organization.

4. Describe the programs and services you plan to create.
5. How will your organization achieve the changes you intend to bring about?
6. What is the unit of change (per person, animal, house, etc.)?
7. How will you measure these changes?
8. Who are your competitors?
9. How much will it cost you to deliver a unit of service?
10. What are your sources of funding?

Grants (Which foundations? How much?):

#	Foundation	Amount
1		
2		
3		
4		
5		

Individual (Who? How much?):

#	Name	Amount
1		
2		
3		
4		
5		

Earned Income (What are your sources of revenue? How much revenue from each source?):

#	Source	Amount
1		
2		
3		
4		
5		

Appendix 4

Business Plan for *Venture* Magazine*

»Summary of Program

This is a plan for a new monthly, general business magazine, called "*Venture* . . . the magazine for entrepreneurs." Included in this plan are a description of the editorial concept, a review of the market for readers and advertisers, and operating plans for the magazine.

Venture will be edited for three principal groups of readers:

- *Existing entrepreneurs*—the owners and managers of entrepreneurial businesses
- *Potential entrepreneurs*—executives and managers of large corporations interested in owning their own businesses
- *Corporate entrepreneurs*—executives and managers of large corporations who perceive their job function as one that requires them to think and operate entrepreneurially

These three groups contain over 10 million potential readers. A quality magazine edited specifically for the entrepreneur does not exist. *Venture's* target audience represents a substantial market for the sale of magazines and advertising for business and consumer products.

Venture's operating plan projects a paid circulation rate basis of 80,000 for the premier issue. The goal of the operating plan is to expand circulation to 320,000 within five years.

The attached exhibits contain projections of management with respect to total investment required and profits. As stated in "Risk Factors," no assurance can be given that these projections will be achieved.

Joseph D. Giarraputo (the "General Partner") offers interests in a limited partnership to be organized under the laws of the State of New York and to be known as The *Venture* Publishing Company (the "Partnership"). Purchasers of such interests will be referred to herein as Limited Partners.

The Limited Partners will contribute the entire capital of the Partnership, and the General Partner will contribute the concept for the magazine. The Limited Partners in the aggregate will receive a 15.0625 percent profit sharing interest in the Partnership, and the General Partner will receive a 84.9375 percent profit-sharing interest. Without the consent of any of the other Partners, the General Partner may raise additional capital by selling additional Limited Partnership Interests in the Partnership up to a maximum amount, including the amount subscribed for hereunder, of $90,000. The sale of these Partnership In-

*Reprinted with permission from Joe Marcuso.

terests shall not dilute the Partnership Interests of the Limited Partners but only that of the General Partner. Thereafter, the General Partner may not raise capital in excess of such amount by selling additional Limited Partnership Interests without the consent of Partners holding in the aggregate a 50 percent Partnership Interest in the Partnership.

Each Limited Partner will receive a capital account equal to the amount of his subscription.

The Partnership will be formed for the purpose of developing and conducting a mailing to test the feasibility of founding a business magazine called "*Venture* . . . the magazine for entrepreneurs." A positive response to the test mailing in excess of 2 percent would generally be required before advancing to the next stage of the magazine's development. If the response falls below this, the project will in all probability be abandoned, and no salvage value is anticipated.

If the test is successful, the next step will be to prepare for the start of regular publication of the magazine, which will involve recruiting a staff, selling advertising, establishing relations with suppliers, commencing direct mail promotion, and raising a substantial amount of additional capital (see "Prepublication Phase").

It is projected that the proceeds of the sale of interests in the Partnership will be expended approximately in the following manner.

Direct Mail Test	
(80,000 pieces)	$24,000
Direct Mail	
Advertising Agency	$ 4,000
Office and Travel	$ 2,250
Magazine Design	$ 1,750
Legal	$ 3,000
	$35,000

Interests in the Partnership will not be registered with the Securities and Exchange Commission. The Partnership is relying on an exemption from registration for the sale of securities, which do not involve a public offering. Accordingly, each purchaser will be required to agree that his purchase was not made with any present intention to resell, distribute, or in any way transfer or dispose of his interest in the Partnership, except in compliance with applicable securities laws, and that he meets the suitability standards described herein.

No person is authorized to give any information or representation not contained in this memorandum. Any information or representation not contained herein must not be relied upon as having been authorized by the Partnership or the General Partner.

≫ Risk Factors

Projections. This Prospectus contains certain financial projections. Although no representations can be made that the circulation or advertising levels indicated by the projections will be achieved or that projected costs or cash flow will correspond even approximately to actual costs or cash flow, those projections reflect the current estimates of management of the results that are likely if circulation or advertising can be increased and the costs controlled as reflected herein. These projections are subject to the uncertainties inherent in any attempt to predict the results of operations for the next five years, especially where a new business is involved.

Additional Capital. Assuming the test projections are successful and publication of the magazine is commenced, it is estimated that at least $1 million of new capital will be required before positive cash flow is achieved. There are no commitments for any of these funds, and no assurances can be given that such funds will be available, and if available, no prediction can be made of the terms and conditions of such additional financing. Partners in the Partnership will be given the right to participate in this additional financing. To the extent this right is not exercised, a substantial dilution of the Partners' interest will probably result.

Staff. *To* commence publication of the new magazine, it will be necessary to recruit a new staff. A full staff has not yet been recruited, and no assurance can be given that a qualified staff can be hired on reasonable terms.

Taxation. For the tax treatment of gains or losses to Limited Partners of the Partnership, see "Federal Income Tax Consequences."

General Risk. Starting a new magazine is a highly speculative undertaking and has historically involved a substantial degree of risk. The ultimate profitability of any magazine depends on its appeal to its readers and advertisers in relation to the cost of production, circulation, and distribution. Appeal to readers and advertisers is impossible to predict and depends upon the interaction of many complex factors.

Competition. The magazine business is highly competitive. In promoting the sale of *Venture,* management will be competing with many established companies having substantially greater financial resources.

Suitability. Because of the lack of liquidity of an investment in this program and the high degree of risk involved, the purchase of limited partnership interests of the Partnership should be considered only by persons who can afford a total loss of their investment.

»Editorial Concept

Venture will be a magazine for entrepreneurs—real ones, would-be ones, corporate ones. It will illuminate the world of new *Ventures* in all its aspects for the 10 million businessmen who are entrepreneurs or have aspirations to be, and the millions more who in the future increasingly will be "running their own businesses" within larger corporations. It is a discrete assemblage with an identity and common interests that are all but ignored by today's major business publications.

Venture will appeal to an influential, upwardly mobile readership. While "business" has its detractors as well as adherents, the entrepreneur retains an admirable image with almost everyone. As a risk-taker, his business *Venture* is one of the closest approximations of true adventure our civilized society offers. Even his success is seldom envied, for it is a reminder to the rest of the world that rags to riches stories are still possible. Dropouts from the corporate world they may be, but entrepreneurs build new worlds in their own image. They are fascinating subjects.

Furthermore, the time for *Venture* is propitious. There is a growing realization that "big will not work." The efficiencies of scale of large organizations, predicated upon planning the actions of everyone from the top, may have peaked. Today, even workers on assembly lines balk at becoming unthinking robots. It is hardly surprising then that managers want to be creators, not mindless functionaries. It is a time when entrepreneurship will flourish inside the large company as well as in the new *Venture*.

Venture will be the month-by-month chronicle of that world and the personalities who inhabit it. It will be Edwin Land (Polaroid), Ross Perot (Electronic Data Systems), Mary Wells Lawrence (Wells Rich Greene), but *Venture* also will be today's climbers who will be tomorrow's celebrities.

It can be Ken Walker, 35, whose master's degree from Harvard is in architecture, not business, a museum-quality painter turned entrepreneur, whose five-year-old design firm, Walker/Grad, is currently handling $20 million in construction money and who is wondering how fast he should continue to grow.

It can be Jim Sheridan, businessman turned designer. A former vice president of Bankers Trust, Sheridan purchased a design firm (Raymond Loewy) last summer and expects to double its volume by the end of the current fiscal year.

It can be Bruce Westwood, 36, vice president of a venture capital firm that put $1 million into a Canadian-based soft-drink firm, who then joined the venture as its president and took it to $27 million in sales, with planned expansion just beginning.

It can be Joe Camp, who learned the film business by producing the feature film *Benji* with $550,000 of borrowed money. *Variety* called it 1975's third largest grosser.

Venture will make an impact on the business of its times. It will unashamedly espouse the cause of the entrepreneur as an alternative to corporate gigantism. Entrepreneurs will be portrayed realistically, warts and all, but the image of success will never be more than a page or two away.

Venture will be a mosaic of news, gossip, and need-to-know information. Personalities, trends, and "how to" will be interwoven in a fashion that will entertain as well as, instruct.

The core of *Venture* will be its feature articles. The format—appropriate for a monthly—will be flexible enough to allow articles, which will be written with style and wit, to run their proper length, whether one page or ten. But each must justify itself as topical and newsy, not merely instructional and significant.

Subjects will include management, financing, how-to-get-started, risks, and rewards.

The relationship between government and entrepreneurial business also will be a frequent area of exploration. Much in the system today mitigates against the fledgling entrepreneur and to the advantage of the large corporation, which often in turn seems to subvert the very nature of a free market system. We will expose attempts to erect unwarranted barriers in the way of new *Ventures* and will speak out strongly against them.

While features will comprise most of *Venture's* editorial columns, each issue will include regular departments, front and back, to give the magazine a familiar look and "feel."

One will be a news section, with a small-column format and staccato news items on People (making it, trying to make it, and going bust); Legislation; Taxes; New Ventures; Franchises.

Other regular stand-alone departments will be Books; Letters; Rewards (a feature showing how to spend the big bucks that our upscale readers will aspire to, and presenting the life styles of successful entrepreneurs); You and Your _____ (Banker, Consultant, Backer, Accountant, Lawyer, Right-hand Man), a feature on building relationships with the entrepreneur's various associates; Capitalists (a regular feature on what the money men are up to and the kinds of *Ventures* they are looking for); Franchises (a rating of opportunities); and How to Start a _____ (Restaurant, Resort, Tennis Club).

Sample tables of contents of issues show more specifically how *Venture's* concept can be translated into a provocative and entertaining magazine.

Contents: Month I

Letters

Newspage

(Sample lead items):

People: Clay Felker, sadder but surely wiser, starts over . . .

Legislation: Going public? The SEC's fuller-disclosure rules could put you at a competitive disadvantage . . .

Taxes: Backers of Broadway musicals find tax shelter benefits as well as glamour . . .

New *Ventures:* Former banker Jim Sheridan's design company is booming . . .

Franchises: The biggest growth will be in recreation, travel, and entertainment . . .

Features:

Who says technology ventures are passé? Take the case of Frederick Adler, who made $6 million on Data General and is busy incubating a host of companies with names like Lexidata that may make him millions more. Shades of '69?

The second time around. Entrepreneurs do not always make it on their first attempt, but almost 3 out of 4 try again if they fail. Here are 6 who came back from disasters to succeed the second time around.

A Venture Capital Paradise—Santa Clara. In all, some 150 *Venture* capitalists live and work in Santa Clara county, California, a place that offers everything entrepreneurs need to succeed. Already more than 100 company founders have become millionaires there and many are not yet 35 years old.

Seymour Cray: His plans are ambitious. Cray already is famous in his field as the original technical genius behind William Morris Control Data Corporation. Now his own Cray Research, Inc. plans nothing less than dominance of the scientific computer market. Cray is contributing his talents— and $1 million of his own money—but he still will be lucky to hold on to two percent of this potential giant.

Half-way House. Corporate executives (at General Mills, GE, and Exxon, among others) sometimes have the chance to act more like entrepreneurs than some of the real ones—and occasionally reap the same kind of rewards.

You do not have to go public to make money. A package of subordinated debentures, convertible preferred, and equity will tide you over in a bad-market pinch.

Franchising's golden dozen. Franchise volume is soaring with sales expected to total $179 billion by 1980. On average, however, sales at individual establishments are abysmally low. Still, the winning industries are well worth your attention.

Departments

Books: *The Entrepreneur's Manual*, Richard M. White, Jr. (Chilton, $15)

Rewards: *The Sporting Life.* Lamar Hunt's professional sports enterprise football, soccer, tennis among others—allow him to live very well indeed. (Who else could have afforded to buy Jim Ling's $3 million chateau?) It also helps that daddy was a billionaire.

You and Your *Lawyer*

Capitalists: *Personality Test. Venture* firms have their own ideas about what kind of personality profile an entrepreneur should have. It is okay to be a misfit but, yes, these days to get a stake you have to be a super guy.

Franchises: McDonald's vs. Burger King

How to Start a *Magazine*

Contents: Month 2

Letters

Newspage

(Sample lead items):

People: Donald Cook, who made plenty of waves as CEO at American Electric Power, is running Lazard Freres' *Venture* capital fund his own way . . .

Legislation: What you hear is true—the Pension Reform Act is hurting companies without records of success . . .

Taxes: The new laws opened as well as closed some loopholes: Shelters today . . .

New *Ventures:* A California book publisher is making money by breaking all the rules . . .

Franchises: Pyramiding, Bait-and-Switch, Sound-Alikes, and other frauds to watch for . . .

Features:

Advice to Corporate Minnows: Being swallowed by a whale isn't all bad. In these times a merger with a larger partner may be the easiest way for backers to turn over their investments. A look at some marriages made in heaven.

Ross Perot: Adjusting to a billion dollar paper loss. But before you pass the hat for him, remember he still has a quarter of a billion left.

The "Entrepreneurial Center." Can these B-School adjuncts—at Wharton, SMU and elsewhere—really show you the ropes in venturing?

The winners are . . . Here is a selling point for your *Venture:* A $1,000 flyer in companies going public can produce some startling dividends if you are lucky. Look at the record. You could have missed Xerox and still be a winner. A 1955 investment of $1,000 in the first public offering of Gearhart Owens, for example, would be worth more than $1 million today.

The small business administration: Getting smaller. Its help for entrepreneurs is shrinking along with everybody else's.

And with the left hand . . . Some of the fastest-stepping managers in some of the largest corporations are doing their own thing on the side. Cases in point: Heinz President Tony O'Reilly, who has his ups and downs with his Irish enterprises and City Investing Executive Vice President Peter Huang, who may soon be cashing in some chips.

How to survive in spite of contract law. Lawyers think every sloppily drawn contract results in a legal battle. Do not believe it. Remember, as an entrepreneur you cannot always afford the legal protection your lawyer says is "Minimal."

Departments

Books: *Running Your Own Business,* Howard H. Stern (Ward Ritchie, $4.95 paper)

Rewards: *Working couple.* Does Mary Wells Lawrence really need a house in the south of France, a ranch in New Mexico, a hideaway in Acapulco, a mansion in Dallas, and an apartment in New York? No. But with her own ad agency she can afford it. Husband Harding Lawrence, Chairman of Braniff, is no slouch in the take-home-pay department either.

You and Your *Banker*

Capitalists: *Sometimes everything is relative.* Face it—first-stage financing isn't apt to come from *Venture* capitalists. But your family and friends are there for the asking.

Franchises: Rating the muffler shops

How to Start an *Art Gallery*

»The Potential Market for *Venture* Readers

Venture will attract its readership primarily from these groups:

- Existing entrepreneurs
- Potential entrepreneurs
- Corporate entrepreneurs

All of its readers will not be businessmen, however. Subscribers will include doctors, dentists, lawyers, government officials, educators, students, and foreign readers with an interest in entrepreneurship.

But existing, potential, and corporate entrepreneurs represent in themselves a large enough group to support a magazine the size of *Venture*. The section that follows, The Circulation Plan, will show how management presently intends to market to these groups.

Existing Entrepreneurs. The number of entrepreneurs is inferred from the number of entrepreneurial businesses or those in which the managers have an equity interest.

We shall assume a business with less than $50 million in revenue is entrepreneurial. Although some larger businesses also are entrepreneurial and some smaller are not, most businesses of this size are entrepreneurial. There are several sources of data on the number of businesses by their size.

The Internal Revenue Service reports there are approximately 13 million proprietorships, partnerships, and corporations in the United States. Most of these businesses are very small and had annual sales of less than $100,000, These very small businesses, while probably entrepreneurial, are not considered a part of the prime market for *Venture* magazine. *Venture* will be too sophisticated for most of this group and it is not the segment of the market *Venture's* advertisers would find most attractive.

Rather than appeal to very small businesses, the existing entrepreneurs *Venture* will seek will be in middle-size businesses. These are businesses with sales of less than $50 million but more than $100,000 for proprietorships and partnerships, and more than $500,000 for corporations. According to the IRS there are approximately 1.1 million businesses in this size range. If it is assumed each of these 1.1 million businesses has three potential readers (an owner and two management-level employees) *Venture's* potential market among existing entrepreneurs would total 3.3 million.

U.S. Commerce Department data, which ranks businesses by number of employees, indicates the number of existing entrepreneurs in *Venture's* prime audience range is closer to 4 million.

That the universe of middle-size and smaller businesses is a potential market for *Venture* circulation may be inferred from data provided by other general-interest publications.

- *Dun's Review* indicates that 55 percent, or 124,000, of its subscribers are from companies with fewer than 1,000 employees.

- *Forbes* indicates that 54 percent, or 346,000, of its subscribers are from companies with fewer than 1,000 employees.

- *Executive Newsweek* indicates that 48 percent, or 239,000, of its subscribers are from companies with sales of less than $50 million.

- *Fortune* indicates that 256,000 of its subscribers are with companies employing fewer than 1,000 people—185,000 are with companies employing fewer than 100 people.

Thus, the total market of entrepreneurial owners and managers is large, and subscription to general business magazines is significant.

The Potential Entrepreneur Market. It is difficult to develop any accurate estimate of the number of potential entrepreneurs. The urge and ambition to become an entrepreneur is wide-spread. Each man's motivation is uniquely his own. One man may be pushed toward entrepreneurship by problems in his present job, while another may be attracted by the chance to make a fortune. Whatever their motivation, potential entrepreneurs undoubtedly outnumber actual entrepreneurs many times over.

However, *Venture* will not attempt to appeal to the entire universe of potential entrepreneurs. Again, the sophistication of the magazine and the reader characteristics advertisers will require preclude this approach. *Venture* will aim at those potential entrepreneurs who are currently executives or managers in large nonentrepreneurial businesses and institutions. These individuals will be equipped to understand the editorial content of *Venture* and, as business decision makers, will be attractive prospects for *Venture* advertisers.

The Corporate Entrepreneur Market. A corporate entrepreneur works in a large corporation as an executive or senior manager. He perceives that success in his job requires him to be able to function entrepreneurially. Specific jobs these corporate entrepreneurs currently fill are varied. Many of them are merger and acquisition specialists, managers who are leading their companies into new businesses and markets. Most profit center managers also envision themselves as entrepreneurs. They are responsible for bringing together many varied resources and orchestrating them into a successful operation. Profit center managers can be presidents of the largest corporations or managers of sales regions.

Many people in the United States fill managerial and executive positions. U.S. census figures indicate that there are more than 9 million people in such positions. The actual number of these managers who will subscribe to *Venture* can only be determined in the direct mail test. However, for editorial and advertising reasons, *Venture* will probably appeal to upper- and middle management corporate entrepreneurs.

»Reaching the Market for Readers: Circulation Plan

Circulation marketing tests, which will be conducted during the first phase of operations, will determine the exact course of the circulation program, but a general description of a plan can be presented.

Venture will be marketed through both subscription and single copy, or newsstand, sales. Subscriptions, however, are expected to account for the predominant share of *Venture's* circulation. It is expected that 90 percent of the magazine's circulation will result from subscriptions. The objective of the Circulation Plan is to attempt to sell approximately 220,000 new subscriptions during *Venture's* first two years of operation. The projected sources of these subscriptions are as follows:

	% Of New Subscriptions
Direct Mail	73%
Reply Cards	12
Catalogue & School Agents	10
Exchange Advertising	4
White Mail	1
	100%

Direct Mail. During the test phase, a direct mail probe of 80,000 pieces will be made. This probe will determine the most responsive mailing lists, copy, and price offers. The types of lists that will be considered for testing include:

- Dun & Bradstreet—particularly those segments of the list selectable by size of business.
- *Business Week, Nation's Business,* and other general interest business publications.
- *Board Room Reports* and other more specific business publications.
- Lists of mail order buyers of self-help business books and other business products.
- Lists of MBAs, GaAs, and certain attorneys.
- Lists of members of organizations such as The Jaycees and National Association of Independent Businessmen.
- Lists of owners and managers of specific types of businesses that fall within *Venture's* size requirements, such as auto dealers, business consultants, and building contractors.

Reply Cards. A significant source of subscribers is expected to be from offers in *Venture* magazine itself. Every issue of *Venture* magazine, newsstand and subscription, will contain a bind-in and blow-in offer for *Venture* magazine. Several successful publishers have made these inserts their most profitable source of new subscriptions.

Catalogue and School Agents.

Subscription agencies are organizations which, for a fee, sell subscriptions to many magazines. They can be useful in building a new magazine's circulation. Past experience indicates that two types of agents produce better revenue and advertising prospects than others. These are catalogue agents, which sell primarily to libraries, and school agents, which sell primarily through students as a fundraising device. *Venture* is expected to use both of these types of agencies in its initial years to gain exposure and build circulation levels.

Exchange Advertising. Another significant source of new orders is expected to be through subscription offers in other general business and trade magazines. This can be a relatively inexpensive method of obtaining subscribers. *Venture* need not pay rate card prices for advertisements in other magazines. Instead of paying cash, it may be possible for *Venture* to trade its own advertising space. (This is a common practice among publishers.) Particularly good sources can be other general business publications. Tests will also be conducted of selected trade publications to determine their responsiveness.

White Mail. Every established magazine receives unsolicited requests for subscriptions. While these will not represent a large portion of the magazine's circulation, they are still very valuable as they require no promotional expenditures.

Several other potential sources of profitable subscriptions for *Venture* have not been included in the projections. All these additional sources have been profitably employed by other publishers. They include the following:

- *Paid Space.* This entails buying advertising in other publications to promote subscriptions.

- *Airline Distribution.* Selected magazines are able to obtain 10,000 to 20,000 subscriptions annually from distribution through airlines. It would appear that *Venture's* editorial content would make it an attractive prospect for this type of distribution.

- *Co-ops.* There are currently in existence several executive co-op mailings. These are mailings, for a variety of products, to groups of business executives. Obviously a magazine like *Venture* could be included in one of these promotions.

- *Sponsored Sales.* Several magazines have successfully worked with organizations in the sale of subscriptions.

Venture could enter into arrangements with organizations such as The Junior Chamber of Commerce or The National Association of Independent Businessmen for the sponsorship of subscription sales.

Shows and Exhibits. Several magazines have been successful selling subscriptions at shows and exhibits related to the editorial concept of the magazine, e.g., a boating magazine at a boat show. Most major cities have an annual start-your-own-business show. It is possible that a subscription booth at these shows would be a profitable source of subscriptions for *Venture*.

While subscriptions from these sources are not included in the projections, there will be continuing attempts to create new profitable sources of subscriptions.

Under the Circulation Plan, *Venture* will attempt to attract about 10 percent of its circulation from newsstand sales. Newsstands can produce profitable sales and newsstand profits can be enhanced by responses to insert offers. *Venture's* operating plan projects total paid circulation of 80,000 for its premier issue—77,000 from subscriptions and 3,000 from newsstand. The goal of the operating plan is to expand circulation to 320,000 within five years—293,000 from subscriptions and 27,000 from newsstand.

»Advertising Plan

Efforts to sell advertising will be directed at a wide range of marketers of business and consumer products and services. *Venture's* editorial environment and reader demographics are expected to make it a desirable forum for those companies currently advertising in other general business publications.

The annual advertising revenue in general business publications is substantial and growing. Publishers Information Bureau (PIB) collects information on advertising revenue of most major magazines. According to PIB, advertising revenue for the general business publications it measures increased from $98 million in 1974 to $101 million in 1975. This represented a 3 percent increase.

General Business Magazines Advertising and Revenue: January–December

	Pages		Revenue (000)	
	1975	1974	1975	1974
Black Enterprise	401	373	$ 3,070	$ 2,787
Business Week	3405	3,698	52,946	51,286
Dun's Review	713	883	3,028	3,321
Forbes	1464	1432	14,901	13,775
Fortune	1432	1679	21,799	23,113
Harvard Business Review	214	246	706	690
Nation's Business	371	297	4,178	3,097
TOTAL	**8,000**	**8,608**	**$100,628**	**$ 98,069**

The general economy and the magazine industry did not experience a particularly good year in 1975. Total advertising in all types of magazines actually declined during the year. General business magazines, however, were able to show an increase in spite of the industry decline. With the recovery of the economy, 1976 developed into an extremely good advertising year for general business publications. PIB data for January through December 1976 issues of the measured magazines follows.

Advertising Pages and Revenue

	Pages			Revenue (000)		
	1976	1975	*Increase*	1976	1975	*Increase*
Black Enterprise	443	401	10%	$ 3,398	$ 3,070	11%
Business Week	3,925	3,405	15	67,428	52,946	27
Dun's Review	727	713	2	3,315	3,028	9
Forbes	1,757	1,464	20	19,452	14,901	31
Fortune	1,599	1,432	12	26,687	21,799	22
Harvard Business Review	274	214	28	927	706	31
Nation's Business	404	371	9	5,054	4,178	21
TOTAL	9,129	8,000	14%	$126,261	$ 100,628	25%

PIB indicates a 25 percent increase in advertising revenue for this group of publications in 1976. Current projections for 1977 call for continued substantial increases in advertising revenue. Advertising revenue for general business magazines actually increased by 24 percent during the first seven months of 1977.

The categories of advertisers that will be attracted to *Venture* magazine will be similar to those currently advertising in existing general business publications. During 1975, advertisers in general business publications were in the following product categories.

PIB Measured Business Publications: 1975 Advertising by Classification

	.0	%
Consumer Services	29,166	29.0
Industrial Materials	20,072	20.0
Office Equip., Stationery, & Writing Supplies	11,936	11.8
Freight	6,349	6.2
Automotive	6,249	6.2
Insurance	4,408	4.4
Travel, Hotels, Resorts	4,357	4.4
Beer, Wine, Liquor	2,904	2.9
Building Materials	2,838	2.8
Publishing, Other Media[*]	2,423	2.4
Aviation, Accessories\Gasoline, Lubricants	2,245	2.2
Gasoline, Lubricants	1,669	1.7

Optical Goods, Cameras	745	0.8
Smoking Materials	641	0.6
Household Equipment, Supplies	587	0.6
Consumer Electronics, TV, etc.	305	0.3
Retail and/or Direct Mail	256	0.3
Sporting Goods, Toys	224	0.2
Food, Food Products	191	0.2
Entertainment, Amusement	122	0.1
Apparel, Footwear, Accessories	109	0.1
All Other	2,820	2.8
	100,616	**100.0**

Black Enterprise, Business Week, Dun's Review, Forbes, Fortune, Harvard Business Review, Nation's Business

The top five classifications of advertisers account for over 70 percent of the total revenue in this market.

Individual advertisers in these top five categories are expected to be *Venture's* prime advertising prospects. Included in these five classifications are banks, brokers, credit cards, communications, computers, office machines, metals, papers, chemicals, foreign and domestic cards, and air, sea, and land carriers.

Among the categories of advertisers selling business products and services, *Venture* may prove to be an excellent medium for those with a special interest in reaching decision makers in medium-size and smaller businesses.

Because its editorial content is oriented toward the individual, *Venture* may be able to compete effectively with general business publications for advertisers of personal consumer products. These categories include automotive, travel, hotels, resorts, beer, wine, and liquor.

Venture's advertising plan calls for obtaining a .06 percent share of the general business magazine advertising market in 1978 and expanding this to a 1.9 percent market share in 1982. If one assumes that this market will grow at a 7 percent annual rate, projected advertising revenues would be as follows:

» *Venture's* Advertising Share

Venture's Advertising Share ($000)

		All General Business	
	Venture	Magazines	*Venture* Share
1978	$ 87.7	$ 143,112	0.06%
1979	487.7	153,130	0.3
1980	1223.0	163,849	0.7
1981	2240.7	175,319	1.3
1982	3607.8	187,591	1.9

»Operational Plan

The Operational Plan for *Venture* is divided into three phases:

1. Testing and Financing
2. Prepublication
3. Publication

Testing and Financing Phase. The major objectives of this phase will be (1) a direct mail test of consumer acceptance of the magazine, and (2) obtaining the capital required to launch the publication and carry it through its initial years. This phase is expected to last from approximately October 1977 through May 1978.

A major portion of *Venture's* subscriptions are expected to be obtained from direct mail promotions. Future response to a direct mail promotion can be tested and predicted with a high degree of accuracy. A direct mail test is planned for December 1977. This mailing will be sent to approximately 80,000 names. The test will attempt to determine the following:

- The validity of the concept
- The most effective copy approaches
- The most productive price at which to offer subscriptions

An experienced direct mail circulation advertising agency has been engaged to plan, execute, and evaluate the direct mail test.

Also during this phase, sources of the capital required to launch the magazine will be contacted and exposed to *Venture* as an investment opportunity.

The expected cost of this phase is $35,000.

Test and Financing Phase Costs

Direct Mail Test (80,000 pieces)	$24,000
Direct Mail Advertising Agency	4,000
Office & Travel	2,250
Magazine Design	1,750
Legal	3,000
	$35,000

Prepublication Phase. After the Testing and Financing Phase has been completed, all information gathered will be carefully evaluated. If this evaluation leads to a decision to proceed with *Venture,* the project will enter a seven-month Prepublication Phase.

During the Prepublication Phase, work will begin in earnest on the actual launch of the magazine. The decision to publish will have been made, the financing obtained, and a substantial portion of the required capital will be committed. The major activities occurring during this period will be:

1. Building the staff
2. Dropping a major direct mail subscription promotion
3. Creating a dummy and initial issues of the magazine
4. Selling advertising
5. Establishing relationships with outside suppliers

1. ***Building the Staff.*** Ideally, the key staff members will be on the job at the start of the Prepublication period, with the remainder of the staff hired during the second, third, and fourth months. *Venture* will be located in New York City. There should be no problem in finding qualified professionals in New York to fill required positions.

2. ***Direct Mail Promotion.*** Current plans call for a direct mail drop in September 1978 of 1.7 million pieces. The preparation of this major promotion will be handled by *Venture's* staff, with the assistance of experienced direct mail advertising agency.

3. ***Creating a Dummy and Initial Issues.*** A dummy, or prototype, of the actual magazine will be required to sell advertising and assist the editorial staff in planning the eventual publication. The dummy will be created by the *Venture* editorial staff. An experienced design consultant will be used to develop the actual look of the magazine.

   Correspondents will be engaged in key areas. Relationships will be developed with qualified free-lance writers and artists. Story and feature ideas will be developed and assigned to staff editors or freelancers. The first issues of *Venture* will be made ready for the printer.

4. ***Selling Advertising.*** Prime potential advertisers will be identified from the lists of the largest advertisers in other general business publications. Sales approaches will be developed. Pricing strategies will be finalized. Sales calls will be made on advertisers and their agencies by the publisher, sales force, and, where indicated, the editor.

5. ***Establishing Relationships with Suppliers.*** Arrangements will be negotiated with printers, typesetters, fulfillment houses, newsstand distributors, subscription agents, and other necessary suppliers.

Publication Phase. The Publication Phase will begin when the first issue of *Venture* is mailed to subscribers in January 1979. Previous sections of this proposal have described plans for the editorial, advertising, and circulation of the magazine.

Reference is made to the exhibits herein for certain financial projections.

Competition. Venture's direct competition is expected to come from the existing general business magazines. These magazines are established and, for the most part, well financed. Comparisons between these publications and projections for *Venture* follow.

» *Venture* Compared to Other Publications

Competitive Data Advertising Rates

Publication	Rate Base		One-Time B/W Page	C P M
Black Enterprise	215		$ 6,190	$ 28.79
Business Week	765		12,940	16.92
Dun's Review	225		4,195	18.64
Forbes	650		9,450	14.54
Fortune	625		12,555	20.09
Harvard Business Review	165		3,170	19.21
Nation's Business	1,030		9,575	9.30
TOTAL	**80**		**$1200**	**$ 15.00**

Subscription and Single Copy Rates

Publication	Issues per Year	One-Year Subscription Price	Subscription Price Per Issue	Single Copy Price
Black Enterprise	12	$ 10.00	$ .83	$ 1.00
Business Week	52	21.50	.41	1.00
Dun's Review	12	12.00	1.00	1.50
Forbes	24	18.00	.75	1.00 – 1.50
Fortune	12	18.00	1.50	2.00
Harvard Business Review	6	18.00	3.00	3.50
Nation's Business	12	13.50	1.13	1.25
Venture	12	12.00		
TOTAL	**8,000**	**8,608**	**$1.00**	**$ 1.25**

»The People Involved

The following people are expected to be involved with *Venture* as the publication develops.

President and Publisher, Joseph D. Giarraputo. Thirty-five years old, Mr. Giarraputo is a graduate of the Harvard Business School. His publishing experience includes positions with the Ziff-Davis Publishing

Co., publishers of *Psychology Today, Popular Photography, Boating, Flying,* and other consumer and business publications. At Ziff-Davis, he was the business manager of the Circulation Division and ran the *Psychology Today* Book Club. Mr. Giarraputo was also Director of Finance at the CBS Education and Publishing Group, and Vice President, Planning and Finance, of CBS Publications. Among the CBS magazines were *Field & Stream, Road and Track, World Tennis,* and others. He is currently Senior Vice President of the Cadence Publishing Division. The company is involved in publishing and publishing services.

Editor-in-Chief. He is currently employed in a senior editorial position with a major weekly business magazine. He has edited and written numerous cover stories for this publication. He is one of four editors who oversee the editorial closing of the magazine on a rotating basis. Prior to this position he served as a bureau manager for this publication. He has also worked as an assistant city editor and reporter for the Dallas *Times Herald*. He graduated with a degree in journalism from the University of Texas, where he was managing editor of the *Daily Texan*, the student newspaper, and president of Sigma Delta Chi, the honorary journalism fraternity.

Direct Mail Consultant. Bloom & Gelb Inc. will function as the direct mail advertising agency. Carl Bloom, President of the agency, has extensive circulation marketing experience, having been Circulation Manager of both *McCalls'* and *Redbook* magazines. Pete Gelb was formerly Circulation Promotion Manager of *Fortune* magazine. Their present clients include *Book Digest* and *New Times* magazines.

Launch Consultant. James B. Kobak is acting as overall publishing consultant with specific responsibility for planning and preparation of projections. Formerly the Senior Partner of J. K. Lasser & Co., Mr. Kobak is now an independent publishing consultant whose client list includes such publishers as McGraw Hill Inc., the *New York Times, Playboy, Book Digest,* and *Firehouse* magazine.

Production Services. Burt Paolucci will be responsible for printing and other production services. Currently an independent consultant, he is a graduate of the Harvard Business School and was formerly Director of Production for Time, Inc. His recent clients include: CBS Publications, ABS Leisure Magazines, *Billboard* Publications, and the *Columbia Journalism Review*.

Finance. Important assistance with respect to finance is being provided by Kenneth Fadner, who was most recently Vice President of Finance of *New York* magazine, the *Village Voice,* and *New West* magazine.

Art Director. David Merrill will function as *Venture's* Art Director. For four years, until August 1977, Mr. Merrill was the Art Director of *Time* magazine.

Probable Auditors. J. K. Lasser & Co.

»Exhibit 1

Venture Basic Assumptions

	Prepublication	Year One	Year Two	Year Three	Year Four	Year Five
Subscription Price (one year only)						
Introductory	10.00	10.00	12.00	13.00	14.00	15.00
Regular	14.00	14.00	14.00	14.00	15.00	16.00
Total Mailings/Year (in millions)	1.7	1.7	2.6	2.4	3.4	2.8
Average Bad Debt Mailings	15%	15%	15%	15%	15%	15%
Average Percent Return Mailings (gross)	3%	3%	3%	3%	3%	3%
Renewal Percentage 1st Renewal (conversion)	_____	50%	50%	50%	50%	50%
Renewal	_____	60%	60%	60%	60%	60%
Newsstand Draw (in thousands)	_____	15	30	35	40	50
Newsstand Percentage of Sale	_____	25%	40%	45%	50%	55%
Newsstand Price/Copy	_____	$ 1.25	$ 1.25	$ 1.25	$1.25	$ 1.50
Average Total Pages/Issue	_____	88	96	104	112	112
Average Advertising Pages/Issue	_____	15	20	33	43	54
Advertising Rate/Black & White Page	_____	$ 1,200	$ 2,560	$ 3,850	$5,340	$6,860
Copy Printing & Paper	_____	19.5	22.8	26.4	30.5	32.6
# Full Time Employees						
Mechanical and Distribution	1	1	1	2	2	2
Editorial	6	6	6	6	6	6
Advertising	4	4	5	6	6	6
Circulation	2	2	2	2	3	3
General and Administrative	6	6	6	6	6	6

This forecast is based on estimates and assumptions contained on this and other pages. No opinion is expressed as to the future accuracy of these projections.

»The *Venture* Magazine Story

The *Venture* magazine business plan is a great example of a very successful business plan in that it helped Joseph Giarraputo raise the $2 million he needed to launch his magazine back in 1979. Beyond the success of the business plan in raising capital, the rise and fall of *Venture* provides an interesting and instructive case study in entrepreneurship.

The idea for the magazine was conceived when Giarraputo read a report by MIT that noted that most new jobs came from small businesses. He decided he wanted to start a magazine about small business, because they were not being covered by *Fortune, Forbes* or *Business Week*. His target market was entrepreneurs. "The idea was to publish a body of information for entrepreneurs—everything from new business opportunities to how to raise and invest money," says Giarraputo, who is now the publisher of *Global Finance* magazine. "We also thought it was a desirable audience in terms of their income levels."[1]

Giarraputo needed funding and wrote the business plan included in this book to get it. This plan is considered to be a model plan, largely because it is very concise and clear and accomplished its mission of raising capital.

Giarraputo raised $2 million from the Christiana Company, a home-building firm that was looking to get into the magazine business. This investment looked good, but later turned out to be a problem for *Venture*. Giarraputo hired Karl Bergen, a senior editor at *Business Week*, as editor-in-chief, and the first issue of *Venture* launched in May of 1979 with a paid circulation of 75,000. The first advertisers were Mercedes-Benz and Johnny Walker. The magazine tended to reflect the dominant view at the time that most entrepreneurs were, and were going to continue to be, men. There were more men's lifestyle ads than business-related ads. One of the magazine's best reporters was a woman, however. Former *Los Angeles Times* reporter Sally Hofmeister covered everything from franchise scandals to get-rich-quick scams.

Everything was looking good for *Venture* magazine, however interest rates began rising dramatically, and this had a negative effect on the magazine's backer, Christiana. Being in the home-building business, Christiana was really feeling the pinch as people began to put off buying homes because interest rates were so high. Christiana was forced to cut back on its efforts to expand into other businesses. It pulled out of *Venture* magazine, forcing *Venture* executives to search for alternative financing. The tightly staffed company had to divert its efforts from putting out a quality magazine to trying to find financing and launch an IPO (initial public offering of stock) to raise desperately needed capital.

Ironically, one of the potential investors Giarraputo approached for funding initially was Bernie Goldhirsh, who at that time was publishing boating magazines. Goldhirsh did not invest in *Venture*,

---

[1] *Folio* magazine, May 1, 2004, Rachel Lehmann-Haupt.

but liked Giarraputo's idea of a magazine for entrepreneurs. Gold-hirsh thought that *Venture's* target market was too small, so he launched a competitor called *Inc.*, which built upon the *Venture* idea by covering both small and medium-sized businesses that were already up and running, instead of just focusing on entrepreneurial start-ups. The success of *Inc.* was a contributor to the downfall of *Venture*.

Giarraputo tried to sell *Venture* to Bertelsmann and *The New York Times*, but the deals fell through. Giarraputo had taken a bridge loan from financier Arthur Lipper for over $2 million and was planning an IPO to raise the money to pay Lipper back. Unfortunately, the economic climate was not right for an IPO. No bank on Wall Street believed that *Venture* would be able to sell all its stock at a decent price. As a result, Giarraputo was forced to cede control of the magazine to Lipper in 1981.

Lipper kept Giarraputo on as the magazine's publisher—but not for long: Giarraputo left the magazine at the end of 1983 over disagreements with Lipper about the direction of the magazine. Editor Karl Bergen left, as well.

Lipper really wanted the magazine to succeed, and as a result, lost his objectivity: "I originally was only interested in the profit of the financing," he says now. "By the time the company had run out of money, I had made the mistake of allowing myself to fall in love with the publication. I viewed and managed *Venture* as a cause."[2] The new editor, Jim Jubak later commented that he felt the financier was overly involved in trying to run the magazine, rather than leaving the writing and choices of cover material, etc., to the staff.

Lipper spent heavily to take paid circulation from 75,000 in 1982 to 450,000 in 1989. He overspent and was forced to sell the magazine to Carl Ruderman of Drake Publishing. Drake closed *Venture* in 1989. According to Lipper, the magazine's natural circulation probably would have leveled off at 150,000. If he were to do it again, he says he would make it a newsletter delivered via the Web. "The pity is that the 150,000 or so natural subscribers were so editorially interesting and demographically desirable and upward bound that a really good business could have been developed."[3]

Case Analysis

1. What consumer need did Giarraputo identify?

2. What was his target market? Why did he feel it was underserved?

3. What mistake did *Venture* magazine make that *Inc.* magazine did not make?

4. What financing decisions led Giarraputo to lose control over his business?

5. What mistakes ultimately cost Lipper *Venture* magazine and forced the magazine out of business?

---

[2] *Folio* magazine, May 1, 2004, Rachel Lehmann-Haupt.
[3] Ibid.

Resources for Entrepreneurs[1]

» Books

On Starting a Business—and Succeeding

101 Businesses You Can Start on the Internet, by Daniel S. Janal (International Thompson Publishing, Inc., 1996).

The Art of the Start: The Time-Tested, Battle-Hardened Guide for Anyone Starting Anything, by Guy Kawasaki (Portfolio, 2004).

Good to Great: Why Some Companies Make the Leap . . . and Others Do Not, by Jim Collins (HarperBusiness, October 2001).

How to Make 1000 Mistakes in Business and Still Succeed: The Small Business Owner's Guide to Crucial Decisions, by Harold L. Wright (The Wright Track, 1995).

In Search of Excellence: Lessons from America's Best Run Companies, by Thomas J. Peters and Robert H. Waterman (Warner Books; Reissue edition, 1988).

Mancuso's Small Business Resource Guide, by Joseph Mancuso (Sourcebooks Inc., 1996).

Online Success Tactics: 101 Ways to Build Your Small Business, by Jeanette Cates (Twin Towers, 2002).

The E-Myth Revisited: Why Most Small Businesses Do Not Work and What to Do About It, by Michael Gerber (HarperBusiness, 1995).

The Young Entrepreneur's Guide to Starting and Running a Business, by Steve Mariotti (Three Rivers Press; Compl. Rev. edition, 2000).

On Thinking Like an Entrepreneur

The 48 Laws of Power, by Michael Greene (Penguin Putnam, 2000).

Focus: The Future of Your Company Depends on It, by Al Reis (HarperBusiness, 1997).

Secrets of the Young & Successful: How to Get Everything You Want Without Waiting a Lifetime, by Jennifer Kushell and Scott M. Kaufman (Fireside, 2003).

The 7 Habits of Highly Effective People, by Stephen Covey (Free Press, 1990).

The Student Success Manifesto: How To Create a Life of Passion, Purpose, and Prosperity, by Michael Simmons (Extreme Entrepreneurship Education Co., 2003).

Success Through a Positive Mental Attitude, by W. Clement Stone (Pocket Books, 1991 re-issue). A classic!

Think and Grow Rich, by Napoleon Hill (Ballantine Books, 1990 re-issue). Another classic!

Think and Grow Rich, by Dennis Paul Kimbro (New York: Fawcett Columbine, 1991). An update of Hill's book by an African American.

---

[1] Please note that the publisher cannot guarantee that URLs will remain active and is not responsible for future changes to the content of Web sites.

On How Other Entrepreneurs Succeeded

Ben & Jerry's: The Inside Scoop: How Two Real Guys Built a Business with a Social Conscience and a Sense of Humor, by Fred "Chico" Lager. The former CEO of Ben & Jerry's describes the company's remarkable history and activism (Crown Publishers, 1994).

Body & Soul, by Anita Roddick—tells the story of The Body Shop (Crown Publishers, 1991).

Entrepreneurs in Profile: How 20 of the World's Greatest Entrepreneurs Built Their Business Empires . . . and How You Can Too, by Steve Mariotti and Michael Caslin with Debra DeSalvo (Career Press, 2000).

Kitchen Table Entrepreneurs: How Eleven Women Escaped Poverty and Became Their Own Bosses, by Martha Shirk, Anna Wadia, Marie Wilson, and Sara Gould (Westview Press, 2004).

Life and Def: Sex, Drugs, Money + God, by Russell Simmons (Three Rivers Press, 2002).

Losing My Virginity: How I've Survived, Had Fun, and Made a Fortune Doing Business My Way, by Richard Branson (Three Rivers Press, 1999).

Steve Jobs: Wizard of Apple Computer, by Suzan Willson (Enslow Publishers, 2001).

Student Entrepreneurs: 14 Undergraduate All-Stars Tell Their Stories by Michael McMyne and Nicole Amare (Premium Press America, 2003).

The Men Behind Def Jam: The Radical Rise of Russell Simmons and Rick Rubin, by Alex Ogg (Omnibus Press, 2002).

Trump: The Way to the Top: The Best Business Advice I Ever Received by Donald Trump (Crown Business, 2004).

Upstart Start-Ups!: How 34 Young Entrepreneurs Overcame Youth, Inexperience, and Lack of Money to Create Thriving Businesses, by Ron Lieber (Broadway; 1st edition, 1998).

On Negotiating

Difficult Conversations: How to Discuss What Matters Most, by Douglas Stone, Bruce Patton, Sheila Heen, and Roger Fisher (Penguin Putnam; 1st edition, 2000).

Getting to Yes: Negotiating Agreement Without Giving In by Roger Fisher, William Ury, and Bruce Patton (Penguin Books; 2nd/reprint edition, 1991).

You Can Negotiate Anything, by Herb Cohen (New York: Bantam Books, 1993).

On Accounting

Accounting the Easy Way, by Peter J. Eisen (Barron's Educational Series, 4th edition, 2003).

The Guide to Understanding Financial Statements, by S. B. Costales (McGraw Hill, 1993).

On Investing, Money Management, and Personal Finance

The Motley Fool Investment Guide for Teens: 8 Steps to Having More Money Than Your Parents Ever Dreamed Of, by David Gardner, Tom Gardner, and Selena Maranjian (Fireside, 2002).

Rich Dad, Poor Dad: What the Rich Teach Their Kids About Money—That the Poor and Middle Class Do Not!, by Robert T. Kiyosaki and Sharon L. Lechter (Warner Business Books, 2000).

The Laws of Money, The Lessons of Life: Keep What You Have and Create What You Deserve, by Suze Orman (Free Press, 2003).

The Millionaire Next Door by Thomas Stanley and William Danko (Pocket, 1998).

Understanding Wall Street, by Jeffrey Little (McGraw-Hill, 2004).

On Marketing

Purple Cow: Transform Your Business by Being Remarkable, by Seth Godin (Portfolio, 2003).

Social Marketing: Improving the Quality of Life, by Philip Kotler, Ned Roberto, and Nancy Lee (SAGE Publications; 2nd edition, 2002).

The 22 Immutable Laws of Branding, by Al Reis and Laura Reis (HarperBusiness; 1st edition, 2002).

The Tipping Point: How Little Things Can Make a Big Difference, by Malcolm Gladwell (Back Bay Books, 2002).

» Magazines

BusinessWeek
1221 Avenue of the Americas
New York, NY 10018
(212) 512–2000

Subscriptions:
(800) 635–1200
www.businessweek.com

Inc. Magazine
375 Lexington Avenue
New York, NY 10017
(212) 499–2000

Subscriptions:
www.inc.com

Entrepreneur
Entrepreneur Media Inc.
2445 McCabe Way
Irvine, CA 92614
(949) 261–2325

Subscriptions:
(800) 274–6229
www.entrepreneur.com

Fast Company
Fast Company Media Group, LLC
77 North Washington Street
Boston, MA 02114

Subscriptions:
(515) 248–7693
www.fastcompany.com

Forbes
60 Fifth Avenue
New York, NY 10003
(212) 620–2200

Subscriptions:
www.forbes.com

Fortune
1271 Sixth Avenue, 16th Floor
New York, NY 10020

Subscriptions:
(800) 621–8000
www.fortune.com

As entrepreneurship has taken hold among women and minorities, several magazines have sprung up to serve those markets. The best are the following:

Black Enterprise
130 Fifth Avenue
New York, NY 10003
(212) 242–8000
www.blackenterprise.com

Hispanic Business
425 Pine Avenue
Santa Barbara, CA 93117–3709
(805) 964–4554
www.hispanicbusiness.com

» Web Sites

BizBuySell at www.bizbuysell.com sends registered users who might want to buy your business e-mails, alerting them that you want to sell.

Business Owners Idea Café at www.businessownersideacafe.com provides a tool for figuring out how much capital you will need to get your business off the ground.

Copyright Office, http://www.loc.gov/copyright CPA Finder at www.cpafinder.com can help you locate a certified public accountant.

Download.com at www.download.com has free software. Be sure to run any software through your virus-detection program before installing it on your hard drive.

E-Commerce Guide, http://e-comm.internet.com

Internal Revenue Service at www.irs.gov You can download any tax form you need from the IRS Web site.

Internet Public Library at www.ipl.org is a good source for industry and market statistics.

InterNIC, www.internic.net, where you can register the name of your Web site.

Practical Money Skills, www.practicalmoneyskills.com

Sell It On The Web, www.sellitontheweb.com

Standards of Corporate Responsibility at
http://www.svn.org/initiatives/standards.html provides ideas on how to make your business socially responsible.

The *Thomas Register* is a giant catalog that lists almost all the manufacturing companies in the United States. (It is composed of about 25 volumes, each about 4 inches thick.) There is a national and regional version of the *Thomas Register*. You can find a copy in most public libraries, or you can use the *Thomas Register* online at

http://www.thomasregister.com/   (national catalog)

http://www.thomasregional.com/   (for regional versions)

» Buying Wholesale

The following is a list of Web sites where you can purchase products wholesale:

American Science and Surplus
http://www.sciplus.com
Science, chemistry, and lab-related toys and equipment.

Craft Catalog
http://www.craftcatalog.com
Provides crafts and art supplies, including brushes, paints, and sewing supplies.

CR's Crafts
www.crscraft.com
Provides crafts, dolls, stuffed animals, and clothing.

Golf Discount
http://www.golfdiscount.com
Golfing clubs, balls, spikes, and shoes.

Johnny's Selected Seeds
http://www.johnnyseeds.com
Supplier of plant, flower, and herb seeds, along with garden accessories.

Night Club Items
http://nightclubs.items.com/
Provider of nightclub bracelets and glow sticks.

OfficeMax Online
http://www.officemax.com
Office supplies.

Off Price Clothing
http://www.offpriceclothing.net/
Provides returned and recycled clothing at low prices.

Oriental Trader
http://www.oriental.com
Large provider of wholesale gift items.

Party Pro
http://www.partypro.com
Party and paper supplies.

Performance Bicycle Shop
http://www.performancebike.com
Bicycling supplies.

Sav-On Closeouts
http://www.sav-on-closeouts.com/
Closeout gifts.

St. Louis Wholesaler
http://stlouiswholesale.com
Sunglasses, jewelry, and toys.

Superior Snacks
http://www.superiorsnacks.com
Provider of wholesale snacks and candy.

Toysmart.com
http://www.toysmart.com
Educational and children's toys.

WholesaleCentral.com
http://www.wholesalecentral.com/
A large collection of categories and subcategories, along with a great search feature.

Xybermart
http://www.xybermart.com
Provides wholesale items primarily to retail businesses and a much
smaller set of categories than WholesaleCentral.com.

Yahoo's Wholesaler list
http://dir.yahoo.com/Business_and_Economy/Companies/Retailers/
Wholesalers/

≫ Additional Resources

The **Small Business Administration (SBA)** is a government agency created
to support and promote entrepreneurs. The SBA offers free and inexpensive
pamphlets on a variety of business subjects. Some local offices offer
counseling to small business owners.

Contact the SBA at
Small Business Administration
409 Third Street, S.W.
Washington, DC 20416
(800) 827–5722

or visit www.sbaonline.sba.gov.

Call this toll-free number to reach the **Small Business Answer Desk,** which
assists entrepreneurs with questions and can help locate local SBA offices:
(800) 368–5855.

The **Minority Business Development Agency (MBDA)** is a federal
government agency created to foster the establishment and growth of minority-
owned businesses in America. MBDA provides funding for a network of
Minority Business Development Centers (MBDCs), Native American Business
Development Centers (NABDCs), and Business Resource Centers (BRCs). The
centers provide minority entrepreneurs with one-on-one assistance in writing
business plans, marketing, management and technical assistance, and financial
planning to assure adequate financing for business ventures.

To find a Minority Business Development Center near you, visit
http://www.mbda.gov.

The **Service Core of Retired Executives (SCORE)** is a group of retired
businesspeople who volunteer as counselors and mentors to entrepreneurs.
To locate an office near you, contact

Service Core of Retired Executives
26 Federal Plaza, Room 3100
New York, NY 10278
(212) 264–4507
www.score.org

The **National Association of Women Business Owners** helps female
entrepreneurs network. You can even join a local chapter of female
entrepreneurs in your area.

National Association of Women Business Owners
1413 K Street, NW, Suite 637
Washington, DC 20005
(301) 608–2590
Fax (301) 608–2596
www.nawbo.org

The *Small Business Reporter* is a series of over 100 pamphlets on entrepreneurial subjects, including financial statements. Each pamphlet is available for a small postage and handling charge. For a free index, write to

Small Business Reporter
  Bank of America
  PO Box 3700, Dept. 36361
  San Francisco, CA 94317

The **Young Entrepreneurs Organization (YEO)** provides learning and networking opportunities worldwide for young entrepreneurs through YEO and the **World Entrepreneurs' Organization** (WEO).

Young Entrepreneurs Organization
  1199 Fairfax Street, Suite 200
  Alexandria, VA 22314
  703–519–6700
  http://www.yeo.org

» Business Plan Competitions

The following organizations run annual business plan competitions. Prizes often include cash that can be used to finance the awardee's business.

NFTE Advanced Entrepreneurship Seminar Business Plan Competition—www.nfte.com

Emerging Business Leaders Summit (EBLS) Business Plan Competition—sponsored by the Department of Commerce's Minority Business Development Agency—www.mbda.gov

Carrot Capital provides capital and management expertise to young entrepreneurs.www.carrotcapital.com

Junior Chamber International is a worldwide organization of entrepreneurs between 18 and 40. It runs the JCI Best Business Plan (BBP) of the World Competition— http://mail.juniorchamber.org/english/bbc/

Fleet Youth Entrepreneur of the Year Award for New York City— http://ccnyc.neighborhoodlink.com/ccnyc/genpage.html?n_id=660130940

» Awards for Entrepreneurs

If you are an entrepreneur under twenty-five, you may qualify for awards that promote youth entrepreneurship. Such sources of start-up capital include the following:

Ernst & Young Entrepreneur of the Year Award— http://www.ey.com/GLOBAL/content.nsf/International/EGC_-_Events_-_EoY

To qualify for the Ernst & Young award, you must be an owner/manager primarily responsible for the recent performance of a privately held or public company that is at least two years old.

Guardian Life Insurance "Girls Going Places" Scholarship Award— http://www.guardianlife.com/womens_channel/girls_going_places/ggp_program_agenda.html

National Association for the Self-Employed Future Entrepreneur of the Year Award—http://benefits.nase.org/show_benefit.asp?Benefit=Scholarship

This scholarship prize of $12,000 is given to a young man or woman who demonstrates leadership and academic excellence, ingenuity, and entrepreneurial spirit. In addition, NASE awards 22 other young individuals with $4,000 scholarships. Since the award's inception, the organization has provided financial assistance of $855,000 to 423 students.

NFIB Free Enterprise Scholars Awards—
http://www.nfibeducationfoundation.org/

The NFIB Education Foundation grants at least 100 NFIB Free Enterprise Scholars Awards per year nationwide in the amount of $1,000 each.

NFTE Young Entrepreneur of the Year—http://www.nfte.com

NFTE graduates can win an all-expense paid trip to New York City for NFTE's annual "Salute to the Entrepreneurial Spirit" Awards Dinner and a grant of $750 (business plan category) or $1,000 (operational business category) to be applied toward the awardee's business or college education.

SBA Young Entrepreneur of the Year Award—http://www.sba.gov

At National Small Business Week, one outstanding entrepreneur is named to represent each state, the District of Columbia, Puerto Rico, and Guam as the state Small Business Person of the Year. From this group, the national Small Business Person of the Year is chosen.

Youth In Action Awards—http://www.youthlink.org/us/awards.php

YouthActionNet gives awards to youth leaders and their emerging projects that promote social change and connect youth with local communities. Awardees receive $500, which includes funds for a disposable camera to photo-document the project for an online photo gallery. Award recipients will also have the opportunity to take part in an online journal and contribute to a booklet of case studies highlighting the work of young people who are bringing positive change to communities around the world.

》Scholarships for Entrepreneurs

Most business schools offer scholarships. If you are interesting in studying business and entrepreneurship in college, contact the business school at the college you would like to attend. Having run your own business will be a big plus on your scholarship and college applications!

Here is a sampling of scholarship programs that focus on entrepreneurship:

Center for Entrepreneurship, Scholarships—
http://www.entrecenter.com/scholarships.cfm

FDU Entrepreneurial Studies Scholarship—
http://www.fdu.edu/academic/rothman/scholarship.htm

For New Jersey students seeking to study entrepreneurship.

Indiana University Kelley School of Business—
http://www.kelley.iu.edu/ugrad/scholarships/index.html

Johnson Scholarship Foundation, Tribal College Entrepreneurship Scholarship Program—http://www.johnsonscholarships.org/
TRJSF_Application.pdf

Minority College Awards Program—http://www.black-collegian.com/news/
ifa402.shtml

Encourages the study of franchising by minority students.

MIT Entrepreneurship Center, Awards and Scholarships—
http://ecenter-sloan.mit.edu/awards_scholarships.php

Williams College of Business, Scholarships in Entrepreneurial Studies—http://www.xu.edu/management/scholarships.cfm

Useful Formulas and Equations

1. Average Unit of Sale = Total Sales/Number of Customers
2. Revenue − COGS = Gross Profit
3. Total Revenue − Total Cost of Goods Sold = Total Gross Profit
4. Return on Investment = Net Profit/Investment
5. Projected Annual ROI = Monthly ROI × 12

   Quarterly (three months) ROI × 4 = Projected Annual ROI
6. The Rule of 72:

   72/annual interest rate = number of years it will take for an investment to double

   Use the rule of 72 to figure out how long it will take an investment to double. Take any fixed annual interest rate, convert it to a decimal, and divide into 72. The result is the number of years it will take for the investment to double.
7. The seven common operating costs can be summarized by the acronym USAIIRD:

   Utilities (gas, electric, telephone, Internet service)

   Salaries

   Advertising

   Insurance

   Interest

   Rent

   Depreciation
8. Return on Sales (ROS) = Net Profit ÷ Sales
9. Payback = Start-Up Investment ÷ Net Profit per Month
10. Debt-to-Equity Ratio: Debt ÷ Equity
11. Debt Ratio: Debt ÷ Assets
12. Breakeven Units = Fixed Costs ÷ Gross Profit per Unit

    To include variable costs: Breakeven Units = Fixed Costs ÷ Gross Profit per Unit −Variable Costs per Unit
13. Stock Yield: Dividend ÷ Closing Price × 100
14. Price/Earnings Ratio: P/E = Price per Share ÷ Earnings per Share
15. Bond Yield: Interest ÷ Price of Bond

16. Owner's Equity (OE) = Assets − Liabilities

    Total Assets = Total Liabilities + Owner's Equity (OE)

17. Quick Ratio: Cash + Marketable Securities ÷ Current Liabilities

18. Current Ratio: Current Assets ÷ Current Liabilities

19. Total Market Value of Company = Amount of Venture Capital Received ÷ Percentage of Company Sold

20. Cash Flow = Cash Receipts − Cash Disbursements

    Beginning Cash + Cash Surplus = Ending Cash Balance

21. Burn Rate: Cash on Hand ÷ Negative Cash Outflow per Month

22. Working Capital = Current Assets − Current Liabilities

Appendix 7 | Accounting Journal Distribution Guide

The following table is a general guide to help you make the best choice when distributing income and expenses in an accounting journal. In some cases there is more than one correct choice. If so, make the best choice for your situation, and then stick with that method. Then apply that decision consistently.

Always use the accounting format ( ) to designate a negative value entry. For example, negative $150.00 is written as (150.00).

Purchases – $ Out

Category	Type of Transaction	Explanation
FC	Accounting/bookkeeping service	
FC	Advertising (all types)	Not driven by sales.
FC	Bank fees	
FC	Brochures	
FC	Bus tickets	
FC	Business cards	
(CAPITAL INV.)	Cash taken out by owner (Draw)	Negative because you're taking money out of the business; Use "( )".
FC	Catalog designed	
FC	Catalog printed	
FC	Cleaning service	
INV. COSTS	Contracted direct labor	Labor paid "per piece" for work directly producing the product or service.
FC	Computer, business only	
FC	Computer supplies, business only	
FC	Consulting fees	
INV. COST	Costs listed in the EOU model	SUS only includes what's in the product. Do not include royalties, outbound shipping in SUS model.
FC	Development of Web site	
(CAPITAL INV.)	Draw of cash by owner	Negative because you're taking money out of the business; use ( ).

Continued

Category	Type of Transaction	Explanation
FC	Electric bill	
FC	Entertainment, business only	Keep good documentation; Frequently questioned by auditors.
Same category used for the wages	Employers share of Social Security tax, unemployment insurance and other payments made for employees.	It is a cost of hiring labor, whether it goes directly to the employee or not. These taxes add approximately, 10 percent to the cost of hiring.
FC or CAP. EQUIP'T	Equipment or machinery	Depends on whether it will last more than one year or not.
FC	Equipment; lasts less than 1 year	
CAP. EQUIP'T	Equipment; lasts more than 1 year	
FC or INV. COST	Fees for use of equipment	Depends on whether or not you are producing product that will be sold.
FC	Flyers	
FC	Furniture, for your own use	
FC	Gas bill, natural or LP	
FC	Gas for vehicle	
FC	Insurance	
FC	Internet Service, ISP	
VC or INV. COST	Labor, direct work on product, incl. paid on a "per unit" basis	Depends on whether it is in your SUS model; either way will work.
FC	Labor, not on product, and paid by the hour	
FC	Legal fees	
Other Costs *	Loan payments (any kind)	
FC	Machinery, last less than 1 year	
CAP. EQUIP'T	Machinery, last more than 1 year	
FC	Market research	
FC	Marketing costs	
FC	Marketing materials	
INV. COST	Materials used up in product or services purchased	
FC	Mechanical pencils; other bookkeeping supplies	
FC	Office supplies	
FC	Other car expense, cost per mile	You normally pay for the use of a nonbusiness vehicle by the mile, including gas; 32 cents/mile is acceptable, but the amount is increased periodically.

Note: Any example of negative value in Other Costs, signified by (Other Costs) is money received that does not fit the existing categories. Such receipts of income could be distributed into an Other Income column for nonrevenue, noninvestment income.

Category	Type of Transaction	Explanation
VC, INV. COSTS or Other Costs	Packing materials, ship end product to customer	Depends on whether it is included in your product price.
INV. COSTS	Packing materials, ship product to subcontractor	Part of your process to create the product or service.
FC	Parking fees	
Other Costs *	Payments on loan (any kind)	
FC	Payroll, general	Not linked to production of product or service.
VC or INV. COST	Payroll for direct labor on product or service	Linked to production of product or service; see EOU model.
FC	Phone bill	
FC	Postage	
FC	Posters	
INV. COST	Product or service to be resold	
FC or Other Costs	Property tax	
INV. COST	Raw materials	
(REVENUES)	Rebates to customers	Is a planned part of the sale and should be averaged in with your sale price; enter as negative value with ( ).
FC	Receipt booklet	
FC	Recycling costs	
(REVENUES)	Refunds on sales	Represents a sale not made, even though not preplanned.
FC	Registration fees	
Use category that reflects what is being paid for	Reimbursements for business expenses (Be sure they are legitimate).	Include a note about the purpose of the reimbursement and keep thorough documentation; frequently challenged by auditors who suspect that people are draining cash out of the business.
FC	Rent	
FC	Repairs, minor	
VC	Royalties owed on sales	Do not count as INV. COSTS because you do not pay unless the product is sold.
FC	Salaries of employees, not direct labor	
INV. COSTS	Salaries of employees, direct labor	Only if 100 percent working on product or service.
FC	Salary of owner	
VC	Sales commissions	
Other Costs	Sales tax collected and then paid to government	Collect sales tax as revenue. Pay out as Other Costs.
FC	Services, any type	
INV. COST	Shipping, inbound for product	

Continued

Category	Type of Transaction	Explanation
FC	Shipping not for product, inbound and outbound	
INV. COST	Shipping of product to and from subcontractor	
VC	Shipping, outbound to customer	
FC	Shop supplies (not direct product)	If used in making the product or service, use INV. COSTS.
FC	Software, business only	
VC	Special packaging not included in the product price	If it is in your EOU model, it is your product price; then use INV. COST.
FC	Subway tokens	
INV. COST	Supplies used on product or service	
FC	Supplies, general	
Other Costs	Taxes, business profit	
FC	Tools, last less than 1 year	
CAP. EQUIP'T	Tools, last more than 1 year	
FC	Transportation, misc.	
VC	Transportation to deliver products to customer	It happens after the sale is made, it cannot be INV COSTS.
INV. COST	Transportation to get products	The same as inbound shipping, only you pay with your time and cash spent.
FC	Trash removal	
Same category used for the wages	Unemployment tax	It is a cost of hiring labor, whether it goes directly to the employee or not.
FC	Vehicle maintenance	
CAP. EQUIP'T	Vehicle purchase	
Other Costs	Warrantees paid	Not part of the original, planned sale; warrantee costs should be watched carefully to see if you have a bad product.
FC	Web site development	
FC	Web site hosting	

Receipts of Money – $ In

Category	Type of Transaction	Explanation
CAPITAL INV.	Additional investment by owner	
CAPITAL INV.	Additional investment from new partner(s)	
REVENUE	Extra charges to customers that are not part of the planned sale	They are still part of the sale.
(Other Costs)	Gain from sale of equipment	Negative because you're bringing in money.
(Other Costs)	Insurance settlement	Negative because you're bringing in money. It is not revenue because it is not normal part of your business.
(Other Costs) *	Receive cash from line of credit; a type of short-term loan	A line of credit (LOC) is a ST loan; include it on the balance sheet under ST liabilities.
(Other Costs) *	Receive cash from loan, less than 1 year; short term	Include in ST liabilities on balance sheet.
(Other Costs) *	Receive cash from loan, more than 1 year; long term	Include in LT liabilities on balance sheet.
Other Costs*	Loss from sale of assets	Enter as a positive value, because it costs you to lose value on an asset. You will make this entry when you receive cash from the sale of the asset.
CAPITAL INV.	Original investment by owners	
REVENUE	Revenue	
(Other Costs)	Sale of other assets, such as intellectual property	Enter as a negative because you're bringing in money, not spending it. Use ( ) to show neg.
CAPITAL INV.	Sale of a percentage of the business, taking in partner(s)	
CAPITAL INV.	Sale of stock to investors	
(Other Costs)	Sale of capital equipment	Enter as a negative because you're bringing in money, not spending it. Use ( ) to show neg.
REVENUE	Sales of your product/service	
REVENUE	Shipping and handling fees charged to customers	
CAPITAL INV.	Start-up capital; original investment	

Appendix 8 | Using Business Plan Pro

In addition to the BizBuilders CD, this book also includes Business Plan Pro planning software that you can use to create a professional-looking business plan. We recommend that you build your business plan using the BizBuilder Business Plan Template found on the CD packaged in this book, because it mirrors the planning process presented in the textbook and contains more detailed questions in some areas than Business Plan Pro that will be helpful to you in the preparation of your plan.

Once you have created your plan using the BizBuilder's Template, it is easy to cut and paste material from your planning document into Business Plan Pro. You may want to do this to get a more professional-looking product and make use of the spreadsheet and wizards for charts and graphs. Business Plan Pro also contains a large number of sample plans that you can review for ideas and alternate formats.

Business Plan Pro includes:

- Over 400 sample business plans for you to study and compare to your business plan. Use the Sample Plan Browser to search the extensive sample plan library.
- Easy Plan Wizard that guides you through writing your plan.
- Spreadsheet tables with columns, rows, and formulas to automatically calculate totals as you enter your numbers.
- Financial statements that you can customize to meet your business's needs.
- Plan Review Wizard that reviews your plan for completeness, compares your financial statements to standard account practices, and checks for errors.
- Pie and bar charts that can be automatically created from your spreadsheets.
- A professional-looking printout of your business plan.
- Links to useful Internet resources.

If you would like to create a plan using Business Plan Pro, you will need to have the following installed on your computer: Microsoft Internet Explorer (6.0 or higher) and Adobe Acrobat Reader (4.0 or higher). You can find both programs online; just be sure to install Internet Explorer before you attempt to install Adobe Acrobat Reader.

The serial number you will need in order to install Business Plan Pro on your computer is on the back of the CD-ROM that came with your book. There is a quick-start tutorial on the CD and more tutorials online at http://www.paloalto.com/su/bp/tutorials/.

Appendix 9 | Glossary

accounts payable   money a business owes its suppliers.

accrue   to increase or grow because interest is being added periodically.

angel   a potential investor who invests in small business and typically does not ask for as high a rate of return as a venture capitalist or a bank.

antidiscrimination law   a statute that protects employees from being treated differently from other employees due to age, race, sex, gender, or sexual orientation.

arbitration   settling a conflict with the help of another individual both parties trust rather than in a court of law.

assets   any item of value. In business, cash, inventory, furniture, and machinery are all examples of assets.

attitude   a way of acting, thinking, or feeling that expresses one's opinion.

audit   a formal examination of accounts conducted by the Internal Revenue Service to determine whether the taxpayer being investigated is paying appropriate taxes.

balance   1. the difference between the credit and the debit side of a ledger; also, the difference between the assets and liabilities of a financial statement. 2. to calculate such differences; to settle an account by paying debts; to keep books properly so credits and debits in an account equal each other.

balance sheet   a financial statement summarizing the assets, liabilities, and net worth (or owner's equity) of a business, so called because the sum of the assets will equal the total of the liabilities plus the net worth (or owner's equity).

benefit   an improvement in one's condition; an advantage gained by doing or accepting something.

board of directors   a group of people who manage or control a business. The board of directors of a corporation is chosen by the stockholders. Unincorporated business owners sometimes appoint a board of directors to advise the business.

bond   an interest-bearing certificate issued by a government or business that promises to pay the holder interest as well as the face value of the bond at maturity.

book value   valuation of a company as assets minus liabilities. This method is the most common one used for valuing companies, and also the simplest.

bootstrap financing   financing a business by creatively stretching existing capital as far as possible, including extensive use of the entrepreneur's time.

brand   a name (sometimes with an accompanying symbol or trademark) that distinguishes a business from its competition and makes its competitive advantage instantly recognizable to the consumer.

breach of contract   failure by an individual who signed a contract to comply with its provisions.

budget   a plan to spend money.

burn rate   negative cash flow; cash on hand divided by monthly operating costs, which is a ratio that indicates how many months a business can cover its overhead without making a profit.

business   the buying and selling of goods or services in order to make a profit.

business card   a small, rectangular card imprinted with a business's name, logo, and contact information (and, often, a slogan).

capital   money or property owned or used in business.

cash balance   cash receipts less cash disbursements at the end of each business day.

cash flow   cash receipts less cash disbursements over a period of time. Cash flow is represented by the cash balance in an accounting journal or ledger.

cash flow statement   a financial statement showing cash receipts less cash disbursements for a business over a period of time, such as one month or one year.

cause-related marketing   marketing that is tied to a social, political, or environmental cause that a business owner wants to support.

charge account   credit extended by a store allowing qualified customers to make purchases up to a specified limit without paying cash at the time of purchase.

checking account   a bank account against which the account holder can write checks.

collateral   property or assets pledged by a borrower to a lender to secure a loan.

commission   a percentage of a sale paid to a salesperson or employee; treated as a variable operating cost.

competition   rivalry in business for customers or markets. Competition in a free market leads to lower prices and produces better quality goods and services for consumers.

competitive advantage a benefit that can be delivered to consumers in a market better than the competition.

compromise a settlement in which each side in a negotiation has given in on some demands.

consumer a person or business that buys goods and services for its own needs, not for resale or to use to produce goods and services for resale.

contingency an unforeseen or unpredictable event.

continuous improvement the idea that constantly seeking to improve quality and efficiency in a business will increase profits.

contract a formal written agreement between two or more people legally binding each party to fulfill obligations as specified.

core competency a fundamental knowledge, ability, or expertise in a special subject area or skill set, which is critical to the success of a business; another term for "competitive advantage."

corporate governance rules and safeguards designed to ensure that a company's executives and employees behave legally and ethically.

corporation a legal "person" (entity), composed of stockholders, that is granted the right to buy, sell, and inherit possessions, and is legally liable for its actions.

cost an expense; the amount of money, time, or energy spent on something.

cost/benefit analysis a decision-making process in which the costs of taking an action are compared to the benefits; if the benefits outweigh the costs, the action should be taken.

cost of goods sold the cost of selling "one additional unit."

creativity the ability to invent something using the imagination, or to perceive an already existing thing or situation in a new way.

credit in bookkeeping, a recording of income. Also, the ability to borrow money.

creditor person who is owed money.

cyclical occurring in cycles, periods when things happen in the same pattern.

database collection of information, such as customer addresses, often stored in a computer.

debit in bookkeeping, a recording of an expense.

debt an obligation to pay back a loan; a "liability."

debt ratio the ratio of debt (liabilities) to assets.

debt-to-equity ratio a comparison that expresses financial strategy by showing how much of a company is financed by debt and how much by equity.

deductible the portion of an insured loss or damage not covered by insurance; the higher the deductible, the lower the insurance premium.

deduction expense incurred during the course of doing business. A business owner may subtract deductible amounts from income when figuring income tax due.

demand the willingness and desire for a commodity together with the ability to pay for it; the amount consumers are ready and able to buy at the price offered in the marketplace.

demographics population statistics.

depreciation the percentage of value of an asset subtracted each year until the value becomes zero; reflects wear and tear on the asset.

discount (referring to bonds) the difference between a bond's trading price and par when the trading price is below par.

dividend each stockholder's portion of the profit per share paid out by a corporation.

donation a gift or contribution to a charitable organization.

draft to write a version of a contract or agreement with the understanding that it will probably need to be developed and rewritten further.

economy the financial structure of a nation or other area that determines how resources and wealth are distributed.

electronic rights protection of a creator's intellectual property (writing, art, music, etc.) from being used on a Web site without payment to the creator.

electronic storefront a Web site set up as a store where consumers can see and purchase merchandise.

e-mail short for electronic mail; messages sent between computers using the Internet.

employee a person hired by a business to work for wages (salary) or commission.

entrepreneur a person who organizes and manages a business, assuming the risk for the sake of the potential return.

Equal Pay Act law passed in 1963 that requires employers to pay men and women the same wage for doing the same job.

equity ownership in a company received in exchange for money invested. In accounting, equity is equal to assets minus liabilities.

ethics a system of morals or standards of conduct and judgment.

export 1. to ship products overseas for sale. 2. *n.* (singular and plural) the products themselves.

external opportunity an opportunity generated by observing the outside world, as opposed to an internal opportunity, which is generated from an interest or hobby.

face value the value printed on a bill or bond; not necessarily its market value.

Fair Labor Standards Act law passed in 1938 requiring employers to pay employees at least minimum wage and prohibiting the hiring of anyone under 16 full time.

fair market value the price at which a property or business is valued by the market; the price it would fetch on the open market.

fax short for facsimile, a machine that electronically sends printed material over a telephone line; *v.* to use a fax machine.

file (referring to taxes) to fulfill one's legal obligation by mailing a tax return, and any taxes due, to the Internal Revenue Service or state or local tax authority.

fiscal year a twelve-month period between settling financial recordkeeping.

fixed costs business expenses that must be paid whether or not any sales are being generated; USAIIRD: utilities, salaries, advertising, insurance, interest, rent, and depreciation.

foundation an organization that manages money donated to it by philanthropists.

franchise a business that markets a product or service developed by the franchisor, in the manner specified by the franchisor.

franchisee owner of a franchise unit or units.

franchisor person who develops a franchise or a company that sells franchises.

fraud intentional failure by a business owner to inform a customer that he or she could be hurt in some way by the business's product or service.

free enterprise system economic system in which businesses are privately owned and operate relatively free of government interference.

future value the amount an investment is worth in the future if invested at a specific rate of return.

goodwill an intangible asset generated when a company does something positive that has value—goodwill can include the company's reputation, brand recognition, and relationships with the community and customers.

gross domestic product (GDP) the annual estimated market value of all products and services produced within a country.

gross national product (GNP) the annual estimated market value of all products and services produced by the resources of a country.

gross profit total sales revenue minus total cost of goods sold.

human resources department of a business that hires, trains, and develops the company's employees.

hyperlink a highlighted or underlined word, phrase, or icon on a Web site that, when clicked on, leads to a new document page anywhere on the Internet.

immigrant a person who settles in a new country or region, having left his or her country or region of birth.

import 1. to bring products from overseas into a country to sell. 2. *n.* (singular and plural) the products themselves.

incentive something that motivates someone to take action—to work, start a business, or study harder, for example.

income statement a financial statement that summarizes income and expense activity over a specified period and shows net profit or loss.

inflation the gradual continuous increase in the prices of products and services, usually resulting from an increase in the amount of money in circulation in an economy.

infringe to violate a copyright, trademark, or patent.

installment payment on a loan or debt made at regular intervals.

institutional advertising advertisements placed by large corporations to keep the name of the company in the mind of the public—not to promote a specific product or service.

insurance a system of protection for payment provided by insurance companies to protect people or businesses from having property or wealth damaged or destroyed.

insurance agent insurance company employee who sells insurance and helps purchasers determine what insurance they need to protect their assets.

insurance policy contract between an insurance company and a person or business being insured that describes the premium(s) to be paid and the insurance company's obligations.

intellectual property intangible property created using the intellect, such as an invention, book, painting, or music.

interest payment for using someone else's money; payment received for lending money.

interest rate money paid for the use of money, expressed as a percentage per unit of time.

Internal Revenue Service the federal government bureau in charge of taxation.

Internet the world's largest computer network, connecting many millions of users.

interoffice something sent from one person to another within the same office, or company, using the office distribution system.

inventory items on hand to be sold.

investment something into which one puts money, time, or energy with the hope of gaining profit or satisfaction, in the future.

invoice an itemized list of goods delivered or services rendered and the amount due; a bill.

ISP abbreviation for Internet Service Provider; services that provide access to the Internet for subscribers' computers. Some ISPs, such as Microsoft Network or America Online, also provide software for browsing the Internet and chatting with other subscribers, among other services.

kaizen Japanese word for "continuous improvement"; the philosophy that continually seeking to improve quality will steadily increase profits.

lawsuit attempt to recover a right or claim through legal action.

layaway store policy allowing a customer to make a down payment on an item to secure it and then make monthly payments on the balance (the store keeps the item until it is fully paid for).

letter of agreement written agreement between parties regarding a business arrangement; less formal and detailed than a contract and usually used for arrangements of brief duration.

letterhead stationery imprinted with the name, address, phone and fax numbers, logo, etc., of a business.

leveraged financed by debt, as opposed to equity.

liability an entry on a balance sheet showing a debt of a business.

liability insurance insurance that covers the cost of injuries to a customer or damage to property caused on a business's property, or by its product or service.

liable to be responsible for lawsuits that arise from accidents, unpaid bills, faulty merchandise, or other business problems.

license legal authorization to perform some specified thing; *v.* to grant the right to use a licensor's name on a product or service.

licensee person granted the right to use a licensor's name on a product or service sold by the licensee.

licensor person who sells the right to use his or her name or company name to a licensee; unlike the franchisor, the licensor does not attempt to dictate exactly how the licensee does business.

limited liability company (LLC) a form of business ownership offering the tax advantages of a partnership as well as limited legal liability; this structure is not available in all states.

limited partnership form of partnership in which certain partners have limited investment in a business and therefore limited liability.

logo short for logotype, a company trademark or sign.

majority interest ownership of more stock in a corporation than all the other stockholders own together.

management the art of planning and organizing a business so it can meet its goals.

manufacture to make or produce a tangible product.

market a group of people potentially interested in buying a product or service; any scenario or designated location where trade occurs.

market clearing price the price at which the amount of a product or service demanded by consumers equals the amount the supplier is willing to sell at that price; the price at which the supply and demand lines cross, also called "equilibrium price."

marketing the development and use of strategies for getting a product or service to consumers and generating interest in it.

marketing mix the combination of the four factors—product, price, place, and promotion—that communicates a marketing vision.

market segment a group of consumers who have a similar response to a particular type of product.

markup an increase in the price of a product to cover expenses and create a profit for the seller.

maturity the date at which a bond must be redeemed by the company that issued it.

media means of communication (newspapers, radio, television, etc.) that reach the general public, usually including advertising.

memo short for memorandum, from the Latin word for "to be remembered"; a brief, concise note from one person to another often "interoffice."

mentor a person who agrees to volunteer time and expertise, or provide emotional support, to help or support someone else, usually younger.

micro-loan a loan of between $100 and $25,000 made to an entrepreneur based not on credit history or collateral, but rather on character, management ability, and business plan. The money can be used to buy machinery, furniture, inventory, and supplies for a new business but may not be used to pay existing debts.

mission statement a short, written statement that informs customers and employees what a business's goal is and describes the strategy and tactics intended to meet it.

modem device that connects a computer to a phone or cable line and translates digital information between them.

monopoly a market with only one producer; the control of the pricing and distribution of a product or service in a given market as a result of lack of competition.

moving assembly line continuously moving conveyor belt in a factory on which workers assemble cars, appliances, etc.

negotiation discussion or bargaining in an effort to reach agreement between parties with differing goals.

net final result; in business, the profit or loss remaining after all costs have been subtracted.

net present value the net amount an investment is worth discounted back to the present.

network to exchange information and contacts.

newsgroup an online discussion group focused on a specific subject.

noncash expenses expenses a business may incur, such as depreciation, that do not require cash outlay.

operating cost a cost necessary to operate a business, not including the cost of goods sold. Operating costs almost always fall into USAIIRD: utilities, salaries, advertising, insurance, interest, rent, and depreciation. Operating costs are also called "overhead."

opportunity a chance or occasion that can be turned to one's advantage.

opportunity cost the value of what must be given up in order to obtain something else.

optimist a person who consistently looks on the positive side of situations or outcomes.

overhead the continuing fixed costs of running a business; the costs a business has to disburse to operate.

owner's equity net worth; the difference between assets and liabilities.

par the face value of a bond.

partnership   an association of two or more people in a business enterprise.

patent   an exclusive right, granted by the government, to produce, use, and sell an invention or process.

payroll tax   employers must deduct this tax from their employees' paychecks.

percentage   literally, "a given part of a hundred"; a number expressed as part of a whole, with the whole represented as 100 percent.

philanthropy   a concern for human and social welfare that is expressed by giving money through charities and foundations.

pilferage   stealing by employees or customers of a business's inventory.

position   to distinguish a product or service from similar products or services being offered to the same market. *n.* the place of a product or service in a market.

premium   the amount above par for which a bond is trading on the open market; the cost of insurance, usually expressed as a regular payment by the policyholder to the insurance company.

present value   the amount an investment is worth discounted back to the present.

press release   an announcement sent to the media to generate publicity.

principal   the amount of a debt or loan before interest is added.

product   something that exists in nature, or made by human industry, usually to be sold.

production-distribution chain   the manufacturer-to-wholesaler-to-retailer-to-consumer process along which a product progresses.

product life cycle   the four stages that a product or service goes through as it matures in the market—introduction, growth, maturity, and decline.

profit   the sum remaining after all costs are deducted from the income of a business.

profit and loss statement   an income statement showing the gain and loss from business transactions and summarizing the net profit or loss.

profit margin   the percentage of each dollar of revenue that is profit; profit divided by revenue times 100.

profit per unit   the selling price minus the cost of goods sold of an item.

progressive tax   a tax that takes a greater percentage of higher incomes than of lower incomes.

projection   a forecast or prediction of financial outcome; business plans include projections of how the entrepreneur expects financial statements to come out.

promissory note   a written promise to pay a certain sum of money on a specified date.

promotion   the development of the popularity and sales of a product or service through advertising and publicity.

proportional tax   a tax that takes the same percentage of all incomes.

prospect   a person who may be receptive to your sales pitch.

prototype   a model or pattern that serves as an example of how a product would look and operate if it were manufactured.

public domain   free of copyright or patent restrictions.

publicity   free promotion, as opposed to advertising, which is purchased.

quality   degree of excellence (of a product or service).

quota   a restriction imposed by the government of a country on the amount of a specified good that can be imported.

rate of return   the return on an investment, expressed as a percentage of the amount invested.

real estate   land or buildings that have value in the marketplace.

recession   an economic downturn; lower than normal employment and business activity.

reconcile   to compare two financial records, item by item, to make sure both have been kept accurately. One may reconcile an accounting journal by comparing the right side to the left, or a checkbook by comparing the entries in the check register to a bank statement.

recruitment   the act of finding and hiring employees.

redeem   to turn in a bond to the issuing corporation at the date of maturity for conversion into cash.

resume (or resumé, or résumé)   a concise summary of a person's education, work experience, and interests.

return on investment   profit on an investment, expressed as a percentage.

risk   with an investment, the chance of losing money.

royalty   a share of the proceeds of the sale of a product paid to a person who owns a copyright; also refers to the fee paid to a franchisor or licensor.

salary   fixed amount of money paid to an employee at regular intervals; treated as a fixed operating cost.

sales tax   consumption tax levied on items that are sold by businesses to consumers. U.S. states raise revenue through sales tax.

savings account   a bank account in which money is deposited and on which the bank pays interest to the depositor.

seasonality scenario   a description of a business's expectations for seasonal changes in cash flow.

self-employment tax   a tax people who work for themselves pay in addition to income tax; includes the Social Security tax obligation for people who are self-employed.

self-esteem   belief in oneself; a good feeling about oneself.

service   intangible work providing time, skills, or expertise in exchange for money.

severance   an extension of salary for a limited time period to an employee who has been let go.

share   a single unit of stock.

shareware free software available on the Internet; shareware is usually the "test" or "light" version of the software.

signatory person signing a contract, thereby legally committing to compliance with it.

small claims court state court where disputes for relatively small amounts of money are settled between complainants who are allowed to represent themselves instead of using attorneys.

socially responsible business a business venture that expresses the entrepreneur's ethics and core values.

Social Security a federal government program that pays benefits to retired people and the families of dead or disabled workers.

sole proprietorship a business owned by one person. The owner receives all profits and is legally liable for all debts or lawsuits arising from the business.

speculative highly uncertain or risky.

start-up cost an expense involved in getting a business going; start-up costs are also called the "original investment" in a business.

statistics facts collected and presented in numerical fashion.

stock an individual's share in the ownership of a corporation, based on the size of the investment.

strategy the plan for how a business intends to go about its own performance and outdo that of its competition.

supply a schedule of the quantities that a business will make available to consumers at different prices.

tactics the hands-on ways in which a business carries out its strategy.

tariff a tax imposed by a government on an import designed to make the import more expensive than a similar domestic product and, therefore, less attractive to domestic consumers.

tax a percentage of a business's gross profit or an individual's income taken by the government to support public services.

tax evasion deliberate avoidance of the obligation to pay taxes; may lead to penalties or even prison.

tax-exempt the condition of an entity that is allowed to produce income free from taxation.

test market to offer a product or service to a limited, yet representative, segment of consumers in order to receive feedback and improve the product or service, before attempting to place it in a larger market.

trade balance the difference between the value of a country's imports and its exports.

trademark any word, name, symbol, or device used by a manufacturer or merchant to distinguish a product.

trade-off an exchange in which one benefit or advantage is given up in order to gain another.

value pricing a strategy based on finding the balance between price and quality that will attract the most consumers.

variable cost any cost that changes based on the volume of units sold; a term sometimes used instead of "cost of goods sold."

venture capital funds invested in a potentially profitable business enterprise despite risk of loss.

Web site an Internet document that can contain sound and graphics, as well as text.

Index

Photo Credits